THE CRADLE

OF THE

CONFEDERACY;

OR, THE TIMES OF

TROUP, QUITMAN AND YANCEY.

A SKETCH OF SOUTHWESTERN POLITICAL HISTORY FROM THE FORMATION OF THE FEDERAL GOVERNMENT TO A. D. 1861.

By JOSEPH HODGSON,
OF MOBILE.

MALIM INQUIETAM LIBERTATEM, QUAM QUIETUM SERVITIUM.

Mobile:
PRINTED AT THE REGISTER PUBLISHING OFFICE.
1876.

TO

HON. JOHN FORSYTH,

OF MOBILE,

LATE ENVOY EXTRAORDINARY AND MINISTER PLENIPOTENTIARY
TO THE REPUBLIC OF MEXICO,

I DEDICATE

THIS HISTORICAL SKETCH,

IN GRATEFUL REMEMBRANCE OF THE

PATRIOTIC SERVICES OF HIMSELF AND OF HIS DISTINGUISHED FATHER,

WHOSE LIVES HAVE ILLUSTRATED

THE

PATRIOTISM OF SOUTHERN STATESMANSHIP,

AND THE

DIGNITY OF SOUTHERN MANHOOD.

PREFACE.

Time has borne us so far from the men and events of the period which ushered in the fratricidal war of 1861-'5 that it is well for a new generation to be taught the truth of Southern History. It is not amiss to review the causes which produced the late war, and by examining the more humble and minute incidents of local discussion and action, to arrive at a correct conclusion as to the motives of those who engaged in the formation of the Southern Confederacy.

It will be seen from the following imperfect sketch that a majority of the people of the South were opposed to secession in 1850, and even in 1860; that the Unionists of the South were driven from their position after a protracted struggle, not so much by the advocates of disunion at the South as by the advocates of disunion at the North; and that the great mass of Southern people were led into acceptance of the Ordinance of Secession under the belief that the remedy they thus sought against grievances, would be acquiesced in by the people of the Northern States and by the Federal Government.

The author will not have had his labor in vain, if he succeeds in saving from the wreck of time, and in preserving in the more durable form of a book, many facts which throw light upon our local history, and which, after a few years, might otherwise be lost to memory. And if the facts here presented should aid in convincing the people of this Republic that the South-Western States were driven by Northern enemies, rather than by Southern leaders, into the act of secession, the author will rest satisfied that he has contributed one important aid towards an obliteration of sectional misunderstanding, and towards a return of that fraternal feeling which should exist between peoples bound together by common language, laws, kindred, and commerce.

CONTENTS.

CHAPTER I.—The City of Montgomery, Alabama—The Birthplace of the Confederacy—Extent and Situation of the Original Confederacy—Her Resources and Population—Independent Spirit of the Slave-Owner—Testimony of Edmund Burke—The Non-Slave-Owners—Traditions Inherited from Patrick Henry—Jealousy of States-Rights—The Immigration from Virginia—Displacement of the Muscogees—Growth in Population and Wealth—The Study of Oratory—Political Customs, Social Habits—General Quitman's Description of a Southern Home—Etc., Etc.,

CHAPTER II.—Discovery and Settlement of the Southwest—Hernando DeSoto—Marquette, Joliet, and DeSalle—Iberville, Bienville, and Sauvolle—The French in Alabama, Mississippi, and Louisiana—The English Successors in Alabama and Mississippi—The Spaniards in the Gulf States—Oglethorpe and his Settlement of Georgia—Condition of the Gulf Country at the Outbreak of the Revolution—Strength and Position of the Indian Tribes—Etc., Etc.

CHAPTER III—Growth of the Idea of Secession—Jealousy of the Commercial Against the Agricultural States—Navigation of the Mississippi—The Whiskey Rebellion—The Jay Treaty—Views of Distinguished men—Frequent Threats and Hopes of Disunion—The Louisiana Purchase—The East Fears the South and West—The Hartford Convention—The Resolutions of '98—Randolph's Reply to Patrick Henry—Etc., Etc.

CHAPTER IV.—Jurisdiction of the United States Over Indian Tribes—The Fee Simple of Lands Occupied by the Tribes—The Yazoo Frauds—The Decision in the Case of Fletcher vs. Peck—Indignation of the People of Georgia—Constitutional Questions Growing Out of that Decision—Etc., Etc.

CHAPTER V.—Relation of the Union to the Indian Tribes—Relation of the State to the Tribes Within its Limits—The Georgia Act of Cession—Non-Observance of the Contract on the Part of the United States—The Treaty-Making and Commerce-Regulating Power—Conflicting Views as to Indian Rights—Practice of the Northern and Eastern States—The New Theory of Equality of Races—Etc., Etc.

CHAPTER VI.—The Treaty of Indian Springs—Murder of McIntosh—General Gaines and Governor Troup—Threatened Collision of State and Federal Forces—The State Sustains Her Position—The Cherokee Nation—An Appeal to the Supreme Court—Its Writ of Error Disregarded—The Question of Coercion—Etc., Etc.

CHAPTER VII.—South Carolina and the Tariff—Continued Contest Between the Agricultural and Commercial States—Calhoun and Nullification—The Force Bill and the Right of Coercion—Inconsistency of President Jackson—Calhoun's Victory—Webster Retires from the Battle—Real Causes for the Proclamation—Etc., Etc.

CHAPTER VIII.—Controversy Between Alabama and the United States—Intrusion on the Creek Lands—Killing of Owens—Message of Governor Gayle—Threats of Resistance to the Military—Resolutions of a Legislative Committee—Mission of Key to the State—Adjustment of the Difficulty—The Federal Government Compromises the Question—Etc., Etc.

CHAPTER IX.—The Federal Party Reorganize upon the Slavery Question—Continued War upon the Agricultural States—Opinions of the Southern People as to Slavery—The Missouri Compromise—The Slade Agitation—The Abolitionist, George Thompson—Views of England—Opinions of Jackson, Marcy, Clay, Everett and others—Drawing of the Geographical Line—Etc., Etc.

CHAPTER X.—Position of the South During the Van Buren and Harrison Administration—Relation and Tenets of Parties from 1840 to 1850—More Territory for the South—New Threats of Division at the North—The Mexican War—Quitman and the Palmettoes—Offer of the Mexican Crown to General Scott—Condition of a Mongrel Population—Etc., Etc.

CHAPTER XI.—Wm. L. Yancey and the Montgomery District—The Alabama Democratic Resolutions of 1848—General Cass and the States-Rights Party—The Nashville Convention and Defeat of Secessionists—The Compromise Measures of Clay—Triumph of the Union Party all Over the South—Defeat of Governors Seabrook and Quitman—The Georgia Resolutions—Union Leaders and Sentiment in Alabama—Etc., Etc.

CHAPTER XII.—The Montgomery District—Contest of States-Rights and Union Men over Yancey—The Georgia Platform—Yancey Retires and Cochran Takes His Place—Report of the Southern Rights Association—Defeat of the Yancey Party—Scheme to Acquire Cuba—Lopez and Quitman—Federal Arrest of a Governor—Reorganization of Parties—The Southern Whigs—The Whig Convention at Baltimore—Reply of Scott and Pierce to the States-Rights Associations—Etc., Etc.

CHAPTER XIII.—The Kansas-Nebraska Bill—Preparing for Battle over the Outpost—Sharpe Rifles—Emigrant Societies—Rise of the American Party—Fillmore and Buchanan in the Southwest—Political Elements of the Elections of 1856—Etc., Etc.

CHAPTER XIV.—The Dred Scott Decision—Condition of Parties in 1858—The Irrepressible Conflict—The John Brown Raid—Leagues of United Southerners—The Southern Commercial Convention—Debate Between Yancey and Pryor—Precipitating the Cotton States into Revolution—Etc., Etc.

CHAPTER XV.—Instructions to Alabama Delegates—Action of the Alabama Legislature—Views of Forsyth, White and others—Meeting of the Charleston Convention—Yancey's Great Address—Withdrawal of Southern Delegates—Position of Political Parties—Yancey at Baltimore—He is offered the Vice-Presidency—Nomination of Breckinridge—Etc., Etc.

CHAPTER XVI.—The Canvass in Alabama--Assaults upon Yancey—Position of the Three Contestants—Yancey's Canvass of the West and North—His Arrival at Memphis—Reception at Knoxville--Speech at Washington—Attempted Fusion in New York—Yancey at New York—His Speech in Faneuil Hall, at Lexington, and at New Orleans--Return of Yancey and Visit of Douglas to Montgomery--Etc.

CHAPTER XVII.—Election of Lincoln--Reception of the News--Mass Meeting at Montgomery--Yancey Declares for Secession--The People Taught that Secession will be Peaceable--Co-operationists and Secessionists--The Crittenden Compromise--Its Rejection and Defeat--Etc., Etc.

CHAPTER XVIII—Effect of Seward's Speech--The Vote for Delegates to the Secession Convention--Meeting of the Alabama Convention--Caucus at Washington--Excitement in the Convention--Parties Nearly Equally Divided—Refusal to Submit the Ordinance to the People—Yancey's Threatening Speech—Counter-Threats—Etc., Etc.

CHAPTER XIX.—Adoption of the Ordinance of Secession—Popular Enthusiasm—Union of all Classes of the People—Assembling of the Southern Congress at Montgomery—Arrival of President Davis—Ratification by the Alabama Convention of the Confederate Constitution—Conclusion.

THE

CRADLE OF THE CONFEDERACY.

CHAPTER I.

The City of Montgomery, Alabama—The Birthplace of the Confederacy—Extent and Situation of the Original Confederacy—Her Resources and Population—Independent Spirit of the Slave-Owner—Testimony of Edmund Burke—The Non Slave-Owners—Traditions Inherited from Patrick Henry—Jealousy of State Rights—The Immigration from Virginia—Displacement of the Muscogees—Growth in Population and Wealth—The Study of Oratory—Political Customs—Social Habits—General Quitman's Description of a Southern Home—Etc., Etc., Etc.

"If slavery was an evil, it bred the best race of men and women the world ever saw."

HORATIO SEYMOUR.

"For this much is certain: That if institutions are to be judged by their results in the composition of the councils of the Union, the slave-holders are much more ably represented than the simple freemen." * * * "In the progress of this affair, the distinctive character of the inhabitants of the several great divisions of the Union have been shown more in relief than perhaps in any national transaction since the establishment of the Constitution. It is perhaps accidental that the combination of talent and influence has been the greatest on the slave side."

JOHN QUINCY ADAMS.

"He is a gentleman of the South; they have no property but land; and I am told his territory was immense. * * * It is not unlikely he may have lost his estates now; but that makes no difference to me. I shall treat him, and all Southern gentlemen, as our fathers treated the emigrant nobility of France."

DISRAELI, in Lothair.

It was on the eventful evening of Saturday, February 16th, 1861, that an immense crowd of human beings, of all classes, sexes and colors, thronged the streets of the little city of Montgomery, in the State of Alabama, and congregated in front of the Exchange Hotel, which overlooks the broad mart. The occasion for this immense assemblage, whose shouts of exultation rent the air, was the arrival in that city of the President elect of the Confederate States—JEFFERSON DAVIS.

In obedience to the call of the people who had assembled to greet him, Mr. Davis appeared upon the balcony of the hotel, accompanied by many distinguished men, whose names had long been eminent in the annals of the Union, and who were yet to become even more distinguished in the history of the ill-fated Confederacy.

Prominent among them was William Lowndes Yancey. Introducing Mr. Davis to the assembled multitude, the voice of the greatest orator ever produced by the South rung out like the notes of a clarion—"*The hour and the man have met!*"

The place of this remarkable meeting, Montgomery, was then a small city of twelve thousand inhabitants, standing at the navigable head of the Alabama river, and in the heart of that fertile band of rolling and wooded prairies which stretches itself, averaging a width of seventy-five miles, from the waters of the Savannah to those of the Mississippi.

Here is the great cotton belt of the Gulf States. Here is grown the larger proportion of the cotton production of the United States. Here it was that broad plantations covered the fairest land under the sky; where great wealth accumulated, and where was developed that highest and best pride of humanity which accompanies the possession of vast landed estates.

The beautiful city of Montgomery was the brightest of gems upon the belt of this fertile and happy region. Midway between the Gulf and the Tennessee, between the Savannah and the Mississippi, she held the key to the Gulf States. North of her, and extending to the Tennessee, was a rolling country, rich in metallic ores, with fertile valleys, salubrious climate, and health-giving waters. South of her, the broad cotton lands rolled down to meet the pine forests of the coast, whose wealth of timber was fringed by groves of magnolia and orange.

It was the habit of many who were proud of the extent of the Union to deride the Confederacy at its earliest organization, when it embraced only the first seven seceding States, because it was so small a fraction of the United States. There was no occasion for derision or contempt. The country of which Montgomery was the immediate centre, covered an area as large as England and France combined.

The entire country of which she was then the capital, contained more than half a million square miles, or more than three hundred and thirty-six millions of acres. It embraced some of the most fertile and productive land to be found in either hemisphere, situated in a mild and healthful climate. It lay circling half around a vast inland sea, which covers a surface nearly as extensive as the Mediterranean, and draining river basins unparalleled in size and variety of products by any of those of the Eastern hemisphere.

This territory, of which Montgomery was the capital, is more extensive than the combined areas of France, Great Britain, Prussia, Bavaria, Belgium, and the Netherlands—countries which contain more than one hundred and five millions of inhabitants. It produces every commodity which is adapted to the soil and climate of these populous European nations; and yields, besides, the valuable staples—cotton, sugar and rice. Its mountains are rich with coal and iron, which lie close to the sea, and are easy of manipulation. At a lower price than elsewhere it is able to grow all the cotton needed for the world. Its production of rice and sugar is limited only by the amount of labor. Its timber for ship and house building is the most valuable in the world. It has every variety of climate, from the Appalachian range of mountains to the semi-tropical groves of Mobile and New Orleans. The health of this vast imperial domain stands as well in the medical reports as that of any other section of the Union.

Such was the site of the city in which was established the government of the Confederate States. The people who joined on the evening of February 16, 1861, in joyful greetings to the President elect were no less distinguished than the soil which gave them birth. They were of the highest type of the Anglo-Saxon.

Here and there throughout this broad dominion remain undiluted remnants of the French and Spanish families who first colonized the Gulf Coast, and other Franco-Latin vestiges of that great wave of adventurists which the empire of Charles V sent forth to the Indies and to the Gulf of Mexico; but these feeble off-shoots of South Europe were long since overshadowed by the great Anglo-Saxon immigration which planted the banner of King George, under Oglethorpe, upon the banks of the Savannah; which swept down from southwestern Virginia along the waters of the Tennessee; and which followed the course of the Ohio and the Mississippi to the bluffs of Vicksburg and Natchez.

It has been remarked that the American descendants of the English Saxons have acquired, as a race, a variety of their own: that in complexion, expression and physique they now differ perceptibly from the parent stock. Although this may be true of the people of the more northern States, it cannot be held true of the people of the South. In the latter region, and especially in those sections where were large landed estates, the race of men has always preserved the highest characteristics of their English ancestry.

Whether or not the institution of African slavery aided in the development of this highest order of Saxon manhood, has been a disputed question; but we have on record that philosophic testimony of Edmund Burke, which, during the civil war in America, arrested general attention. That great statesman, seeking to dissipate the hope that less resistance to the encroachments of Great Britain would be found in the Southern colonies than in the Northern, uttered this language:

"There is, however, a circumstance attending the "[Southern] colonies, which, in my opinion, counterbal- "ances this difference, and makes the spirit of liberty "still more high and haughty than in those to the "Northward. It is, that in Virginia and the Carolinas "they have a vast multitude of slaves. Where this is "the case in any part of the world, those who are free "are by far the most proud and jealous of their freedom. "Freedom is to them not only an enjoyment, but a kind "of rank and privilege. Not seeing there that freedom, "as in countries where it is a common blessing, and as "broad and genial as the air, may be united with much "abject toil, with great misery, with all the exterior of "servitude, liberty looks among them like something "that is more noble and liberal. I do not mean, sir, to "commend the peculiar morality of this sentiment, which "has at least as much pride as virtue in it; but I cannot "alter the nature of man. The fact is so; and these "people of the Southern colonies are much more strongly, "and with a higher and more stubborn spirit, attached to "liberty than those to the Northward. Such were all "the ancient commonwealths; such were our Gothic "ancestors; such in our days were the Poles; and such "will be all masters of slaves, who are not slaves them- "selves. In such a people the haughtiness of domination "combines with the spirit of freedom, fortifies it, and "renders it invincible."

Throughout the cotton belt, where, at the blast of a horn, the master could be surrounded by a regiment of slaves, the spirit of freedom and domination in the descendants of the Cavaliers and Huguenots was such as to develop the frame, and inflame and intensify the pride of the individual to the highest extent known to the human race. Such Herculean deeds of valor as were drawn forth in the terrible conflict which shook the North American continent testified to the sagacity of the English philosopher, and to the manhood of the Southern Saxons.

Nor was this spirit of personal dignity and independence confined to the actual slave-owners. The non slave-owners, who had been crowded by superior wealth or energy from the rich cretaceous lands of the interior, and from the equally rich alluvium of the rivers, and who had taken up more humble abodes among the hills of north Alabama, or in the pine forests of the coast, felt an equal pride in that distinction of race which made the Saxon a master. With such jealousy did they cherish the spirit of personal liberty and local independence, that the policy which looked to the extremest license of State-rights always found among them the most enthusiastic, the most numerous, and the most persistent supporters. They received no pecuniary advantage from African slavery, and were so careless as to its continuance that at no time were they willing to enter into a war for separation of the States to secure its firmer establishment; but they perceived with that subtle instinct which belongs to the average Saxon, that the overthrow of African slavery would leave in the heart of their State a host of citizens foreign to their ideas, antagonistic to their labor, and cherishing under the influence of designing leaders the fretful jealousy of race—a jealousy which the history of mankind had shown to be the precursor of violent and constant hostility.

These non slave-holders were not, as has been supposed, the dupes or the deluded followers of the slave-owner. They were so numerous as to control the politics of the State. They gave political leaders to the slave-owners. From their midst sprung men like Patrick Henry, Andrew Jackson, Calhoun and Clay. They gave warriors of renown, at whose head stands Stonewall Jackson. They furnished the rank and file of armies, and concluded with glorious honor a contest entered into with unanimity, and prosecuted it with unparalleled devotion, gallantry and endurance.

The ancestors of these men had served in the Revolutionary war, and had won the independence of the colonies: an independence which they were so careful not to surrender to a new, overshadowing, government that their fears of the proposed Constitution of the United States could only be allayed by the then clearly defined and clearly understood reservations of the annexed amendments.

Patrick Henry, the eloquent commoner who infused this spirit into the masses of Southern people, perceived the doubtful constructions which ambitious men might place upon the Federal powers. He opposed the adoption of the Constitution. Believing that in a national government the liberties of the people would be gradually lost, he saw that the only hope of the multitude of Anglo-Saxon people who were destined to fill this continent was in a confederated republic of independent States. Hence, he asked in the Virginia convention, "Why is it that the preamble of the Constitution is "made to read '*we, the people*,' instead of '*we, the* "*States?*'" "If," he declared, "the States be not the "agents of this compact, it must be one great, consoli- "dated, national government of the people of all the "States." He protested against the language of the preamble as containing the germ of absolutism. Beginning with this solemn protest, the wisdom of which has been justified by the events of the succeeding eighty years, the Virginia patriot raised a warning voice which appears to us of to-day the inspiration of prophecy. The checks and balances of the three co-ordinate departments of the Federal Government appeared to him as specious, imaginary balances—"rope-dancing, "chain-rattling, ridiculous ideal checks and contriv- "ances," which could be annulled by the power of Congress to throttle the judiciary, or by the power of the President at the head of a standing army to throttle States, Congress and Courts. "Can he not at the head "his army beat down every opposition? Away with "your President, we shall have a king: the army will "salute him monarch; your militia will leave you, and "assist in making him king, and fight against you;

"and what have you to oppose this force?" The State legislatures would be shorn of their consequence, being forbidden to legislate upon any but the most trivial affairs. They are not to touch private contracts, and "cannot be trusted with dealing out justice between "man and man." A stamp act was authorized. Federal collectors could seize the papers and property of citizens, and call in the army to enforce the most dangerous and alarming practices. The Federal judiciary could overshadow the States, oppress the citizen by onerous costs, summon juries from a great distance, and, in the hands of bad men, sustained by the Federal Executive, could destroy the last vestige of popular government. The State was at the mercy of a Federal judge—the creature of the Federal Executive.

The fears of Patrick Henry were those of the people. They were only quieted by those amendments which were supposed to studiously guard against the dangers which he had portrayed so eloquently.

From this orator of the Revolution the people of the South inherited a deadly opposition to a national consolidated government, a fear of concentrated Federal power, and an earnest resolve to resist to the last the abrogation of State-rights. The slave-holder and the non slave-holder alike were inflamed by this traditionary antagonism; and when LINCOLN declared after his election to the presidency that the relation of a State to the Federal Government was simply the relation of a county to a State; and when SEWARD, a little later, declared that old things had passed away and all things had become new, the Anglo-Saxons of the Gulf, with no special reference to African slavery, except as an incident in the impending conflict, arose as one man, from the mountains to the sea, and, in the language of the last battle-order of General Gordon, lowered at Appamattox the Cross of St. Andrews only amid the huzzas of victory and before a routed foe. As an organization, they were conquered; as individuals, they were still freemen. This spirit of personal independence and pride of race could not be crushed by the most appalling catastrophe that ever befell a people.

The central and most fertile lands of the Gulf States received at Augusta, Georgia, the tide of immigration from Virginia and the Carolinas, which followed swiftly upon the steps of the departing Muscogees. This noble tribe of Indians (better known as Creek Indians, from the abundance of water courses upon which they lived), in the year 1721 occupied that entire country from the Savannah to the Tallapoosa and Coosa rivers, which afterwards became the garden spots of Georgia and Alabama. In 1733 General Oglethorpe met the Muscogees on the bluff of Yamacraw, on the Savannah. They agreed in formal council to yield to the colonists all the lands below tide water between the Savannah and the Altamaha. Six years later, Oglethorpe again visited them on the Chattahoochee, and by a new treaty they acknowledged themselves subjects of Great Britain; ceding to the English, with some reservations, the coast from the Savannah to the St. Johns as far into the interior as the tide flows. During the American Revolution the Creeks adhered to the British. After the conclusion of peace the Georgians claimed, that by treaties concluded in 1783, 1785 and 1786, the Muscogees had ceded to Georgia a considerable part of their lands south and west of the Oconee. The Creeks, under their able leader, McGillivray, whose father was a

Scotchman, denied the validity of these treaties, and, although his people had always been allies of the English against the Spaniards, they now entered into close relation with the Spanish government of Florida. They numbered 6000 warriors, and were well supplied with fire arms. In 1787 war broke out between them and the Georgians, and the colonists suffered severely. In 1789 they entered into negotiations with the United States, and acknowledged allegiance to the Federal Government; but soon after broke off negotiations, and renewed hostilities when they discovered that the commissioner did not propose to restore their lands. By the treaty of 1796 the Creeks admitted the eastern boundary, as defined by the treaty of Hopewell in 1756, "from Tugals river, thence a direct line to the "top of Currohe mountain; thence to the head of the "south fork of the Oconee river."

Between this eastern boundary, and the western boundary of Line creek in the county of Montgomery, Alabama, the Creeks cultivated their fertile lands in a rude way, and remained at peace eighteen years. But at the outbreak of the war of 1812 with Great Britain, a large portion of the nation—incited it is said by Tecumseh, and probably receiving encouragement from other quarters—took arms without the slightest provocation, and at first committed great ravages. They received a severe chastisement at the hands of General Jackson, and in August, 1814, surrendered a large part of their best territory. In 1818 they made another large cession of lands, and in February, 1825, they ceded all their lands in Georgia. On March 2, 1832, the Creeks ceded to the United States all their lands east of the Mississippi.

It was thus that during the first quarter of the present century the immigration from Virginia and the Carolinas, crossing the Savannah at Augusta, pushed before it the fated Muscogees, until finally by treaty and by battle driving the savages beyond the Mississippi, they spread the broad wave of civilization and industry over the entire Gulf States.

This occupancy was not marked by the circumstances of frontier life. It met upon the west below and beyond Montgomery an old and refined society which had been planted by Iberville and Bienville, and which had received accessions from the fugitives of Waterloo. It brought with it the wealth, energy and enlightenment of half a century of industry upon the banks of the Savannah, the memories of the American Revolution, and the manly independence and honesty which had been engendered by the political education of middle Georgia.

Thirty years' use of the cotton gin had raised to wealth and respectability persons who before the introduction of Whitney's invention, had been depressed by poverty and sunk in idleness. Debts had been paid off. Slaves had been imported in great numbers under the clause of the Federal Constitution which forbid the discontinuance of the African slave trade until 1807. Capital had increased. The sons of the planters had been liberally educated at Cambridge, New Haven, Litchfield, Princeton and Charlottesville. Lands had grown enormously in value, and railroads were even had in contemplation to convey to Savannah and Charleston the cotton bales of that broad belt which reached from the Savannah to the Mississippi.

The parish of St. Paul, which was afterwards known as

the county of Richmond, and from which the county of Columbia was constructed, was one of the wealthiest in the State of Georgia. Its county seat, Augusta, was the centre of a very populous and prosperous community. Among its eminent sons it numbered such men as Edward Telfair, William H. Crawford, John Forsyth, Richard Henry Wilde, William Cumming, the Holts, Longstreets, Glasscocks, the two Generals Twiggs (father and son), Abram Baldwin, Nicholas Ware, George Walton, John Milledge, Freeman Walker and Thomas W. Cobb.

Within the limits of the present county of Columbia was Carmel academy, which was for some years conducted by the celebrated Dr. Waddell. At this academy John C. Calhoun, William. H. Crawford and Thomas W. Cobb were pupils. Here Calhoun, supported by the proceeds of his own labor alone, was prepared in two years for the junior class of Yale college.

Immediately after the Revolution this region received a large accession of population from Virginia. The leader of this wave of immigration, GEORGE MATHEWS, a man of sterling worth, but of limited education, had been colonel of the 9th regiment of Virginia troops in the continental service. His knowledge of frontier life recommended him to the notice of Gen. Washington, and at the head of his regiment he distinguished himself at Germantown. He was high in favor with the army as a vigorous and undaunted officer. In 1785 Col. Mathews purchased a tract of land on Broad river, and removed to it with his family. By his advice, Traviss Merriwether, Benj. Taliaferro, Peachy Gilmer and John Gilmer also emigrated from Virginia to the same region. These families became prosperous, rose to distinction, gave governors to Georgia, and were honored by having their names perpetuated in counties.

Mathews was the principal man of all that section. His military reputation made him governor of Georgia one year after his settlement in the State. He had become personally known to the people some years before while serving under Gen. Greene. From 1785 to 1795 the lands upon Broad river were settled mainly by the friends and relatives of Mathews and those who first accompanied him from Virginia. The descendants of these Virginians followed the retiring Muscogees, and settled in the heart of the richest prairies between the Chattahoochee and Line creek in Alabama.

This society of middle Georgia, born in the hills of Virginia and nurtured upon the banks of the Savannah, extended in full vigor to the fresher lands of central Alabama.

The men of this region, from the beginning of the century to its fifth decade, were such as no country ever saw before; and such as, it may be feared, will perhaps never be seen again. The first settlers were comparatively rude and uncultivated. The eight years of Revolution had debarred an entire generation from all education except that of the camp and the battle field. There was then no rapid road to wealth. Somewhat later, however, the cotton gin added new value to agricultural labor, and began to bring gold into the hands of the planter. The log cabin soon gave way to the substantial framed house, or to the more pretentious country mansion surrounded by elegance and taste. The squad of slaves increased into companies and regiments; school houses and churches arose in every settlement, and the trading villages swelled into wealthy commercial towns.

The population was almost entirely agricultural. There were few mechanics, and but a small number engaged in commercial pursuits. The professions were not crowded. Although the sons of planters generally pursued legal studies, it was seldom with a view to active practice; more generally it was to serve as an entrance to political life.

Sir James Mackintosh, speaking of the English nobility as the most powerful order of men in Europe, surrounded by every circumstance which might seem likely to fill them with arrogance, and to teach them to scorn their inferiors, and which might naturally be supposed to extinguish enterprise and to lull every power of the understanding to sleep, has asked the question: "What has preserved their character? what "makes them capable of serving or adorning their "country as orators and poets, men of letters and men "of business, in equal proportion to the same number "of men in the commercial and professional pursuits of "life?" The answer is: Where the ordinary incentives to action are withdrawn, a free constitution excites it by presenting political power as a new object of pursuit. By rendering that power in a great degree dependent on popular favor, it compels the highest to treat their fellow-creatures with decency and courtesy, and disposes the best of them to feel that inferiors in station may be superiors in worth, as they are equals in right. What is true of the English nobility, was true of the most opulent and well-born of the Southern planters. They looked to the people at large for preferment, and from a nearer plane. The richest among them had been poor but recently, and the most aristocratic in feeling could boast of no ancestry which antedated the Revolution in distinction. The only aristocracy which could maintain itself was one either of wealth or genius. But as wealth was an accident to which any one might attain, and as the honors of the Republic lay within the reach of the youth born in poverty equally with him who was born in opulence, it became essential that the men who sought the ear and favor of the people should cultivate all the graces and courtesies which are found among the political aspirants of England. Oratory was cultivated as the most effective means to reach the popular ear. Newspapers being rare, the rostrum became the source of political information, and a people who had ample leisure delighted to witness the contests of the intellectual gladiators.

There was no official dishonesty in those days. To be suspected even of selfishness in office was to be discarded from public favor. The voice of the people was supreme. No officer dared set himself above the wishes of his constituents, nor resist the power of public opinion. The man with clean hands was caressed and honored. The man with soiled hands sunk to obscurity, and died in shame. The peculiar election laws of Virginia had moulded a lofty public sentiment, and impressed upon her children in the other Southern States a purity of political morals which lives now only in tradition. The manner of voting was *viva voce*. The voter was a free-holder. On the day of election the candidates sat with the judges, and in turn harangued the multitude in elevated and courteous language. The free-holder in an open, frank and manly manner announced his preference. He had a choice, and he was brave enough to let the world know it. There was no equivocation, double-dealing and shuffling. It was the voter's pride that he sustained great fundamental principles, or honored men of great worth, or maintained the dignity of his State in the Union by elevating to representative positions the wisest and the best in the land. In the dignity and worth of his governor or representative in Congress he recognized his own importance. He blushed with shame at an unworthy representative. So strong had become the pride of the voter, and so firmly rooted had become this elevated view of statesmanship, that it remained steadfast long after the subdivision of property and the gradual extension of suffrage to the non-land-owner. This lofty sentiment accompanied the Virginian and Carolinian wherever he went. It was renewed and strengthened by the aristocratic tendency of African slavery. It made him the most independent of mankind. He was the patron of the politician and statesman, and not the recipient of governmental favors and bounty. He bore himself with all the majesty of the perfect freeman, dispensed a generous hospitality, and displayed a loftiness of soul which respected and alleviated honest misfortune. He was quick to rebuke an unworthy act, and to revenge the slightest affront. He was haughty to the proud, kind to the unfortunate, gentle to the poor, stubborn in opinion, patient under affliction, and unostentatious in prosperity. He was a fair specimen of a class of men which could be developed only by great agricultural prosperity, under a system of laws which encouraged and compelled the highest exhibition of political candor and boldness.

Although the generation which immediately followed the Revolution was comparatively rude and uncultivated, it possessed those splendid qualities of patriotism, patience, and endurance which invariably lay broad and deep the foundations of States. In the midst, and immediately under the shadow, of great events the human mind becomes more comprehensive in its grasp, and the human soul more enlarged in its aspirations, and more steadfast in its principles. Nothing impresses the mind more permanently with the glory of humanity than the exhibition of splendid acts of devotion occurring within its experience. The immortal deeds which shine out brilliantly from a patriotic war stir the heart of the beholder with an ambition to emulate such virtue, and a pride in being worthy to claim it as a heritage. When the political causes which occasion war have been lost to memory in the mass of uncertain historical facts, the deeds of gallantry which emblazoned its annals will live fresh and green in the enthusiastic bosoms of succeeding generations. The fathers of the Revolution exhibited in their struggle for freedom the most heroic qualities. The mothers forgot the feebleness of their sex and bore with fortitude the most appalling dangers, from the open foe, the secret enemy at their door, and from the merciless savage.

In the Carolinas and in Georgia the sufferings and misfortunes of the patriots were most intense. The army of GREENE, the little bands of MARION and SUMTER, struggled against fearful odds, and at times seemed to be struggling against destiny itself. Such patience, such endurance, was the cradle of a race of men of enlarged intellect and iron will. They were found in every settlement where the Continental soldier had hung up his musket. They carved an empire out of the forest; they thrust the Indian backward towards the Pacific. They organized and conducted State and municipal governments which were models of simplicity, vigor and purity. There were but few books in their cabins; but the lives of WASHINGTON and of MARION, by WEEMS, were in the hand of nearly every child. The events described in these little books formed the character of the rising generation. It grew to be jealous of personal dignity and anxious for the security of municipal privileges. It chafed at the interference of a Federal executive. It was suspicious of a government whose authority was not derived directly from themselves. Above all it yearned for military glory. All wars were popular with them; and no politician could win the popular applause more surely than by appealing to the final arbitrament of arms.

The succeeding generation, that which was born with the present century, inherited the manly qualities of their fathers. To these, prosperity added education, with its refining influences and its expansion of the grasp of intellect. With them society was simple and orderly. There was no dissipation, thriftlessness, no want. The thief and the beggar were rarely known.

The slave which had escaped the club of the captor found a home where labor was accompanied with abundant food and clothing, and where the law and public opinion alike protected him from cruelty and oppression. If it was a crime to have brought him from Africa, the crime did not rest with these planters. Under OGLETHORPE, slavery had been prohibited in all Georgia, stretching from the Savannah to the Mississippi, but the greed of merchants on the coast and of ship owners from New England, abolished the prohibition and engrafted the traffic for twenty years, even on the face of the Federal Constitution. Was it better, in the development of mankind, that this race should have remained in Africa, free to live like the veriest beasts they slaughtered, or should have become useful as slaves, under an enlightened sky? In that day slavery was regarded as an evil—but so difficult of removal that no plan was ever seriously contemplated for its cure. It was many years later that the constant assaults upon the slaveholder by citizens of distant States drove him in his pride and defiance to the proposition that slavery was a moral, political and social blessing. Compared with his situation in Africa, slavery was undoubtedly a political, moral and social blessing to the slave. Whether it was such to the master will remain one of those vexed questions which will be answered according to the sentiments with which habit, education, prejudice and custom have clothed each one of us. Certain it is, that taking the slave-owning planters of that day as a body, there was nowhere under the broad sun a more moral race of men, with purer and more elevated social habits, or with more liberal and benign political institutions.

Major General Quitman, a native of New York, wrote in 1822, when but a youth, to his father, the following description of Southern life:

"Our bar is quartered at different country seats—"not boarding; a Mississippi planter would be insulted "by such a proposition, but we are enjoying the hospi-"talities that are offered to us on all sides. The awful "pestilence in the city brings out, in strong relief, the "peculiar virtues of these people. The mansions of "the planters are thrown open to all comers and goers "free of charge. Whole families have free quarters "during the epidemic, and country wagons are sent "daily to the verge of the smitten city with fowls, veg- "etables, &c., for gratuitous distribution to the poor. I "am now writing from one of these old mansions, and "I can give you no better notion of life at the South "than by describing the routine of a day. The owner "is the widow of a Virginia gentleman of distinction— "a brave officer who died in the public service during "the last war with Great Britain.

"She herself is a native of this vicinity—of Eng- "lish parents, settled here in Spanish times. She is "an intimate friend of my first friend, Mrs. G., and I "have been in the habit of visiting her house ever "since I came South.) The whole aim of this excellent "lady seems to be to make others happy. I do not "believe she ever thinks of herself. She is growing "old, but her parlors are constantly thronged with the "young and gay, attracted by her cheerful and never- "failing kindness. There are two large families from "the city staying here; and every day come ten or a "dozen transient guests. Mint juleps in the morning "are sent to our rooms, and then follows a delightful "breakfast in the open veranda. We hunt, ride, fish, "pay morning visits, play chess, read or lounge until "dinner, which is served at 2 P. M., in great variety, "and most delicately cooked in what is here called "Creole style—very rich, and many made or mixed "dishes. In two hours afterwards everybody, white "and black, has disappeared. The whole household is "asleep—the *siesta* of the Italians. The ladies retire "to their apartments, and the gentlemen on sofas, set- "tees, hammocks, and often gipsy fashion, on the grass "under the spreading oaks. Here, too, in fine weather "the tea-table is always set before sunset; and then "until bedtime we stroll, sing, play whist or croquet. "It is an indolent, yet charming life, and one quits "thinking and takes to dreaming.

"This excellent lady is not rich, merely independ-"ent; but by thrifty housewifery and a good dairy and "garden she contrives to dispense the most liberal hos-"pitality. Her slaves appear to be in a manner free, "yet are obedient and polite, and the farm is well "worked. With all her gayety of disposition and fond-"ness for the young she is truly pious; and in her own "apartments every night she has family prayers with "her slaves, one or more of them being often called "upon to sing and pray. When a minister visits the "house, which happens very frequently, prayers, night "and morning, are always said; and on these occasions "the whole household and the guests assemble in the "parlor; chairs are provided for the servants. They "are married by a clergyman of their own color; and "a sumptuous supper is always prepared. On public "holidays they have dinners equal to an Ohio barba-"cue; and Christmas, for a week or ten days, is a pro-"tracted festival for the blacks. They are a happy, "careless, unreflecting, good-natured race, who, left to "themselves, would degenerate into drones or brutes; "but subjected to wholesome restraint and stimulus be-"come the best and most contented of laborers. They "are strongly attached to 'old massa' and 'old missus,' "but their devotion to 'young massa' and 'young "missus' amounts to enthusiasm. They have great "family pride, and are the most arrant coxcombs and "aristocrats in the world. At a wedding I witnessed "here last Saturday evening, where some one hundred "and fifty negroes were assembled—many being in-"vited guests—I heard a number of them addressed as "governors, generals, judges and doctors (the titles of "their masters), and a spruce, tight-set darkey, who "waited on me in town, was called 'Major Quitman.' "The 'colored ladies' are invariably Miss Joneses, "Miss Smiths, or some such title. They are exceed-"ingly pompous and ceremonious, gloved and highly "perfumed. The 'gentlemen' sport canes, ruffles and "jewelry; wear boots and spurs; affect crape on their "hats, and carry huge cigars. The belles wear gaudy "colors, 'tote' their fans with the air of Spanish seno-"ritas, and never stir out, though black as the ace of "spades, without their parasols.

"In short, these 'niggers,' as you call them, are the "happiest people I have ever seen, and some of them, "in form, features and movements, are real sultanas. So "far from being fed on 'salted cotton seed,' as we used "to believe in Ohio, they are oily, sleek, bountifully "fed, well clothed, well taken care of, and one hears "them at all times whistling and singing cheerily at "their work. They have an extraordinary facility for "sleeping. A negro is a great night-walker. He will, "after laboring all day in the burning sun, walk ten "miles to a frolic, or to see his Dinah, and be at home "and at his work by daylight the next morning. (This "would knock up a white man or an Indian.) But a "negro will sleep during the day—sleep at his work—"sleep on the carriage box, sleep standing up; and I "have often seen them sitting bare-headed in the sun, "on a high rail fence, sleeping as securely as though "lying in a bed.) They never lose their equipoise; "and will carry their cotton baskets or their water ves-

"sels, filled to the brim, poised on their heads, walking "carelessly and at a rapid rate, without spilling a drop. "The very weight of such burdens would crush a white "man's brains into apoplexy.

"Compared with the ague-smitten and suffering "settlers that you and I have seen in Ohio, or the sickly "and starved operatives we read of in factories and in "mines, these Southern slaves are indeed to be envied. "They are treated with great humanity and kindness."

This is a true picture of the home and surroundings of the Southern planter of that day, drawn by an intelligent spectator of Northern birth and education. Such were the homes of Middle Georgia and of Middle Alabama. If the character of the people was not marked with that quiet refinement, that gentle grace and perfect command over every movement of person and every expression of countenance and speech which belonged to the older communities of the coast cities, and which can only be acquired by constant contact with the highly educated, it was at least marked with an unselfishness and a candor, a vigor of mind and a purity of thought and action, which could often shame and put to flight the cold, calculating spirit of the fashionable world. It was not an aristocracy of education and hereditary wealth, but a nobility of nature. The child obtains the imprint of character from the mother. The daughters of that day received a home education. Their constitutions were robust; their health vigorous. They were devoted to the claims of home, husband and children. They were affectionate, industrious, proud and pious. Their world was the home circle; and their occupation was in the broad field of domestic duties. They taught their sons and daughters the simple purity of their own lives—the former to look upon woman with the most chivalric tenderness, and the latter to cultivate that delicacy of sentiment and action which takes alarm at the first approach of whatever is coarse and vulgar. The man of mean conduct was despised and discarded. The man of cruelty was shunned. The drunkard, the liar, the libertine was ostracised. The silly and the froward woman was rebuked, and she who overstepped the bounds of maiden propriety lost caste forever. The slightest whisper against a woman's character, if true, blasted a life and caused the heads of a family to hang in shame for generations; if false, the life of the accuser paid the forfeit for an accusation so revolting to the sentiment of the domestic circle.

Religion is the cement which holds together the constituent elements of society. The generation which immediately succeeded the Revolution lived in sparse settlements and was cut off from the word of God. It would seem that in the face of great dangers and calamities the religious element would be strengthened, but strangely enough, during periods of war familiarity with death appears to rob the grim monarch of his terrors. The soldier falls with the triumphant huzza upon his lips and a smile of defiance mocking the pallor of the last adversary. He is buried with the honors of war; a volley of musketry is fired over his grave, and his comrade, with a single tear for his memory, rushes in another hour to the arms of a like fate. With the generation which succeeded our war for independence that skepticism and infidelity which accompanied the rise and progress of the French Revolution, increased the indifference of its American sympathisers to matters pertaining to the life beyond the grave. There was still another reason for carelessness in religious affairs; men high in authority and possessed of the affections of the people were known to entertain irreligious opinions. Beside this, there was no immediate means by which such an unhealthy condition of society could be remedied. The Parish of St. Paul's was no more. The Anglican Church lost its power and popularity with the Revolution, and its Episcopal successor had not only to struggle against the prejudice which had attached to the relation of its predecessor with the English government, but against the stronger prejudice which a rude and uncultivated people entertained against the ritual. The services were too complicated, the forms and ceremonies too cumbersome. The prayer-book appeared to them to require as much study as an Indian dialect.

JOHN WESLEY had been sent by the Anglican Church as a missionary to Georgia, and the renowned WHITEFIELD had followed him, but notwithstanding their labors, as late as 1769, there were but two churches in Georgia, and these were one hundred and fifty miles apart. Soon after the Revolution the Baptists obtained some foothold on Kiokee creek in Columbia county, where was established the first Baptist church in Georgia. The first Methodist society was formed in Augusta as late as 1799. It may be said that for twenty years, or one generation after the Revolution, there were no churches in Georgia. With the opening century, however, when the introduction of the cotton gin had increased the comforts, wealth and opportunities of the people, a new condition of religious affairs began. The labors of WESLEY and WHITEFIELD had been seed sown in fruitful ground, destined after a long time, but finally, to bear abundant fruit. The Baptists and Methodists were the missionaries of the Word. The simple practices and faith of these churches adapted themselves to the rude customs of the early settlers. Devoid of show and ceremony, they appealed to the emotional nature of man. Woman is more religious than man, because her emotional nature is more delicately organized. So an appeal to the emotions more readily captivates an unlettered and simple people than one more highly educated. The humble ministers of God passed to and fro, holding divine services in the log schoolhouses, in the cottages, under the wide-spreading trees beside the cool springs. They inculcated those divine precepts which society recognizes, so soon as announced, as the corner-stone of its structure, the key-stone of its arch—to love one's neighbor, to live virtuously, to do no wrong. Here and there churches were erected, but churches no longer could contain the multitudes who crowded to listen to the men of God—men often of the most captivating eloquence, always of a zeal which if it could not arouse the attention by beauties of rhetoric and logic, wrought the heart into a frenzy by the electricity of enthusiasm. To accommodate the multitudes camps were resorted to. Great arbors covered with brush, and under which were rough seats of logs and coarse boards, constituted the audience room. Often several preachers were occupied in exhorting different congregations at the same hour. From morning until midnight the groves resounded with prayer and song. The whole country assembled at these meetings. The tents witnessed the most profuse hospitality. In the intervals of service the families of the neighborhood mingled together, and as the conversation was naturally directed towards the events of the occasion, the conduct and language of the people partook of a religious discretion and fervor. Amid such scenes were educated the most exalted sentiments of human nature. From such a presence the impure of heart, the disturber of public peace, the man of lasciviousness and violence slunk abashed.

The memory of revolutionary deeds excited this people to bravery; their political customs educated them to candor and honesty; their free institutions inflamed their pride and independence; but their camp-meetings did more than all else to make of them a peaceful, orderly and virtuous society.

CHAPTER II.

Discovery and Settlement of the Southwest—Hernando DeSoto—Marquette, Joliet and DeSalle—Iberville, Bienville and Sauvolle—The French in Alabama, Mississippi and Louisiana—The English Successors in Alabama and Mississippi—The Spaniards in the Gulf States—Oglethorpe and his Settlement of Georgia—Condition of the Gulf Country at the Outbreak of the Revolution—Strength and Position of the Indian Tribes, &c., &c.

"What a substratum for empire! Compared with which the foundation of the Macedonian, the Roman and the British sink into insignificance. Some of our large States have territory superior to the island of Great Britain, whilst the whole together are little inferior to Europe itself. Our independence will people this extent of country with freemen and will stimulate the innumerable inhabitants thereof, by every motive, to perfect the acts of government and to extend human happiness."

DAVID RAMSEY.

"The time will come when one hundred and fifty millions of people will be living in America, equal in condition, the progeny of one race, owing their origin to the same cause, preserving the same civilization, the same language, the same literature, the same religion, the same habits, the same manners, and imbued with the same opinions, propagated under the same forms."

DE TOCQUEVILLE.

Hernando DeSoto, a native of Spain, in early youth enlisted under the banner of Pizarro, and acquired distinction in the conquest of Peru. Returning to Spain, he was made governor of Cuba in 1538, and adalentado of Florida. A year after, he sailed for Florida with an expedition of nine vessels and six hundred men. It was his ambition to establish on the northern coast of the gulf, an empire equal to that of Peru and Mexico. The story of his adventure is soon told.

Landing at Tampa bay, Florida, he marched in the direction of Tallahassee, one of his captains, in the mean time, having discovered the Bay of Pensacola. Entering Georgia, he crossed the Ockmulgee, Oconee and Ogechee rivers, and marched up the Savannah to a point in Habersham county. Thence he marched westwardly across Georgia to the head waters of the Coosa, and along the course of the Oostenaula to the sight of the present town of Rome. Still moving down the Coosa he reached the Indian town of Tallassee, and was met by the son of Tuskaloosa, a powerful chief, whose rule extended from the Coosa and Alabama to the Tombigbee. Accepting an invitation from Tuskaloosa, DeSoto met the great chief at a village upon Line creek, in the county of Montgomery. Thence he passed through the counties of Montgomery, Lowndes and Dallas, and crossing the Alabama, moved southward through Wilcox. Tuskaloosa, the chief of the Mobiles, while accompanying DeSoto in this march, secretly dispatched his couriers in every direction to alarm and concentrate his warriors. On October 18, 1540, DeSoto and Tuskaloosa arrived at the capital of the chief, the town of Mobile, situated upon the north bank of the Alabama, at Choctaw bluff, in the county of Clarke. It was here that DeSoto was attacked by Tuskaloosa. The battle lasted nine hours, and eighty-two Spaniards were killed. Forty-five horses were also slain and the camp baggage destroyed by fire. The town of Mobile was burned, and it is said that Tuskaloosa perished in the flames. After this disastrous victory the Spaniards *were anxious to march directly for Pensacola, where their ships were awaiting* them with stores, but DeSoto, unwilling to surrender the enterprise, took up his march toward the northwest, passing through the counties of Clarke, Marengo and Greene, and at last reaching the banks of the Black Warrior, near the village of Erie. It was there that he was again attacked by a large force of the Mobiles, supposed to number eight thousand warriors. The result was like that of all the contests between naked savages, armed with bows and arrows, and cavalrymen, armed with guns. The Indians were driven off. Crossing the Tombigbee, DeSoto marched westwardly through Mississippi, and at last reached the great father of waters, of which he was the first European discoverer. His ranks had been thinned by constant engagements with the brave Indians and by disease. The energy of his men was gone, and his own stout heart had failed him. In May, 1542, DeSoto died upon the banks of the Mississippi, and his body was buried in the waters. The remnant of his ill-fated expedition constructed boats and set sail down the river, July 2, 1543. But three hundred and twenty men were then left of the army of one thousand who had sailed from Cuba. As they descended the river they were attacked by fleets of canoes, and lost twelve in killed or drowned, and twenty-five in wounded. In sixteen days they reached the gulf and put to sea, landing at Panuca, on the Mexican coast, September 10, 1543, after four years of wandering through Florida, Georgia, Alabama, Mississippi and Arkansas. Such was the fate of the first attempt to colonize the southwest.

It was not until 1673 that a new attempt was made to found a colony of Europeans upon this gulf coast. It was in that year that two Canadians, Father Marquette, and Joliet, a trader, sought the great father of waters, of which they had heard vague rumors. Leaving the lakes, they ascended Fox river, crossed to the Wisconsin, and made their way in canoes to the Mississippi, and southwardly as far as the Arkansas. Joliet returned to Quebec and announced the result of his explorations. LaSalle organized an expedition and followed the Mississippi to the gulf, taking formal possession of the country, April 9, 1682, in the name of King Louis XIV. Upon information by LaSalle, of his discoveries, the French government fitted out an expedition to assist him in planting a colony near the Mouth of the Mississippi. They saw the importance of connecting their Canadian possessions by a chain of colonies and military posts with the Gulf of Mexico. LaSalle's little fleet failed to find the mouth of the great river, but landed the expedition upon the coast of Texas. There a colony was planted, and LaSalle, with a few companies, set out in search of the Mississippi. Doubt, hardships and famine led to his murder, by his own men, on the headwaters of the Trinity. A few of the adventurers made their way to Canada, and the rest perished on the coast of Texas.

Six years later commences the history of the three Canadian brothers, who were the actual founders of Mississippi, Alabama and Louisiana. Iberville had won some rank as a naval officer in the service of Louis XIV. He was commissioned in 1668, with a small fleet, to prosecute the search instituted by LaSalle, and was accompanied by his brothers, Bienville and Sanvolle. Discovering the mouth of the Mississippi, he explored the river some distance, penetrated the lakes, and finally established a colony at Biloxi. Sanvolle was appointed governor, and Bienville, lieutenant governor of Louisiana. They at once built a fort upon the Mississippi, to hold the river against the claim to the entire gulf coast set up by the Spanish Governor at Pensacola. In 1701, Bienville broke up the establishment at Biloxi, and moved the colony to Mobile Bay.

The growth of these feeble settlements was slow, and for a long time uncertain. The fear of the savages, and of sickness from the more fertile lands of the interior, caused the colonists to hug the coast closely, and to depend for subsistence upon barter with the Indians and upon contributions from the home government. Ten years after Iberville had planted his flag at the mouth of the Mississippi, the condition of the colony of Louisiana was extremely precarious. Of officers and soldiers there were one hundred and twenty-two, and of civilians there were but one hundred and fifty-seven. In 1712, the King of France granted Louisiana to one of his favorites, Crozat, a wealthy speculator, who hoped to build up a splendid name by developing this extensive region. Crozat sent out as governor Lamotte Cadillac, who, in his dispatches to Count Pontchartrain, represented Bienville's colony as being "a mass of rapscallians, from Canada, a cut-throat "set, without subordination, with no respect for religion, "and abandoned in vice with Indian women whom they "prefer to French girls." This picture of the earliest settlements of the gulf coast is no doubt overdrawn, but enough of it is true to convince the reader that these colonies did not possess the enterprise to lay broad and deep the foundation of a vigorous government and a flourishing commerce.

While they remained weak and apathetic, the English colony of the Carolinas was extending its arms westward and seeking alliances. That colony was forty-four years old when Crozat assumed charge of the gulf, and had for a long time conducted trade with the great tribe of Muscogees, who extended from the Savannah nearly to the Warrior, and even with the brave Chickasaws, who held for a century later undisputed sway over north Mississippi.

In 1716, Bienville established a military post at Natchez, which became the nucleus for the settlement of west Mississippi. This was the only inportant event of the Crozat regime. In the following year his charter was annulled, and Louisiana was handed over to a West India company, of which the celebrated Law was chief director. This adventure also signally failed, the new colonists imitating their predecessors in hugging the coast and abstaining from agriculture. But war accomplished what peace had failed to do. When hostilities began between Spain and France, in 1719, the French saw the importance of strengthening the population and resources of their colony if they would save the great river from the hands of the Spaniard. The home government offered special inducements to settlers, and succeeded in increasing the population of the colonies very rapidly. Negro slaves were sent over in large numbers, and the cultivation of rice, indigo and tobacco was encouraged.

After the peace between Spain and France and the spread of French traders more frequently through the Indian tribes, the collisions between them and the English traders from the Carolinas became more and more serious. Each tried to inflame the savages against the other. The cordon of French military posts extended at this time from Fort Toulouse, upon the Coosa, a few miles north of the present city of Montgomery, to La Harpe's Station, upon Red River.

The Indians complained that their peltries brought better prices from the English than from the French, and that the goods which they received from the English posts were of better quality and cheaper price than that furnished at Mobile and New Orleans. Thus early did the great question which controls civilized nations, affect the sentiments of these savages. The Chickasaws and the Muscogees allied themselves with the English. The Choctaws adhered to the French, and the Alabamas preserved an armed neutrality. Governor Perrier, who succeeded Bienville, in a dispatch to the home government, used this language:

"The English continue to urge their commerce into "the very heart of the province. Sixty or seventy "horses laden with merchandise have passed into the "country of the Chickasaws, to which nation I have "given orders to plunder the English of their goods, "promising to recompense them by a present."

In the year 1728, the province of Louisiana was guarded by 800 soldiers, and employed 2000 African slaves in labor. Her exports of indigo, cotton, tobacco, grain and lumber were becoming considerable. This growth in agriculture and trade was clouded but not checked by the massacre by the Indians of the Natchez settlement during the following year.

The English Carolinas were desirous of interposing a barrier between themselves and the Spaniards of the Floridas on the one hand and the French of Louisiana on the other. To carry out this desire, James Oglethorpe proposed to establish a colony upon the western bank of the Savannah. In February, 1733, Oglethorpe landed on that river with thirty families, numbering one hundred and twenty-five persons, and immediately laid out the city of Savannah. Calling the chiefs of the Lower Creek Nation together, he obtained from them a cession of all the lands between the Savannah and the Altamaha. During the following year this colony was increased by a company of forty Jews; of three hundred and forty-one Germans, and by many Scots, who settled at Darien. Two years later the town of Augusta was laid out, and a fort established there. At once, Augusta became the scene of an active trade with the Indians. Over six hundred whites were engaged in this trade. A highway was constructed between Augusta and Savannah, and boats plied between those towns and Charleston. We have seen how feeble were the settlements of Bienville after an existence of twenty years. Only five years had elapsed from the landing of Oglethorpe, before the colony of Georgia had received more than one thousand settlers from the trustees of the Company, and several hundred more who came at their own expense.

The rapid growth of Georgia alarmed the Spanish Government, and led to a series of skirmishes between the English and Floridian Spaniards. Oglethorpe wisely formed alliance with the Lower Creeks. In their treaty it was stipulated that no one but the trustees of the colony of Georgia should settle the lands between the Savannah and the mountains. The Upper Creeks being under French and Spanish influence, did not unite in this treaty. They never recognized the cessions to Oglethorpe made by the Lower Creeks; and although the English held a garrison at Ocfuskee, on the eastern bank of the Tallapoosa river, within forty miles of Fort Toulouse, planted by Bienville, they succeeded in converting to their cause but few of the Upper Creeks.

It was in May, 1736, that Bienville determined to destroy the last vestige of the Natchez tribe, who had fled from French arms upon the Mississippi, and who were now hospitably entertained by the Chickasaws in the hills of North Mississippi and North Alabama. These Natchez refugees bore a deadly hatred to the French for the destruction of their tribe, and lost no occasion to instil animosity against their conquerors in the breasts of the brave mountaineers. The English fanned the flame, until the French were goaded by constant attacks upon their settlements to launch an expedition against the Natchez village, which had been established in the heart of the Chickasaw nation.

It was planned that D'Artaquette should lead a force of French, with their allies of the tribes of the Miamis and the Illinois, from a point upon the Mississippi, and should march eastward toward the heart of the Chickasaw tribe, while Bienville should move up the Tombigbee from Mobile and march westward to the same point. The two forces were to unite and extinguish the Natchez survivors, and destroy English influence with the mountain tribes.

D'Artaquette reached the point of contemplated junction of forces, but could hear nothing of Bienville. He determined to make the attack alone and reap all the glory. His force consisted of one hundred and thirty Frenchmen and three hundred and sixty Indians. He charged the Natchez town and found himself confronted by a body of thirty Englishmen and five hundred Chickasaws. The Miamis and Illinois fled at once and the French were shot down by scores. Most of the officers were slain, and D'Artaquette himself fell into the hands of the enemy and was subsequently burned to death But a small remnant of the expedition escaped. The French guns and ammunition captured on the field were afterwards turned against Bienville.

With an army of five hundred and fifty French and six hundred Choctaw allies, Bienville embarked at Mobile, and ascended the Tombigbee to the head of navigation, now known as Cotton-Gin Port. Not hearing from D'Artaquette, he marched westward twenty-seven miles and encountered the first Chickasaw village. To his astonishment he found it well fortified by stockades, with loop-holes for musketry, and with the English flag flying over the fort. Bienville attacked the village and was most disgracefully driven back. His Choctaw allies gave him no assistance in the battle. He left his dead and wounded on the field of Pontotoc, and hastily reached the river and descended to Mobile. This disastrous expedition terminated the official career of Bienville.

In 1752, war broke out between England and France. The Chickasaws remained true to the English, and Bienville's successor, the Marquis De Vaudreuil, determined to chastise them. He pursued the route followed by Bienville, landed with his army at Cotton-Gin Port, marched westward against the Chickasaw villages, and was beaten as disastrously as his predecessor had been. He returned to Mobile with no laurels

At the conclusion of the French and Indian war, by

treaty of February 18, 1763, France ceded to Great Britain all of her Canadian possessions, and all of Louisiana lying on the eastern side of the Mississippi, as far south as Bayou Iberville. She ceded also the port and river of Mobile. Spain, the ally of France, ceded to Great Britain her province of Florida. The northern boundary of West Florida was declared to be the line 32 degrees, 28 minutes, which, commencing at the mouth of the Yazoo river, extended through points near the towns of Demopolis on the Tombigbee, and of Columbus on the Chattahoochee. Alabama, south of that line, was in British West Florida; and Alabama, north of that line, was in British Illinois. As soon as the fertile lands of Alabama and Mississippi passed into English hands, and a British Governor was stationed at Mobile, Anglo-American colonies sprang up in every direction. A colony of North Carolinians settled between Manchac and Baton Rouge. Virginians came down the Ohio and the Tennessee. Many immigrants came in from England, Ireland, Scotland and the British West Indies. All along the Mississippi, and covering a belt of fifteen miles, settled adventurers from New Jersey, Delaware, and Virginia, and colonies of Scots and of Germans, many of whom assumed French names. The British government industriously supplied these settlers with African slaves.

In June, 1773, the Creeks and Cherokees met the English at Augusta and ceded to them all the territory upon the head waters of the Ogeechee and northwest of Little river.

Lachlan McGillivray, a young Scotch trader, had married an indian girl, the daughter of Marchand, by an Indian woman of the tribe of the Wind. Marchand had been commander of Fort Toulouse. The son of Lachlan by the Indian princess, Alexander McGillivray, became a powerful man among the Creeks. He was carefully educated at Charleston, and at the age of 30 was elected Chief of the Creek Nation. This was just at the outbreak of the American Revolution. The British commissioned him a colonel, and thus early secured his favor. He was active in confederating the Indians against the Whigs, and led many expeditions of Tory Refugees and Indians against the white settlements of the Gulf.

As soon as Spain was embroiled in the war with Great Britain, she resolved to re-take Florida, and restore the Spanish flag over the country which De-Soto had discovered. Don Galvez attacked and reduced Fort Bute at Manchac and carried his arms to Baton Rouge. The forts along the river were surrendered by the British. Thence Don Galvez sailed for Mobile, reduced Fort Charlotte, and received the surrender of the city with all the territory from the Perdido to Pearl river. With the exception of Pensacola, the Spaniards were now in possession of the British Province of West Florida. On May 9, 1781, Pensacola was also conquered by the everywhere victorious Galvez.

By the treaty of Paris, Great Britain stipulated as the southern boundary of the American colonies now free, the line of thirty-one degrees, beginning at the Mississippi, extending due east to the Chattahoochee, down that river to the mouth of the Flint, thence to the St. Mary's, and along that river to the sea. Great Britain ceded East Florida and confirmed West Florida to Spain.

The territory between thirty-one degrees and thirty-two degrees twenty-eight minutes, although not ceded to Spain by Great Britain, was claimed by that power in virtue of the line adopted, under conquest by Galvez, as the northern boundary of West Florida.

The colony of Oglethorpe continued to enlarge its proportions. In 1783, commissioners from the Georgia Legislature, by treaty at Augusta, acquired from the Cherokees the country west of the Tugaloo, including the head-waters of the Oconee. A small delegation of Creeks agreed to this treaty, but a larger portion of the nation repudiated it.

After the acquisition of East and West Florida by Spain, the Indian chief McGillivray, who represented the Creeks and Seminoles, allied himself with Spain and agreed that there should be concert of action in the interest of Spain between the Creeks, Chickasaws, Choctaws and Cherokees. As soon as Georgia attempted to occupy the lands ceded under the Augusta treaty, a border war commenced. The Provisional Congress appointed Commissioners to treat with McGillivray, but only a few of the chiefs attended at the appointed place. Georgia protested against the interference of the Provisional Congress, and so soon as the Federal Commissioners took their departure, she treated with the few assembled Creek chiefs for a cession of all the territory lying on the east side of a line to run from the junction of the Oconee and Ocmulgee to the St. Marys river, including all the islands and harbors. In thus repudiating the Congressional Commission, the State of Georgia, at the earliest day, while the articles of Confederation were the league between the States, denied the right of Congress to make treaties with the

Indian nations who resided within what she claimed to be her territory. The articles of Confederation gave Congress the power to make treaties with and to manage affairs with Indians not dwelling within the boundaries of a State. When the Federal Constitution was adopted, in 1787, the year following the Augusta treaty its language gave Congress the power to regulate commerce with the Indian tribes; but in ratifying that instrument Georgia never for a moment suspected that the absence from the Constitution of the qualifying phrase contained in the articles of Confederacy was intended to give the new Federal Congress authority to make treaties and regulate commerce with Indians resident in a State. The Georgia Legislature, in 1786, declared by resolution that the attempt of Congress to treat with the Creeks was subversive of the rights of the State. It also instructed its members of Congress to insist on a revocation of the powers of the Federal Commission.

The Upper Creeks, who had never occupied the Oconee lands, waged incessant skirmish against the Georgians who dared to settle upon the disputed territory. McGillivray was active in every direction. He sent a detachment of Creeks to the rescue of the Cherokees, who were being pushed back by the North Carolinians, and after collecting the demoralized warriors, attacked a body of the Franklin troops and completely routed them. But three of the Americans escaped.

At last McGillivray, in hope of being restored to the

two thousand warriors he attended the Commission, at Rock Landing, on the Oconee, but finding that the basis of treaty did not contemplate a return to the Creeks of the Oconee lands, he abruptly terminated the conference.

General Washington, now President, was at first inclined to declare war against McGillivray and defend the Oconee settlements, but finally concluded to attempt further peaceable measures. He despatched Col. Marinus Willett, a native of Long Island, and distinguished as an officer in the Canadian war and in the Revolution, to meet McGillivray and to invite him and his chiefs to a conference at the seat of Government. The chiefs accepted the invitation and visited New York. When they reached that city, they were received by the Tammany Society, in the full dress of their order, and conducted to the presence of the President and Congress. A treaty was concluded whereby it was agreed that the Creeks and Seminoles should be under the protection of the United States, and that they should make no treaties with any State, and that the Oconee lands should remain with Georgia. By private understanding, McGillivray was to be made agent of the United States, with the rank and pay of Brigadier General, and the various chiefs were to be paid annually $100 each, and to be furnished gold medals. Such was the inauguration of that pernicious system of bribery which ever since that day has kept the Indian standing in presence of the Government with a bloody scalp extended in one hand and the other hand stretched out for his annual subsidy of gold.

Upon his return to the Coosa, McGillivray found a

large portion of his people hostile to his New York treaty, and he therefore delayed carrying out its provisions. At the first convenient time, he visited Mobile, New Orleans and Pensacola, and entered into a new alliance with the Spaniards. He was made Spanish agent over the Creeks at a salary of $3,500 per annum. Professing to be desirous of carrying out the New York treaty, he remained silent and apathetic while the Spanish officers incited the Indians to renewed hostilities upon the Cumberland and the Oconee. The Spanish Government forbid free navigation to the mouth of the Mississippi, claimed thirty-two degrees twenty-eight minutes as the North boundary of West Florida, remonstrated against the running of the line around the Oconee lands, claimed surveillance over the affairs of the Creeks, and declared that she would protect them against the pretensions of Georgia.

On February 17, 1793, McGillivray died at Pensacola. He had been a Colonel in the British service, and at one and the same time Brigadier General in the Spanish and United States service.

After McGillivray's death hostilities between the Creeks and Georgians increased, until Governor Edward Telfair, of Georgia, determined to raise a large force and invade the Creek nation. President Washington remonstrated with Telfair and claimed that Congress alone had the right to prosecute such a war. But the Georgian denied the claim of Congress and continued his military preparations. So intense was the feeling against the pretensions of the President, that Washington, notwithstanding his eminent services to his country, was regarded with deep animosity by the people of Georgia of that day.

It was in June, 1796, that the Federal Government concluded a treaty with the chiefs of the whole Creek nation, ratifying that made by McGillivray at New York. The Creeks admitted a new entering wedge into their territory by giving the Federal Government the right to establish posts between the Oconee and the Ocmulgee, although denying such permission to be a cession of lands.

Thomas Pinckney, United States Minister at Madrid, in October, 1795, concluded a treated with Spain, in which the line of thirty-one degrees was defined as the northwest boundary of West Florida. Thus another large domain lying between thirty-one degrees and thirty-two degrees, twenty-eight minutes, and stretching from the Mississippi to the Chattahoochee, became the acknowledged property of Georgia.

In 1798, Congress, by the consent of the State of Georgia, organized the territory of Mississippi, comprising the country bounded between thirty-one degrees and thirty-two degrees twenty-eight minutes, and between the Mississippi and Chattahoochee rivers. This organization by Congress, it was stipulated, was not to impair the rights of Georgia in the soil. President Adams appointed Winthrop Sergeant, Governor; John Steele, Secretary; and John Tilton, of New Hampshire, and Thomas Rodney, of Delaware, Judges.

The Natchez District was formed into two counties, Adams and Pickering. The population of this district numbered six thousand. They cultivated the banks of the Mississippi, and the bayous and larger streams flowing into that river. The Chickasaw and others of the bravest Indian tribes dwelt upon the north, east, and west of these settlements, and the Spanish Government held the country to the south.

The Alabama District was organized into one county, Washington, which covered an area from which twenty counties in Alabama and twelve in Mississippi have been since constructed. The population of the entire territory, excluding Indians, was at that time about ten thousand.

In 1802, the Federal Government acquired from Georgia all of her rights in territory west of the Chattahoochee. It was agreed that Georgia should be paid the sum of one million two hundred and fifty thousand dollars, and the Federal Government stipulated that the Indians should be removed as soon as possible from the territory of Georgia. The purchase money which was to be paid could not be considered a ruling motive for this cession on the part of Georgia, since it was to be paid from proceeds of the sale of lands within the ceded territory. The true motive by which Georgia was actuated was the pledge by the Federal Government to remove the Indians from her limits.

So soon as land offices were established by the Government and the boundaries of old French, Spanish and English grants had been fixed and recognized by law, the territory of Mississippi received a large and constantly increasing population. It came from all sections of the United States, but chiefly from Georgia, the Carolinas and from Virginia.

In 1801, Napoleon compelled Spain to cede the province of Louisiana to France; but burdened by European possessions and not being able to protect and defend so distant and at that time unprofitable colony, he readily consented, in consideration of fifteen millions of dollars, very greatly needed by his camp chest, to cede Louisiana to the United States. This cession took place April 30, 1803, and at once large numbers of settlers flocked into the territory of Louisiana from the States, and planted settlements from the Kansas river to the mouth of the Mississippi. On Dec. 20, 1803, General Wilkinson and the troops of the United States took possession of New Orleans.

The people of the territories of Louisiana and Mississippi, impatient of the Spanish garrison and commercial restrictions at Mobile, and anxious to occupy the lands about Bayou Sara, Baton Rouge and Manchac, on the east bank of the Mississippi, and the lands on the Tombigbee and Alabama, south of thirty-one degrees, and as far as the gulf, both of which regions fell within the latest Spanish definition of West Florida, contended that the cession of Louisiana by Spain to France, in 1801, was a cession of that Louisiana of which Bienville had been the founder and which France possessed before 1792, and that when Napoleon, in 1802, ceded to the United States all the territory acquired by France from Spain, he ceded not only the region then known as Louisiana, but also that other region extending from the Perdido to Bayou Iberville, embracing Mobile, which was once a part of Louisiana, but which afterwards became known as a part of Florida. The United States supported this claim.

Some border troubles occurred between the Americans and the Spaniards. So intense was the popular feeling against the Spanish pretension and continued occupation of Baton Rouge and Mobile, that John Randolph, of the Committee on Foreign Relations, reported a bill in Congress to raise an army to repel the Spaniards. President Jefferson, however, exerted his influence, effectually, to defeat such a warlike measure.

The animosity against the Spanish occupancy continued to grow for several years, during which the population of Louisiana and Mississippi multiplied in every direction, until at last, in August, 1810, a band of Americans, styling themselves patriots, and under the lead of the Kempers, who had suffered cruelty at the hands of the Spaniards, organized at St. Francisville, made a dash upon Baton Rouge and took that place by surprise, killing Governor Grandpre in the assault. The other posts were captured in succession, and the Spanish forces departed for Pensacola.

The territory thus captured was bounded by thirty-one degrees on the north, Bayou Iberville on the south, the Mississippi on the west and Pearl river on the east. It embraced the present parishes of West and East Feliciana, East Baton Rouge, St. Helena, Livingston, Washington and St. Tammany, in Louisiana, a territory comprising nearly eight thousand square miles, and equal in extent to the State of Massachusetts.

A Declaration of Independence was published by the patriots in convention, and steps were taken to establish a government independent of the Union. The adventure of Aaron Burr, a few years previous, had inspired a wide-spread ambition to organize new governments after the model of the United States, from either unoccupied territory of the United States or from neighboring territory.

The new republic commissioned Reuben Kemper to organize a force upon the Tombigbee to expel the Spaniards from Mobile and all the territory between

Pearl and Perdido rivers. A considerable body of men was soon organized and moved down the river. Halting one mile above Blakely, they sent a note to Governor Folch, demanding the surrender of Mobile. While awaiting an answer the expedition threw off all military restraint and precaution, and were surprised by a Spanish force. A number were killed and the rest took to flight. A few captives were confined five years in Moro Castle. The United States frowned upon these proceedings of the Kempers, and sent a force to Mobile for the protection of the Spaniards. Had this adventure succeeded, and the country between the Pearl and Perdido been added to the already free republic of Iberville, the dominion of that Government would have been so extensive and favorably situated as to become at once self-supporting and prosperous.

But the failure of the expedition against Mobile resulted at once in a relinquishment of all plans for an independent republic upon Lake Pontchartrain, and in the annexation of that region to Louisiana.

Spain continued to hold the country south of thirty-one degrees, and to shut the Americans from the gulf, but the United States made valuable acquisitions of territory in other directions. In 1805 nothing but an Indian trail led from the Oconee to the Alabama river, at Lake Tensaw. To open a better avenue to the settlements on the Tombigbee, the Federal Government obtained from the Creeks the right to open a horse-path through their country. The chiefs agreed to establish bridges and houses of accommodation. In the same year the Cherokees granted the right for a mail route from Knoxville to New Orleans by way of the Tombigbee, and also a cession of three hundred and fifty thousand acres of land, lying in the bend of the Tennessee river, and embracing the present county of Madison. In that year, also, the Choctaws ceded five millions of acres between the Alabama and Tombigbee rivers, and stretching from the Tombigbee to the Natchez settlements. It was thus that the fairest of his lands were being acquired from the Indian, and highways constructed through the remainder, which tended surely to further conquest or removal.

When war broke out between England and the United States, in 1812, the continued occupancy of the gulf coast by the Spaniard was considered dangerous to our Government, as Spain was believed to be in secret league with England. Under orders, General Wilkinson, with six hundred men, sailed from New Orleans, in April, 1813, and on the 13th took position in the rear of Fort Charlotte. Captain Perez, the commandant, surrendered the fort, and the Spanish garrison retired to Pensacola. At last the whole territory of what is now Louisiana, Mississippi and Alabama was free from foreign dominion, and nothing was left to prevent its entire occupancy by Americans except the continued residence of warlike tribes of Indians, whom the Federal Government, as long ago as 1802, had stipulated with Georgia to remove.

Notwithstanding the non-observance of this stipulation, the country was rapidly settled by a brave and enterprising people. In 1810 the population of Louisiana was 76,556; that of Georgia was 252,438, and that of the Mississippi territory was 40,352. The total population of this new region thus embraced more than 369,000 souls. Ten years later, in 1820, just as the Indian agitation, the slavery agitation and the free-trade agitation had begun to divide the people of the United States into well defined political parties, we find that the population of these gulf States was as follows: Georgia, 340,975; Mississippi, 75,448; Alabama, 127,901; and Louisiana, 152,923. They had grown in ten years from a population of 369,000 to one of 697,000, notwithstanding the fierce Indian war which had occurred in the meantime.

This population represented a voting power two-thirds as great as that of Virginia, more than half as great as that of New York, much greater than that of Massachusetts, and more than one-third as great as that of all New England. If in the short period of one generation this new power in the southwest was able to command a political position so imposing, would not her continued growth in a few years restore to the South and to the agricultural States that preponderance in the government which had already shifted from Virginia to Massachusetts?

The unjust political plans devised to curb this growing empire were the causes which led to the establishment at Montgomery, in 1861, of the Southern Confederacy.

CHAPTER III.

Growth of the Idea of Secession—Jealousy of the Commercial against the Agricultural States—Navigation of the Mississippi—The Whiskey Rebellion—The Jay Treaty —Views of Distinguished Men—Frequent Threats and Hopes of Disunion—The Louisiana Purchase—The East Fears the South and West—The Hartford Convention—The Resolutions of '98—Randolph's Reply to Patrick Henry, etc., etc.

"An effort has often since been made to represent it as one of many malicious and entirely ungrounded calumnies, that there was at this time any serious thought of a disruption of the Union. This is only one instance of the white-washing tendencies and decorative coloring characteristic of the greater number of historical works. In the letters of the Federalists we find not only that wishes to this end were expressed, but that formal plans were devised."

VON HOLST'S Constitutional History of the United States.

"The Federal Government, then, appears to be the organ through which the United Republics communicate with foreign nations and with each other. Their submission to its operation is voluntary; its councils, its engagements, its authority, are theirs, modified and united. Its sovereignty is an emanation from theirs, not a flame in which they have been swallowed up. Each is still a perfect State, still sovereign, still independent, and still capable, should the occasion require, to resume the exercise of its functions in the most unlimited extent."

TUCKER'S Blackstone [1803.]

The growth of the southwest was looked upon with disfavor by the political leaders of the Northern States from the very hour when the Constitution recently adopted began to show signs of vitality; and this disfavor was intensified by the acquisition of Louisiana. Washington himself, even as late as 1784, did not regard the possession of the Mississippi river as a matter essential to the confederation, and was accustomed, like the entire body of the Congress, to limit his attention to the thirteen colonies. The outlying lands were regarded simply as a convenience for payment of the public debt. Few if any of the statesmen of that day contemplated the possibility of the expansion of this outlying territory into populous States, whose votes in the Federal Congress might soon decide the balance of power against the North.

The first issue between the South and North was distinctly and positively made when Spain, in 1785, refused to yield the free navigation of the Mississippi, but at the same time offered a treaty, which otherwise would have been favorable to the commercial interests of the Middle and Northern States. The Secretary of Foreign Affairs, Mr. Jay, recommended a waiver for thirty years, of all claim to the free navigation of the Mississippi. The seven Northern States voted for this stipulation, and the five Southern States, with the exception of one member, voted against it. Delaware was not then represented. Thus early were geographical lines drawn upon a question in which the South exhibited a comprehensive statesmanship, and in which the North exhibited an unpatriotic jealousy at the expansion of the confederation. Jefferson, writing from Paris, to Madison, in 1787, says: "I have had great "opportunities of knowing the character of the people "who inhabit that country, and I venture to say that "the act which abandons the navigation of the Missis- "sippi is an act of separation between the eastern and "western country. It is a relinquishment of five parts "out of eight of the territory of the United States— "an abandonment of the fairest subject for the pay- "ment of our public debts, and the chaining of those "debts upon our own necks, in perpetuation. I have "the utmost confidence in the honest intentions of "those who concur in this measure, but I lament their "want of acquaintance with the character and physical "advantages of the people who, right or wrong, will "suppose their interests sacrificed on this occasion to "the contrary interests of that part of the confederacy "in possession of present power."

Unquestionably on this occasion the interests of all the settlements upon the waters of the Mississippi were sacrificed to the jealousy of that part of the confederacy which was then in power. In the language of John Adams, this unpatriotic attempt at waiver for thirty years, of all claim to the free navigation of the Mississippi, "gave rise to rankling jealousies and fester-"ing prejudices, not only of the North and the South "against each other, but of each section against the "ablest and most virtuous of the other."

The jealousy which thus began under the confederation continued after the adoption of the Constitution. The smaller commercial States, at the outset, while John Adams was President, for the most part repudiated the right of secession, and denounced the resolutions of the Kentucky and Virginia Legislatures, which set up the doctrine that in the last resort, the State was the sole umpire as to all Federal questions; but so soon as it appeared that the Federalists would lose control of the government, they hastened to advocate and threatened disunion upon every question which tended to diminish their already waning power. There was not at that day a horror of disunion, and no man was stigmatized as traitor who threatened it. The States had made the Union, just as they had made the confederation, and it was difficult to understand how the one compact was more sacred in its origin or its objects than the other. The confederation had signally failed of its purpose, and the Union might be equally as defective.

As an illustration of the temper of the times it is interesting to note that the suppression of the whiskey insurrection, during Washington's administration, gave rise to prophecies of civil war, and of the overthrow of the administration. It was said that the insurgent district of Pennsylvania would secede from the Union, and that the coercive action of the Government would justify such secession. JEFFERSON feared that the excise law would produce disunion. WOLCOTT expressed a hope that the insurgent district would be either chastised or rejected from the Union. HAMILTON was chagrined to find that the march of the militia to enforce the excise law was greeted by the people with laughter and derision. EDMUND RANDOLPH expressed a fear that the insurgents would call England to their aid and thus bring about disruption of the Union.

Another illustration of the indifference with which the Union was regarded by the States whenever Federal laws interfered with their peculiar interests, may be found in the denunciation of the treaty negotiated with Great Britain, by Jay, in 1794. The friends of the French Revolution in the House of Representatives, in retaliation against the British Orders in Council of 1793, which forbade the commerce of foreign nations with France, had adopted a resolution in Congress forbidding the purchase of British manufactured goods until the western posts were surrendered and reparation had been made for a violation of the neutral rights of the United States. Fortunately better councils prevailed;

but, pending the question of this embargo, there was the most intense excitement among the people. The material interests of the Federalists and a fear of her power bound them to England. Sympathy with the Republican purposes of the French bound the anti-Federalists or Republicans to France. New England was for peace with Great Britain and acceptance of Jay's treaty. The Middle States and the South were a unit against the treaty. DWIGHT declared that the people of New England would take no part in a war with Great Britain. Said he, in a letter to WOLCOTT: "Sooner would ninety-nine out of a hundred of our "inhabitants separate from the Union than plunge "themselves into an abyss of misery." WOLCOTT writing to NOAH WEBSTER, expressed his impatience at the antagonism between the agricultural South and the commercial East, and his belief that "the great sec-"tions of the United States will not long continue to "be agitated as they have been."

Jefferson, in the fourth volume of his Memoirs, says that John Q. Adams called upon him during this controversy over the embargo laws and declared that he had information of the most unmistakable character that certain citizens of the Eastern States, Massachusetts particularly, were in negotiation with the British Government, the object of which was an agreement that the New England States should take no further part in executing the embargo laws against the hostile British Orders in Council, and that without formally declaring their separation from the Union, they would withdraw from all aid and obedience to it. In other words they would resort to nullification.

A report by Mr. Gore, in the Massachusetts Legislature, which was adopted by the unanimous vote of the Federal party, declared the war enforcing the embargo "unjust, oppressive and unconstitutional, and not "binding." Here was a plain and explicit nullification of a Federal law. If the laws in question were "not "binding," the State had a clear right, and it was her duty to resist them if she saw proper to do so.

The political economist, MATHEW CAREY, writing just after the peace with Great Britain, sets forth very pointedly the reasons which inflamed the sectional jealousy of the North against the South.

"The naked fact is, that the demogogues in the "Eastern States, not satisfied with deriving all the "benefit from the Southern section of the Union, that "they would from so many wealthy colonies; with "making princely fortunes by the carriage and expor-"tation of its bulky and valuable productions, and "supplying it with their own manufactures and the pro-"ductions of Europe and the East and West Indies, to "an enormous amount, and at an immense profit, have "uniformly treated it with outrage, insults and injury. "And, regardless of their vital interests, the Eastern "States were lately courting their own destruction, by "allowing a few restless, turbulent men to lead them "blindfold to a separation, which was pregnant with "their certain ruin. Whenever that event takes place "they sink into insignificance. If a separation were "desirable to any part of the Union, it would be to the "Middle and Southern States, particularly the latter, "who have been so long harassed with the complaints, "the restlessness, the turbulence and the ingratitude of "the Eastern States, that their patience has been tried "almost beyond endurance. 'Jeshuran waxed fat "and kicked'; and he will be severely punished for his "kicking in the event of a dissolution of the Union."

The next issue between the South and North was upon the acquisition of Louisiana. Here, again, the North exhibited an unpatriotic jealousy against expansion of territory. In this matter the question of slavery was not mooted. The objection was to the acquisition of any portion of Louisiana—that at the head waters of the Mississippi, as well as that at its mouth. Again, Congress and the country were divided by geographical lines, and the two discordant elements became even more embittered against each other than they had been upon the Mississippi Navigation and the Embargo questions. It was openly declared from Northern sources that separation from the Union would be preferable to acquisition of Louisiana. Plummer, of New Hampshire, said: "Admit this "Western World into the Union, and you destroy at "once the weight and importance of the Eastern States "and compel them to establish a separate and inde-"pendent empire." Griswold, of Connecticut, regarded as a leader of the Federal party, said: "The vast, "unmanageable extent which the accession of Louisiana "will give to the United States, the consequent disper-"sion of our population, and the distribution of the "balance, which it is so important to maintain between "the Eastern and Western States, threatens at no very "distant day, the subversion of our Union."

The disunion design of the Federal party, in consequence of the acquisition of Louisiana is thus shown by John Quincy Adams, who in 1828 wrote: "This "design had been formed in the winter of 1803 or "1804, immediately after, and as a consequence of the "acquisition of Louisiana. * * This plan was so "far matured that the proposal had been made to an "individual to permit himself at the proper time to be "placed at the head of the military movements which "it was foreseen would be necessary for carrying it into "execution. The project, I repeat, had gone to the "length of fixing upon a military leader for its exe-"cution."

Mr. Adams' information was obtained from Senator Tracy, of Connecticut, who, although he disapproved the project, was made acquainted with it in all its particulars. The Northern Confederacy was to extend, if practicable, so far South as to include Maryland. The Susquehanna was suggested as another boundary, but if New York could not be won over, the Hudson was to be the boundary. Mr. Adams gives incidents of a visit to Rufus King, in 1804, and says: "I found "there sitting Timothy Pickering, who, shortly after I "went in, took leave and withdrew. Mr. King said to "me, 'Col. Pickering has been talking to me about a "project they have for a separation of the States, and "a Northern Confederacy.' "

Governor Plummer, of New Hampshire, was an open and pronounced secessionist. In a letter to Mr. Adams, he admitted that he "was a disunionist at that "period; in favor of forming a separate government in "New England; that he was consulted on such a plan "by Federal members of Congress from New England." In his journal, Governor Plummer mentions that in 1804, Timothy Pickering, James Hillhouse and himself dined with Aaron Burr; that Hillhouse "unequivocally "stated that it was his opinion that the United States "would soon form two distinct and separate govern-

"ments." Again he says: "When the late Samuel "Hunt intimated to me the necessity of seceding "from the Union, he observed that the work must "commence in the State Legislatures, so that those "who acted should be supported by State laws."

When Hillhouse denied the statement of Adams, Governor Plummer made the following entry in his journal: "There is no circumstance in these publica-"tions that surprises me so much as the letter of James "Hillhouse. I recollect and am certain that on return-"ing early one evening from dining with Aaron Burr, "this same Mr. Hillhouse, after saying to me that New "England had no influence in the government, added "in an animated tone, 'The Eastern States must and "will dissolve the Union, and form a separate govern-"ment of their own, and the sooner they do this the "better.' But there was no man with whom I con-"versed so often, so fully, and so freely as with Roger "Griswold. He was without doubt or hesitation deci-"dedly in favor of dividing the Union and establishing "a Northern Confederacy."

Gov. Plummer speaks of walking for hours with Pickering, who said "that he thought the United "States too large and their interests too diversified for "the Union to continue, and that New England, New "York, and perhaps Pennsylvania might and ought to "form a separate government. He then paused, and "looking me fully in the face, awaited my reply. I "simply asked him if the division of the States was "not the object which General Washington most pa-"thetically warned the people to oppose. He said, "'yes, the fear of it was a ghost that for a long time "haunted the imagination of that old gentleman.'"

From the day of the ratification of the Federal Constitution, the Southern States saw themselves outstripped by the Northern and Eastern States, in population and wealth. But at the opening of the present century the agricultural interests of the South received an impetus from the increased value of cotton planting, and it was just then that a combination of circumstances attracted to the South and West the attention of the country and inflamed that jealousy at the North which had survived the acquisition of the Mississippi river and the adoption of the Jay treaty.

The experiments which were being made for cheapening the production of cotton, by applying machinery to the removal of the seed promised a speedy and rapid appreciation of Southern lands and power. The efforts which had been made by General WASHINGTON and Governor TELFAIR, to remove from the gulf country all the Indian tribes; the cession by Georgia to the United States of all the territory between the Chattahoochee and the Mississippi; the prospect of a speedy erection of this territory into at least two States; the fortunate acquisition by President JEFFERSON of LOUISIANA and the great territory stretching from the Mississippi river to the Pacific Ocean, capable of erection into a hundred States and certain of giving birth to at least two more States within a few years—all alarmed the political leaders of New England as to a continuance of their power.

For some years to come they might control the popular branch of Congress, but, if these schemes were to be permitted, the new States would soon overshadow the old in the Senate. The labors of New England were therefore still more ardently directed towards curbing the power of the great southwest.

So long as the commercial States controlled by New England prevailed in the Federal Government, the desired curb was to be found in an exercise of the power of Congress. When Virginia and Kentucky protested in their celebrated resolutions of 1798 against the alien and sedition laws, and declared that as there was no umpire to settle disputes between the State and Federal Government, each State must decide for itself the measure of its grievances and the mode of redress, all of the commercial States at once denied the doctrine. No matter that JEFFERSON, the author of the Declaration of Independence, had written the one set of resolutions, and MADISON, the father of the Constitution, had written the other, every one of these States admitted the power of Congress to enact the alien and sedition laws. The agricultural States denied that power.

But when the growth of the southwest was observed, and the acquisition of Louisiana was impending, the very men and the very States, who in order to vindicate the alien and sedition laws, denied to the States all power to decide for themselves against any Federal act, however oppressive or iniquitous, now openly and boldly advocated a dissolution of the Union.

From his seat in Congress, JOSIAH QUINCY, a leading statesman of Massachusetts, declared that if the bill for the purchase of Louisiana became law it was a virtual dissolution of the Union, that it would free the States from their moral obligation; and as it would be the right of all, it would be the duty of some to prepare for a separation—amicably if they could, violently if they must. The doctrine of secession and nullification thus obtained its first practical application in New England. The embargo affected their maritime interests. Therefore they went so far as to designate the man who was to be the military chief of their secession movement. The acquisition of Louisiana threatened their political supremacy. Therefore they declared that the extension of our territory justified violent separation; and we find AARON BURR, a prominent statesman of New York, relying upon the tacit consent of the North and the possible forbearance of the South, organizing an armed expedition to make New Orleans the capital of a great southwestern republic.

This spirit of sectionalism acquired additional growth at the North, and especially at the East, during the war of 1812. It had not as yet appeared at the South. While the South rallied as one man to the aid of the oppressed seamen of the United States (all of northern birth), the States of New England, at first clamorous for war, so soon as they saw that their ships were left idle and their commerce destroyed, were as ardently clamorous for peace. They defamed President MADISON, and held up to him, "the Island of Elba! or a "halter." The acts of nullification at the outbreak of the war were numerous. The resolutions of their legislatures went as far as the more celebrated but not more pointed resolutions of '98. The executives of Connecticut and Massachusetts refused to place their militia, when called into service, under command of the President, as required by the Constitution. The Governor of Vermont ordered the return of the militia of that State, which had gone upon the expedition to Canada. Nothing was left undone to embarrass the financial operations of the Government, to prevent the enlistment of troops, to keep back the men and money of New England from the service of the Union, and to force the President from his seat. Illicit trade was carried on with the enemy, and free traffic was conducted between Massachusetts and Great Britain through a separate custom house. Beacon fires were lighted as signals to the enemy. The fall of Detroit was openly rejoiced at The acts of individuals soon became the acts of government. The Massachusetts Legislature authorized delegates to meet like delegates from other New England States, at Hartford, to consult upon the subject of "their public grievances and "concerns," and upon "the best means of preserving "their resources." Chief among the recommendations of that convention was—that an amendment be proposed "for restraining Congress in the exercise of an "unlimited power to make new States and to admit "them into the Union." Through all their proceedings the under-current of complaint was at the loss of political power by the growth of the States. It was the old jealousy of the small States against the large States which had so seriously obstructed the formation of the Constitution.

A clergyman of Boston expressed the sentiment of the hour when he said—"The Union has long since "been virtually dissolved, and it is full time that this "part of the dis-united States should take care of "itself." Another doctor of divinity thus addressed his flock: "The Israelites became weary of yielding "the fruit of their labor to pamper their splendid "tyrants. They left their political woes. They sep-"arated; where is our Moses? Where the rod of his "miracles? Where is our Aaron? Alas! no voice "from the burning bush has directed them here."

An irrepressible conflict was admitted at that day as existing between the smaller States of the East, which were engaged in commercial pursuits, and the larger States of the South, which were engaged more especially in agriculture. "Events may prove," says the Journal of the Hartford Convention, January 4, 1815, "that the causes of our calamity are deep *and permanent.* They may be found to proceed, not merely from "blindness of prejudice, pride of opinion, violence of "party spirit, or the confusion of the times; but they "may be traced to implacable combinations of individuals or States, to monopolize power and office and "to trample without remorse upon the rights and "interests of *the commercial sections* of the Union."

"Whenever it shall appear," continues the Journal, "that these causes are radical and permanent, a separation by equitable arrangement will be preferable to *an* "*alliance by constraint among nominal friends but real* "*enemies, inflamed by mutual hatreds and jealousies,* "*and inviting by intestine divisions, contempt and* "*aggressions from abroad.*" The Hartford Convention, having thus announced that there were such serious conflicts of interest between the commercial and agricultural States, the maritime and the inland, as to threaten a permanent calamity to the States of New England, proceeded to announce the remedy for the evil. The remedy proposed was precisely that suggested by the Virginia and Kentucky resolutions. The Convention said: "That Acts of Congress in violation "of the Constitution are absolutely void, is an undeniable position. It does not, however, consist with "the respect from a confederate State towards the "general government, to fly to open resistance upon "every infraction of the Constitution. The mode and "the energy of the opposition should always conform "to the nature of the violation, the intention of the "authors, the extent of the evil inflicted, the determi-"nation manifested to persist in it, and the danger of "delay. But in cases of deliberate, dangerous, and "palpable infractions of the Constitution, *affecting the* "*sovereignty of the State*, and the liberties of the "people; it is not only the right, but the duty, of such "State to interpose its authority for their protection, in "the manner best calculated to secure that end. When "emergencies occur, which are either beyond the reach "of judicial tribunals, or too pressing to admit of delay "incident to their forms, STATES WHICH HAVE NO COMMON "UMPIRE, MUST BE THEIR OWN JUDGES AND EXECUTE THEIR "OWN DECISIONS."

It will be observed that the Convention recognized the possibility of emergencies beyond the reach of judicial tribunals, and for the settlement of which there is no common umpire. In the debate between MR. WEBSTER and MR. HAYNE, in 1830, at the session of Congress during which the question arose as to the conflicting jurisdiction of the State of Georgia and the Federal Government, the umpire declared by MR. WEBSTER, in all cases affecting the powers of the general government, was the Supreme Court of the United States. MR. HAYNE insisted that courts, whether supreme or inferior, are the mere creatures of the sovereign power designed to expound and carry into effect its sovereign will, and that no independent State ever yet submitted to a Judge upon the bench the true construction of a compact between itself and another sovereign. In proof that the judiciary were not designed to act as umpires it is only necessary to observe that in a great majority of cases the Supreme Court could manifestly not take jurisdiction of the matters in dispute. "Whenever it may be designed by the Federal "Government," prophesied Mr. Hayne, "to commit a "violation of the Constitution, it can be done and "always will be done in such a manner as to deprive "the court of all jurisdiction over the subject." Likewise MR. MADISON, in his report upon the Virginia Resolutions of '98, says: "But it is objected that the "judicial authority is to be regarded as the sole expos-"itor of the Constitution in their last resort; and it "may be asked, for what reason the declaration by the "general assembly, supposing it to be theoretically "true, could be required at the present day, and in so "solemn a manner? On this objection, it might be "observed, first, that there may be instances of usurped "power which the forms of the Constitution would "never draw within the control of the judiciary depart-"ment; secondly, that if the decision of the judiciary "be raised above the authority of the sovereign parties "to the Constitution, the decisions of the other depart-"ments, not carried by the forms of the Constitution "before the judiciary, must be equally authoritative "and final with the decisions of that department."

These views of MR. HAYNE and of MR. MADISON, accord with the opinion which prevailed at the Hartford Convention, as to the impotency of the Supreme Court to decide grave questions affecting the sovereignty of a state. A few years later than the great WEBSTER-HAYNE debate, it was seen that the Supreme Court refused to decide as to the legitimate sovereignty of Rhode Island, referring the whole question to the political department of the government, and following its decision. To us, of the present day, who have seen the Supreme Court shorn of its powers, or increased in members, by the political department of the government, at pleasure, in order to secure a decision one way, or to defeat a decision another way, it is evident that the Supreme Court of the United States is no umpire between the States and the Federal Government.

The spirit of sectionalism thus owed its birth to New England, and found the only basis for its independence in those principles of State sovereignty which remained undisputed for forty years from the foundation of the government. MR. JOHN QUINCY ADAMS, then Minister to Russia, writing from St. Petersburgh, October 24th, 1813, says: "If New England loses her influence in "the councils of the Union, it will not be owing to any "diminution of her population, occasioned by these "emigrations: it will be from the partial, sectarian, or "as Hamilton has called it, clannish spirit, which "makes so many of her political leaders jealous and "envious of the West and South. This spirit is in its "nature, narrow and contracted, and it always works "by means like itself. *Its natural tendency is to excite "and provoke a counteracting spirit of the same char- "acter; and it has actually produced that effect in our "country.*" Such is the testimony of one of New England's representative sons against his own people.

Is it surprising that this partial, selfish, clannish spirit of sectionalism which planted itself boldly on the extremest doctrines of State rights, should arouse a counteracting spirit in the people of the Gulf States and lead them to assert the sovereignty of their rightful State laws over every inch of their territory, even though it should be in the face of a writ of error from the Supreme Court of the United States and in the face of Federal troops?

The greater part of the southwest was finally and completely opened up to settlement by annexation to the United States, as we have seen, just as the constitutional questions which divided the friends of Jefferson from those of Hamilton, were the subject of violent party contention. The most vital of these questions affected this district closely, and the people were educated in politics by practical experience of the operation of the Constitution as construed by one party or the other. Their first lesson in constitutional law came from that doctrine of Jefferson and Madison, set forth in the resolutions of 1798, which was a few years later incorporated in the resolutions of the Hartford Convention.

The Virginia Resolutions, adopted by her Legislature, December 24th, 1798, were written by James Madison, who has been styled "the Father of the Constitution." The most important paragraph of those Resolutions is the one which declares that "in case of a deliberate, "palpable, and dangerous exercise of other powers not "granted by the said compact, the States who are "parties thereto, have the right and are in duty bound "*to interpose* for arresting the progress of the evil, and "for maintaining within their respective limits the "authorities, rights, and liberties, appertaining to "them."

The Kentucky Resolutions, adopted by that State, November 10th, 1799, were written by JEFFERSON, after consultation with MADISON. The language made use of was not so guarded as that of the Virginia resolutions. It declared that the Federal Government "was not made the exclusive or final judge of the "extent of the powers delegated to itself, since that "would have made its discretion, and not the "Constitution, the measure of its powers: but that as "in all other cases of compact between parties having "no common judge, each party has an equal right to "judge for itself, as well of infractions as of the mode "and measure of redress." The Resolutions went on to define the manner in which this principle might be put into practice, by declaring that "the several States who "formed that instrument [the Constitution] being sov- "ereign and independent, have the unquestionable "right to judge of the infraction: and that a nullifica- "tion by those sovereignties of all unauthorized acts "done under color of that instrument, is the rightful "remedy."

At a later day, when the sentiment in favor of Union had become strengthened by time and by the growing greatness of the Republic, it was endeavored to argue away the plain meaning of these celebrated resolutions. Madison, in 1831, asserted that his Resolutions were merely declaratory of opinion, that they pointed out no mode of correcting illegal Federal acts, that the words "to interpose" meant legal interposition, and that the word "nullification" which appears in the Kentucky Resolutions was not to be found in the Virginia Resolutions. BENTON, in his "Thirty Years' View," attempts a defense of Jefferson, by asserting that he was not the author of the Kentucky Resolutions. The publication of Jefferson's Works at a later day refutes the denial of Benton, and the evasions of Madison. There were found among his papers, two original drafts, in Jefferson's own handwriting, of the Kentucky Resolutions. In one of them is this resolution: that when the general government assumes powers "which have not been delegated, a nullification "of the Act, is the rightful remedy: that every State "has a natural right, in cases not within the compact "[*casus non fœderis*,] to nullify of their own authority, "all assumptions of power by others within their "limits."

Although the Virginia Resolutions used the words "to interpose," where Kentucky used the word "nullify," there is not room for a shadow of doubt that both meant the same thing. Jefferson says that the conference on the Kentucky Resolutions took place between him and the two brothers Nicholas, and he adds: "I think Mr. Madison was either with us, or "consulted, but my memory is uncertain as to the "minute details." The two sets of resolutions bear upon their face evidence of consultation and unity of sentiment between the two distinguished authors. Von Holst, professor at the University of Freidburg, in his Constitutional History of the United States, very justly says, with reference to these Resolutions: "In a word, "as the principles advanced in the Resolutions were the "same, they led to the same logical conclusions, which "were clearly expressed in the Kentucky Resolutions, "namely, the right of the States, through the organ of "their Legislatures, to 'resolve' that laws of Congress "were unconstitutional, and therefore void and of no "effect."

Jefferson wrote to Madison, November 17th, 1798,

enclosing him a draft of the Kentucky Resolutions, and we have nowhere, in evidence, any protest against, or difference of opinion, as to the use of the word "nullification," expressed by Madison, until the lapse of more than thirty years, when South Carolina, under the teachings of Calhoun, put in practical effect the doctrines of the Kentucky Resolutions. John Quincy Adams, in his eulogy on Madison, said: "Concurring "in the doctrine that the separate States have a right "to interpose in cases of palpable infractions of the "Constitution by the government of the United States, "and that the alien and sedition acts presented a case "of such infraction, Mr. Jefferson considered them "as absolutely null and void, and thought the State "Legislatures competent, not only to declare but to "make them so, to resist their execution within their "respective borders by physical force and to secede "from the Union rather than submit to them, if at- "tempted to be carried into execution by force."

Whatever doubt there may be as to what MADISON meant by the right and duty of the State "to interpose" to prevent Federal infractions of the Constitution, there is no doubt as to what JEFFERSON meant, and not the least doubt as to what Virginia meant The State of Virginia meant precisely what the State of Kentucky had said. At this time HAMILTON wrote to DRAYTON, Speaker of the House, charging that the Virginia Resolutions meant the overthrow of the Government, and that her hostile declarations had been followed up by preparations for the use of force. He declared that Virginia had taken steps to put her militia on a war footing, and had established magazines and arsenals. The truth of this charge is not denied by Randall, the biographer of Jefferson. Indeed, at a somewhat later day, John Randolph admitted in Congress that there was no longer any cause for concealing that the great armory at Richmond was built to enable the State of Virginia to resist by force the encroachments of the then administration upon her indisputable rights.

The views of the anti-Federalists were well expressed by John Randolph when in March, 1799, he debated with Patrick Henry at Charlotte Courthouse, Virginia. Mr. Henry, at the request of Washington, had come from his retirement and offered himself as candidate for the legislature, with the purpose of defending the acts and doctrines of the Federal administration under ADAMS. RANDOLPH was a mere youth, and his reply to HENRY was the first of a long series of brilliant addresses. He had been educated in the ideas of Jefferson and Madison. Said he: "In questions of *meum* "and *tuum*, where rights of property are concerned, "and some other cases specified in the Constitution, I "grant you that the Federal judiciary may pronounce "on the validity of the law. But in questions involv- "ing the right to power, whether this or that power "has been delegated or reserved, they cannot and "ought not to be the arbiter; that question has been "left, as it always was, and always must be left, to be "determined among sovereignties in the best way they "can. Political wisdom has not yet discovered any "infallible mathematical rule by which to determine "the assumptions of power between those who know no "other law or limitation, save that imposed upon them "by their own consent, and which they can abrogate "at pleasure." He continued: "Shall the creature "of the States be the sole judge of the legality or con-"stitutionality of its acts, in a question of power "between them and the States? Shall they who "assert a right be the sole judges of their authority to "claim and to exercise it? Does not all power seek to "enlarge itself?—grow on that it feeds upon? Has "not that been the history of all encroachment, all "usurpation?"

Mr. Henry had said that the remedy for unauthorized Federal laws, when the Federal judiciary had no cognizance of the case, would be found in the privilege and right of petition. "Petition! Whom are "we to petition?" replied Randolph. "Those who "are the projectors of these measures, who voted for "them and forced them upon you in spite of your will? "Would not those men laugh at your petition, and, in "the pride and insolence of new born power, trample it "under their feet with disdain?"

From this brief review of the opinions and wishes of political leaders of both of the early parties, it is seen that the right of nullification and secession was recognized by either party whenever the administration was in the hands of its opponents, or whenever the tendency of events pointed to a diminution of the power and influence of the section in which its strength lay. The friends of Jefferson might threaten secession one day because of the sedition act; but it was the party of Adams which threatened disunion on the next day because of the extension of territory or of an embargo upon commerce. Under these leaders the Southwest came into existence and began its wonderful growth. At their very birth the Gulf States had seen a desperate attempt by New England to strangle them under the continued rule of Spain and of the Indian savage. The first political lesson learned in infancy was that they were a bastard offspring, regarded with aversion by the mother who should have nourished them. The first political cry that met their ears was the cry from Massachusetts, that their accession to the Union was justifiable cause for disunion, and a similar cry from Virginia that each State has the right to judge for itself of an infraction of the Constitution and to assert the mode of redress.

CHAPTER IV.

Jurisdiction of the United States Over Indian Tribes—The Fee Simple of Lands Occupied by the Tribes—The Yazoo Frauds—The Decision in the Case of Fletcher vs. Peck—Indignation of the People of Georgia—Constitutional Questions growing out of that Decision, &c.

"Congress have the exclusive right of pre-emption to all Indian lands lying within the territories of the United States. * * * The title is in the United States by the treaty of peace with Great Britain, and by subsequent cessions from France and Spain, and by cessions from the individual States; and the Indians have only a right of occupancy and the United States possess the legal title subject to that occupancy, and with an absolute and exclusive right to extinguish the Indian title of occupancy either by conquest or purchase."

KENT'S COMMENTARIES ON AMERICAN LAW.

"Randolph was in Georgia at the time of the perpetration of this villainy, and participated in the shame and mortification of his friends at seeing persons reputed religious and respectable, effecting a public robbery, by bribing the legislature of the State, and reducing them to the horrors of treachery and perjury. A more detestable, impudent, and dangerous villainy is not to be found on record."

GARLAND'S LIFE OF RANDOLPH.

Under the Articles of Confederation the United States had the power to manage all affairs with the Indian nations not members of a State. The language of the article conveying the power was this: "The United "States in Congress assembled, shall also have the sole "and exclusive right and power of * * regulating "the trade and managing all affairs with the Indians, "not members of any of the States, provided that the "legislative right of any State within its own limits be "not infringed or violated."

It was claimed under this grant that the Federal Government could manage all Indian affairs of whatever character, except affairs relating to individual Indians who may have subjected themselves to State laws and become citizens of the State. In all other cases, whether the Indian tribe resided within or without the limits of a State, the United States alone could regulate and rule them. It was seen at once that this Federal jurisdiction must conflict with the right of a State to rule the people of every class within its own limits, and that interminable confusion would result from the subjection of one class of the people within a State to one set of laws, and those of another to another set. When, therefore, the Constitution was framed, the States declined to renew this grant; but contented themselves simply with adopting this provision, the only one in that instrument referring to the Indian:

"The Congress shall have power * * to regu-"late commerce with foreign nations, and among the "several States and with the Indian tribes."

The plain meaning of this section is that the United States should regulate commerce with those Indian tribes which dwelt upon lands not belonging to a State, and which were outside the jurisdiction of a State. This is evident from the fact that commerce with the Indian tribes alluded to is placed in connection with commerce between the States and foreign governments. The right to manage all affairs with the Indians, such as the United States possessed under the articles was withdrawn under the Constitution, and yet the Federal Government proceeded under the Constitution to exercise the authority it wielded under the articles, to regulate commerce with Indian tribes, both within and without the limits of a State, and also to manage all Indian affairs, without regard to whether the tribes were within or without the State.

Such a claim, and an attempt to enforce it, was the occasion of serious difficulty between the Federal Government and the State of Georgia from an early day. The questions which sprang from this claim, agitated the people of Georgia, Alabama and Mississippi, from the year 1795 to the close of the administration of President Jackson, a period of more than forty years. Notwithstanding the denunciations which have been hurled at the State of Georgia for her action and position in these Indian questions, a review of the facts and the law, must convince every dispassionate reader that at each step of the controversy, the people of the Southwest are vindicated.

The first question which arose between the State of Georgia and the Federal Government was, who possessed the fee simple of the lands lying within the boundaries of the State, but occupied by Indian tribes? An answer to this question is found in the International Law which prevailed among Christian Powers at the period of the discovery of America.

When the American Continent was discovered by the Europeans, the several nations who settled it with colonies united in the declaration that discovery gave a title to the government by whose subjects it was made, against all other European governments whose title might be consummated by possession. The nation making the discovery was recognized among Christian people as having the sole right to make terms with the Indians, and to plant settlements. The Indians were admitted to be the rightful occupants of the soil with a legal, as well as just, claim to retain possession of it, and to use it according to their own discretion; but their rights to complete sovereignty were necessarily diminished, and their power to dispose of the soil at their own will, to whomever they pleased, was denied by the original fundamental principle, that discovery gave exclusive title to those who made it.

While the different nations of Europe respected the rights of the natives, as occupants, they asserted the ultimate dominion to be in themselves: and claimed and exercised as a conveyance of this ultimate dominion, a power to grant the soil while yet in possession of the natives. These grants have been understood by all, say the Supreme Court of the United States, to convey a title to the grantees, subject only to the Indian right of occupancy.

Spain, in all her discussions with France, Great Britain and the United States, based her title on the rights given by discovery. Upon the same basis rested the claim of Portugal to the Brazils: and upon this basis, France claimed all Canada and Acadie, as well as Louisiana, when her population was insignificant, and when the Indians occupied nearly all the country. Holland based its title to the New Netherlands, upon the discovery by Hudson.

Great Britain recognized with equal distinctness the rights of discovery. In 1496 Cabot was commissioned to take possession in the name of the King of England of all countries he might find, "then unknown to all "Christian people." Here we find asserted the right to take possession of the country, notwithstanding the occupancy of the natives who were heathens, and at the same time admitting the prior title of any Christian people who may have made a previous discovery. The charter granted to Sir Humphrey Gilbert in 1517 authorizes him to discover and take possession of such remote, heathen and barbarous lands as were not possessed by any Christian prince or people. This charter was afterwards renewed to Sir Walter Raleigh, in nearly the same terms. In 1606, by charter, afterwards enlarged in 1609, James I granted to colonists all the lands between the thirty-fourth and forty-first degrees of north latitude, along the sea coast and into the land from sea to sea. In all of this territory the soil, at the time the grants were made, was occupied by the Indians; yet almost every title within these boundaries is dependent on these grants. It has never been objected to any of these original grants that the title as well as possession was in the Indians when it was made, and that it passed nothing on that account.

Under all the treaties which affected the possession of this country by European states, the title given by discovery was relied upon, and the fact that the territory was largely, often entirely, occupied by Indian tribes, was ignored as of no importance. Such was the case under the treaty of Utrecht, in 1703, when France ceded Nova Scotia to Great Britain; and under the treaty of 1763, when Spain ceded Florida to Great Britain; and also under the secret treaty when France ceded Louisiana to Spain. All the nations of Europe have invariably asserted for themselves and recognized in others the exclusive right of the discoverer to appropriate the lands occupied by the Indian.

The American States have recognized the principle thus inherited from the old world. At the close of the Revolution, Great Britain conveyed all of her rights, proprietary and territorial, to the colonies, and thereby all of her rights to the soil passed to the States. "It "has never been doubted," says Chief Justice Marshall, in his opinion in the case of Johnson vs. McIntosh, "that either the United States or the several "States had a clear title to all the lands within the "boundary lines described in the treaty, subject only "to the Indian right of occupancy, and that the ex- "clusive power to extinguish that right was vested in "that government which might constitutionally exer- "cise it."

Virginia in 1779 passed an act declaring her exclusive right of pre-emption from the Indians, of all the lands within the limits of her chartered territory, and denying the right of any person to buy lands from the Indians. The territory ceded by Virginia to the Federal Government was occupied by numerous and warlike tribes of Indians, but the exclusive right of the United States to extinguish their title and to grant the soil has never been doubted.

In 1845, in a case before the Supreme Court of the United States, (United States vs. Rogers,) Chief Justice Taney used this language: "It is our duty to "expound and execute the law as we find it, and we "think it too firmly and clearly established to admit of "dispute that the Indian tribes residing within the ter- "ritorial limits of the United States are subject to their "authority; and where the country occupied by them "is not within the limits of one of the United States, "Congress may by law punish any offence committed "there, no matter whether the offender be a white man "or an Indian.

Assuming a right over all of her lands which thus

far had never been denied, and which had been acted upon by all of the thirteen original States, the General Assembly of Georgia, in 1798, authorized a conditional sale of the larger portion of her territory lying between the Chattahoochee and the Mississippi. Three companies were organized by speculators to acquire these valuable lands. The "South Carolina Yazoo Company" agreed to pay sixty thousand dollars for five millions of acres, now embracing the middle counties of Mississippi. The Virginia Company agreed to pay ninety-three thousand dollars for seven millions of acres, embracing what are now the northern counties of Mississippi. The "Tennessee Company," for forty-six thousand dollars agreed to purchase three millions five hundred thousand acres, now lying in north Alabama.

Steps were being taken to occupy the several purchases, when a question arose as to the right of Georgia to sell the lands claimed by Spain, between thirty-one degrees and thirty-two degrees twenty-eight minutes. A still more serious question, and one to which attention has already been called, arose, as to the right of Georgia to dispose of the fee simple of lands occupied still by Indian tribes, with whom the Federal Government had treaties, and who had never granted to the whites the lands which the State was now claiming her right and power to convey to speculating companies. The Union had just been formed, and President Washington was unwilling that anything should be done to embroil the infant republic with a foreign power. He was also fearful of the effect upon the Union of a general Indian war. But the chief motive for his opposition to the Yazoo sale may be found in the jealousy which he entertained for the power of the Federal

Government as against the claims of a State. He had seen during the continuance of the preceding weak Government, that under the articles of confederation the United States had the right to make treaties with the Indian tribes (or nations as they were improperly styled) not residing within a State, and he either failed to observe that that clause was excluded from the new Federal Constitution, or construed its absence as meaning that the new Government were to make treaties with and have exclusive charge of Indian tribes both outside as well as within a State. He still believed that the old practice of treating with the tribes as though they were independent sovereigns should be continued by the general Government, and that the States being precluded from making treaties, could not properly deal with the Indian people, and could not legally alienate the lands they occupied. The question which puzzled Washington was that which puzzled the Government for many years after his day, and which will be practically solved at last only by the subjection of the Indian to the laws which rule every other citizen of the Republic, of whatever color or race.

The President issued a proclamation against the attempt of the companies to occupy the lands, and as they all failed to pay the purchase money within the time stipulated, the State rescinded the sale.

In December, 1794, the Legislature of Georgia, by a majority, passed a new bill contracting for a sale of the Yazoo territory. This bill was vetoed by Governor Mathews because of the inadequacy of the consideration offered, and on the ground that it would create a monopoly. A few days subsequently, Governor Mathews gave way to the importunities of the

Assembly and signed another bill in January, 1795, which was designed to accomplish the purpose of the first, but which was more guarded in some of its expressions. This "Yazoo Act" set out that the Articles of the Confederation had stipulated that each State was to retain her territory: that by the treaty with Great Britain, the boundary of Georgia was confirmed as being the same claimed by her repeatedly and recognized by the convention between South Carolina and Georgia, held at Beaufort, in 1787: that the State had the right of pre-emption over all the lands within her borders occupied by Indian tribes: that the treaty claimed to have been made at New York, between McGillivray and the Federal Government, had never been recognized by Georgia: that the confederation had no right to make that treaty with Indians, resident within a State: that President Washington had no right to agree with McGillivray and his chiefs, and to guarantee all the territory west of the Oconee, to the Creeks: and that the State had the right to convey fee simple titles to all of her territory, whether to individuals or to companies.

The importance of these positions taken by Georgia, will appear hereafter. The claim thus set forth by her in the preamble to the Yazoo Act, has been recognized as correct by the Supreme Court of the United States in various decisions, but at that day it was denied strenuously by President Washington and the Federal party. We will see how it became the occasion for prolonged hostility between the Gulf States and the Federal Government, and for the development of that responsive spirit of jealousy on the part of the State against the unjust pretensions of the Union, which educated the people of this section, from the earliest day, in the doctrines of State rights, nullification, and finally secession, as the only remedy against Federal usurpation.

Four Yazoo companies were formed under this Act, and for the sum of five hundred thousand dollars, twenty-one millions and five hundred thousand acres of land were conveyed. The companies paid promptly into the State treasury one-fifth of the purchase money and obtained titles from the Governor. They hastened at once to re-sell the lands to those who might, in case of a repeal by the State, set up a title as innocent purchasers without notice. As soon as this sale was consummated, President Washington laid a copy of the Yazoo Acts before Congress, saying—"These Acts "embrace an object of great magnitude, and their con-"sequences may deeply affect the peace and welfare of "the United States." Congress instructed the Attorney General to investigate the title of Georgia to the lands in question.

Before, however, any action could be taken by the Federal Government, the people of Georgia themselves effectually disposed of these Yazoo Acts. While they acknowledged the right of the State to the fee simple of the lands involved, they repudiated the sale so far as lay in their power, as having been secured through bribery and corruption.

The opponents of the Act denied the power of the Legislature to sell, and denounced the scheme as transferring the richest part of the territory of Georgia with all the inchoate rights of the settlers to the tender mercies of a speculative corporation. They contended with great reason, that the members had not been elected with a view to such a proposition, and that the people should be consulted at a new election before passing upon such a momentous subject. So deep was the popular indignation that several of those who voted for the Act were actually slain upon their return home: some had their dwellings burned: others fled the State: and one was even pursued and killed in Virginia. All of them were repudiated and spurned by the people. Their votes were held as affixing a mark of disgrace to themselves and entailing infamy for years upon their children.

There were men of virtue and high position who advocated and supported the Yazoo Acts. They held that the sale of the western territory to different companies would be productive of a more rapid settlement of the lands, the erection of new States, and the speedy building up of an interest quite equal to the task of compassing the extinguishment of the whole Indian tribe. There can be no question that these men were deceived as to the character of those who managed the business of securing the sale, however honest they may have been as to the merits of the question itself. WILLIAM FEW, then a Senator in Congress from Georgia, bears this testimony: "In fact Georgia was invaded and overrun by a horde of speculators and other "adventurers, just after the close of the Revolution, and "was as completely changed for a time as to character, "sentiment, or conduct, as ever was England after the "Saxon or Norman invasion." He declared further, that "it is hardly susceptible of proof, that any persons, born or bred in Georgia, were any more than "dupes in the fraud." MR. FEW was doubtless correct. We have seen in another day, and after a fiercer revolution, an invasion of similar adventurers, and the perpetration of similar frauds, without the connivance or consent of the native population. There is no reason to believe that Governor Mathews was corrupted. But so bitter was the feeling against all who aided directly or indirectly in the passage of the obnoxious Acts, that to this day no county of Georgia has been named for one of its first and most gallant governors; and never since that day has a member of a Georgia Legislature, elected by the Anglo-Saxon population, dared to exercise his office corruptly. One of the first lessons of the century in the Gulf country taught honesty in political life. It was remembered for generations.

The people of Georgia made the expressed opinion of a politician with reference to the validity of the Yazoo sale a test of his fitness for office. If he held that the Legislature had the right to sell the territory, and that the purchasers acquired title by the sale, he sank to an obscurity from which he could never rise. JAMES JACKSON, a young man of great tact and ability and boldness, who had served with distinction in the Revolution, and who was elevated to the gubernatorial chair at an unusually early age, was now a member of Congress. He was of ardent temperament, the soul of honor, and chivalrous in the highest degree. Of commanding and graceful figure, eloquent in expression, a determined enemy and an impulsive friend, positive in thought and act, and holding in utter contempt every species of deceit and treachery, he wielded a wide influence throughout South Georgia. Resigning his seat in Congress, this young "Bayard," without fear and without reproach, announced himself as a candidate for the State Legislature, declared that "Repeal of the Yazoo sale" should be the rallying cry of the honest sons of Georgia, and proceeded to visit every section of the State, addressing popular assemblies and calling for an uprising of the people to rebuke the first corrupt scheme that ever passed a Georgia Legislature. He inspired the multitudes with his own enthusiasm, was elected to a seat in the Assembly, proposed and secured a repeal of the Yazoo sale, and then at the head of a procession of members of both houses, bore the manuscript of the repealed Act to the public square, and with a sun glass burned it to ashes. Henceforth the rising young men of Georgia knew that to preserve popular favor they must keep the robes of office unsullied.

The "Yazoo Fraud" question did not make its appearance again until after the State of Georgia, in 1802, had ceded to the United States all of her lands lying between the Chattahoochee and the Mississippi.

In the "Articles of Agreement and Cession" between Georgia and the United States, was a proviso that the latter may dispose of or appropriate a portion of the lands covered by the Yazoo grants, not exceeding five millions of acres, or any part thereof, for the purpose of satisfying, quieting, or compensating any claims other than those recognized in the Articles of Agreement, which may be made to the said lands. It was under this provision that the New England and Mississippi Land Company, who, in the meantime, had purchased the title of the original grantees of a corrupt Legislature, petitioned Congress to satisfy their claim by a fair purchase or commutation. In the session of 1802–3 this subject was first brought to the attention of Congress. Mr. Madison and Mr. Gallatin, members of the Cabinet, and Mr. Levi Lincoln, were appointed commissioners to investigate the subject. They made an elaborate report and concluded with a proposition that so much of the five millions of acres as shall remain after having satisfied the claims of settlers and others, not recognized by the agreement with Georgia, which shall be confirmed by the United States, be appropriated for the purpose of satisfying and quieting the claims of the persons who derive their titles from the Act of the State of Georgia, passed Jan. 7, 1795.

The head of this New England and Mississippi Land Company was Gideon Granger, then Postmaster General. He was the agent of the Company to prosecute the claim before Congress. Referring to Mr. Granger and his application to Congress in this case, Mr. John Randolph said: "The first year I had the honor of a "seat in this House, an act was passed somewhat of a "similar nature to the one now proposed. I allude to "the case of the Connecticut Reserve, by which the "nation was swindled out of three or four millions of "acres, which, like other bad titles, had fallen into the "hands of innocent purchasers. When I advert to "the applicants by whom we were then beset, I find "among them one of the persons who styled them-"selves the agents of the New England and Mississippi "Land Company, who seems to have an unfortunate "knack of buying bad titles. His gigantic grasp em-"braces with one hand the shores of Lake Erie, and "with the other stretches to the Bay of Mobile. * * "Mr. Speaker, when I see the agency which is em-"ployed on this occasion, I must own that it fills me "with apprehension and alarm. The same agent is at "the head of an Executive Department of our Gov-"ernment, and inferior to none in the influence at-"tached to it. * * This officer presents himself at "your bar at once a party and an advocate. Sir, when "I see such a tremendous influence brought to bear "upon us I do confess it strikes me with consternation "and despair. Are the heads of Executive Depart-"ments, with the influence and patronage attached to "them, to extort from us now, what we refused at the "last session of Congress."

Mr. Granger and his friends professed great indignation at the opposition of Randolph, and threatened to canvass New England in the interest of the company who now claimed to hold as innocent purchasers under the rescinded Yazoo law. Prominent among those who aided and sympathized with the company was AARON BURR, who doubtless was in league with the claimants to add their portion of the Yazoo territory to the country which he hoped to erect into an independent Southwestern Republic.

In order to establish their claim, a case was made by the claimants for adjudication by the Supreme Court of the United States. James Gunn and others, who held one of the grants, sold certain lands to John Peck, who in turn sold to Robert Fletcher. Peck made a deed to Fletcher, and Fletcher sued Peck for breach of covenant, in that the State of Georgia at the time of passing the Yazoo Acts, had no good right to sell and dispose of the lands in question. One of the covenants of the deed from Peck was that all the title which Georgia ever had in the lands had been legally conveyed, and another was that the title to the lands had in no way been impaired by virtue of the subsequent rescision of the Acts by a new Georgia Legislature.

Thus the questions came up which were to have so marked an influence upon Southwestern politics. (1). As to the right of a State to the fee simple of lands occupied by Indian tribes. (2) As to the right of a State to interfere with vested rights by rescision of a contract.

The Supreme Court refused to say that bribery of a General Assembly would invalidate an Act. "It "would be indecent in the extreme," said the Chief Justice, "upon a private contract between two indi-"viduals, to enter into an enquiry respecting the corrup-"tion of a sovereign power of a State. If the title be "plainly deduced from a Legislative Act, which the "Legislature might constitutionally pass, if the act be "clothed with all the requisite favors of a law, a court, "sitting as a court of law, cannot sustain a suit brought "by one individual against another, founded on the "allegations that the Act is a nullity, in consequence "of the impure motives which influenced certain mem-"bers of the Legislature which passed the law."

The Supreme Court decided that the constitutional inhibition forbidding a State to enact a law invalidating a contract, applied to this case. It was the unanimous opinion of the Court that the repealing Act did not deprive purchasers from the Yazoo grantees of rights under the Acts of 1795, and that the lands in controversy having passed into the hands of a purchaser for valuable consideration and without notice, the rescisive Act of the State of Georgia was inoperative, null and void as to such innocent purchaser.

To sustain the rights of the purchasers in this case,

it was necessarily held also that Georgia had a right to sell the lands in question, although then occupied and claimed by Indian tribes. It was found by the Court that the grant of Carolina by Charles I, to the Earl of Clarendon and others, comprehended the whole country from thirty-six degrees thirty minutes, to twenty-nine degrees, and from the Atlantic to the South Sea. Seven of the eight proprietors of the colonies surrendered to George I, in 1729, who appointed a governor for South Carolina.

In 1732, George I granted to the Lord Viscount Percival and others, seven-eighths of the territory between the Savannah and the Altamaha, and extending west to the South Sea, the remaining eighth part, which was still the property of the heir of Lord Carteret, one of the original grantees of Carolina, was afterwards conveyed to them. This territory was constituted a colony, and called Georgia. The Governor of South Carolina continued to exercise jurisdiction south of Georgia. In 1752, the grantees surrendered to the crown, and in 1754 a governor was appointed by the crown, with a commission defining the boundaries of the colony. In 1765, a commission was issued to the Governer describing the boundaries of Georgia, as extending westward to the Mississippi. The lands involved in the case of Fletcher vs. Peck, lay within the boundary defined by the commission of 1763. It was thus held to be the exclusive property of Georgia, inherited and acquired by the right of conquest. Chief Justice Marshall, in passing upon this branch of the case, said: "The question whether the vacant "land within the United States became joint property, "or belonged to the separate States, was a momentous "question, which at one time threatened to shake the "American confederacy to its foundation. This im- "portant and dangerous contest has been compromised, "and this compromise is not now to be disturbed." In conclusion of his opinion, he says: "The majority of "the Court are of opinion that the nature of the "Indian title, which is certainly to be respected by all "Courts until it be legitimately extinguished, is not "such as to be absolutely repugnant to seizin in fee on "the part of the State."

Although the Supreme Court was thus cautious in its language in 1810, when this decision was rendered, we find that Chief Justice Tracy and the Court had become positive in 1845. There was at that day no longer a doubt as to the seizin in fee by the State of all lands within her limits occupied by Indian tribes. This right to the soil was recognized by Kent in his Commentaries, as early as 1826, as will be seen by reference to the paragraph from his writings quoted at the beginning of this chapter.

The importance of this decision of *Fletcher vs. Peck*, was at once understood by the States It was the first adjudication which announced that the control by a State of its own territory is not unlimited, but that the General Government has the right in certain cases to restrain the State from annulling its own patent. The Court declared that when a law is in its nature a contract, a repeal of the law cannot divest the rights acquired under it by innocent purchasers without notice, and that their title shall not be impaired. The Court held that a grant by a State is a contract within the meaning of the Constitution, and a party is always estopped by his own grant. A party cannot pronounce his own deed invalid whatever cause may be assigned for its invalidity, even though that party be the Legislature of a State. A grant amounts to an extinguishment of the right of the grantor, and implies a contract not to reassert that right. A grant from a State is as much protected by the operation of the provision of the Constitution as a grant from one individual to another; and the State is as much inhibited from impairing its own contracts, or a contract to which it is a party, as it is from impairing the obligation of contracts between individuals.

Such was the decision of the Supreme Court of the United States. No matter that the voice and consent of Georgia had been obtained through misrepresentation on the part of her General Assembly. No matter that bribery and corruption had extorted a shameful sacrifice of most valuable property from the accidental representatives of the people No matter, said the United States Judiciary to the innocent people, whether the grant was made rightfully or wrongfully, "you are "not to be the judge of that question; you are "estopped from questioning anything but the existence "of your patent." No wonder the people of Georgia were indignant at such a decision, so unexpected, so novel, so antagonistic to the theory of State sovereignty in which they had been educated.

The opponents of the decision contended that the inhibitory clause of the Federal Constitution simply applied to cases of contract between man and man, and not to cases in which a sovereign State directly or indirectly was a party. It appeared to them monstrous that a State should be bound by the unauthorized acts of her ageuts, simply because a citizen had acquired a vested right thereby. Could it not be left safely with the State to make compensation for injury to innocent parties in such case? Before the States would ratify the Constitution they insisted upon an amendment forbidding the judicial power of the United States to any suit in law or equity by the citizen of another State or of a foreign country against any of the States. If the State could not be compelled to abide by a contract made with a citizen of another State or a foreigner, how could she be compelled by the United States to abide by a contract with one of her own citizens? The people of the State were filled with indignation against the alleged encroachment by the General Government against their rights.

The Federal party which had adhered to the administration of WASHINGTON, from this day began to fall away more rapidly than ever. The Republican party of Georgia grew with wonderful rapidity, and soon there appeared upon the stage such men as JOHN FORSYTH, WILLIAM H. CRAWFORD, THOMAS W. COBB, DUNCAN G. CAMPBELL, AUGUSTUS CLAYTON, ELI S. SHORTER, JOHN M. DOOLY, FREEMAN WALKER, JOHN M. BERRIEN, STEPHEN W. HARRIS, and GEO. M. TROUP. Into every political campaign entered the principles of Government involved in the Yazoo transaction. The people were on the side of Georgia, and this splendid array of youthful intellect was on the side of the people. The current all set towards the sovereignty of the State; there was barely a perceptible eddy in the other direction.

CHAPTER V.

Relation of the Union to the Indian Tribes—Relation of the State to the Tribes Within Its Limits—The Georgia Act of Cession—Non-Observance of the Contract on the Part of the United States—The Treaty Making and Commerce Regulating Power—Conflicting Views as to Indian Rights—Practice of the Northern and Eastern States—The New Theory of Equality of Races, &c., &c.

"But the project of ultimately organizing them [the Indian tribes] into States, within the limits of those States which had not ceded or should not cede to the United States the jurisdiction over the Indian territory within their bounds, could not possibly have entered into the contemplation of our Government. Nothing but express authority from the States could have justified such a policy, pursued with such a view."

WILLIAM JOHNSON, Associate Justice Supreme Court U. S.

"The main point involved, was not the rights of the Creeks, but the corner-stone of the legal foundation of the whole Union. It is true that there was no danger that this corner-stone would be broken and shattered on the instant. But the demand of *principiis obsta!* was again urged upon the Federal Government, and in a more pressing way than ever before."

VON HOLST'S CONSTITUTIONAL HISTORY, p. 449.

A majority of the States represented in the convention which framed the Constitution, either ceded to the United States the soil and jurisdiction of their western lands, or claimed it to be remaining within themselves. Congress assented as to ceded, and the States as to the unceded territory, their right to the soil absolutely and the dominion in full sovereignty, within their respective limits, subject only to the Indian occupancy, not as foreign States or nations, but as dependent on, and appendant to the State governments. Before the convention took action, Congress erected a government in the Northwestern territory containing numerous and powerful tribes. It was ordained that the territorial laws should extend over the whole district, and divisions were created for the execution of the civil and commercial law. Although the Indians were, for a long time, and generally, permitted to regulate their internal affairs in their own way, it was not by any inherent right acknowledged by Congress or reserved by treaty, but because Congress did not see proper to exercise its full powers of sovereignty. This complete sovereignty was declared and asserted in all the regulations of Congress, from 1775 to 1788, in the Articles of Confederation, in the Ordinance of 1787, in the Proclamation of 1788, and in the case of the Southwestern Indians in the Treaty of Hopewell in 1785.

In the Act of Cession made by Georgia to the United States in 1802 of all lands claimed by her west of the line designated, one of the conditions was: "that "the United States should, at their own expense, "extinguish for the use of Georgia, as early as the "same can be peaceably obtained, on reasonable terms, "the Indian title to lands within the State of Georgia."

Finding that the Federal Government delayed to carry out their part of the stipulation, and were adopting measures looking to the perpetual occupation of these lands by the Indians, such as the erection of school houses and churches, the parcelling out of farms among them, and their education in the arts of civilized life, the State of Georgia resolved to extend her laws over the entire Indian territory within her borders. She claimed, as has already been seen, a fee simple title to these Indian lands. She claimed and exercised the right to sell these lands to the Yazoo speculators; and the Supreme Court of the United States, in 1810, had decided that she had a right to make the sale, and should not annul it. There could be no higher recognition of her right to sovereignty, over the vast territory covered by the Yazoo Acts, than the opinion of Chief Justice Marshall in the case of Fletcher vs. Peck.

If Georgia, as was admitted by a majority of the court in that cause, had a fee simple title to the soil, it was a worthless title so long as the Federal Government recognized a right on the part of the Indian tribes to occupy the soil at will. The analogy of an estate in remainder or reversion could not apply, since no time or circumstance was fixed for the reversion to happen. There could not be two concurrent sovereignties. The State repeatedly remonstrated to the President, and called upon the Federal Government to take the necessary steps to fulfil the stipulations as to removal. She complained that while the Indian title to immense tracts of country had been extinguished elsewhere, but little if any effort had been made in that direction within the limits of Georgia. This delay was attributed either to a want of attention on the part of the United States, or to the effect of its new humanitarian policy towards the red man. In one or more of the treaties, titles in fee simple to certain reservations of land were given by the United States to individual Indians. This was complained of by Georgia as a direct infraction of the condition of the cession.

Georgia complained also that the policy of the Government in advancing the cause of civilization among the tribes, and inducing them to assume the forms of a regular government and of civilized life, was calculated to promote an attachment to the soil they inhabited, and to render the purchase of their title more difficult, if not impracticable. Mr. Jefferson in 1809, in a letter to the Cherokees, recommended them to adopt a regular government, that crimes might be punished and property protected. He pointed out a mode by which a council should be chosen, who should have power to enact law; and he also recommended the appointment of judicial and executive officers, through whom the law should be enforced. In the treaty of 1817, the Cherokees were encouraged to adopt a regular form of government, and they thereupon adopted a government modelled on that of a State. Subsequently a law was passed by Congress making an annual appropriation of $10,000, as a school fund for the education of Indian youths. Missionary labors among the Indians were also sanctioned by the Government, by granting permission to reside in the Indian country to those who were disposed to engage in such work. The means thus adopted by the United States to reclaim the savage from his erratic life, and induce him to assume the forms of civilization, no doubt tended to increase his attachment to the soil, and the difficulty of purchasing it as the United States had agreed with Georgia to do. It was not contemplated by the State at the time of the cession that any obstructions to the fulfilment of the contract should be allowed, much less sanctioned, by the United States.

Georgia denied that the power of the United States to make treaties authorized the Government to treat with Indian tribes as though they were sovereign and independent nations. The Indian tribe was in no sense a nation. It did not own the fee simple of the lands it hunted over. It occupied, said Chief Justice Marshall, towards the State in whose limits it was included, or to the United States, if it lay without the borders of a State, the relation of a ward to a guardian. Assuredly a guardian could not treat with his ward. In the treaty of Hopewell, March 15, 1875, just after the Revolution, the Commissioners of the United States expressed themselves in these terms: "The Commis-"sioners Plenipotentiary of the United States give "peace to all the Cherokees, and receive them into the "favor and protection of the United States, on the "following conditions." This was the language of conquerors and sovereigns, and not the address of equals to equals. Such an agreement was simply a promise or contract, and in no way worthy or deserving of the title of treaty. In designating the country to which the Cherokees should be confined, the Commissioners used this language: "The boundaries allotted "to the Cherokees for their hunting grounds." The concession was all on the side of the United States. No right of possession of the soil in the Indian was recognized. Down to that day the tribes did not claim to be recognized as nations, and no nation on earth had ever looked upon them as sufficiently sovereign to become parties to what is technically known as a treaty. If they should declare war, and issue letters of marque or reprisal, no one would respect their commissions. In the treaty of Hopewell, the Cherokees renounced every attribute of sovereignty. They received as a boon the territory allotted to them: the right of punishing intruders into that territory was conceded by the conqueror, not asserted by the tribe, and the sole and exclusive right was claimed by the conqueror of regulating their trade and managing all their affairs in such manner as the Government of the United States should think proper. To leave no question as to the subjection of the tribes, the United States in the so-called treaty of Hopewell provided: "For the benefit and "comfort of the Indians, and for the prevention of "injuries and aggressions on the part of the citizens "or Indians, the United States, in Congress assembled, "shall have the sole and exclusive right of regulating "the trade with the Indians, and managing all "their affairs in such manner as they shall think "proper."

Georgia claimed under this Hopewell treaty that the United States had plenary power to do with the Indians as they might think proper. A similar and equal power to that which the United States possessed over Indian tribes outside of Georgia, clearly belonged to the State as regards those tribes within her limits. The Federal Government had only the power which it inherited from the State. The treaties that followed that of Hopewell, namely, those of Holston and Tellico, referred to and confirmed that of Hopewell.

The use of the word "treaty," as applied to these agreements, contracts or stipulations made with Indian tribes is of no significance. Thus in the second article of the Holston treaty, so-called, occurs these words: "That the said Cherokee nation will not hold any "treaty with any foreign power, individual, State, or "with individuals of any State." The application of the word treaty to an agreement with an individual is evidence that it was not used in its strict technical sense, and was not intended to mean a contract between sovereign powers. Georgia protested that these agreements with conquered and dependent Indian tribes were not such treaties as were made by the Constitution the supreme law of the land, and therefore the Federal Government, under color of these so-called treaties had no right to interfere with the State of Georgia in managing every foot of her own soil and every person resident within her borders.

A memorial of the Georgia Legislature in 1819, urged the President to hasten the fulfilment of the agreement of 1802. The Administration professed willingness to carry out the stipulation, but the Indians refused to sell. A council of Creek chiefs at Tuckebachee declared, May 25, 1824, that the lands still in their possession were only sufficient for the support of the tribe. Said they: "We have guns and ropes, and "if any of our people shall break these laws, those "guns and ropes shall be their end." On the 29th of October, of the same year, a council of chiefs met again and passed a resolution of the same tenor, and committed it, "confiding in the magnanimous disposi-"tion of the citizens of the United States to render "justice to the Indians"—to a newspaper for publication, "so that it may be known to the world." In reply to the Commissioners of the United States, Duncan G. Campbell and James Merriwether, who conferred with them at Broken Arm, in the following December, John Ross and the Creek chiefs used decided language.

It was suggested to the Indian, by the Commissioners, that but two courses were left him. He must consent to removal to hunting grounds beyond the

Mississippi, or he must be incorporated in the State government. To the first of these propositions was given an emphatic no. To the second, it was replied that the happiness which the Indians once enjoyed by a quiet and undisturbed ease, before the face of the white man was seen upon the continent, was afterwards poisoned by the bad fruits of the civilized tree which he had planted around them. Wars arose, the mountains and plains were covered with carnage, and the Elysian fields drenched with blood; and many noble tribes, whose unfortunate doom it was to have been overshadowed by the expanded branches of this tree, drooped, withered, and are no more. The Indian tribes have become extinct whenever merged into the white population. Invariably they have fallen an early and easy sacrifice to the ambition, pride, and avarice of the civilized man. Defrauded out of their rights; treated as inferior beings, because of their poverty, their ignorance and their color, they have been thrown with the most degraded of society, from whom they imbibed habits of debauchery and intemperance, with all the vices that follow in their train Their lands have been swept from under their feet by the ingenuity and cunning of the white man, and being left destitute of a home, ignorant of the arts and sciences, and possessing no experience in the occupations of a laborious and industrious life, they have become vagrants among strangers. By successive and constant oppressions, their spirits have been depressed and broken, and finally, they have been urged by misery to hasten the period of a troublesome existence by resort to intemperance and every description of sensuality. Such have been the causes which fixed the doom of extinction to many of the proudest Indian tribes; and such, they protested, would be their own doom if incorporated into the family of the white man.

If we concede that it is impossible for the Indian to practice the arts of peace and civilized life, these men undoubtedly spoke the language of truth. It is amusing, after the lapse of half a century, to recur to the reasons assigned by Governor MURPHY, of Alabama, for arriving at the conclusion of Ross and his braves. In his message to the Alabama Legislature he seriously said:

"To civilize a people from a rude and barbarous "condition, they should be removed from the influence "of the vices and luxuries which prevail in civilized "life, and subjected to that discipline and instruction "by which a change of life, manners and mental "improvement is gradually produced. The virtues "must first be cultivated, and the mind strengthened "against the seductions of vicious gratification. Such "is the natural order of things; and experience only "confirms what they might justly predicate on a cor- "rect knowledge of human nature. Such has been "the evidence of history; for the provinces farther "removed from the vices, refinements and luxuries of "Rome, but subjected to its laws and instructed by its "arts, made the most solid, if not the most immediate "progress in civilization. This necessary course can "not be pursued with the Indians whilst they remain "within our limits; they have continued access to "whatever tends to corrupt them; they have con- "stant testimony that their condition is regarded as "inferior to others, than which nothing is more "destructive to virtuous pride and generous emulation;

"and the abandoned part of our people (who alone can "mingle freely with the nation as a body without "losing their standing in society), will introduce our "vices and prevent the introduction of our virtues."

More candid and much more philosophic was the view taken of this difficult problem by Governor TROUP, of Georgia. He held that if such a scheme as the incorporation of the Indian and his amalgamation with the society of the Anglo Saxons, was practicable, the utmost of rights and privileges which public opinion would concede him would be a middle station between the white man and the negro slave; that if he should survive this degradation, without the possibility of attaining to the position of the former, he would gradually sink to the condition of the latter, would intermarry and amalgamate with the negro, and thus extinguish his proud race of huntsmen by transforming it into a loathsome hybrid without the docility of the mother nor the pride of the father.

The State of Massachusetts had been earliest to enact a law against intermarriage between the Indian and the Anglo-Saxon. It was entitled "An Act for the better preventing of a spurious or mixed issue." Our forefathers, understanding the inferior character of the colored races, refused to permit amalgamation, and visited it with the severest penalties of law. They possessed a lofty pride of race which, in a great measure, has been lost to their descendants. Their firm resolve to preserve the purity of the race, and to continue its dominion over the land, was strengthened by the aspect presented by Central and South America, and the Spanish isles. There the races had been received into political fellowship; the white blood had been adulterated, and government had become a by-word and reproach. The Pilgrims Fathers who came flying from persecution, piously returned thanks to God for the wonderful dispensation of His Providence in sweeping away whole tribes of Indians with pestilence. The Indian was considered by them an incumbrance upon the land, and the mode of dealing with him was entirely discretionary. The whole of Rhode Island was bought for fifty fathoms of beads. But the colonies invariably claimed possession under the royal charters, and not by purchase. In war, the Indian was never treated as a civilized enemy. The male adults were exterminated. The females and children were reduced to slavery. Massachusetts sold the son of King PHILIP into slavery. In Virginia, Massachusetts, Connecticut, Maryland and Pennsylvania, laws were passed, some still existing, to regulate, to protect and to punish Indians. In Massachusetts the intermarriage of an Indian and white was forbidden as debasing the Anglo-Saxon blood. The white man by his oath could purge himself of a charge brought by an Indian. In Connecticut as late as 1774, we find a statute enacted which provides that if any Negro, Indian or Mulatto servant is found wandering out of the town of his residence without a written pass, he is made liable to seizure and return to his master. At a recent day Maine had passed an Act "for the regulation of the Penobscot and Passamaquoddy tribes." Everywhere the laws of the State were extended over the Indian. The difference between his condition North and his condition South, was that at the North he was placed upon the level of a slave, and at the South he was treated simply as an uncivilized freeman.

He had no rights at the North which a white man was bound to respect. Georgia proposed to give him every right which the laws extended to the whites.

Understanding perfectly the absolute sovereignty which had been claimed and exercised by the other States in this matter Georgia repudiated definitely and finally the idea of admitting the Indian to her political family. There was no place for him intermediate between the slave and the master. He was a weed, indigenous to the soil it is true, intended doubtless for a good purpose in the economy of nature, but not for a moment to be tolerated among the life-giving and health-preserving plants of a cultivated garden. Not all the logic nor all the rhapsodies of the new generation of humanitarians, who looked to equal political and civil rights between the white man and the Indian could convince the bold Saxons who won their independence from Great Britain that it was their duty to adulterate their white blood and sink to a level with the descendants of the Castilian of the Southern Continent. No Federal agent to the Indian tribes could convince them that such was their duty. The Indian must go. There had been enough said about the noble red man, his happy hunting grounds, and how his untutored mind sees God in the clouds and hears him in the wind. All that was very pretty in poetry; but in plain prose the Indian was a murderous, treacherous savage, who flattened his skull between boards and hung brass trinkets from his nostrils, who sang the most remarkable noises and beat the most discordant tunes on the harshest sorts of instruments, who traded off a league of land for a glass necklace and wore a flap around his middle, who stuck fish bones through his ears and painted himself like a zebra, who jumped about like an idiot in what he called a war dance or a corn dance, and lived like the beasts of the field, leaving behind him not a trace of the purpose of his creation. Georgia was the only one of the original States burthened with the presence of this nuisance; and she concluded it was time to devote her soil to something better.

Georgia prosecuted her efforts to obtain from the Creeks their consent to removal. A portion of the chiefs who represented the Southern Creeks were friendly to the Georgians. The Upper Creeks, who had united with Tecumseh and waged war against the United States, had been conquered, and had never been recognized as having a voice in treaties or negotiations with the States or Federal Government. The chiefs of the Lower Creeks, representing the nation, signed a treaty of sale at Indian Springs. This treaty, despite the objections of the Indian agents, was ratified by the United States Senate and signed by the President. It thus became, according to the theory of Mr. Adams and the party who agreed with him as to the dignity of such treaties, the supreme law of the land.

But even if this Indian Springs treaty had not been completed with the only recognized Creek chiefs, and ratified by the Government at Washington, the State of Georgia had high ground upon which to stand as to her abstract right to extend her laws over her own soil, whether occupied by whites, Indians or Negroes. Under the treaty-making power, the United States guaranteed to the Indians the integrity of their territory, and held, apart from the treaty-making power, that the power to regulate commerce among the Indians and between the United States, was sufficient to establish a guardianship over the tribes, represented by an agent who was to act as a minister plenipotentiary near the Royal Wigwam. These claims appeared to the Georgians to be fallacious and unwarranted.

Judge George Walton, an eminent jurist, in his charge to the grand jury of Richmond county, in regard to the settlement made by General CLARKE, in 1795, within the Indian reservation, while condemning the settlement as an infraction of Georgia laws, had said:

"Soon after the accession of all the States to the "present Federal Constitution, I stated my doubts to a "grand jury, also of Wilkes county, as to treaties "with savages being of the same rank as those of civ-"ilized nations; and was inclined to be of the opinion "that they ought not to be considered in the list of "supreme laws, and of equal efficacy with those in the "statute book; but the construction of the United "States has been otherwise."

How the tribes of Indians having simply an *usufruct* of the woods, and holding them originally by permission of the colonies, and afterwards by that of the States, could enter into treaties with the Union, and those treaties become the supreme law of the land to the exclusion of every right of sovereignty of the State, was difficult to be understood. If this were the law, where would the treaty-power end? Could a colony of foreigners enter one of the States, and claiming to be a tribe or nation, enter into a treaty with the General Government? Could treaties be made with wandering tribes of gypsies, and thus be made the supreme law of the land? All of the other original States had dealt with Indians as their subjects, and had extinguished their claims without the interference or interposition of the Washington authorities. Several of the Northern States had extended their laws over the Indian reservations and incorporated the tribes among the citizens. But now the Federal Government must enter upon the soil of Georgia, treat with her subjects as though they were independent nations, and deny to the Georgia authorities even entrance upon their own territory.

Nor could the people of Georgia understand how a power to regulate commerce among the Indian tribes could carry with it a power to exclude white traders from the Indian country, to establish Federal agencies for their Government with the powers of a pro-consul, and to regulate all the domestic and municipal affairs of the territory. The article of the Constitution which gave Congress the power to regulate commerce with the Indians, at the same time granted power to regulate commerce with foreign nations and between States. It has never been contended except by extreme Federalists, that the right to regulate commerce between the States would justify the United States in excluding traders from one State or another, or to appoint official traders throughout a State, to the exclusion of all other citizens. Yet this was the power claimed in the case of commerce with Indians, and which is practiced down to the present day.

The Georgians contended that, even if their State had not been one of the original colonies, the United States would not have had jurisdiction over the vacant and unpatented lands within her borders. It was held that the Indian was not an occupyer. He was simply an overrunner, and had not the faintest claim, except such as Georgia might permit, to the soil upon which he hunted. In the matter of vacant lands within the limit of a State, the right of the United States to their possession has been often seriously questioned by even those States which have been constructed from territory undoubtedly possessed by the United States. Mississippi, Illinois and Indiana have all contended that on the organization of a State and its admission into the Union, it entered, in the language of the Act of Congress accepting the territorial claim from the States, "with the same rights of sovereignty, freedom, and "independence as the other States." Could the State of Indiana be as independent, or as sovereign as the State of Connecticut, if a large part of her territory, unlike the territory of Connecticut, remained in the possession of the United States? Could the United States, owning large bodies of unpatented or vacant lands in the heart of a State, set up a government to regulate the same, as independent of that of the State, as are the navy yards, the barracks, or the forts? To ask such a question appeared to the sovereign people of the State of Indiana, in 1829, to justify an instant and decisive answer in the negative. If, then, a question could arise as to the right of the Federal Government to retain ownership of vacant lands in a State framed from a territory, how much stronger was the question when applied to one of the original colonies, and to an Indian reservation? Georgia contended that she had absolute dominion over the Indian lands, and could, at pleasure, extinguish the Indian title by extending to their reservation the municipal regulations of the State. The case of FLETCHER and PECK confirmed this claim, so far as to establish the doctrine that the Indians are to be considered merely occupants. It established, also, as has been seen, the doctrine that over the Indian lands which lie within the common territory, the United States possess the legal title, subject to that occupancy, and with an absolute and exclusive right to extinguish the Indian title of occupancy, either by conquest or purchase. Clearly, then, if the United States, by virtue of their sovereignty over the common territory, could extinguish the Indian occupancy at pleasure, it followed that Georgia had the right to extinguish in like manner the Indian claims within her own borders.

It was better that the central power of the Government, at Washington, should deal with all the Indian tribes. If that power had to deal only with tribes outside the States, leaving it to the State authorities to deal with those inside, it was clear that in military movements there could not be that concert of action necessary for prompt defense of an extensive frontier against a wily and nomadic enemy. Hence it was that Georgia in her patriotic cession to the United States, stipulated that the United States should extinguish the Indian title as soon as possible. Here was a distinct compact between the State and the General Government. Georgia consented for the Federal Government to do what she herself might have done, but which she well knew could be done more speedily, more satisfactorily, and more peaceably by the powers at Washington. In extinguishing the claims herself, the Indian would still be within her borders; the money received by him for the cession would be soon spent; his hunting grounds would be filled with white settlers, and becoming a vagrant, he would soon be a burden to the

State. The United States, in extinguishing the title could give him better and more extensive hunting grounds beyond the Mississippi, and hence Georgia was content to surrender her magnificent territory to the United States, provided they would remove the Indian at once. In consenting thus to restrict her right of soil and her sovereignty, Georgia looked, with confidence in the plighted faith of the Union, to the prompt removal of the Indians, and the speedy settlement of the vacant territory.

It was in 1802 that the cession was made. Twenty years had passed away. New States had been organized and received into the Union from even beyond the Mississippi river, and still the Federal Government, as though determined to prevent the development of the Gulf States, had not extinguished the Indian titles in Georgia, nor in Alabama and Mississippi. Still the savages hovered on the Georgia frontier and pressed back the step of civilization. It was as though a deadly miasma rested upon the brow of the State; and energy, enlightenment and progress held back from the contagion. Is it wonderful that Georgia at last resolved to do what the United States, after accepting her imperial grant, had failed to do?

The slavery agitation had begun to raise its head. The Missouri question had aroused the Freesoilers to active exertions, and growing out of that body of agitators was a class of humanitarians who believed, or affected to believe, in the equality of all men before the law. With them the Caucasian, the Negro and the Indian were entitled to the same consideration; and they would listen to no argument drawn from the difference in origin, habits and circumstances of the races antagonistic to their optimistic theories. While some of these men were engaged in advocating the freedom of the Negro, others had penetrated the Indian nations, and were using every argument and artifice to induce them to withhold their consent to a relinquishment of their lands. These men contended with the people of Georgia that the Indian was a man and brother; that he should not be damned for a skin not colored like their own; and that having been once lords of the forest and free as the winds, they should be received into the political family of the State, endowed with the privileges of citizenship, and mingled in blood with the other races which had visited and populated the land. It was cruel, they contended, to treat these innocent and simple natives as a lower order of humanity, destitute of the claims of society, and unfit for alliance with the white man. It was brutal to drive them from their hunting grounds and transport them to unknown wilds far distant from the scenes of their birth. The true policy, dictated by reason and humanity, was to permit the Indian to retain his native lands, to force him to possess them, not as an usufruct held in common, subject to the council, but by allodial tenure; in fine, to make him a citizen living on his own farm and to extend over him the laws of the State. If he should alienate his land and wander out among the whites, so much the better, for the bond of tribe would be broken. He would sink or rise with the great body of citizens of whatever color, and that prejudice which would have been arrayed against the tribe, would refuse to visit itself against the individual. The French Revolution had developed *les amis des Noirs*. Liberty, fraternity and equality were to cover all classes, conditions and races of the people alike. The Caucasian, the Malay, the Indian, the Mongolian, and the Negro were all to stand alike—side by side, and hand in hand—under the broad banner of a common Republic. Such were the views of heavenly philanthropy; mixed with a large quantity of mortal cunning. The humanitarians were generally traders and teachers, and a few missionaries from the North. Some of them were pious men, but others divided their time in administering to the Indian sinner ghostly consolation and bad whiskey. The agents were generally men who, finding their positions profitable in the way of trade, were exceedingly anxious to preserve the autonomy of the Indian tribe; and failing in that, to get possession of the Indian lands, by having them allotted to the simple-minded savages. In all events, they were deadly hostile to the removal of those upon whom they lived and thrived.

There were others who believed that the only solution of the Indian problem was in absorption of the aboriginees by the whites—men who were true friends of Georgia and of undoubted purity of character. Of such was WILLIAM H. CRAWFORD, one of the ablest and noblest of Georgia statesmen. As Secretary of War, in 1816, it was his opinion, that when every effort to introduce among the Indians ideas of separate property, real as well as personal, had failed, the Government should encourage inter-marriage between them and the whites. While declaring that the extinction of the Indian race was abhorrent to the feelings of an enlightened and benevolent nation, it appears that he was willing to extinguish them by contaminating the blood of the progressive white man with the imbecility of one of the feeblest of peoples. It does not appear, however, that he proposed for the mongrel race to which he would have given birth, to be admitted to the full rights of citizenship enjoyed by the Anglo-Saxon conqueror.

The thunders of the New England church and rostrum which had agitated the Missouri question on behalf of the black man, were now hurled at the head of Georgia in behalf of the red man. Petitions to Congress were circulated through the New England States for signatures, addressed to congregational clergymen, with instructions to have them filled with as many names as could be obtained. These petitions, starting from the pulpit, supplicated Congress to protect the Indians in the occupancy of their land and the civil regulations they might adopt for their own guidance, as against the laws of the States of Georgia, Alabama and Mississippi. These very Christians were aware that among those Indian regulations were many which were destructive to peace and order, and abhorrent to virtue. Polygamy was allowed by usage and law. A man, overtaking a horse thief, might slay him. An assault with intent to murder or rape, was dismissed with a small fine. Any Indian leaving his home and offering to emigrate, forfeited all right to his property. Any Indian who might enroll his name as an emigrant with the United States agent, forfeited his citizenship, and any one buying his lands was punished with a hundred lashes. If any Indian who had enrolled, should dare to remain fifteen days within the tribe, he might be slain. These were the regulations which the New England clerical politicians besought Congress to sustain as against the beneficent laws of

Georgia. Circulars signed by women and bidding the Congressmen read, "with a view to eternity," also aided in these appeals for the preservation of polygamy.

The same line of argument, the same claim of national power, the same straining of constitutional grants, the same partisan cries, the same fanatical delusion, the same incendiary appeals from the pulpit, which many years afterwards illustrated another political question, were resorted to during John Q. Adams' administration with reference to the sovereignty of a State over any and all of its inhabitants.

The claims of State sovereignty set up by Georgia, Alabama and Mississippi in that day were not imaginary and vain. They were substantial and of supreme importance to the very existence of those commonwealths. Chief McIntosh and his council of braves, representing the Creek Nation, under the usual forms of their law ceded their lands in Georgia, by the treaty of Indian Springs. The party opposed to the sale became violent and appealed to Washington for an annulment of a treaty which they declared was procured by bribery. The administration of James Monroe had ceased, and with it had ceased for a time that scrupulous regard for the rights of the States which marked the immediate successors of Jefferson. John Quincy Adams was now President, and the policy of his administration was to curb the pride of the States, to reduce their governors to the position of sheriffs, and to repress the growing empires of the Southwest. The power of the South was to be broken, and one of the surest means to strangle the incipient giant was to leave the Indian tribes as a constant menace to the growth and civilization of the Gulf country. There was another consideration which controlled the philosopher of BRAINTREE. The greater the importance and dignity with which the Indian might be clothed, the greater the probability that antagonisms of race and prejudices of color would weaken year by year, and finally vanish in a recognition of an universal brotherhood. Already the ideal republic of PLATO, and the actual commune of ROUSSEAU were visible in the near distance to the radical politicians of 1825. Already the foundation was being laid for the erection of an imperial edifice, dedicated to an absolute fraternity and equality, upon the ruins of the autonomy of the States.

CHAPTER VI.

The Treaty of Indian Springs—Murder of McIntosh—General Gaines and Governor Troup—Threatened Collision of State and Federal Forces—The State Sustains Her Position—The Cherokee Nation—An Appeal to the Supreme Court—Its Writ of Error Disregarded—The Question of Coercion, &c., &c.

"When the United States, under the treaty-making power, claimed the right to settle with Great Britain the northern boundary of Maine, Governor LINCOLN, of that State insisted upon the right of Maine to assert her own boundary. Fortunately for Governor LINCOLN, he lived in a favored region: and his doctrine of State rights and sovereignty brought down no invectives upon his head, although in theory, and in language, too, he did not lag far behind the fiery Georgian."

SENATOR JOHN FORSYTH, 1831.

"The European journals, especially the English ones, which had followed the struggle with lively interest, had to listen to many a sneering remark about the short-sightedness which, springing from their hostility to everything Republican, had already led them to think they saw the United States bathed in the blood of her citizens, and the Union shattered forever."

VON HOLST'S CONSTITUTIONAL HISTORY.

"I entreat you most earnestly, now that it is not too late, to step forth, and having exhausted the argument, to stand by your arms."

GOVERNOR TROUP'S MESSAGE.

All Georgia was in a blaze of excitement. The hostile Creeks declared they would not respect the treaty. The State of Georgia took steps at once to make a survey of the lands relinquished by the treaty, and to throw them upon the market. The Georgians complained that the agents had excited the Indians to violate the stipulations of the treaty. The President commissioned Colonel Andrews to investigate the complaints made against the agents. General Gaines was instructed to suppress any hostilities on the part of the Indians, and to seek some way by which an understanding could be arrived at with them.

General Gaines proceeded to the scene of hostilities, and as his intercourse was most closely with the Government agents, his views of the situation were very soon turned against the pretensions of Georgia. He reported to his Government that the INDIAN SPRINGS treaty was a fraud. He represented the people of Georgia as longing to rob the Indian of his lands, and as resorting to the foulest means of cunning and deceit to manufacture a treaty, plausible on its face, but unjust and tyrannical at heart He intimated that McINTOSH was but an instrument of Governor TROUP, and that he had been used for the base purpose of giving a color of consent for the Creek Nation when ninety-nine hundredths of them were utterly opposed to a cession of their lands.

To this it was replied by the people of Georgia that it was true they wanted the lands of the Indian, but they did not seek to obtain them by robbery. The INDIAN SPRINGS treaty gave the Creeks better and more extensive lands in the West. It gave them means of transportation and a vast sum of purchase money. The Georgians wanted the lands of the Indian to make them subserve the purposes of a civilized rather than savage life. This was no robbery. It was simply exercising the right of conquest, without imposing a single condition of hardship upon the subject. It was extending the area of Anglo-Saxon enlightenment and progress, and rendering compact and homogeneous the power of the republic from the Atlantic to the Mississippi. They asserted also that McIntosh, the chief of that branch of the Creeks which was true to the United States in the late war, and which had conquered and subdued their enemies, the Red Sticks, alone had the right to speak for the Nation. That right had been recognized by the General Government in a letter from the Secretary of War, of the 17th March, 1817. In conformity to that recognition, McIntosh and the friendly chiefs had been in the habit of speaking and still spoke for the Creeks. That the Red Sticks assassinated the faithful friends of the whites was no reply to the force of this argument. They further contended that President Monroe had recognized, and the Senate had ratified the Indian Springs treaty; that the Georgia Legislature, in pursuance of that ratification had enacted a law for the survey and distribution of the ceded territory; that citizens had acquired vested rights under this treaty and the laws made in pursuance thereof, which were the supreme laws of the land; and that by virtue of the decision of Fletcher aginst Peck, those vested rights could not be disturbed, however the treaty might have been secured. They contended, moreover, that the treaty was secured fairly; that if money was used to bribe the chiefs, it was nothing more than had been done from the discovery of America. What John Smith and William Penn could do for a few ounces of beads and a dozen or so red blankets, had now to be done, in the present advanced state of Indian ideas, with a more substantial largess. It was denied that the chiefs had been bribed by the State. The Governor could pay no money from the State treasury unless specially appropriated; no appropriation had been made for any such purpose; the contingent fund was barely enough to keep cattle out of the capitol grounds and to pay the hire of servants about the offices of State; and finally, the treasury of the State was not able to pay one-tenth of the sums which the enemies of Georgia had set as the price of the treaty.

The true motive for the ratification of a treaty so favorable to the Georgians, might have been found in the relationship existing between the Governer of Georgia and the great Creek chief. George M. Troup was born in 1780, at McIntosh Bluff, on the west bank of the Tombigbee river, in what is now the State of Alabama. His grandfather was a captain in the royal army, and chief of the McIntosh clan of Scotland. For valuable services in Florida, he was rewarded by King George with a grant of McIntosh Bluff and extensive lands in Mississippi. This Captain McIntosh had one son and one daughter. The son was, like his father, a British officer. The daughter married an officer of the British army named Troup, while on a visit to England. Upon her return to her father's home, Governor Troup was born at McIntosh Bluff. Captain McIntosh, the father of Mrs. Troup, had a brother named Roderick McIntosh, also an officer in the royal army. He was a man of great physical stature and courage, and the embodiment of chivalry. He took part with the Royalists in the Revolution. His cousins, John and Lachlin McIntosh, took part with the Whigs. Roderick, or "Old Rory," as he was called familiarly, took to himself a squaw of the Creek Nation, and was the father of Chief William McIntosh. The chief partook of the characteristics of the McIntosh family. He was brave as a lion. His stature was above that of ordinary men. His intellect, naturally strong, became cultivated by association with white men of position and education. These scions of the McIntosh clan were born to command. They were chiefs in Scotland, chiefs in the royal and patriot armies, and chiefs in the Indian tribes. The near relationship between the Governor and the Indian chief, might have suggested to President Adams a reason for the friendly treaty of Indian Springs more powerful than bribery.

The claim of Georgia under the treaty of Indian Springs was undisputable. The compact of 1802 bound the United States, in consideration of the cession of a princely domain, to extinguish for Georgia all the Indian claims within her borders. When, through their agents, the contract of Indian Springs was negotiated, and the Government had ratified the bargain, the right of Georgia became irrevocably vested; the authority of the United States was then at an end. The power was executed and the Government was *functus officio* as to the subject. The United States had conferred no right upon Georgia: they had simply removed an incumbrance to a pre-existing right, and they could not now replace that encumbrance by a new contract with the Indians.

Georgia denied that the Indian Intercourse Act applied to this subject. It applied to the intrusion of unauthorized individuals, and not to the acts of the sovereign State. This was obvious from its terms and from the fact that the passport of the Governor of the State, equally with that of the President, dispensed with some of its penalties.

That the title of Georgia to the fee simple of Indian lands was unquestionable is evidenced by the second article of the agreement and cession wherein, through abundant caution on the part of the State, the United States "cede to the State of Georgia whatever claim, "right or title they may have to the jurisdiction or soil "of those lands." If that language meant anything, it meant that the United States were debarred from questioning the right of Georgia to enter upon her own soil at her own pleasure for the purpose of survey. The soil and jurisdiction being in Georgia, it was no more lawful for the United States to introduce other persons there, than it would have been for them to introduce into the settled portions of Georgia a colony of free persons of color, of Indians or of white people. The utmost allowable to the United States in this respect was the settlement within the territory of such officers as were necessary for the regulation of commerce with the Indians. The United States, nevertheless, by permission and toleration, even by encouragement, had introduced there from time to time, white persons and others who had made settlements, exercised ownership over the soil and cultivated it in the same manner as though the United States, and not Georgia, possessed the right of soil and jurisdiction. These very persons, so illegally occupying the soil of Georgia under the protection of the United States, were chiefly instrumental in preventing the Indians from leaving the country.

Prominent among these disturbers of the peace was the United States agent. This person, indebted for his lucrative office to the administration, lost no opportunity to fortify his present position and to recommend his loyalty to the new administration. He not only inflamed the Creeks against McIntosh, but went out among the people of Georgia electioneering against Troup. The Governor in his next annual message alluded to his conduct, in the following language:

"I had for the first time come into office when a "subject of peculiar delicacy presented itself, and "being intimately connected with the independence of "the elective franchise (without which it would be in "vain for Georgia to claim for herself the attributes "of a sovereign State), it was made known to the "President that on occasion of the election just then "terminated, an officer in his employ, bearing a high "and dignified commission, and being a citizen of "another State, had abandoned his post to mingle in "the strifes of that election, had espoused the cause of "one of the parties to the prejudice of the other, and "by the weight and influence of his office, united with "the most enthusiastic ardor, had rendered himself so "signally conspicuous, that the chief magistrate could "not conscientiously forbear, among his first acts, to "complain to the executive government of the Union "of this outrage upon the most sacred of all the rights "of sovereignty.

The President paid no attention to this remonstrance. It was evident that the agent by positive instruction or implied consent, was authorized to leave his station, assail the Governor of Georgia, and teach the Indians that their Great Father at Washington was not the friend of the Governor of Georgia, nor of those Indians who were his allies. He labored to prevent the treaty at Indian Springs, and failing in that, misrepresented it at Washington. All the mischiefs, disorders, and heart-burnings, which followed this treaty were organized and fostered by this man. In justice to him, he should be considered, however, as the instrument of the administration; for whatever he said or did was approved by his principal. No evil report of him would be listened to; the word of no man taken against him; all testimony in his favor was eagerly received; all against him promptly discredited. If one of the foreign governments should request another to remove its ambassador for language and conduct unbecoming his mission, the request would be instantly granted, however much the conduct of the minister might be subsequently approved by his government. In this case, however, when the Governor of Georgia had denounced the agent as an enemy to her interests, a fomenter of disturbance, a breaker of treaties, the Federal Government disregarded the wish of the State, and the agent himself treated it with derision and contempt. Failing in his effort to defeat the ratification of the Indian Springs treaty, this Indian agent, in the face of the action of the President and of the Senate, returned from Washington and proceeded to agitate for its annulment. How could it be annulled? McIntosh was President of the National Council; he was authorized to make the treaty. Not only was he recognized by the Indian nation as the officer to negotiate, but the Federal Government had time and again declared that he was the only competent authority for that purpose. There was only one way to set it aside. It must be made to appear that the act of McIntosh was unauthorized. Not by an appeal to usages, customs and laws; but by an appeal to the higher law, the sword, or rather the bow and arrow. Independent of the treaty, McIntosh and his chiefs had consented that Georgia should survey the lands, some months prior to the period set for removal. The agent seized upon this agreement to array the Indians and the Federal Government against the State. The treaty was supreme law, according to the broad Federal idea, now that it was ratified; but as McIntosh's consent to the survey was not a part of the treaty, the agent, on that ground, advised the Indians to resist the survey. This advice, coming from the agent of the Great Father, was equivalent to a mandate. McIntosh saw his danger. The life of this splendid chief, in whose veins flowed the blood of Indian kings and Scottish princes, whose breast was adorned with the badge of a general of the United States army, who had served gallantly under Jackson, and who had been the unflinching, unfailing, constant friend of the white man, was now imperilled by the cunning machinations of an Indian agent. The Red Sticks remembered that it was McIntosh who held them in check; although by the interposition of his iron hand, he had saved them from the ruin to which Tecumseh would certainly have led them. They were savages, and needed only an occasion for vengeance. The agent furnished the occasion. They notified the Georgia surveyors that they must desist from running their lines. To the number of three hundred they surrounded the house of McIntosh at night, and sent a hundred bullets through the body of this defenceless man. The assassins declared to the wife of the chief that they were supported and encouraged in their murderous mission by the agent.

The Governor called out the militia to enforce the treaty, and to protect the surveyors under the supplemental agreement. Generals Wimberly, Shorter and Miller were ordered to hold their divisions in readiness.

The President of the United States, at this juncture, interferes and commands the survey to cease. Whence came the authority for this virtual annulment of a treaty ratified by Congress? The President had sworn to execute the laws, and here he was setting himself against what, by his own logic, was one of the supreme laws of the land. As a pretext for his interposition he alleged that it was made in accordance with the eighth article of the treaty which guarantees protection to the friendly Indians. Under that guaranty the United States passively suffer McIntosh and his friends to be murdered; in the hour of peril no arm is lifted to protect or save; after the commission of the foul deed no voice comes from Washington for vengeance. The danger past, the chiefs massacreed, their property ravished, the surviving friends of McIntosh in exile in Georgia asking bread and protection, after abandoning every valuable to the insurgents, the United States now step forth with their armed power to defend, under the eighth article of the treaty, the so-called friendly Indians against their enemies. It might be supposed that the enemies to be defended against were the assassins, in the employment of Opothleyoholo. No, the Federal administration find the enemies contemplated by the treaty to be the people of Georgia, at whose firesides the friendly Indians were then resting. Could the force of absurdity go farther? It was supposed that the Federal Government at its creation was a government of delegated powers expressly stated, or of powers necessarily implied for the support and maintenance of those expressly stated. Yet, here, the Government was straining the treaty-making power in order to dispose of the Indian most effectually and according to whatever policy might suit its pleasure; it was at the same time using the commerce-regulating power to acquire possession of the territory of a State and to confine the benefit of trading posts to the friends of the agent. Worse than all, while denying the validity of a treaty which the Senate had approved, and which stood on the statute book as one of the supreme laws of the land, it was now seeking under a clause of that treaty which was intended to protect friendly Indians from the violence of hostile Indians, actually to defend the unjust pretensions of the hostile Indians who stood before them with the blood of the friendly Indians still dripping from their hands. The indignation of the State was aroused against these alleged usurpations of the General Government, and the hills and valleys of Georgia, from the mountains to the sea, rang with the cry of "TROUP AND THE TREATY."

The man with whom General GAINES was to deal upon reaching Georgia, was GEORGE M. TROUP. It was a a case of flint meeting steel. From the time he reached his majority, TROUP had been in public life as a representative of the people. He supported the claims of JEFFERSON against ADAMS when a member of the Georgia Legislature. As Representative in Congress he combatted the compromise made by the Federal Legislature with the Yazoo speculators. As chairman of the Committee on Military Affairs, he was a leading spirit in the war of 1812. As Senator in Congress, he pleaded for the removal of the Indians. He was always active, fervid, and faithful. Every interest of his people found in him a stubborn and determined advocate.

General GAINES was received by the people of Georgia with great courtesy. While at Milledgeville, he informed the Governor that his instructions from Washington were that no survey was to be made until the removal of the Indians under the treaty. The only point of controversy then existing was the authority of the chiefs to permit a survey outside of the letter of the treaty. Certainly if the Indians who made the treaty did not object, Georgia had a clear right to survey her own fee simple. It was a matter with which the United States had nothing to do. The reply of TROUP to this letter was courteous but decided. While deploring the vascillating conduct of the administration at Washington, he said: "On the part of the govern- "ment of Georgia, the will of its highest constitutional "authorities has been declared, upon the most solemn "deliberation, that the line shall be run and the survey "executed. It is for you, therefore, to bring it to an "issue; it is only for me to repeat that, cost what it "will, the line will be run and the survey effected."

At the same time the Governor suggested that the Georgia commissioners should be present at the council to be held by General Gaines at BROKEN ARROW, so as to meet and repel any charges or misstatements preferred by the agent or the hostile Indians. To this General GAINES objected. He was to arrive at the truth by an *ex parte* examination. It appeared as though the approaching council was not for the purpose of ascertaining facts, but to carry out a policy already decided upon by President ADAMS. Upon reaching Flint river, General Gaines held a council with leading chiefs, and forthwith dispatched to the Governor a certificate of two persons of doubtful character to the effect that neither General McINTOSH nor the chiefs had ever consented to a survey. General GAINES added, in a letter, that this certificate "proves that your excel-

"lency has been greatly deceived in supposing that the "McIntosh party ever consented to the survey of the "ceded territory being commenced before the time set "forth in the treaty for their removal," and that it became "his duty to remonstrate against the surveys "being commenced until the Indians shall have re-"moved, agreeably to the treaty." Down to this time not a word had been said as to the illegality or annulment of the treaty itself. On every occasion General Gaines advised the Indians to entertain no hope as to its rescision. The stopping of the survey was designed, however, simply as a pretext for the entire abrogation of the treaty.

Governor Troup so understood it. General Gaines perhaps did not at that time understand the purpose of President Adams' cabinet.

Governor Troup very justly felt aggrieved that Georgia was refused an audience at the council; that her two eminent citizens, Campbell and Merriwether, who had negotiated the treaty of Indian Springs, on the part of the United States, were cavalierly excluded from vindicating their mission; and now that an *ex parte* examination of, and certificate from, two Indians should be set forth as conclusive testimony, without application to the Governor of Georgia to know what evidence was in his possession to the contrary.

The Governor replied: "The certificate of Mar-"shall, no matter how procured, is one of the most "daring efforts that ever was attempted by malignant "villainy to palm a falsehood upon credulity." At that very moment the Governor had in his possession the agreement of McIntosh to the survey. He offered to make oath to the fact, and concluded his letter as follows: "I very well know from the late events which "have transpired under the eyes of the commissioners, "that the oath even of a Governor of Georgia may be "passed for nothing, and that any vagabond of the "Indian country may be put in requisition to discredit "him." This was hot language, and barely to be palliated on the ground of deep popular excitement.

General GAINES responded to this letter, through the public press. He tried to sustain the character of the two persons who had signed the certificate, and declared that the "malignant villainy" was all on the part of those who had secured the treaty. As to the question of the Governor's veracity he used this remarkable language: "If you will take the trouble to read the "newspaper essays with which the presses have been "teeming for some years past, you will find that many "of the essayists have had the hardihood to refuse "credence to the word of their chief magistrate, and "yet we have no reason to despair of the Republic."

To this unmilitary letter Governor TROUP responded curtly by forbidding the General to have any further intercourse with the Georgia government And now the Secretary of War, alleging intrigue and deceit in the procurement of the treaty, addressed the Governor as follows: "I am, therefore, directed by the Presi-"dent, to state distinctly to your excellency that for "the present he will not permit such entry or survey "to be made." To this the Governor replied by saying that no Indian treaty had ever been negotiated in better faith; that if there had been corruption in its procurement, the principles of the case of FLETCHER and PECK, estopped the United States from annulling it; and furthermore that he would advise the Georgia Legislature on its first meeting "to resist any effort which might "be made to wrest from the State the territory ac-"quired by that treaty, no matter by what authority "that effort be made." Remonstrating against the conduct of General Gaines, the Governor wrote to the President of the United States, as follows: "In the "enclosed gazette you will find another insolent letter, "dated the 16th instant, addressed by your agent, "Brevet Major General GAINES, to the chief magis-"trate of this State. Having been betrayed by his "passions into the most violent excesses, he is pre-"sented before you at this moment as your commis-"sioned officer and authorized agent, with a corps of "regulars at his heels, attempting to dragoon and over-"awe the constituted authorities of an independent "State, and on the eve of a great election, amid the "distractions of party, taking side with the one polit-"ical party against the other, and addressing election-"eering papers almost weekly to the chief magistrate "through the public prints, couched in language of con-"tumely and insult and defiance, and for which, were "I to send him to you in chains I would transgress "nothing of the public law." In conclusion the Governor said, "I demand, therefore, as chief magistrate of "Georgia, his immediate recall, and his arrest, trial and "punishment, under the rules and articles of war."

The President replied through the Secretary of War that he could not accede to the demand for GAINES' arrest; but at the same time sent a letter of rebuke to the General.

Upon the assembling of Congress, President Adams rehearsed in his message the events connected with the Indian Springs treaty. He said that happily distributed as the sovereign powers of the people of this Union have been between their General and State governments, their history has already too often presented collisions between these divided authorities with regard to the extent of their respective powers. No instance, however, had hitherto occurred in which this collision had been urged into a conflict of actual force. No other case was known to have happened in which the application of military force by the Government of the Union had been prescribed for the enforcement of a law, the violation of which had, within any single State, been prescribed by a legislative act of the State. In the present instance he held it to be his duty, if the State of Georgia still persisted in making a survey of the Indian lands, to enforce the law and fulfil the duties of *the nation* by all the force committed for that purpose to his charge.

Upon the convening of the General Assembly of Georgia, Governor TROUP held no less decided language. The Committee on Relations with the Federal Government submitted a report in which the complaints of Georgia were fairly and forcibly set out. "We have "been insulted," they said, "by petty agents; we have "been brow-beaten and derided by Indians. Our "chief magistrate at home and our Representatives in "Congress, while in the public service and under the "very eye of the General Government, have been com-"pelled to brook the insolence of half-breeds; we have "been prevented, nay, ordered to desist from surveying "our own lands when no possible harm could ensure, "and when, too, the General Government under pre-"cisely similar circumstances was carrying on its own "surveys among Indians unremoved from recently ac-

"quired lands, a privilege heretofore uninterruptedly "enjoyed by every new frontier State, and questioned "only for the first time in the case of Georgia, one of "the original thirteen States; we have had our Indian "allies—those who long defended Georgia from the "tomahawk of the very Indians who are now so high in "favor—murdered in cold blood, their families exiled "from home, made wanderers and outcasts from the "very country which but nine years ago was declared "to be exclusively theirs, under the plighted faith and "solemnly written guaranty of the General Govern-"ment, and all these misfortunes, cruelties and hard-"ships, they have been destined to endure from no "other cause, as we verily believe, than that of being "the unswerving friends of Georgia."

The resolutions of the committee maintained, 1st, that Georgia owns exclusively the soil and jurisdiction of all her territory, and with the exception of the right to regulate commerce among the Indian tribes, claims the right to exercise over any people, white or red, within those limits, the authority of her laws; 2d, that threatening a State with an armed force and actually stationing troops upon her borders is contrary to the spirit and genius of our Government—a fundamental principle of which is that the military is subordinate to the civil authority; 3d, that the President's protest against the survey is an instance of dictation and Federal supremacy unwarranted by any grant of power to the General Government.

In the meantime President ADAMS went to the length of declaring the Indian Springs treaty null and void, and proceeded to negotiate a new treaty with certain of the hostile Creek chiefs at Washington. By this second treaty the removal of the Creeks would be only partial, and the boundary of Georgia somewhat restricted. The State protested against this new treaty. A collision appeared imminent. The surveyors appointed by the General Assembly were ordered to be on the ground by a certain day, and at sunrise to commence their work. Governor TROUP had classified the militia, and ordered his generals to hold themselves in readiness to take the field. General GAINES was ready with the Federal forces to meet those of the State.

Fortunately, in the army of GAINES were three Georgians devoted to their State, and connected with some of her most distinguished people: Col. DAVID E. TWIGGS, Col. JOHN S. MCINTOSH, and Col. DUNCAN CLINCH. ZACHARY TAYLOR was Lieutenant-Colonel of CLINCH'S regiment. All of these men were ardently Southern. The three Georgians wrote to the President tendering their commissions if ordered to take arms against Georgia. This letter was sent to Washington by a person who had much influence with Mr. ADAMS; and it is said that the representations made by this person as to the temper of the Southern people, and particularly of the Federal army officers of Southern birth, was such as to induce him to change his policy, and to acquiesce in the claims of Georgia, under cover of a new treaty. The new treaty was in substance the old treaty so far as Georgia was concerned, and it was finally confirmed by the Senate—the Georgia Senators voting against it; but the State of Georgia, without regard to the proceedings at Washington, continued the survey and took and held possession of all the lands ceded by the Indian Springs treaty. The treaty of Washington was simply a pretext to enable the President to escape from his coercive policy. Its terms were never intended to be carried out, and were never regarded by the State, except so far as they conformed to the former treaty.

To cap the climax of the triumph of Governor TROUP, it was proven that those immaculate friends of the red man who had denounced and sought to annul the Indian Springs treaty on the ground of bribery and corruption, had actually secured the Washington treaty by giving bribes to the leading hostile Indians. Mr. BENTON, in his "Thirty Years in the United States "Senate," has given an interesting account of the manner in which he made the discovery that the war department had agreed to divide one hundred and sixty thousand dollars among the murderers of McINTOSH, in order to induce them to do what they alleged they had slain McINTOSH for consenting to do Mr. Benton says: "When the President sent in the treaty of January, "and after its rejection by the Senate became certain, "thereby leaving the Federal Government and Georgia "upon the point of collision, I urged upon Mr. JAMES "BARBOUR, the Secretary of War (of whose department the Indian office was then a branch), the necessity of a supplemental treaty ceding all the Creek "lands in Georgia; and assured him that with that "additional article, the treaty would be ratified and the "question settled. The secretary was very willing to "do all this, but said it was impossible—that the chiefs "would not agree to it. I recommended to him to "make them some presents, so as to overcome their "opposition, which he most innocently declined, as it "would savor of bribery. In the meantime it had "been communicated to me that the treaty already "made was itself the work of great bribery; the sum "of $160,000 out of $247,000, which it stipulated to "the Creek Nation, as a first payment, being a fund for "private distribution among the chiefs who negotiated "it. Having received this information I felt sure that "fear of the rejection of the treaty and the consequent "loss of these $160,000 to the negotiating chiefs would "insure their assent to the supplemental article without "the inducement of other presents. I had an inter-"view with the leading chiefs, and made known to them "the inevitable fact that the Senate would reject the "treaty as it stood, but would ratify it with a supple-"mental article ceding all their lands in Georgia. With "this information they agreed to the additional article, "and then the whole was ratified as I have already "stated."

Thus it was that President Adams negotiated a treaty with the hostile chiefs, which was the counterpart of that made with the friendly chiefs, except that the Indians were not to remove from a small part of the Georgia territory included in the former treaty. The hostile chiefs were bribed to accede to it, and when their appetite was whetted for the bribe money, almost in their grasp, the bags of gold were held up beyond their reach until they had ceded every acre of Georgia territory. What then? Were the shameful terms of the compact held good by the high contracting parties? One would suppose there would be honor between briber and bribed. Not so in this case. Mr. Benton continues the narrative in the most ingenuous manner:

"But a further work remained behind. It was to "balk the fraud of the corrupt distribution of $160,000 "among a few chiefs; and that was to be done in the "appropriation bill, and by a clause directing the whole "treaty money to be paid to the Nation instead of the "chiefs. The case was communicated to the Senate in "secret session, and a committee of conference was ap- "pointed (Messrs. Benton, Van Buren and Berrien) "to agree with the House committee upon the proper "clause to be put into the appropriation bill. It was "also communicated to the Secretary of War. He "sent in a report from Mr. McKinney, the Indian "Bureau clerk, and actual negotiator of the treaty, "admitting the fact of the intended private distribu- "tion; which in fact could not be denied, as I held an "original paper showing the names of all the intended "recipients with the sum allowed to each, beginning at "$20,000 and ranging down to $5,000, and that it "was done with his cognizance.."

The Indian Springs treaty ceded all the Creek lands in Georgia, and to the Coosa river in Alabama; but the Washington treaty ceded simply the Georgia lands. Georgia came out of the controversy with all she had ever demanded. It was Alabama that suffered. While the Governor of Georgia had exhausted the argument and was standing by his arms, the Governor of Alabama was content simply to advise the gentle savage that to civilize a people from a rude and barbarous condition they should be removed from the influence of the vices and luxuries which prevail in civilized life; and that the provinces farthest removed from the vices, refinements and luxuries of Rome made the most solid progress in civilization. In this whole difficulty with the Creeks, beyond a simple resolution instructing her members in Congress to use their best efforts to procure for Alabama the immediate execution of the Indian Springs treaty, nothing was done to assert, prosecute or defend her rights thereunder. And thus the fairest part of Alabama remained in the hands of savages for twelve years longer.

Although the Creeks had been removed, and the country opened up to civilization between the Oconee and Chattahoochee, there yet remained ten thousand Cherokees in Georgia. The Cherokee country of Georgia is one of the most fertile, healthful and beautiful on the western continent. The Indians were greatly attached to it, especially as under the teachings of Jefferson they had adopted many of the methods of civilized life. Had the plans of that wise philanthropist been left undisturbed, the Indian tribes would eventually have become useful citizens of the States; but the desire of the Federal party to keep those of this section as a breastwork against Southern advance, created reciprocal hostility between the white man and the red man, and finally defeated every scheme for their culture.

The Georgians having overrun the lands of the Creek, now turned wistful eyes to the lands of the Cherokee. Did the Federal Government have no intentention to extinguish the Cherokee title in accordance with the cession of 1802? Twenty-five years had now elapsed since that cession, and Georgia witnessed the same delay which almost plunged the State into hostilities with the Federal Government in the case of the Creeks. Not only was no step being taken for removal of the Cherokees, but the policy of President Adams and his friends appeared more pronounced in this case than in the other. Every effort was being put forth by the administration to fasten the Cherokees to the soil, by instructing them in those peaceful avocations which strengthen the attachments of family and home.

Georgia by a law of December 20, 1828, added all of the Cherokee territory lying within her limits to certain counties of the State, and extended over it her criminal jurisdiction. The object of this law, and of a subsequent one passed in the following year, was to parcel out the territory of the Cherokees, to subject it to the laws of Georgia, to abolish the Cherokee laws, to make it murder for a death sentence to be executed under Cherokee law, and to authorize the use of the Georgia militia in executing all processes over the Cherokee territory. The Cherokees sent a delegation to Washington, which presented to the President a protest against the encroachments of the Georgians; but Mr. Adams, just on the eve of retiring from office, took no action in the matter.

The views of the party opposed to the Adams theory of government were well expressed in the first annual message of President Jackson. He called the attention of Congress to the fact that the Indian tribes had lately attempted to erect an independent government within the limits of Georgia and Alabama. These States claiming to be the only sovereigns within their territories, had extended their laws over the Indians, and the latter had called upon the United States to interpose between the tribe and the State. Under these circumstances the question presented was, whether the General Government had a right to sustain the tribe in their pretensions? The Constitution declares that "no "new State shall be formed or erected within the juris-"diction of another State" without the consent of its Legislature. If the General Government is not permitted to tolerate the erection of a confederate State within the territory of one of the members of the

Union, against her consent, much less, said President Jackson, could it allow a foreign and independent government to establish itself there. Georgia became a member of the confederacy, which resulted in our Federal Union, as a sovereign State, always asserting her claim to certain limits, which having been originally defined in her colonial charter, and subsequently recognized in the treaty of peace, she has ever since continued to enjoy, except as they have been circumscribed by her own voluntary transfer of a portion of her territory to the United States in the cession of 1802. Alabama was admitted into the Union on the same footing with the original States, with boundaries which were prescribed by Congress. There is, said the message, no constitutional, conventional, nor legal provision which allows them less power over the Indians within their borders than is possessed by Maine or New York. Would the people of Maine permit the Penobscot tribe to erect an independent government within their State? And if they did, would it not be the duty of the General Government to aid the State in resisting such an an attempt? Would the people of New York permit each remnant of the six nations within her borders to declare itself an independent people under the protection of the United States? Could the Indians establish a separate republic on each of their reservations in Ohio? And if they were so disposed, would it be the duty of the Federal Government to sustain them? "If," said General Jackson, "the principle involved in the obvious answer to these "questions be abandoned, it will follow that the objects "of this Government are reversed; and that it has "become a part of its duty to aid in destroying the "States which it was established to protect."

Actuated by this view of the subject, President JACKSON, reversing the policy of his predecessor, informed the Indians inhabiting parts of Georgia and Alabama, that their attempt to establish an independent government would not be countenanced by the executive of the United States, and advised them either to emigrate beyond the Mississippi or submit to the laws of the State. Instead of bribing the Indian chiefs and going through the absurd formality of treating with them as independent nations, the President called upon Congress for the passage of an act to enable him to provide for their removal. Upon this proposition the two parties arrayed themselves. The Representatives in Congress from the Southern States, aided by a few votes from the North, succeeded in enacting such a law as the President requested. The opposition was led by Mr. FRELINGHUYSEN, in the Senate, and with him was found nearly all the Northern Senators.

The Indians, instigated by the half-breeds and missionaries who inclined to the Federal party, took counsel and legal advice with a view to get the question into the Supreme Court of the United States. WILLIAM WIRT, late Attorney General, was retained as their counsel. GEORGE R. GILMER was then Governor of Georgia. As soon as it became evident that the Indian Bill, as proposed by the President would become law, the Cherokees were persuaded that the right of self-government could be secured to them by the power of the Supreme Court of the United States, in defiance of the legislature of the State and National Government. At that time the idea does not appear to have been entertained by WIRT or by his cotemporaries of the Federal school of politics, that in the event the Supreme Court might show an inclination to interfere, that august tribunal might be brought to terms by an act of Congress curtailing its powers or increasing its members.

Judge A. S. CLAYTON of Georgia, in whose circuit the Indian counties lay, in his charge to the grand jury, assured the Indians of protection from the State, warned them against the intermeddling agents and missionaries who used their influence improperly in governmental matters, and predicted the futility of applying for relief to the Supreme Court. With respect to those who had counselled resistance to the State law, he said: "Meetings have been held in all directions to express "opinions on the conduct of Georgia, and of Georgia "alone," when her adjoining sister States had safely done precisely the same thing; and which she and they had done in the rightful exercise of their State sovereignty. The judge showed that one of those intrusive philanthropists had endeavored to enlist European sympathy in behalf of the Cherokees; and quoted from the address of the Reverend Mr. MILNER of New York, to the Foreign Missionary Society of London: "That "if the cause of the negroes in the West Indies was "interesting to that auditory—and deeply interesting "it ought to be—if the population in Ireland, groaning "beneath the degradation of superstition, excited their "sympathies, he trusted the Indians of North America "would also be considered as the objects of their Christian "regards. He was grieved, however, to state that there were those in America who acted towards them in a different spirit; and he lamented to say, at this very moment, the State of Georgia was seeking to subjugate "and destroy the liberties both of the Creeks and "Cherokees." Thus was it sought to defame a Southern State which was simply seeking to extend its laws throughout its limits as had been done by every Northern and Eastern State which had dealt with the Indians within its borders. And so ignorant was this pseudo philanthropist of what he was discussing that he seemed not to know that the Creeks, at the time he was speaking, had been gone five years from Georgia. Instead of the Cherokees, who still remained, being deprived of their liberties, they were offered a large price for their lands if they chose to remove across the Mississippi. If they preferred to remain they were simply to be subjected to the same laws with the whites. With respect to the Supreme Court, Judge CLAYTON declared that he should pay no attention to its mandate—holding no writ of error to lie from the Supreme Court of the United States to his State court, but would execute the sentence of the law, whatever it might be, in defiance of the Supreme Court. This bold position of the Georgia judge was maintained with the same firmness it was enunciated.

A Cherokee half-breed, GEORGE TASSELS, instigated by the political opposition to the policy of JACKSON, committed a homicide in resisting the execution of the Georgia law. He was tried for murder, condemned, and sentenced to be executed on a certain day. A writ of error to bring the case before the United States Supreme Court was obtained, and Mr. WIRT endeavored to secure the consent of Governor GILMER that the whole question should rest upon an agreed statement of facts. Governor GILMER replied: "Your suggestion "that it would be convenient and satisfactory if your-

"self, the Indians and the Governor could make up a "law case to be submitted to the Supreme Court for "the determination of the question whether the Legis- "lature of Georgia has competent authority to pass "laws for the government of the Indians residing "within its limits, however courteous the manner and "conciliatory the phraseology, cannot but be considered "exceedingly disrespectful to the government of this "State. No one knows better than yourself that the "Governor would grossly violate his duty and exceed "his authority by complying with such a suggestion, "and that both the letter and the spirit of the powers "conferred by the Constitution upon the Supreme Court "forbid its adjudging such a case."

The proceedings before the United States Supreme Court are of supreme interest when considered in relation to the alleged right of the Federal Government to coerce a State. MR. WIRT, in his application for an injunction to restrain the State, discussed the question with great ardor and ability. His argument has been pronounced the most brilliant of his life. "The great "interest excited by the controversy," says a writer in the North American Review, "was naturally to be "expected from the novelty of the case, the dignity of "the parties, and the high importance of the principles "in question. The scene wore, in some degrees, the "imposing majesty of those ancient debates, in which "the great father of Roman eloquence sustained before "the senate the rights of allied and dependent, but "sovereign princes, who had found themselves com- "pelled to seek for protection and redress from the "justice of the mighty Republic." Miss MARTINEAU, in her graceful description of the Court, alludes to the scene—" I have watched the assemblance when the " Chief Justice was delivering a judgment, the three " judges on either hand gazing at him more like " learners than associates, Webster standing firm as a " rock, his large, deep set eyes wide awake, his lips " compressed, and his whole countenance in that intent " stillness which easily fixes the eye of the stranger; " Clay, leaning against the desk in an attitude, whose " grace contrasts strangely with the slovenly make of " his dress, his snuff box for the moment unopened in " his hand, his small gray eye and placid half-smile, " conveying an expression of pleasure which redeems " his face from its usual unaccountable commonness; " the Attorney General, his fingers playing among his " papers, his quick black eye, and thin, tremulous lips " for once fixed, his small face pale with thought, con- " trasting remarkably with the other two. These men, " absorbed in what they are listening to, thinking " neither of themselves nor of each other, while they " are watched by the group of idlers and listeners " around them: the newspaper corps, the dark Chero- " kee chiefs, the stragglers from the far West, the gay " ladies in their waving plumes, and the members of " either House that have stepped in to listen; all these " I have seen constitute one silent assemblage, while " the mild voice of the aged Chief Justice sounded " through the Court."

At the outset of the case, was suggested the difficulty as to how the injunction was to be enforced in the event it should be awarded and the State should refuse to obey. " It will be time enough," said Mr. Wirt, " to meet the question when it shall arise."

Chief Justice Marshall, ever ambitious to make the

Supreme Court the arbiter of all constitutional questions, and by the force of former political association ever leaning to the views of the Federal party, held that the Court had full jurisdiction to pronounce upon the validity of the Georgia laws. The Court declared the Cherokee Nation a distinct community, occupying its own territory, with boundaries accurately described, and in which the laws of Georgia could have no force. It declared void the act of Georgia, under which the plaintiff in error was prosecuted, that the judgment of the State Court was a nullity, and that the plaintiff "was entitled to the protection of the Constitution, "laws and treaties of his country."

Thereupon arose the question, how was this decision to be enforced? Could the United States coerce a State?

The State of Georgia treated the decision as a nullity. No further action was taken by the Supreme Court; no effort made to enforce its decision. Chief Justice MARSHALL and his associates, by non-action, tacitly admitted that the United States had no constitutional power to enforce a decision against a sovereign State.

The State of Georgia did not appear as a party to these proceedings. The Chief Justice cited the State by writ of error "to show cause, if any there be, why "the judgment [of the State Court] should not be "corrected." The Governor laid the writ before the General Assembly, saying that he would not regard commands of the Federal Court which interfered with the constitutional jurisdiction of the State, and would oppose any attempt to execute them. The General Assembly sustained the Governor, and adopted a series of resolutions to the effect that the action of the Chief Justice of the United States was "a flagrant violation "of the rights of the State;" that the Governor should pay no attention to the mandate; but that he was bound "to resist and repel any and every inva- "sion, from whatever quarter, upon the administration "of the criminal laws" of the State, with all the "force "and means" entrusted to him by the laws of Georgia. They declared that "the State of Georgia will never so "far compromise her sovereignty as an independent "State, as to become a party to a case sought to be "made before the Supreme Court of the United States "by the writ in question," and that the Governor should acquaint the sheriff of Hall county with these resolutions, as far as was necessary to ensure the full execution of the laws in the case of George Tassels. The sentence of the State court was executed by the hanging of Tassels, Dec. 28, 1830.

Depending upon a statement of G. N. Briggs of Massachusetts, who was at the time a member of Congress, Greeley, in "The American Conflict," vol. I, p. 106, relates that President Jackson said: "John "Marshall has made his decision; now let him enforce "it!"

In accordance with the Georgia law of December 22, 1830, a missionary named Worcester, with other white persons who persisted in disobeying the statute, was sentenced to four years' imprisonment at hard labor. Worcester took the case before the Supreme Court of the United States, and the State of Georgia was once more cited to appear at Washington, before the Federal judiciary. Governor Lumpkin informed the Legislature that he would present a "determined resistance" to such "usurpation." The Supreme Court once more attempted to annul the action of the State, but the State court refused to grant a writ of habeas corpus, and paid no attention to the decision. No effort was ever made by the Federal Government to enforce the decision.

The Government at Washington and the country at large, by acquiescing in the failure of the Federal Government to carry out the mandate of the Federal court, admitted that Georgia had the right to extinguish any title to her lands remaining in the occupancy of the savages, that she was right in refusing to appear at the bar of the Supreme Court, and right in executing her statutes in these cases, notwithstanding interference from the Federal Government. In the debate over the Force Bill, in 1833, two years later than the events here referred to, we find the verdict of the people expressed in the language of Senator Miller of South Carolina. "No reproof of her [Georgia's] refractory "spirit was heard; on the contrary, a learned review of "the decision came out attributed to executive coun-"tenance and favor." It is to be borne in mind that the executive alluded to was the same who one year later, proposed at a public dinner at Washington, the toast, "The Federal Union, it must be preserved."

CHAPTER VII.

South Carolina and the Tariff—Continued Contest between the Agricultural and Commercial States—Calhoun and Nullification—The Force Bill and the Right of Coercion—Inconsistency of President Jackson—Calhoun's Victory—Webster Retires from the Battle—Real Causes for the Proclamation, &c., &c.

"Why should we fetter commerce? If a man is in chains, he droops and bows to the earth, because his spirits are broken; but let him twist the fetters from his legs and he will stand erect. Fetter not commerce! Let her be as free as the air. She will range the whole creation, and return on the four winds of Heaven, to bless the land with plenty."

PATRICK HENRY.

"To the Northern politician, who, during Monroe's administration recalled the past annals of the republic, the future was without hope. Incited by his devotion to Unionism, he had tried to strengthen the central power at Washington, but had been defeated on the occasion of the Alien and Sedition Acts; he had looked with disfavor upon the free navigation of the Mississippi, but the river had been bought; he was disinclined to territorial expansion, but Louisiana had been purchased; he had resisted the admission of new States from that purchase, but one after another, they were coming in."

DRAPER'S CIVIL WAR, vol. I, p. 360.

While the difficulty between Georgia and the Federal Government was still pending, the people of the United States, by a large majority, threw off the remaining vestiges of Federalism as represented by Adams, and elected Andrew Jackson to the Presidency by an electoral vote of one hundred and eighty-three, as against eighty-three for Adams. It is worthy of observation, however, that the victory of Jackson was not strictly upon principle. In New York, Pennsylvania, and in the West generally, Jackson was supported as the firm friend of the protective tariff, and of internal improvements by the General Government; whereas, in the South he was zealously sustained by those who denied the right and constitutionality of those things, as being the friend of those Southern interests which were believed by them to be seriously injured by the laws protecting home industry.

The new President's inaugural address was extremely vague upon the question of the tariff. His first annual message was not much more explicit. It favored a modification of the protective features of the tariff, but at the same time suggested that a desire for successful competition of American products with foreign should furnish "the general rule to be applied in graduating "the duties." The friends of Calhoun lost confidence in the purpose of President Jackson to carry out the free trade views upon which they had voted for him.

The first protective tariff, that of 1816, was advocated by Calhoun and opposed by Webster. It was at that time believed that the South would establish factories, and that the building of this Chinese wall around New England would destroy her carrying trade. The question of principle was lost sight of; and policy alone attached Calhoun to a doctrine which he afterwards condemned, and caused Webster to advocate free trade, which his section a few years later repudiated. Between 1816 and 1824, New England took advantage of the tariff and invested largely in factories. In 1824 the protective system was championed by HENRY CLAY, and still resisted by DANIEL WEBSTER. Virginia, the Carolinas, Georgia and the Southwest were unanimous against it, while Pennsylvania, New York, Ohio and Kentucky were unanimous for it. Massachusetts, under the lead of Webster, gave all her votes except one against it. It was not until four years later that Webster gave in his adhesion to the American system of CLAY.

In 1828 the question had assumed a most serious sectional aspect. When Jefferson was President, the maritime States of the North had bitterly opposed the embargo laws, which virtually kept their ships rotting at the wharves. They boldly declared that the enforcement of the embargo was adequate cause for dissolution of the Union. But now, in 1828, and in 1830, they favored a protective tariff, which operated upon the agricultural States as the embargo had upon the maritime States. Its operation was claimed to be even more severe. No one pretended that it was simply a tariff for revenue. It was intended to protect certain branches of industry by paying them a bonus wrung from other branches, and especially from the agricultural labor of the South. It was spoken of as a Bill of Abominations. All that the South asked was that she might buy her cotton gins, her ploughs, her hoes, and her clothing at moderate and just prices, and not be compelled to pay a subsidy to Massachusetts for the one article, or to Pennsylvania for another. African slavery had made the South purely agricultural, and all agricultural States naturally and necessarily favor free trade. Perhaps under other circumstances, however violative of the spirit of the Constitution, the South might have found a protective tariff an incentive to manufactories of iron in Tennessee, Georgia, Virginia and Alabama, of cotton goods in nearly all of the Atlantic and Gulf States south of the Chesapeake, and of leathern goods in the vast pine forests of the coast, as it was certainly an incentive to the production of sugar in Louisiana. But while agriculture was the sole occupation of the Southern people, the tariff fell upon the cotton States with crushing burthen. With one-third of the population they paid two-thirds of the revenue of the Union.

The opening of richer cotton fields in Alabama had diminished the value of land in South Carolina, and the commercial importance of Charleston had receded, it was said, before the blighting effects of the tariff. Within a few years past a thriving foreign commerce had been carried on direct with Europe, but now the forty ships which had sought the harbor of Charleston had all disappeared. The ship yards had been broken up; the merchants had become bankrupt or had sought other pursuits; mechanics were thrown out of employment, and the very streets were assuming the silence of inactivity. Said Mr. Hayne: "If we fly "from the city to the country, what do we there behold? "fields abandoned; the hospitable mansions of our "fathers deserted; agriculture drooping; our slaves, "like their masters, working harder and faring worse; "the planter striving with unavailable efforts to avert "the ruin that is before him."

If there had been a necessity for such protection to the interests of one branch of industry at the expense of another, the case would not have appeared so bad; but it was shown from the custom-house books that many species of our manufactures, and especially those of cotton, were going abroad to distant countries, and sustaining themselves there against all competition and beyond the fostering care of our laws. The only effect of protective duties in such cases was clearly to cut off importations, to create a monopoly at home, and to enable manufacturers to sell their goods higher to their own fellow-citizens of the South who produced the raw material than to the distant inhabitants of the Mediterranean and of India.

JOHN C. CALHOUN saw very plainly that the question of free trade was that which, keeping the more dangerous question of slavery in the back ground, was destined to divide the republic into two great parties. Upon this question he could rally the agricultural States to his standard, and would have the advantage of fighting on a higher level than he would be compelled to stand upon were the issue simply upon slavery. He had given up all hope that President Jackson would aid him in destroying the protective system by ordinary parliamentary measures. On July 26, 1831, at Fort Hill, he issued an address to the people of South Carolina, setting forth the declaration of the Virginia resolutions and asserting the right of interposition, "be it "called as it may, State right, veto, nullification or by "any other name." In 1832 the tariff had received the sanction of the President. Calhoun in a letter to Governor Hamilton of South Carolina reviewed the situation quite elaborately and announced the doctrine of nullification. "Nullification," said he, "is the great "conservative principle of the Union." "Not a pro-"vision can be found in the Constitution authorizing "the General Government to exercise any control over "a State by force, by veto, by judicial process, or in "any other form—a most important omission, designed "and not accidental." That Calhoun regarded nullification as a peaceful remedy appears throughout his letter. The calling out of the military power of the

Union, he said, would be useless because no opponents would be found, for "it would be * * * a con-"flict of moral, not physical force." He insisted that the legal relation between the Federal and State governments would not be broken up.

He denied the right of a State Legislature to nullify a Federal law. It must be done by a State convention. A motion was made in the South Carolina Legislature to call a State convention, but failed of the regular two-thirds vote. Another effort was more successful, and a convention was called to meet at Columbia, November 18th. A nullification ordinance was adopted November 24th, declaring that the tariff of May 19, 1828, and that of July 24, 1832, were null and void, and instructing the Legislature to pass laws necessary for enforcing the ordinance, after the first day of February next, for preventing the collection of duties imposed by the nullified laws. The convention announced that every measure of coercion on the part of the Federal Government would be regarded "as inconsistent with "the longer continuance of South Carolina in the "Union." The convention then adjourned until March to await the action of Congress.

There were many leading men of the South, who, while sympathizing with those who complained of the obnoxious tariff and not denying the right of a State in the ultimate resort to judge of the measure of its grievances and the mode of redress, nevertheless held that South Carolina had placed herself in a wrong attitude by passing her ordinance at a time when the Presidential election, two weeks before, had gone overwhelmingly against CLAY'S American system, and when a large majority of opponents of the odious tariff had been returned to Congress under a pledge for its repeal or modification. A majority of the people of the South believed that the case was not such an one as was described in the resolutions of '98, and in those of the Hartford convention, as a "deliberate, palpable "and dangerous" exercise of powers not granted by the compact. It was not a deliberate act of the United States; because after full debate in Congress, and an appeal to the country in a Presidential canvass in which the tariff was a leading question, the verdict of the people of the United State had been against it. It was not a dangerous act because the verdict of the election being adverse, it was now certain that its dangerous and oppressive features would be removed. Recognizing the fact that the Constitution itself was a bundle of compromises, these patriotic citizens of the South were willing to endure all burdens of Government which were not absolutely too grievous to be borne and without remedy, rather than rush to unknown evils beyond the confines of the Federal system. They believed in an appeal to the judiciary whenever the question could be reached in that way; if it was a question which could not be so reached, they appealed to the people at the next election. Hence they now protested against the hasty action of South Carolina.

Another large body of Southern people held that the remedy adopted by South Carolina was not the proper one. To secede from the Union was one thing; to remain in the Union and nullify a Federal law was quite another thing. Nullification would make the Union "a rope of sand," and place her precisely in the position she occupied under the articles of confederation when she had power to enact laws but no power to enforce obedience to them. The Constitution was clearly intended to enable the Federal Government to enforce obedience to her laws within those States which remained in the Union. To escape such laws, the remedy, as was asserted by these opponents of nullification, was by secession from the Union.

It is interesting to know that many of these Southern opponents of the principle of nullification were those who but a few years previous had stood by Governors TROUP and GILMER in their determined and successful nullification of the Indian treaties. The apparent inconsistency of their course is explained by reference to the distinction which they made between a Federal law of merely local operation which might be met by the local authorities without affecting the general interests of the Union, and a Federal law of general operation affecting all the States. The former could be opposed, they said, by State action within the Union; the latter could be met only by separation from the Union. While the Georgian, however, could consistently deny nullification as a remedy, in the case of the tariff, the New Englander who had advocated nullification of the embargo law, and of the acts declaring war against Great Britain, was morally estopped from such denial.

There was still another class of Southern men who held that the protective tariff was not only not unconstitutional and dangerous to the States, but actually within the scope of the Constitution, and conducive to the prosperity of the whole country. This class of men were numerous throughout the West, powerful in Louisiana and strong throughout the Gulf States. When the policy of protection was first broached, and the discriminating tariff of 1816 enacted, New England denounced it as unjust and oppressive, and the South advocated it almost as a unit. As has been already mentioned, CALHOUN was then for protection, and WEBSTER was for free trade. The South looked to the day when she might build up factories in her cotton fields; but New England feared that a protective tariff would lessen the imported cargoes which fostered her shipping. Public sentiment was not aroused upon this question until 1824, and not until then was a doubt expressed as to the constitutionality of protection. Four years later, New England had changed her investments from the West India shipping trade into factories, and was beginning to reap a golden harvest. The Western States, also, were giving birth to villages and cities where furnaces and water-wheels were in perpetual motion. The hemp factories of Kentucky and Missouri were supplying bagging and rope to the Cotton States, and Louisiana was furnishing the whole Union with sugar. With an exception here and there, the American system had been sustained from 1820 to 1832 by the New England States, by those north and west of the Alleghanies, and by the State of Louisiana. It is not surprising that it had ardent supporters among those intellects at the South, who, looking into the future, desired to diversify her industries and make her self-supporting in peace and in war. It was for these reasons that a large class at the South opposed the nullification act of South Carolina as hasty, inconsiderate and illegal.

President JACKSON issued his proclamation on the 11th of December, 1832. Congress was then in session. In his annual message, the President had expressed an opinion that the proceedings in South Carolina would come to an end if the tariff were simply put upon a revenue footing. South Carolina still persisting in her course, notwithstanding the favorable disposition of the administration and of Congress, the "revenue collection," or "force bill," as it was called, was introduced into Congress, January 31st, 1833, giving the President full power to meet the acts of the nullification legislature. The whole country was plunged into the wildest excitement. Those at the South who protested against the course of South Carolina, protested as strongly against the use of force towards her by the Federal Government. Upon this bill arose the great debate between CALHOUN and WEBSTER. Has the Federal Government the right to coerce a sovereign State into obedience to a law which she holds to be unconstitutional and oppressive? Our wisest statesmen had often warned their countrymen, in the most solemn terms, that our institutions could not be preserved by force, and could only endure whilst concord of feeling and a proper respect by one section for the rights of another should be maintained. MADISON, in this spirit, had observed in the Federal Convention that, "any Government for the United States, "formed upon the supposed practicability of using "force against the unconstitutional proceedings of the "States, would prove as visionary and fallacious as the "government of [the old] Congress." Senator TYLER of Virginia, well expressed the sentiment of the whole South when he said: "Yes, sir, the Federal Union "must be preserved. But how? Will you seek to "preserve it by force? Will you seek to appease the "angry spirit of discord by an oblation of blood?

"Suppose that the proud and haughty spirit of South "Carolina should not bend to your high edicts in "token of fealty; that you make war upon her; hang "her Governor, her legislators and her judges, as trai-"tors, and reduce her to the condition of a conquered "province—have you preserved the Union? This "Union consists of twenty-four States; would you "have preserved the Union by striking out one of the "States—one of the old thirteen? Gentlemen had "boasted of the flag of our country, with its thirteen "stars. When the light of one of these stars shall "have been extinguished, *will the flag wave over us, "under which our fathers fought?* If we are to go on "striking out star after star, what will finally remain "but a central and burning sun, blighting and destroy-"ing every germ of liberty? The flag which I wish "to wave over me, is that flag which floated in triumph "at Saratoga and Yorktown. It bore upon it thirteen "stars, of which South Carolina was one. Sir, there is "a great difference between preserving the Union and "preserving the Government; the Union may be anni-"hilated, yet Government preserved; but, under such "a Government, no man ought to desire to live."

This idea of Mr. Tyler, for the first time advanced in the American Senate, that the coercion of a State would leave it at the feet of the Federal Government as a conquered province, was scouted by those Senators who sustained the bill. Mr. BENTON speaks of his language as "vituperative." Mr. WEBSTER at all times declared that whatever might be the coercion employed by the Federal Government, it could not operate upon the State, but would simply preserve the peace among the people of the State, and prevent their interference with the regular process of an act of Congress. Thus far only, declared the Federalists, could the force bill go. The Federal Government could no more overthrow and destroy the State, than the State could nullify an act of. Congress.

Affairs were in a critical state, and the whole Southern people undoubtedly stood ready in the event of hostilities between South Carolina and the United States to array themselves with the former. In this crisis, Virginia delegated BENJAMIN WATKINS LEIGH, as commissioner to intercede, with South Carolina and to urge her either to rescind her ordinance or to postpone action until the close of the session of Congress. His mission was successful. In view of the probable reduction of the tariff to a revenue standard, action upon her ordinance was postponed from February 1st to March 4th. It was then that Clay offered his compromise measure, securing adequate protection for nine years, and less protection beyond that term. The manufacturers denounced him, as having yielded to a storm which in a few years would sweep protection away entirely; and his Northern supporters fell from him in multitudes. It was said to him that by compromising protection he had forfeited his chances for the Presidency. "I would rather be right than be President," replied the patriot. While Webster, proud of the power of the opulent North, and impatient of what he held to be the factious disturbance of ambitious politicians, refused to be a party to the compromise, CLAY remembered that the Union itself was a compromise and that no document, like the Constitution, could be so perfect, that a resort to mutual concessions might be discarded when questions of conflicting jurisdiction arise between the State and Federal Government. To the mind of this great man it was clear that it was better to solve political questions by compromises which endangered no great interest and which applied to their cure the soothing influence of time, than to resort to civil war with its waste of treasure and blood, its distortion of principles, and the bitter seed it would sow for generation after generation.

Referring to the spirit of that day, the attitude of South Carolina finds an apology in the temper of the North. While she believed that the protective tariff was dangerous to the Union and oppressive to her people, and that its retention would justify resistence, her enemies on the other hand believed that the abolition of protection would be ruinous to the welfare of the Union and would justify its dissolution. The threats of South Carolina were met by counter threats from the manufacturing regions. If treason lurked in the oratory of CALHOUN, and in the proclamations of HAYNE, it showed itself fully to view in the language of Northern politicians. CLAY had distinctly declared that danger to the Union was more to be feared from a surrender of the American system than from its retention. Of the friends of that system he said: "Let "them feel that a foreign system is to predominate, "and the sources of their subsistence and comfort "dried up; let New England, the West and the middle "States, all feel that they too are the victims of a mis-"taken policy, and let these vast portions of our "country despair of any favorable change, and *then* "*indeed might we tremble for the continuance and* "*safety of this Union.*"

JOHN M. CLAYTON, Senator from Delaware, said that

"*the Government cannot be kept together if the princi-*
"*ple of protection were to be discarded in our policy,*" and that he "would pause before he surrendered that "principle, *even to save the Union.*"

Thus it was that whereas South Carolina was ready to resist the Federal Government in the levying of imposts for what she believed to be an unconstitutional object, her defamers were ready to dissolve the Union if the imposts were simply directed towards raising revenue. The cause for which South Carolina would fight was a violation of the Constitution; the cause for which her enemies would fight was not a violation of the Constitution, but simply a curtailment of their extravagant profits in business.

That profound student, Von Holst, in his able work on the Constitutional History of the United States, has not failed to observe the inconsistency between the action of President Jackson towards South Carolina and that towards Georgia, only a few years previous. "Why was that now so great a crime," he asks, "upon "which the President then looked with scarcely con- "cealed satisfaction? Did not his oath of office im- "pose the same duties upon him then? Was the "supremacy of a tariff law of a higher sort than that "of treaties? Why must a sovereign State now most "obediently entreat the United States Supreme Court "to inform it of the limits of its rights, when, then, "a State no more sovereign could angrily reject the "decision of that Court, made in all form, as a revolt- "ing assumption, without receiving even a warning re- "proof from President or Congress? South Carolina "knew that no answer could be given to all these ques- "tions, and therefore did not fail to put them."

The answer to these questions is that President Jackson was carried away by his personal animosity to Calhoun, and having resolved to antagonize him and vindicate his determination to maintain a personal government, he hastened into an inconsistency, and assumed an attitude against State-rights which he afterwards desired to explain away. When Calhoun was elected to the Vice-Presidency with Jackson, it was not known to the latter that when a member of Monroe's Cabinet, the former had expressed the opinion that the General ought to be brought to trial for his conduct in the war against the Seminoles. When the truth was made known to Jackson, he submitted the charge to Calhoun's inspection and was informed that it was true. From that day General Jackson was the implacable enemy of Calhoun. He even threatened him with the halter—and to show his hostility, he reorganized the Cabinet, giving a majority of the Secretaryships to the friends of Van Buren, and the enemies of Calhoun.

Calhoun at once resigned the Vice-Presidency and was elected to the United States Senate to succeed Hayne, who had given up his seat in order to accept the Governorship of South Carolina. Upon taking his seat in the Senate, Calhoun at once took issue with the President's proclamation. That proclamation had already been received with loud laughter and jesting commentaries by the South Carolina Legislature. This was to be expected; but it was also received with doubt, hesitation, or opposition by a vast multitude, who did not sympathize with South Carolina. Henry Clay wrote December 12th, to Judge Brooks: "As to the "proclamation, although there are good things in it, "especially what relates to the judiciary, there are "some entirely too ultra for me, and which I cannot "stomach."

Before its adjournment the South Carolina convention issued an address to the people of the United States, in which it declared that so far as lay in its power matters would not come to bloodshed, and that to avoid such result, the State would secede from the Union. Whatever doubt was entertained by the States-rights advocates as to the right of the State to remain in the Union and nullify Federal laws, it does not appear that there was any doubt among them as to the right of peaceable secession. In the Legislature of South Carolina the proclamation of Jackson was severely commented upon by Barnwell Smith, as containing "the tyrannical doctrine that we have not even the "right to secede." The address proceeded to set forth a plan of taxation which would satisfy the State and lead to a repeal of the nullification ordinance. This concession was offered by the State, "provided she is "met in due time and in a becoming spirit by the "States interested in the protection of manufactures."

President Jackson, in his message of December 4th, recommended the removal of such duties as were found to fall unequally upon any of the community. This was a concession made in the face of the ordinance of South Carolina. On December 27th the committee to whom this part of the message was referred reported a bill decreasing the revenue $13,000,000 compared with the tariff of 1828, and $7,000,000 compared with that 1832. As this reduction was to take place within two years, it amounted to an abandonment of protection. The manufacturers were alarmed, and Webster opposed the bill with all his power. He declared that Jackson was not in favor of any concessions to the nullifiers, but had been pressed forward by his party who feared the effect of the doctrines developed in the proclamation.

Pending these proceedings the President asked for extraordinary powers to enforce the collection of customs as against the ordinance; and "in case of an at-"tempt otherwise to take the property [attached for "non-payment of duties] by a force too great to be "overcome by the officers of the customs," he applied for authority to use the land and sea forces to execute the law. On January 21st, the judiciary committee reported the bill known as the "force bill," to make possible the collection of customs. The bill was furiously assailed by all the States-rights advocates. The debate had continued fourteen days, and threatened to be almost interminable when Clay asked the Senate to permit him to bring in a bill to modify the tariff. Benton relates that Clay had advised Webster of his intentions, but that the latter had opposed the proposed bill, saying: "It would be yielding great principles to fac-"tion, and that the time had come to test the strength "of the Constitution and the Government."

Calhoun sustained the proposed bill, saying that the minor points of difference would present no difficulty if men met each other in the spirit of mutual compromise. That Calhoun did not yield consent to this proposition simply to escape personal danger, appears from his speech of February 15th and 16th against the force bill, in which he declared that should that bill become law and an effort be made to enforce it, "it will "be resisted at every hazard—even that of death "itself." On February 18th the Senate ordered the force bill to a third reading by a vote of thirty-two to eight. On February 25th, on motion of Letcher, the bill of Verplanck, then pending in the House, was stricken out, and Clay's bill substituted for it. The bill, on the next day, passed the House by a vote of one hundred and nineteen against eighty-five.

The House then took up the Senate bill. Already the Judiciary Committee of that body had, on February 8th, denounced the message of President Jackson, and declared that the use of force towards South Carolina would be unjust and impolitic from every point of view. The committee did not pass upon the question of right, but they evidently believed that the Federal Government had no such right. The House did not carry out the views of the committee, but after waiting to see the fate of the Clay tariff bill, in the Senate, they yielded assent to the Senate force bill. When the force bill came up in the House, McDuffie asked what practical aim the bill now had, and Foster asked any member to rise in his seat who imagined any further resistence by South Carolina possible after every Senator and Representative from that State had voted for the tariff bill. Notwithstanding these objections, the passage of the two bills was tacitly regarded as a mutual concession, and the House ordered the force bill to a third reading, by a vote of one hundred and twenty-six to thirty-four. The Senate thereupon passed the tariff bill by a vote of twenty-nine to sixteen. The President signed both bills on the 2d of March, and on March 16th, South Carolina repealed the ordinance of nullification.

The people of the South saw in this settlement a victory for South Carolina. The exhibition of resistance to a Federal law by a single State had resulted in a surrender by the Federal Government of the law in question. It is true that the passage of the force act was an assertion by the United States of the principles of the proclamation—but that assertion was weakened by a denial on the part of Jackson's intimate advisers of the apparent meaning of the proclamation, and was destroyed several years later by the adoption of substantially the very resolutions with which Calhoun had met and defied that proclamation.

A portion of Jackson's adherents objected to his course, because they saw in his proclamation the consolidation ideas of the old Federalists. The *Congressional Globe* met the reproaches of this faction with a long "authorized" article in which the President let it be stated that he recognized not only in the States but in the State Governments, the rights claimed in the Virginia and Kentucky resolutions. The article said:

"Its [the proclamation's] doctrines, if construed in "the sense they were intended, and carried out, incul-"cate * * that in the case of the violation of the "Constitution of the United States and the usurpation "of the powers not granted by it on the part of the "functionaries of the General Government, the State "Governments have the right to interpose and arrest "the evil, upon the principles which were set forth in "the Virginia resolutions of 1798, against the alien "and sedition acts; and finally that in extreme cases of "oppression (every mode of constitutional redress hav-"ing been sought in vain) the right resides with the "people of the several States to organize resistance "against such oppression."

The editor of the Globe, Francis P. Blair, who was

authorized to explain away the generally understood meaning of the proclamation, proceeded in this article to say that during the debate on Foote's resolutions between Hayne and Webster, and while he was editor of a journal in Kentucky, he received from the Post Master General the speech delivered by Mr. Livingston, accompanied by a letter saying that the views contained in it were sanctioned by the President, and might be considered as exhibiting the light in which his administration considered the subject under debate. The following extracts from that speech will serve to illustrate the principles upon which the President then took his stand, and to explain the more condensed view given of them in his proclamation:

"It is a *compact* by which the people of each State "have consented to take from their own Legislatures "some of the powers they had conferred upon them, "and to transfer them, with other enumerated powers, "to the Government of the United States, created by "that compact."

"Yet I am far from thinking that this [Supreme] "Court is created an umpire to judge between the "General and State Governments."

"In an extreme case * * * the injured State "would have a right at once to declare that it would no "longer be bound by a compact which had been thus "grossly violated."

John Tyler in his memoir of Roger B. Taney, says that when the proclamation was presented to President Jackson, he disapproved the principles and doctrines contained in it. But as the conclusion suited him, he determined to issue it at once, without waiting to correct the erroneous doctrines contained in it.

The South did not believe Jackson entertained the principles of his proclamation. It was against his views and conduct in the Creek controversy. It was antagonistic to the Virginia Resolutions of 1798, which he professed to endorse. It ran counter to the above expressed views of Livingston, who is said to have written the proclamation. They attributed his course to purely personal hostility against Calhoun, and they attributed the concession of the United States on the Tariff question as a recognition of the correctness of the views of South Carolina. The condition of the public faith as to the umpire in disputes between the States and the United States was well expressed by Clay in his letter of January 17th, to Brooks: "As "to politics we have no past, no future. After forty "years of existence under the present Constitution, "what single principle is fixed? The bank? No. "Internal improvements? No. The tariff? No. "Who is to interpret the Constitution? We are as "much afloat at sea as the day when the Constitution "went into operation."

Not only did the actual victory rest with South Carolina in this controversy, but the intellectual and moral victory rested with the champion of South Carolina. On January 22d, 1833, CALHOUN introduced into the Senate his celebrated series of resolutions which gave rise to the remarkable debate between himself and WEBSTER. The first resolution against which the thunders of Webster were directed, reads as follows:

"*Resolved*, That the people of the several States "comprising these United States, are united as parties "to a constitutional compact, to which the people of each "State acceded as a separate sovereign community, each "binding itself by its own particular ratification; and "that the Union of which the said compact is the "bond, is a Union *between the States* ratifying the "same."

From this compact the other resolutions deduced the doctrine of the resolutions of '98, that in this case as in all other cases of compact among sovereign parties, without any common judge, each has an equal right to judge for itself as well of the infraction as of the mode and measure of redress. These resolutions of CALHOUN were aimed directly at the President's proclamation. Webster so accepted and so treated them. He argued that "the Constitution means a Government, and not "a compact." "Not a Constitutional compact but a "Government." "If compact, it rests on plighted "faith, and the mode of redress would be to declare the "whole void." "States may secede, if a league or "compact."

Seizing upon this admission of Webster, that a State may secede if the Constitution is a compact, Calhoun in his response called attention to the language used by Massachusetts in ratifying the Constitution. She speaks of it as a "solemn compact." He called attention to Webster's own language in his great speech three years before, upon the Foote resolutions, when he alluded to "accusations which impute to us a disposition to evade "*the Constitutional compact.*" So complete was Calhoun's argument that Webster never offered a rejoinder. ALEXANDER H. STEPHENS, in his "War between the "States," speaks of it as "a crusher, an extinguisher, "an annihilator," and says—"This speech of his was "not answered then, it has not been answered since, "and in my judgment never will be, or can be answered "while truth has its legitimate influence, and reason "controls the judgments of men."

That Webster felt the force of Calhoun's argument is evident from the change in his own views within the next few years. In 1839, in the case of the *Bank of Augusta vs. Earle,* Webster used such language as this: "I am not prepared to say that the States have no "national sovereignty." "The Constitution treats "States as States." "The States of this Union, as "States, are subject to all the voluntary and customary "laws of nations." The language of the Supreme Court in this case was: "They are sovereign States." "A corporation created by one sovereignty is per-"mitted to make contracts in another, and to sue in its "courts." "The same law of comity prevails among "the several sovereignties of this Union." Thus the Supreme Court held that sovereignty is still retained by the several States of the Union under the Constitution. Webster admitted it. The great "expounder "of the Constitution," in 1839, was immeasurably behind his successor of 1861, who held with Lincoln that the relation of a State to the United States was simply that of a county to a State—without one shadow or spark of sovereignty.

Subsequently, in his letter to the Barings, bankers of London, who enquired as to the right of States to issue bonds and borrow money, Webster recognized in the State this high privilege of sovereignty. "Every "State," said he, "is an independent, sovereign, politi-"cal community, except in so far as certain powers, "which it might otherwise have exercised, have been "conferred on a General Government." Again, in

1851, Webster expressed similar views in a speech made at Capon Springs, Virginia. He said:

"How absurd it is to suppose that when different "parties enter into a compact for certain purposes, "either can disregard any one provision, and expect, "nevertheless, the other to observe the rest."

"I have not hesitated to say, and I repeat, that if "the Northern States refuse, wilfully and deliberately, "to carry into effect that part of the Constitution "which respects the restoration of fugitive slaves, the "South would no longer be bound to observe the com- "pact. A bargain cannot be broken on one side and "still bind on the other."

The Resolutions of Calhoun in 1833 did not express more distinctly than this language of Webster, that the Union is a Union of States, that the Union is founded upon compact, and that a compact broken on one side does not continue to bind the other side. No vote was taken upon the Calhoun resolutions of 1833, but on December 28, 1837, only four years later, Calhoun introduced to the Senate a new set of resolutions, the first of which, in these words, set forth the very idea of those of 1833.

Resolved, That in the adoption of the Federal "Con- "stitution, the States adopting the same, acted severally "as free, independent, and sovereign States; and that "each for itself, by its own voluntary assent, entered "the Union with the view to its increased security "against all dangers, domestic as well as foreign, and "the more perfect and secure enjoyment of its advan- "tages, natural, political and social."

It will be observed that this resolution is in direct conflict with the Websterian doctrine as announced in

1833, and with the generally accepted meaning of Jackson's proclamation. Calhoun here announced that the Union is a compact springing from the States acting as States, and not a government springing from the people. This resolution was adopted by a vote of thirty-two Senators against thirteen. Eighteen States voted for it; and Senators representing only six States voted against it. One State was divided and one did not vote. Thus more than two-thirds of the States, through their Senators, vindicated the political ideas of Calhoun, and this verdict was given only four years after the ordinance of nullification, and after Jackson's proclamation.

CHAPTER VIII.

Controversy between Alabama and the United States—Intrusion on the Creek Lands—Killing of Owens—Message of Governor Gayle—Threats of Resistance to the Military—Resolutions of a Legislative Committee—Mission of Key to the State—Adjustment of the Difficulty—The Federal Government Compromises the Question, &c., &c.

"Allegiance, a word brought from the Old World, of Latin origin, from *ligo*, to bind, means the obligation which every one owes to that power in the State, to which he is indebted for the protection of his rights of person and property. Allegiance and sovereignty, as we have seen, are reciprocal. 'To whatever power a citizen owes allegiance, that power is his sovereign.' To what power are the citizens of the several States indebted for protection of person and property, in all the relations of life, for the regulation of which governments are instituted? Certainly not to the Federal Government."

ALEXANDER H. STEPHENS.

"The use of force against a State would look more like a declaration of war than an infliction of punishment, and would probably be considered by the party attacked as a dissolution of all previous compacts by which it might be bound. * * Any government for the United States formed on the supposed practicability of using force against the unconstitutional proceedings of the States would prove visionary and fallacious."

JAMES MADISON, IN THE CONVENTION.

The lands occupied by the Creeks in Alabama were laid off and organized into nine counties, by an act of the General Assembly, so as to put the entire machinery of the State Government into full operation. This was in accordance with the action of Georgia, in pursuance of the Constitution of Alabama, and consistent with the views of President Jackson, as understood at the time the treaty was made, and before his views had become affected by the tariff difficulty in South Carolina. Several of these counties contained a population of six or eight thousand whites, and the aggregate white population was not less than twenty-five thousand.

The treaty by which the Creek Indians in March, 1832, ceded to the United States their possessions in Alabama, contained this stipulation:

ARTICLE 5th.—"All intruders upon the country "hereby ceded shall be removed therefrom in the same "manner as intruders may be removed by law from "other public land, until the country is surveyed and "the selections made; excepting however from this "provision, those white persons who have made their "own improvements, and not expelled the Creeks from "theirs. Such persons may remain till their crops are "gathered. After the country is surveyed, and the se- "lections made, this article shall not operate upon that "part of it not included in such selections. But in- "truders shall, in the manner before described be re- "moved from the selections, for the term of five years "from the ratification of this treaty, or until the same "are conveyed to white persons."

It will be seen that, by this article, the Government assumed upon itself the obligation of removing intruders from this land, in the same manner as intruders might be removed by law from other public land. The "*manner*" was prescribed in the Act of Congress, passed March 3d, 1807, entitled "An Act to prevent "settlements being made on lands, ceded to the United "States, until authorized by law." This Act provided for the interposition of the Marshal and the employment of military force, under orders of the President, and furnished the authority by virtue of which the proceedings in Alabama, in relation to this subject, took place.

There were two limitations to this obligation. One excepted from its operation "those white persons, who "have made their own improvements, and not expelled "the Creeks from theirs; such persons may remain till "their crops are gathered." As the season alluded to had passed away, and the crops had been gathered, this provision was no longer applicable to any settler upon these lands. The other limitation confined the obligation of the Government, to remove intruders, to the tracts located for the Indians "after the country is surveyed "and the selections made," and leaving the duty of removal imperative over the whole cession, until both of these objects were accomplished.

It was now denied by Alabama as it had been by Georgia, that the Act of 1807 applied to intrusions upon lands lying within a State. As early as the year 1785, when Colonel Harmar was engaged in removing intruders from the public lands in the western country, the commissioners of Indian affairs directed him to employ such military force as he might judge necessary in driving off persons attempting to settle on the lands of the United States, "not within the limits of any "particular State."

It was claimed that the settlers upon these vacant lands, hunted over by the Creeks, had the same rights of occupancy and pre-emption permitted by the laws of the United States in the case of any other vacant lands. Under a series of Acts of Congress, extending from the Act of May 10th, 1800, down to that of 1830, persons who had settled upon public lands in anticipation of a sale, were entitled to the right of pre-emption. The Act of 1830 provided—"that every "settler or occupant of the public lands, prior to the "passage of this Act, who is now in possession, and has "cultivated any part thereof, in the year 1829, shall "be, and he is hereby authorized to enter with the "register of the land office, for the district in which "such lands may lie, by legal subdivisions, any number "of acres not more than 160, or quarter section, to "include his improvement, upon paying to the United "States the minimum price of the land."

In this continued succession of Acts, embracing and running through a period of thirty years, all conferring upon settlers the valuable privilege of pre-emption, is shown the settled policy of the Government to encourage citizens to settle and occupy the public lands. This class of population had always been esteemed highly meritorious, and the exclusive right to purchase at private sale was extended to them in consideration of, and as a reward for, the services they had rendered by these settlements, in testing the value and productiveness of the soil; and in affording facilities to purchasers to examine it.

Notwithstanding this claim of Alabama to jurisdiction of her State laws over the Creek territory, and notwithstanding the fact that the "treaty" doctrine had been exploded for several years, and the pre-emption rights of settlers had been respected for thirty years, the Federal Government announced its purpose to remove the so-called "intruders" upon Creek territory, numbering now twenty-five thousand souls, by the strong arm of military force.

Alabama had sustained President Jackson in his contest with South Carolina on the tariff question, and the Governor of the State, JOHN GAYLE, had been elected to the executive chair as an opponent of the theory of nullification; but, notwithstanding the ardent desire of the people of the gulf country to strengthen the Union, they were constantly met by stubborn facts which tended to repress that desire. Governor Gayle had no disposition to bring about a collision between the Federal Government and the State of Alabama, but the theory as to the treaty-making and commerce-regulating powers of the General Government, as applied to Indian tribes and lands, was so repugnant to the rights of the States and to the interests of the people, that he was borne along by the same current of argument and events which carried Governor Troup to the edge of battle. The honest and patriotic spirit which actuated the Governor of Alabama is exhibited in his letter dated at Tuscaloosa, October 2d, 1833, and addressed to Lewis Cass, Secretary of War. In that letter he says:

"If the General Government have the right to regu-"late the conduct of our people in relation to their "land—if it can rightfully expel a citizen who tres-"passes upon the landed possession of his neighbor, by "the summary interposition of a military guard, with-"out even the forms of military investigation, what is "to restrain it from the exercise of the same power in "relation to trespassers upon personal property? From "this the transition would be easy to the taking cog-"nizance of all irregularities, misdemeanors, and crimes, "the right to punish which, has heretofore been con-"sidered as belonging exclusively to the State tribu-"nals. If, by the treaty-making power, the ordinary "operation of our laws upon the persons and property "of our own citizens can be suspended, as will be the "case if the 5th article of the treaty is executed in "the mode prescribed in your late order to the marshal, "the whole field of State jurisdiction may be consid-

"ered as occupied; *and State sovereignty, the reserved* "*rights of the States, &c.*, are but unmeaning sounds, "totally unworthy of serious consideration.

"I know that these terms are used by many as mere "cant expressions, and that they have been brought "into disrepute by the extravagant pretensions and "absurd doctrines of a sister State? but they imply "things that are still worth preserving, and as long as "the blessings of this Union are justly appreciated, "they will command the best and highest exertions of "the patriot. It is often difficult to trace, with precise "accuracy, the boundary which separates the jurisdic-"tion of the State and Federal Governments. We can "at all times, however, determine nearly where it lies. "But this treaty is for giving it a new direction. It "crosses the line designated in the Constitution, at "right angles, and runs into the very heart and centre "of our domestic concerns.

"But, sir, there is another view of this subject, "which will expose in a light still more glaring, the "utter incompatibility of this treaty with the jurisdic-"tive rights of the State of Alabama.

"As before observed, the right of extending our "laws over the country from which our people are "ordered to be expelled, is admitted to the fullest "extent. This necessarily implies the right of employ-"ing the means that are indispensible to its exercise. "What are these means? As enumerated in the Con-"stitution of this State and the laws made in pursu-"ance thereof, they are, that the State shall be laid off "into counties, and convenient circuits, that the circuit "courts shall be held in each county at least twice in "every year, that the counties shall be divided into "small districts, in each of which there shall be ap-"pointed two justices of the peace and two constables, "that there shall be, in each circuit, a judge of the "circuit court, who shall reside in his circuit, that there "shall be for each county a judge of the county court, "that there shall be also in each county, a sheriff, "clerks of the circuit and county courts, a coroner, "notaries public, commissioners of roads and revenue, "&c.; and that there shall be summoned, previous to "every circuit court, a competent number of grand and "petit jurors, and a like number of petit jurors for the "county courts. All these ministers of our law are "required to reside in the counties to which their office "belongs. These are the ordinary means by which our "State government is put in operation, and effect given "to our laws. And yet the late instructions to the "marshal absolutely prohibit the use of them.

"The General Government has not only admitted "the right of Alabama to extend her jurisdiction "over the ceded country, but it has invited and encour-"aged such extension by sundry documents to which "it is unnecessary to refer. No sooner, however, is the "country organized and the necessary steps taken to "this end, than an armed forced is collected on the "banks of the Chattahoochee for the purpose of expel-"ling from this large and flourishing section of the "State all 'white persons,' including of course all civil "officers and other persons whose agency is necessary "to the execution of our laws.

"We will have no power to punish any offences "committed by the Indians, or to subject them in any "respect to the restraints of the law, because our "courts will have been suppressed in all the counties in "which they reside. Now, sir, if your order be car-"ried into effect, will not an instance have occurred in "our country, and the first instance, too, of the gov-"ernment of a State being put down and destroyed, in "nine of its counties, by military force? Will not the "alarming spectacle be exhibited of the laws of one of the "States of this Union, in their ordinary operation, being "compelled to yield in time of profound peace, to the "dominion of the sword—to give way to the capricious "will of a deputy marshal, whose favorite modes of "punishment seem to be the conflagration of dwellings "and the application of the bayonet.

"I respectfully request that this project, so fatal in "its tendency to civil liberty, and so directly subver- "sive of the acknowledged rights and sovereignty of "the State of Alabama, be abandoned. I protest "against it as unconstitutional interference with our "local and internal affairs, and as a measure of revolt- "ing injustice and oppression towards that portion of "our inhabitants who have not injured the Indians. "Put away, sir, the sword which has been unneces- "sarily and too quickly drawn against this large and "unoffending community. It is the appropriate arbiter "in contests of ambition, but not in questions of con- "stitutional right. It is not to be forgotten that the "American people, on a recent occasion, pronounced "emphatically, that questions of jurisdiction between "the foreign and domestic branches of our government, "are to be settled by the tribunals which the Constitu- "tion vests with the power of expounding the laws. "To these tribunals I appeal on behalf of the good "people of this State."

In August, 1833, a citizen of the county of Russell, by the name of Owens, was killed by a party of soldiers who had been placed under the direction of the deputy marshal for the Southern District of Alabama, for the purpose of removing from the Creek country such persons as had intruded upon Indian possessions. These officers had previously made frequent incursions with the soldiers of the United States, and their action, after the murder of Owens, kindled an excitement that rapidly extended over the whole of the new counties, and in some degree, throughout the State. Governor Gayle was at once satisfied that the mode adopted by the Government to carry the stipulation of the treaty into effect, and to evict intruders, could not fail to produce serious and unpleasant difficulties, and that it would lead to unhappy, and perhaps dangerous excesses.

He wrote to the Secretary of War protesting against the action of the soldiery. but received no other response than that the settlers must be removed.

The greatest agitation existed in the new counties. Everywhere public meetings were called, at which was represented the incalculable injury in which their removal would involve them. It was perceived, when the business of *burning houses and delivering crops to the chiefs* should commence, that the exasperated feelings of the people would urge them to stand by their wives, their children and their property, that bloodshed would be the inevitable consequence, and that many valuable lives would be lost. In the meantime, the troops of the United States had taken their position at Fort Mitchell, and active preparations were making to move in upon the settlers. At this period, apparently so gloomy, the Governor issued a proclamation to the inhabitants of the new counties, recommending and exhorting them to look with unshaken confidence to the law for protection, to submit to any process from the courts of the United States, and to abstain from attacks or unlawful violence towards the Indians. The civil officers were advised to issue, promptly, all necessary process for the apprehension of offenders, and the people generally were instructed to look to the courts as affording more certain protection than they could expect from a confused and disorderly resort to arms.

This step had the effect, at once, to quiet the citizens, to inspire confidence in the efficacy of the laws, and to put a stop to the contemplated movement of the troops;

thus affording, says Governor Gayle, "a practical and "impressive illustration of the great truths so often and "so ably advocated by the President himself—that the "Constitution of the United States, and the constitutions "and laws of the several States, as they are understood "by the common sense of mankind, are sufficient for "any emergency, and that the laws in their usual and "customary operation will stay the hand of encroach-"ment, in whatever quarter it may appear."

The grand jury of Russell county returned a bill of indictment for murder against the soldiers and officers who were concerned in the death of Hardeman Owens, and application in due form was made to the commanding officer at Fort Mitchell to deliver them over to the civil authorities. The application was rejected. The Governor, in his message to the General Assembly, November 19, 1833, said: "The officers and troops "of the United States, at this post, have set our laws "and our courts at defiance, and the power of the "county is not sufficient to arrest the offenders. "Though full power is conferred on the executive by "the Constitution, to call forth the militia in cases of "this kind, yet sincerely desirous of avoiding all col-"lision with the Government or any of its officers—"and not doubting that they would be ordered to be "delivered up for trial—I have deemed it unnecessary "to take any other step than transmit the despatches "to the War Department, for consideration of the "President, which was done on the 23d ult."

The Secretary of War, in a letter to Senators King and Clay, of Alabama, as early as December, 1832, had distinctly acquiesced in the continuance of the so-called intruders upon the Creek lands, provided they interfered with no Indian rights. Mr. Cass had said:

"Taking into view the facts that the season for agri-"cultural labor will not arrive for some time—that the "surveys are nearly completed, and that as soon as "they are received, the locations of the individual "reservations will be made, and the tract selected for "each will be assigned and delivered to him, I do not "see that any injury would result to the Indians, by "permitting those persons who obtained peaceable pos-"session of the land on which they live, and do not "retain it to the exclusion of any Indian, justly "entitled to it, to occupy those tracts till the several "selections are made. If, however, any of them are "selected for the Indians, it will be expected that the "occupants relinquish possession, within thirty days "after such selection is made. This arrangement "seems to me to be an equitable one, and I trust will "be satisfactory to all persons interested in the subject. "I hope, further, that after the locations are made, "quick possession will be relinquished to the Indians, "so that the Government will not be compelled to resort "for that purpose to measures which I am anxious to "avoid"

Letters of similar tenor had been addressed to Honorable Gabriel Moore and other citizens of Alabama.

Referring to the letters of the Secretary, Governor Gayle placed the responsibility, for the condition of affairs, upon the Federal Government, using this language:

"After the publication of those letters, no one, what-"ever his respect for the laws and for the rights of "others, could have supposed he was doing wrong or "violating any of the duties of a good citizen, by "making a settlement in this part of the State; and it "is submitted to the impartial judgment of all candid "minds, whether the great body of the settlers have "not been involved in their present difficulties without "any fault on their part.

"When the act of the last session was passed, laying "this country off into counties, the letters of the Sec- "retary of War were before the Legislature.

"Without this measure, the people would have been "deprived of separate representation for the next six "years, and it was obvious that our laws could not be "made to operate with effect upon a population so "large and so rapidly increasing. The policy and the "views of the administration in relation to the Indians "were made known, and the act, while under considera- "tion, was regarded as being in strict accordance there- "with. The treaty extinguished the Indian title to "land, and the Indians had become citizens of the "State, and amenable to its laws, by their own con- "sent, thereby obviating all objections growing out of "our former relations with their people. All saw and "acknowledged the necessity of the measure, and none "objected to it. The General Assembly were influ- "enced in their course by considerations of public duty "and public policy, and it certainly never entered the "mind of any one that they were encroaching upon "the *property rights* of the United States.

"It is difficult to anticipate the effects that would "result from the abolition of these counties. All crim- "inals and persons indicted for offences, will be dis- "charged; all suits will be discontinued; the courts "and all offices abolished; officers will lose their places, "and in fine, such is the intimate connexion between "these and the other counties of the State, that to "destroy them would embarrass and derange the "administration of justice generally, and introduce "perplexing confusion through the whole machinery of "the State government."

The conclusion of Governor Gayle's message indicates the change of political sentiment which was being brought about in Alabama by the new pretensions of the Federal Government. So long as the question of usurpation agitated a sister State, the people were content to follow those leaders who exalted the Union, and strengthened Federal power; but now that the usurpation had come home to themselves, we find an executive message using this language:

"In the present controversy, my situation has not "been free from difficulty and embarrassment. Yield-"ing as I had done, for the last ten years, a sincere "and disinterested support to the distinguished citizen "who now fills the presidency, it was with the utmost "reluctance that I felt myself constrained to oppose "the course he had adopted. The country, too, had "but recently emerged from the gloom of a threatened "conflict with a sister State, and it was foreseen that "even a difference of opinion with the administration "would tend to awaken the fears and alarm the appre-"hensions of many good citizens.

"The suppression of the State government, or the "maintenance of its laws in eight flourishing and pop-"ulous counties, were the alternatives presented, and I "embraced that to which I was directed by the solemn "obligation I had assumed as the chief magistrate of "one of the independent States of this Union. With-"out resorting to force, which I cannot believe neces-"sary, unless the process of our courts be altogether "disregarded, I have maintained the integrity of these "counties and kept the laws steadily in operation."

Before this controversy had reached the point when it was suggested that force might be used to protect the civil organization of the eight counties against the pretensions of the War Department, Governor Gayle had been re-elected to the executive chair without opposition. In delivering his inaugural address, December, 1833, before the General Assembly, the governor declared that to execute the order of removal, "power is claimed to suppress by military force the "government of the State in eight of its counties, to "regulate, at the point of the bayonet, trespasses by "our citizens upon the possessions of each other, and "in effect to establish military tribunals as substitutes "for our courts." Commenting on this inaugural, the Mobile *Register*, of date December 6, 1833, defied any man in South Carolina to indite a better nullifying paragraph: "And yet," said that journal, "his excel-"lency, not ten days before, took occasion to denounce "nullification in good set terms; perhaps he has a pre-"judice against the phrase; it may be that he thinketh "it unpopular, or that a rose by any other name "would smell as sweet."

A special committee was raised by the General Assembly to report upon the grave matters submitted in the message and inaugural.

Near the end of December, the chairman of this committee, Mr. BREEN, made their report and submitted the following resolutions for the consideration and adoption of the House:

1st. *Resolved*, That the order of the Secretary of War, directing the removal, by military force, of the whole white population, from the counties contained in the territory ceded by the Creek Indians, was unnecessary for the protection of the Indians, that its execution would be destructive of the prosperity of the citizens, subversive of the jurisdiction of the State, and ought not to be carried into effect.

2d. *Resolved*, That in the opinion of this General Assembly, the Act of Congress, of 1807, was not intended to have effect within the limits of States of the Union; that the execution of the provisions of said Act, by the military force, would be subversive of the rights of the citizens, destructive of free government, and incompatible with the jurisdiction and sovereignty of the States.

3d. *Resolved,* That the General Government has no constitutional power to interfere with the internal municipal affairs of the State, that when the Government has parted with the public lands, it has no further control over them, and that trespasses by the citizens of the same State, upon the property of each other can be regulated and corrected alone by the laws and authorities of such State.

4th. *Resolved,* That the power conferred by the Constitution of the United States upon the President and two-thirds of the Senate to make treaties is limited and restrained by the grants of power therein contained, and that all treaties which encroach upon the reserved rights of the States are usurpations of power, subversive of the Government and destructive of civil liberty.

5th. *Resolved,* That this General Assembly do approve of the principles avowed, and the propositions assumed by the Governor of this State, in his proclamation dated on the 7th day of October last; addressed to the citizens of the Creek country and in his recent correspondence with the Secretary of War, and that he is hereby authorized and requested to see that the laws and jurisdiction of the State, be maintained in full force and effect in the said counties.

As indicating the wide-spread interest manifested by citizens of other States, both North and South, in the progress of this controversy, the Richmond *Enquirer* used this language: "We know of no event, which "would cover the friends of our Federal Institutions "with so deep a gloom, as the actual collision between "the Federal and the State authorities in this instance, "and the shedding of the blood of our fellow citizens "in a civil contest between the troops of the United

"States and the militia of Alabama. Here is a President of the United States, who has distinguished himself by his manly vindication of the rights of Georgia in the case of the Cherokee Indians. We should expect from him a course in relation to the Creeks, which may manifest his strict respect for the rights of Alabama. Here, also, is the Governor of a State, who has avowed himself one of the most decided opponents of nullification, in the whole Southern country. Who better calculated to settle this dispute than these two citizens? To respect, on the one hand, the sacred and inalienable rights of the States, in relation to State jurisdiction over the Indian tribes, and on the other, to avoid all rash and hasty recourse to violent measures against the agents of the United States. We put it freely to all, that, if under such favorable circumstances, a direct issue should be made up between the two; if blood should be shed in this civil war; how much would it gratify the enemies of our Federal system, who predict that the machine is too complicated to play freely, and that the parties must inevitably clash with each other? And what disconsolation would it not impart to the real friends of the Republic?"

Governor Gayle, among other letters of encouragement received the following* from a number of young men of Hudson, New York:

HUDSON, NEW YORK,
Dec. 29, 1833.

To His Excellency,

JOHN GAYLE,

Governor of Alabama.

SIR.—A number of young men of this city, sensible of the injustice with which Alabama is threatened in the proposed forcible removal of the settlers from the Indian territory, have appointed us a committee to offer their and our services to your Excellency in the anticipated contest. We propose to raise a company of volunteers, to act as the service may require. If you, sir, are willing to receive our aid, please inform us as soon as convenient.

With great respect,

Your most obedient servants,

J. VANVLECK,
N. T. ROSSETER,
E. CLARK,
F. N. CADY,
C. S. JORDAN,
R. H. BURTON.

The committee sustained their resolutions with an able report, in which they held, that to drive out the 30,000 white settlers at the point of the bayonet, would be a cruel and unparalleled usurpation; that a government whose laws are carried into effect without the

*This letter is among the correspondence of the late Governor Gayle, kindly submitted to the author by his accomplished daughter, Mrs. Thomas L. Bayne, of New Orleans.

intervention of courts, by military authority, is a despotism, by whatever name it may be called; that whether a tract of land is public or private property is strictly a judicial question which every citizen has a right to have investigated according to the known and established forms of law; that the doctrine that the rightful jurisdiction of a State can be taken away by virtue of a treaty has been so uniformly repudiated by President Jackson, both by his declarations and by his practices, that it could not with any propriety be advanced by the Secretary of War; that such a doctrine has not been seriously contended for by the great Federal party of our country, since the period of Jay's treaty, and it is to be regretted that any attempt should be made to renew it now? If the rights of the State, urged the committee, can be bartered away by the President and Senate under the form of a treaty, there could have been no object in inserting any provisions in the Constitution limiting the General Government to certain specific objects for the security of the State and the people. According to such a doctrine it would be in the power of President and Senate to change the form of our government.

It was the earnest desire of the Alabama Representatives in Congress, who, with Governor Gayle, had opposed the nullification measures of South Carolina, that there should be no breach with the President. William R. King and Gabriel Moore of the Senate and Messrs. John Murphy, Dixon H. Lewis and Clement C. Clay of the House, exerted themselves to bring about a compromise of the matters in controversy. Upon reaching Washington, they hastened to call upon the President, and to lay before him the distress that would be caused by a strict compliance with the order of removal. While conciliating the President by removing from his mind the idea that the Governor of Alabama was desirous of following in the steps of South Carolina, they, at the same time, opened the way for an adjustment, by assuring Governor Gayle that the executive order was never intended to be carried into full effect, but was simply framed to cover every case that might possibly arise under the treaty. The language of Ex-Governor Murphy to Governor Gayle was: "I believe it was never intended to expel all the people from the ceded Creek territory. This would evidently be carrying the thing beyond the justice or necessity of the case. The order issued was general in its nature to apply to what had taken place, or might possibly afterwards take place, and to cover every stipulation of the treaty intended for the benefit of the Indians. It was merely asserting the control of the Government over the subject, should there arise the necessity to exercise it; but evidently the execution of the order would be governed by that necessity. Why remove the whole population while only a few individuals have been guilty of trespass, and indeed while the Indians for whose benefit all this was done had no desire that any but a very few should be removed? It never could have been necessary, and therefore could never have been intended." Mr. Murphy continues in his letter of December 3d, 1833: "The nullifiers have endeavored to make much of this excitement. They entertained great hopes from it for their cause."

Early in December, 1833, Mr. King called upon the President and received assurances that "no measures "should be taken for the removal of the settlers who "had not interfered with the possessions of the Indians," and these assurances were at once conveyed to Governor Gayle. On the next day Representatives Clay and Samuel W. Mardis accompanied Senator King upon a visit to the Secretary of War, LEWIS CASS, and represented to him, as Mr. King and Mr. Murphy had already done to the President, the condition of affairs in Alabama. The Secretary acceded to the views and wishes of the delegation, and requested them to submit to him an address in writing. The address was drawn up and submitted to the Secretary. The President appointed Francis S. Key, author of "the Star-spangled "Banner," a commissioner, to visit Alabama and adjust all the questions in dispute. Mr. Key was a man of most captivating address, learned in the law, of high personal character and great prudence of action. A better agent could not have been selected to mediate in a dispute which had almost reached the point of armed collision.

To prepare Governor Gayle for the conciliatory communications borne by Mr. Key, Mr. Murphy reviewed the whole controversy elaborately in a letter to the Governor, and closed by intimating that his course would lead to a breach between him and President Jackson, and the result would be that he would find himself drifting out of the Republican party and into the ranks of the opposition. Writing, February 28, 1834, in reply to Murphy, Governor Gayle said: "As "straws show which way the wind blows, some small "occurrences, too unimportant to mention, have pro-"ceeded towards me from the President, which induce "me to suppose he is tired of the Creek controversy, "and wishes to mend the breach which that affair has "produced. My feelings have had no effect to change "the favorable light in which I have always regarded "the prominent measures of General Jackson's admin-"istration, or his qualifications and fitness for the office "he fills, but I can never yield him the zealous and "active support, which I have heretofore extended, "under the charges of corrupt speculation and furnish-"ing a combination with the nullifiers, which were dealt "out against me some time since by the *Globe*, as it is "understood, with the approbation, if not at the "instance, of the President."

A letter from Senator KING to Governor Gayle, dated March 18, 1834, was evidently intended to heal the breach between the Governor and the President and to pave the way for the success of Mr. Key's mission. The Senator wrote as follows:

"In the controversy in which you conceived it your "duty, from your official situation, to engage with the "General Government, no man knew better than your-"self the view which I took of the matter. Actuated "by a strong feeling of personal and political friendship, "I felt that I could, without offence, speak to you "plainly on a subject of such absorbing interest. I "did so in a spirit of frankness and friendship. I "was, as you know, anxious that as far as practicable "all discussions should be avoided by the legislature, "then about to meet. I feared no good would come "of it, and the event has, I am sorry to say, in some "measure realized my apprehensions. I saw Mr. Key "at Montgomery, and had a free conversation with "him. I did, I trust, ample justice to the purity of "your motives and pure Republican principles. I pre-

"pared him to meet you in the undisguised spirit of "political confidence and personal respect. I took the "earliest occasion to remove from the mind of the "President and the authorities here any unfavorable "impression which the excitement growing out of the "discussion might have produced. I know that I suc-"ceeded, as you have some evidence in the altered "tone of the Secretary of War. As to the publica-"tions or strictures which appeared in the *Globe*, you "must not take them as conveying either the senti-"ments of the President or of any responsible person "connected with the administration. The editor of "that paper is perfectly reckless in his course, and "although it is considered in the country as the official "paper, God help the administration, if it is to be held "responsible for all of Blair's indiscretions. In the "very few communications I made to members of the "Legislature while the subject was under consideration "I held but one language—'put an end to debate; "divide not our party; respect the feelings of our "Governor; impair not his well-earned popularity; "give not currency and strength to the doctrines of "nullification by divisions amongst ourselves.' Sir, no "political considerations would have induced me to "make this plain detail of my motives and conduct "throughout this whole business. But I had seen with "deep regret statements intended no doubt to produce "alienations, if not the destruction of our ancient friend-"ship. The course pursued by some of those with "whom I stand connected, but as you know radically "differing with me on many of the great subjects of "policy which mark the distinctions of party in our "country, was, no doubt, under the circumstances, cal-

"culated to produce unpleasant feelings for the "moment. I am happy to learn they have passed "away with the occasion which called them forth."

It is interesting to know that the breach between the President and Governor Gayle was never cured, and that the latter, after retiring from the gubernatorial chair, threw his influence for Judge White for President, as against Mr. Van Buren, and subsequently supported General Harrison and the Whigs. He was an elector upon the Whig ticket in 1840, and in 1847 was elected by the Whig party a Representative in Congress from the Mobile District. In 1849 he was appointed by President Taylor, United States District Judge for Alabama, which office he held until his death in 1859. In November, 1841, Governor Gayle received fifty-five votes in the Alabama Legislature for United States Senator, against seventy-two for Mr. King.

Secretary Cass, in pursuance of the modified views of the President, transmitted to the Governor a letter informing him that as soon as the report of the death of Owens reached the War Department, a communication was sent to the deputy marshal informing him that instructions had been given the military commanding officer to facilitate, by all the means in his power, any investigation which the civil authorities might consider necessary. He supposed, until recently, that Major McIntosh, the officer in command, had followed these instructions; but it appears that there was some mistake in the transmission of the orders. The President had now instructed McIntosh directly to submit to all legal process. The Secretary said: "These "orders were given some days since, and I have the "honor to enclose you a copy of them. I transmit "also an extract from the instructions to Mr. Key, who "has been employed to aid the District Attorney of "the Southern District of Alabama, in the legal inves-"tigations growing out of this subject, by which you "will see that the supremacy of the civil authority will "be asserted and maintained as far as depends on the "executive. These orders and instructions will be suf-"ficient to insure the due submission of the troops now "in Alabama, to all legal process, and I trust will be "satisfactory to your excellency."

Mr. Key, in a communication, dated at Tuscaloosa, December 16th, 1833, to the Governor, informed him that the reservations allotted to the Indians would be laid off by January 15th, and that the settlers upon all the lands outside of these allotments would be released from the stipulations of the treaty, and no longer subject to removal. Those settlers who were upon the reservations would have it in their power to purchase the right of the Indians whose lands they occupy.

In view of the early day at which the titles of the settlers would be assured, and of the fact that the order for removal was virtually withdrawn, and the further fact that the jurisdiction of the State Courts over the soldiers who killed Owens was admitted, Governor Gayle sent a special message to the General Assembly, December 20th, in which he said that "the principal "object of this unpleasant controversy having been "obtained, by asserting and vindicating those great "principles which were established by the Constitution "for the security of the people and for the protection "of the States, in the exercise of their rightful juris-"diction, it cannot fail to be a source of the highest "satisfaction to our fellow citizens in these new coun-"ties, that the calamity with which, at one period they "were threatened, has been averted, and of pride and "patriotic exultation to our people everywhere that the "supremacy of the civil over the military authority "has been successfully maintained."

Mr. Hopkins, of the House, in his reply to the advocates of the resolutions of Mr. Beene's committee, said that the modification of the orders of the Secretary of War as conveyed to Governor Gayle by Mr. Key, must satisfy ninety-nine out of every hundred of the people of Alabama. If this compromise were not accepted and these nullifying resolutions of the committee were carried out, there would inevitably be a collision between the State and Federal Government, and Alabama would fall before the power of the national arms; or, if successful in the struggle, she would soon become the prey to internal dissensions and to ambitious men. He moved, therefore, that the resolutions be indefinitely postponed. The vote was, 33 for postponement and 34 in the negative. A motion was then made to lay the resolutions on the table. The vote was, nay 39, yea 30. A motion was then made to refer them to a select committee. This motion was adopted by a vote of, yea 36, nay 33. The compromise offered by Key having been accepted by the Governor, and having received the approbation of the press and of the people, the select committee never reported upon the resolutions. The controversy between Alabama and the Union was not settled upon principle, but was smothered by a compromise; and the people once more witnessed the Federal Government yielding the point at issue to the hostile demonstrations of the State.

CHAPTER IX.

The Federal Party Reorganize upon the Slavery Question—Continued War upon the Agricultural States—Opinions of the Southern People as to Slavery—The Missouri Compromise—The Slade Agitation—The Abolitionist, George Thompson—Views of England—Opinions of Jackson, Marcy, Clay, Everett and others—Drawing of the Geographical Line, &c., &c.

"Adverse fortune and ill-judged policy had brought the Federal party to its end. Its leaders saw that all was over. New and living issues must be sought for. Not without wisdom did they select another standpoint and prepare to combat their adversaries in his most vulnerable part. A compact and an unmistakable formula, of which the purport is easily understood, is invaluable as a party war-cry. To restrain slavery, and eventually to destroy it, became their dogma. It gathered irresistible power, because it was in unison with the sentiments of the times."

DRAPER'S CIVIL WAR IN AMERICA.

"The [Missouri] question is a mere party trick. The leaders of Federalism are taking advantage of the virtuous feeling of the people to effect a division of parties by a geographical line; they expect that this will ensure them, on local principles, the majority they could never obtain on the principles of Federalism."

THOMAS JEFFERSON.

"You are kindling a fire which all the waters of the ocean cannot extinguish; it can be extinguished only in blood."

THOS. W. COBB, IN CONGRESS, 1819.

Down to the year 1819, a period of over thirty years from the adoption of the Constitution there had been no objection to the admission of a State to the Union because of the existence of slavery. Objection had been made to the Louisiana purchase upon other grounds, but not upon that of slavery. Louisiana,

Mississippi, Alabama, Kentucky and Tennessee had all been admitted with constitutions recognizing slavery.

Down to this period the existence of slavery in a free Republic had not been held by any large number of people to be repugnant to our theory of government. Nowhere in the Union had it been regarded as violative of moral or Christian law, or opposed to the rights acquired by conquest and capture. No political party, or fraction of a party, had denounced the slave-holding States as unworthy members of the Union. But now, the Federalists, casting about for a new subject upon which they might rally their scattered forces, and upon which they might draw the lines around the agricultural States, seized upon the question of slavery.

The people of the Southern States had inherited their slaves. They had grown up upon the plantations and had passed from father to son by the laws of descent. The ancestors of these slaves had been brought into the Southwest against the wishes of Oglethorpe. One of the earliest laws of the colony of Georgia was that forbidding the introduction of African slaves—but the greed of traders had broken through all laws until the ships of Old England and of New England had filled the South with a vast number of negroes. Nothing in the history of the world, down to the present century had taught the people of this unhappy section, against whom had been launched the poisonous weapons of a defeated political party, that slavery was a moral wrong or a social evil. They saw it recognized by all the ancient nations, kingdoms and republics; by the Mosaic law; by the Roman empire; by the Gospel of Christ; by all the more modern peoples; by the councils of the Catholic church; by the leaders of the reformation; by English law and custom; everywhere throughout the world, in all ages and climes. They saw it recognized in the Federal Constitution which permitted the importation of African slaves for twenty years after its ratification.

In nearly every household throughout the South, if there were no other book, might be found the family Bible. That Bible told the reader of Abraham's slaves, bought with his money; of the Angel of the Lord who commanded the fugitive slave, Hagar, to return to her mistress and submit herself; of the tenth commandment of the Decalogue, which spoke of the master's property in man servants and maid servants; and of the Mosaic laws which recognized and regulated slavery in its severest forms The reader of the New Testament looked in vain for any allusion to slavery by Christ; for any word of censure for an institution then tolerated throughout the world; for any word, on account of it, of condemnation of Cæsar, whose empire, according to the historian, Gibbon, then embraced sixty millions of slaves. They read the precepts of Paul, in which he told the slaves to be obedient to their masters, and in which he warned the masters to give unto their slaves that which is just and equal, since they also had a Master in Heaven. The preachers of the Gospel throughout the South, while inculcating lessons of mercy, justice and kindness between the master and slave, could not stultify themselves by denouncing the moral or Christian legality of Slavery. Before them were the writings of churchmen from the earliest ages, and nowhere, down to that period when the wild orgies of the French Revolution had upturned the foundations of society, could be found any denial of the rectitude of an institution which had been coeval with the ages and coextensive with the habitable globe. Jerome, one of the oracles of the ancient church, writing at a time when the church was at peace and there was no longer occasion to conceal sentiments, commenting on 1 Cor. 7, 21, said: "The condition of a slave cannot "be opposed to the Christian religion." Augustine, Bishop of Hippo, said that slavery could result from iniquity, as in the case when God cursed Canaan, and from purchase, as in the case of the sale of Joseph, and also from capture in war, and that Christ "does not "make free men of servants, but He makes good "servants of bad servants." "How much," adds St. Augustine, "do the wealthy owe to Christ who regu-"lates their home." The great Chrisostom, Bishop of Constantinople, the orator of the "Golden Mouth," writes: "For even as circumcision profiteth nothing, "and uncircumcision hurteth nothing, so even does "slavery or liberty, and in order that he [the Apostle "Paul] might teach this yet more plainly, he saith— "'but if thou mayest be made free, use it rather.' "That is serve rather. But why does he command "him that might be free, to remain a slave? Because "he desired to show that slavery does not hurt, but "even profits. We are not ignorant, indeed, that some "interpret the words, 'use it rather,' as referring to "liberty, saying, 'if thou mayest be freed, be free.' "But this is very contrary to the meaning of Paul, for "his design being to console the slave by showing that "his condition was no injury, he would not have "ordered him to become free."

Gregory the Great, Bishop of Rome, in his book concerning the "pastoral care," lays down this rule to the clergy: "Slaves should be admonished in one way "and the masters in another. The slaves, to-wit: that "they should always in themselves regard the humility "of their condition: but the masters, that the memory "of their nature, in which they are created equally "with their slaves, must not be forgotten." There is extant a deed of gift by Gregory, conveying one of his slaves to the bishop of Porto, who had charge of a suburban diocese near Rome. The bill of sale recites: "so that you may have and hold him, and preserve "and maintain your right to him, and defend him as "your property, and do, by the free right of this dona- "tion, as his master, whatsoever you will concerning "him. Against which charter of our munificence, you "may know that neither we nor our successors are ever "to come."

The Apostolic canons; the Clementine constitutions; the Council of Gangra in Asia Minor; the Councils of Agde, Narbonne and Orleans, in France; the Councils of Epone and Macon, in Burgundy; the Council of Toledo, in Spain; the Council of Berghamstead, near Canterbury, in England; the Councils of Aix-le-Chapelle and Worms, in Germany—all recognized slavery, taught obedience to the master, ordered the rendition of fugitive slaves to their owners, and in no instance denied the rightfulness of the institution. Slaves were owned not only by kings, princes and nobles, but by citizens of every class and condition, by churches, monasteries, bishops and the clergy.

Melancthon, Calvin, Luther; and the commentators, Patrick, Lowth, Whitby, Henry, Scott, Clarke and Doddridge; all, construe the language of St. Paul precisely as the Christian church had construed it from the beginning down to the reformation.

The change from a labor system of slavery to one of freedom was gradually brought about in Europe, but very slowly and without appeals to moral or religious sentiments. As late as A. D. 1545, the Turks, taken prisoners at Lepanto, were made slaves to the victorious Spaniards. They were divided among the victors in the proportion of one-half to Philip, and one-half to the Pope and Venice. Don John received as a present one hundred and seventy-four slaves. The number of slaves allotted to Philip, in chains, was three thousand six hundred. At least seven thousand two hundred slaves were divided out among Christians. At that day the universal judgment of christendom was that there was no sin in holding slaves.

It was as late as 1772, that England took the first step towards declaring against slavery in her courts of law. In the celebrated case of the negro Somerset who sued for his freedom, having been brought to London from the West Indies, that distinguished lawyer, HARGRAVE, declared in his brief that however reasonable it may be to doubt the justice of domestic slavery, however convinced we may be of its evil effects, it must be confessed that the practice is ancient and has been almost universal. The negro, Somerset, was declared free on the ground that no slavery but that of villeinage had ever existed in England by common or statute law, and that the last villein had either died or been manumitted a century and a half previous. Not a word was said about slavery being against moral or natural law. Disuse, in the case of villeinage, had destroyed it as a fact.

The first article of the treaty of Utrecht, A. D. 1713, stipulated that the English-African company should bring into the West Indies one hundred and forty thousand negroes within a period of thirty years, one-fourth part of the profits of the traffic to go to the King of Spain, and one-fourth to the Queen of England. If it was true, according to Lord Mansfield's decision in the celebrated Somerset case, that the soil of England could not tolerate a slave, it is singular that Queen Anne and a British company, chartered under English laws, could legally engage in the African slave trade and stock the colonies with slaves. Let it be observed that the period at which this stipulation was to terminate was the year 1749, less than twenty-two years before the decision of Lord Mansfield, and before the period at which the American colonies entered upon the Revolution! The stipulation was studiously observed by George I and George II; and when it expired, in 1749, the slave trade was thrown open by statute to all British subjects. So great was the influx of negroes into the colonies, under this statute of George II, that South Carolina and Georgia passed laws forbidding the importation; but the British Government abrogated the colonial acts, and reprimanded the Governor of South Carolina for having given assent to them.

In view of Lord Mansfield's decision, it is still more singular to find the British Parliament after the American war, in 1787, authorizing the exportation of certain merchandise from the English islands to any foreign colony, and that in the list of merchandise is included rum and negroes. When the Somerset case was decided, there is said to have been, in London alone, fourteen thousand negro slaves. The decision of Lord Mansfield was held not to be law by such distinguished jurists as Lord Hardwicke and Lord Stowell. WILBERFORCE declared that all the British bar was against his efforts at emancipation. It was not until 1833, the period at which we have just arrived in our sketch of the States-Rights agitation in Alabama, Georgia and South Carolina, that Great Britain emancipated her slaves in the West Indies.

The American colonies having slavery fastened upon them by the treaty of Utrecht, and for the benefit of the purse of the Christian Queen Anne, grew up to believe in its rightfulness, and down to the American Revolution not a doubt as to its propriety, except here and there, was expressed. Lord Dartmouth, in 1774, immediately after the decision in the Somerset case, declared: "We cannot allow the colonies to check or "discourage in any degree, a traffic so beneficial to the "nation." A few enlightened and benevolent minds lamented such a state of affairs, but their regrets were lost in the universal desire for gain. Laurens, of South Carolina, said: "I am devising means for manu-"mitting my slaves. * * * Great powers oppose "me—the laws and customs of my country, my own, "and the avarice of my contrymen." In the draft of the Declaration of Independence, Jefferson bitterly complained that the King of Great Britain had forbidden attempts "to prohibit or restrain this execrable "commerce." Patrick Henry, writing to a Quaker, said: "Would any one believe that I am master of "slaves of my own purchase? I am drawn along by "the great inconvenience of living without them. I "will not, I cannot justify it."

According to the census of 1790, there were slaves in all the States of the Union. Only six were reported in Massachusetts. There were two thousand seven hundred and fifty-nine in Connecticut; three thousand seven hundred and thirty-seven in Pennsylvania; twenty-one thousand three hundred and twenty-four in New York; eleven thousand four hundred and twenty-three in New Jersey; nine hundred and fifty-two in Rhode Island. At that day there were more slaves in Pennsylvania than in Tennessee, and as many in New Jersey as in Kentucky. After the slave trade had ceased, slavery became unprofitable to the Northern States, and the greater value of the cotton fields, from the invention of the gin, drew southward the remaining slaves of the Northern States. Yet the complete abolition of slavery at the North was very slow. As late as 1840, Massachusetts, Maine, Vermont and Michigan were the only States which contained no slaves at all. In that year the number of slaves in the so-called free States amounted to one thousand one hundred and twenty-nine.

When Virginia, in 1784, ceded to the United States her great Northwestern territory, Jefferson moved a plan for its government. The plan declared that after the year 1800, "neither slavery nor involuntary servi-"tude" should exist there. This plan was not adopted; but in 1787 an ordinance was passed by Congress forbidding slavery in all that territory and providing for the rendition of fugitive slaves. Notwithstanding these advances made towards emancipation, we find that in 1785, Hopkins complained that "some New England States and other States" had again begun to import slaves from Africa. In 1800,

Waln of Pennsylvania admitted in Congress that the slave trade was carried on in great part by Rhode Island, Boston and Pennsylvania; and Broun, of Rhode Island, said the encouragement of the trade "ought to "be a matter of national policy since it would bring in "a good revenue to our treasury."

Very soon the West began wishing for slaves to till the fertile lands north of the Ohio. The territory of Indiana labored, from the year 1802, to induce Congress to suspend for a term of years the prohibition imposed by the ordinance of 1787. The request was rejected; but subsequently it was reported upon favorably by the committees of both Houses, although it failed to meet the approval of Congress. There were later attempts also to introduce slavery into Illinois.

The breeze of war around the harbor of Charleston had just blown safely past, when the people of the South were destined once more to have their constitutional rights assailed, and now at a more vulnerable point. By the Missouri Compromise, an attempt had been made to exclude the people of the South from removing with their slave property to the territory North of thirty-six degrees, thirty minutes, north latitude. All the States north of that line must be non-slaveholding; all south of that line might be such, or not, as the people establishing the territory into a State should determine. It was not probable, nay, even possible, that the people of the South would desire or attempt to transport their slaves from the mild and rich lands of the Gulf to the bleak prairies of the Northwest. Yet the application of the settlers of Missouri for admission into the Union, with a constitution recognizing slavery, was made a pretext for assaulting the whole people of the South as slave propagandists, and of establishing the precedent that Congress has power to prohibit slavery in the common territory. The Constitution of Missouri happened to be framed by her first settlers, who had emigrated from Kentucky and Virginia, as growers of tobacco and hemp. So far as she was concerned, had the question been left alone, it was not probable that she would have remained a slave State beyond one generation. The Free-Soilers, not satisfied with their victory in excluding the property of the South from all the northern territories, now proceeded, insidiously and systematically, to agitate, not so much for the abolition of slavery, as for a dissolution of the Union.

Down to this day the people of the South were not banded together in support of slavery. They differed among themselves as widely upon that subject as they did upon other political questions. It was not the South who sprung the Missouri question. The settlers of Missouri, like those of Louisiana, Mississippi, Tennessee and Kentucky, had framed her constitution, and they alone were responsible for its features; just as the settlers of Indiana a few years previous, and not the people of the North, generally, were responsible for her application to Congress to do away with the feature of the ordinance for the government of the Northwest territory proscribing slavery. Down to the period of the unhappy nullification ordinance of South Carolina, and even a few years later, Virginia, Kentucky and Tennessee were earnestly engaged in practical movements for the gradual emancipation of the slaves. In 1832, Virginia was on the verge of emancipation.

Both of the leading Richmond newspapers; all of the most prominent statesmen, and perhaps a majority of the people favored the policy and the justice of the measure. THOMAS JEFFERSON RANDOLPH, grand son of Thomas Jefferson, a delegate from Albemarle, one of the wealthiest and largest of the slave-holding counties, brought forward a bill in the House of Delegates to accomplish this object. The bill was freely and fully discussed, and advocated by many leading members. Not a voice was raised in defense of slavery. Mr. RANDOLPH did not press his measure to a vote, but the House resolved by a vote of sixty-five to fifty-eight that they were sensible of the evils arising from the condition of the colored population of the commonwealth, but that further action for a removal of the slaves should await a more definite development of public opinion. Mr. RANDOLPH'S course was approved by his constituents, and at the next election he was returned to the Legislature as an advocate of this very measure.

Unfortunately, at this moment, when emancipation hung quivering in the balance, as though to prevent what was in process of accomplishment through peaceful and constitutional means, the anti-slavery agitation was set on foot by English and New English agents. It assumed such an alarming aspect for the peace and security of the Southern people, that an immediate reaction against emancipation was the result. Mr. RANDOLPH, a short time thereafter, expressed a confident belief to JAMES BUCHANAN, that but for this interference, the General Assembly of Virginia, at no distant day, would have passed a law for gradual emancipation.

The moderate tone of Southern sentiment, at that period, is further evidenced by the fact that the Constitution of Mississippi was amended by a clause prohibiting the introduction of slaves into her territory. The General Assembly of Alabama had also forbidden the introduction and sale of slaves from other States. At several sessions of the Legislature of the latter State, there was an open advocacy by the "lobby" of gradual emancipation—a proposition seriously entertained by the more intelligent and independent members. It was a notable fact that the agents of certain cotton factories, owned by Quakers, travelled through the State, seeking and purchasing only such cotton as was produced by free labor, their religious and moral scruples forbidding them to encourage slavery by investing in its products. This practice was tolerated, barely drawing forth an adverse criticism from those who were thus passed by as men violating the moral law.

As early as 1825, Governor Israel Pickens, of Alabama, in his message to the General Assembly, calling attention to resolutions transmitted to him by the State of Ohio, recommending a plan for emancipation and colonization, criticised the proposition in fair and temperate language, exhibiting an appreciation of the evils of slavery, and a desire for its removal, whenever a practical plan might be suggested. He said:

"Should the national government, at any future pro-"pitious moment see proper to offer a plan, it is to be "hoped that while it is characterized by justice to our "citizens, it will be worthy of national philanthropy; "that preparatory to the free condition, proper nurser-"ies shall be provided for instruction in the necessary "branches of industry, in the arts and in literature, "as far as may be requisite to form useful members of "society and government."

A still stronger evidence that the South not only tolerated, but actually participated to a wide extent in the anti-slavery sentiment, at that time and for many years after, is the support given HENRY CLAY, who, in his Lexington speech of September, 1836, denounced slavery as a curse to master and man; as altogether wrong and a thing which no possible contingency could make right. The statesman who announced this sentiment, received in the slave States three hundred and eighty-one thousand four hundred and six votes, as against four hundred and five thousand one hundred and seventy-eight cast for Mr. POLK. In Alabama, Mr. CLAY received his strongest support in the slave-holding counties.

The leaders of the slavery agitation, in New England and in old England, knew that there could be no dissolution of the Union so long as the Southern people were divided among themselves. A large section of the country must stand united in sentiment, and with contiguous territory, before secession could be practically accomplished. It has been the habit of Northern politicians to say that CALHOUN and other leading spirits of the South schemed to unite that section upon the slavery question when it was found not to be a unit upon the tariff and nullification questions. History does not substantiate this charge. There was no wide-spread slavery excitement until the British agents of Exeter Hall established a newspaper in Boston, and flooded the South with incendiary documents. The motive of Great Britain in beginning this crusade was the same which was afterwards admitted, under other circumstances, by a distinguished English statesman. "My reason," said Mr. ROEBUCK, "for desiring the "acknowledgment of the South, was this: I wanted "the great Republic of America split into two. I "honestly and openly confess it, and if it had been so "it would have been better for us."

The controlling motive of New England was to be found in the fact that by CLAY's compromise measure, the protective tariff had a certain existence of only nine years; that after that period, a union of the votes of the South with those of the West and North, who opposed protection, would, in their opinion, inevitably reduce the duties to a revenue standard, and place the factories of America in competition with all the world; and that a separation of the slave States from the Union would be the salvation of that protective system, which Clay and Clayton had declared to be dearer to the manufacturing regions than the Union itself.

That this agitation owed its origin to others, and not to the Southern people, and that it was not confined to an insignificant class of the American people, is evident from the official messages of Presidents and Governors. President JACKSON saw proper to call the attention of Congress to the painful excitements in the South by attempts to circulate, through the mails, inflammatory appeals addressed to the passions of the slaves, in prints and various sorts of publications, "calculated to stimu-"late them to insurrection, and to produce all the "horrors of civil war." Governor MARCY, of New York, in his official message, said that he could see no object which the Abolitionists could have in view so far as they propose to operate by disseminating incendiary appeals, but to embark the people of New York, under the sanction of the civil authority or with its connivance, "in a crusade against the slave-holding States "for the purpose of forcing abolition upon them by "violence and bloodshed." "If such a mad project," said Governor Marcy, "as this could be contemplated "for a single moment as a possible thing, everyone "must see that the first step towards its accomplish-"ment would be the end of our confederacy and the "beginning of civil war." Governor EVERETT, of Massachusetts, in his message, said that the country has been greatly agitated during the past year in relation to slavery, and that the patriotism of all classes of citizens must be invoked to abstain from a discussion which exasperated the master, rendered the condition of the slave more oppressive, and tied the hands of those at the South who favored emancipation. Such agitation, he feared, would "prove the rock on which "the Union will split." CLAY, who was by no means an alarmist, or disposed to do injustice to any class of Northern people—remarked from his place in the Senate that "abolition should no longer be regarded as an "imaginary danger." Said he: "The Abolitionists, "let me suppose, succeed in their present aim of unit-"ing the inhabitants of the free States, as one man, "against the inhabitants of the slave States, union on "the one side will beget union on the other. And "this process of reciprocal consolidation will be "attended with all the violent prejudices, embittered "passions and implacable animosities which ever de-"grade and deform human nature. A virtual dissolu-"tion of the Union will have taken place, while the "forms of its existence remain. The most valuable "element of union; mutual kindness; the feelings of "sympathy; the paternal bonds which now happily "unite us, will have been extinguished forever. One "section will stand in menacing, hostile array against "another; the collision of opinion will be quickly fol-"lowed by the clash of arms."

It was clear that the purpose and tendency of this agitation was to array the people of the Union by geographical lines. Every intelligent mind at the North saw and appreciated this fact. At first, the great mass of the people deplored and denounced it; but, gradually the manufacturing interest glided into the movement on the plea that the salvation of the tariff depended on the ostracism of the South. Then, here and there, a few honest, but misguided humanitarians took up the cry. Then the pulpit issued, in the same direction, its hebdomadal flow of irrelevant philanthropy. Then the young politicians, such as WILLIAM H. SEWARD has been described to be in the funeral oration delivered by CHARLES FRANCIS ADAMS, chiming in with the prejudices of his section, chose slavery agitation as the prolific means of obtaining local power at once, and national power after the irrepressible conflict should have been fairly inaugurated. From a small beginning, this agitation assumed most fearful proportions. The pulpit; the press; State Legislatures; State and county conventions; anti-slavery societies; and abolition lectures, were all brought into requisition to drive in the wedge between the sections. Abolition petitions flowed into Congress, signed by hundreds of thousands of men, women and children. The people of the South had every epithet of contempt, hatred and indignation hurled at their heads. If they took up a Northern magazine, their sentiments were shocked by the pages they read; if they travelled with a servant, they ran the risk of being mobbed. They were not to derive consolation from the Word of God unless they believed it to be an anti-slavery Bible; they were not to commune as Christians, except in an anti-slavery church; and there were grave doubts whether they would be admitted into any but an anti-slavery Heaven. Ex-President JEFFERSON, who was no friend to slavery, and who would have listened respectfully to any plan by which it might be removed constitutionally, was alarmed from the very outset of this agitation, at the manner in which it was set on foot, and the motives which prompted it. He charged the leaders of Federalism with taking advantage of the virtuous feelings of the people "to effect a division of "parties by geographical lines." "They expect," said he, "that this will insure them on local principles the majority they could never obtain on principles of "Federalism." If Mr. JEFFERSON had been possessed of the powers of prophecy, he could not have more distinctly pointed out the methods by which the patriotic and virtuous passions of the people of the North were to be directed, whenever occasion required, through their prejudices against slavery and the acts of the slave-holder, towards concentration of power in the Federal Government, and towards the absolute supremacy of Congress.

The controlling spirit of this effort to array North and South on geographical lines was GEORGE THOMPSON, a man of genius, who had been sent from London upon an abolition mission to this country. He had been a member of Parliament, and was a vigorous thinker and writer. J. B. MORSE, of telegraph fame, published about that time a letter giving a statement from General WILSON, a British officer employed by his government in the arrangement for emancipation in the West Indies, to the effect that Great Britain sought a footing by this act of emancipation, from which to promote dissensions between the North and South in regard to slavery, so as by disunion, if possible, to advance her manufacturing interests. In furtherance of this object we find THOMPSON coming to America immediately after the West India Act, and repeating in conversations that "every slaveholder should have his throat cut." LLOYD GARRISON, another British subject, became editor of the "Liberator." In the Massachusetts House of Representatives he appeared before a committee of the General Assembly, an immense audience being present, and said: "I feel myself, Mr. "chairman, like PAUL in the presence of AGRIPPA. "They tell us, sir, that if we proceed in our course we "shall dissolve this Union. But what is the Union to "me? I am a citizen of the world." The motto which he displayed at the head of his paper was: "THE CONSTITUTION—A COVENANT WITH DEATH, AN "AGREEMENT WITH HELL."

The States of VIRGINIA, GEORGIA, NORTH CAROLINA, SOUTH CAROLINA and ALABAMA, transmitted to all the State Legislatures a series of resolutions asking that all petitions for the abolition of slavery be laid on the table of Congress without reading or printing. The twenty-fourth Congress agreed to this reasonable request; but the twenty-fifth Congress had barely convened when the agitation was renewed from a Northern quarter, and rose at once to a pitch of unprecedented fury. In defiance of the adjustment made by the preceding Congress, a member from New England created intense excitement by presenting two abolition petitions, and attempting to debate their merits. The Southern members, the next day, offered a rule by which all such petitions should be laid on the table without being read, printed or debated, and that no further action be had upon them. This rule was adopted by a vote of yeas, one hundred and twenty-two, to nays, forty. The number and character of the petitions which came flooding the tables of Congress were sufficient to create the most intense excitement and uneasiness at the South. BENTON says that they were signed by "hundreds of "thousands—many of them women who forgot their "sex and their duties to mingle in such inflammatory "work; some of them clergymen who forgot their "mission of peace to stir up strife among those who "should be brethren." BUCHANAN says that they were directed not only at slavery in the District of Columbia and at the forts, dock yards, and arsenals of the United States, which might have been a legitimate and constitutional object; but also against the introduction of any more slave States; and some of them went so far as to petition for a dissolution of the Union itself.

Without provocation, other than the inheritance of a species of property transmitted to them by their fathers, the people of the South, without a note of warning, upon the heels of the partial defeat of the protective tariff, and immediately after West India emancipation, thus found themselves ground between the upper and the nether millstone—between the fear of New England at the loss of her manufactures, and the hope of Old England that the dissolution of the American Union would place the South at least in the condition of one of her own colonies, a rich consumer of her wares. From the Chesapeake to the Gulf, a peaceful, intelligent, brave and proud people, found themselves defamed in the halls of Congress, rebuked from pulpit, denounced from press, and threatened on all sides with the knife and the torch. "Sir," said Senator BUCHANAN, in the midst of this intense agitation: "Touch this question of slavery seriously—"let it once be made manifest to the people of the "South that they cannot live with us, except in a state "of continual apprehension and alarm for their wives "and their children, for all that is near and dear to "them upon the earth, and the Union is from that "moment dissolved. It does not then become a ques-"tion of expediency, but of self-preservation. It is a "question brought home to the fireside, to the domestic "circle of every white man in the Southern States."

Following close upon this furious crusade—which relaxed a little of its violence when General HARRISON, the hope of the protectionists, ascended the Presidential chair, only to be resumed when the elevation of President TYLER dashed the cup from their lips—was a decision of the Supreme Court of the United States, which aroused exultation on the part of the agitators, and corresponding indignation on the part of the South. The Constitution had made it mandatory that a fugitive slave "shall be delivered up" on claim of the master; and according to the doctrine of coercion, as held by the Federalists, it became the duty of the authorities of the State to which the slave had fled to deliver him up. If the State should omit to enact laws, or should obstruct such delivery, it followed from the coercion theory that Congress could compel the

State authorities to carry out the mandate of the Constitution. The Constitution provides that the States shall elect members to Congress. Suppose, said the advocates of coercion, the State should refuse to do so, would not Congress have the power to compel her to carry out a provision so necessary for representative government? The class of politicians who have, at a recent day, decided this question in the affirmative, did not hesitate to deny, in 1843, the right of Congress to compel the State to carry out the constitutional mandate respecting fugitive slaves. In that year the Supreme Court held, in the case of "Prigg against the "commonwealth of Pennsylvania," that the State magistrates were not bound to aid the master so far as to grant warrants of arrest upon application.

If the master could have no aid from the local authorities, it was manifest, from the scarcity of Federal officers, that no arrests could be made, and that the provision of the Constitution would be nullified. This decision of the Court was claimed by Judge STORY as a "triumph for freedom." He should rather have claimed it as a "triumph for nullification." So soon as the local magistrates were commanded to stand aside, a new and furious agitation was commenced against the continuation upon the statute book of the fugitive slave law of 1793, which required the Federal judges and magistrates, as well as those of the State, to carry its provisions into effect. Let it be remembered that this law was enacted by those who framed the Constitution, and during the administration of Washington. The Legislatures of several States passed laws prohibiting their magistrates from assisting in its execution. The use of State jails was denied for safe-keeping of the fugitives. Personal liberty laws were enacted, imposing insurmountable obstacles to the recovery of slaves. Every means was resorted to to nullify the constitutional provision. The life and liberty of the pursuing masters were placed in jeopardy. They were often imprisoned and sometimes murdered.

Thus the people of the South, for no fault of their own, were doomed to see their States insulted, their property destroyed, their lives menaced, the laws of the Union reviled and the Constitution spurned. Is it strange that this persecution produced its inevitable result? Is it strange that emancipation was no longer mooted, that he who even suggested it was suspected as an enemy, that the stranger who wandered through the land was often treated with hasty indecency, that the reins were tightened upon the poor and innocent slave, that the geographical line became so distinct that to all intents the two peoples were separate nations, that the value of the Union became a question of discussion, that the wish for separation sought out and welded together arguments in support of the right of secession, and that the Southern people, from looking at slavery as a necessary evil, flung back into the teeth of their tormentors that it was a necessary good?

CHAPTER X.

Position of the South during the Van Buren and Harrison Administration—Relation and Tenets of Parties from 1840 to 1850—More Territory for the South—New Threats of Division at the North—The Mexican War—Quitman and the Palmettoes—Offer of the Mexican Crown to General Scott—Condition of a Mongrel Population, &c., &c.

"There is a political force in ideas which silently renders protestations, promises and guarantees, no matter in what good faith they may have been given, of no avail, and which makes Constitutions obsolete."

DRAPER'S "CIVIL WAR IN AMERICA."

"I have never read reasonings more absurd; sophistry more gross; "in proof of the Althanasian creed or transubstantiation, than the "subtle labors of Helvetius and Rousseau, to demonstrate the natural "equality of mankind. The golden rule, do as you would be done "by, is all the equality that can be supported or defended by reason, "or reconciled to common sense."

JOHN ADAMS.

"But nature's laws are stronger than bayonets. She made the "Saxon and she made the Indian; but no mixed race called Mexican "will she support. Already we are told that the Indian blood pre-"dominates; of course it will; but give the so-called nation another "century, and then let us consider what must happen. The Castilian "blood will be all but extinct, the Indian predominating; but by "that time the Anglo-Saxon, true to his go-ahead principle, seizes "Mexico; but no Saxon will mingle with dark blood; with him the "dark races must be slaves or cease to exist."

KNOX'S "RACES OF MEN."

Towards the close of Van Buren's administration, political parties, which had been in somewhat chaotic condition from the entrance of Alabama into the Union in 1819, now began to assume definite shape. The followers of CALHOUN, who, although seated voiceless in the chair of the Vice-President, had spoken by Hayne in his great debate with Webster, and who had himself subsequently from a seat in the Senate, repeated and strengthened the argument, had never cordially affiliated with either the CLAY Whigs or the JACKSON Democrats. They called themselves *par excellence,* the "States-Rights" party. All the parties professed to be advocates of States-Rights; but this party, alone, defiantly and proudly, planted themselves on the premises laid down by Hayne, and undauntedly held their faces to the inevitable conclusion of the argument. They believed in the right of both nullification and secession. The State might choose either mode of redress; for the resolutions of '98 had distinctly stated that each State had a right to judge for itself "as well "of infractions, as of the mode and measure of redress." General JACKSON had mortally offended Mr. CALHOUN. Whatever may be said of the explanations made by Blair and the "Globe," it is certain that the proclamation against South Carolina had stigmatized secession and nullification as treason. It declared, with respect to nullification, that it would be the abrogation of all Federal authority, and with respect to nullification that it would be nothing more nor less than an act of revolution. It said that these doctrines can only be advocated through gross error, or "to deceive those who "would pause before they made a revolution or incur "the penalties consequent upon a failure."

In CALHOUN'S opposition to General Jackson's administration, the States-Rights party allied themselves with that branch of the old National Republican party, who were now being called for the first time, WHIGS. CALHOUN and CLAY were apparently in close alliance, and remained so, until the elevation of VAN BUREN to the Presidency. There was no common ground of principle for this alliance. The opposition of Clay was to all the Democratic measures of Jackson, since they all ran counter to his "American System;" whereas the opposition of Calhoun was confined to the questions growing out of the alleged right of nullification. Upon questions of policy within the Union, Calhoun was in general accord with the adherents of Jackson. While disclaiming any connection with any party, the South Carolinian had given victory to Clay and Webster in many hard fought battles against the Jackson Democrats. Now that his old enemy had passed from the chief magistracy, Calhoun advanced to the side of the Van Buren administration, and sustained it in those financial measures which gave it character.

The slavery agitation having subsided for a while, the great question before the country was, how the Federal revenue should be deposited, and in what kind of money. The Whigs contended for a national banking system which should be the depository of the public funds, and that taxes should be payable in bank notes equally with coin. This system they contended would be of great convenience to the people in affording them a medium of exchange which would not fluctuate in value; in doing away with the ruinous discounts which prevailed in the exchange of the money of one State for that of another; and in distributing throughout the States the Federal monies for which there was no immediate use by the Government. Banks, based upon Federal deposits, secured by Government pledges, affording wide-spread and equal accommodation and confidence to business men, appeared to the WHIGS to be not only a convenience, but a necessary protection from those pecuniary panics which had so often swept over the country from the insecurity and recklessness of State banks. On the other hand, the Jackson Democrats, and now the Calhoun States-Rights party, held that a national bank system tended to a consolidation of Federal power; that it gave undue weight and influence to the Federal agents; that it tended to drive gold and silver from circulation; and that it placed all industrial interests at the mercy of the banks, and held the banks themselves at the mercy of the Secretary of the Treasury and of the President. In one word, it would place not only the purse of the Government, but the purse of every citizen at the mercy of the Executive. Believing that a national bank system would endanger the rights of the States, the followers of Mr. Calhoun sustained President VAN BUREN in his recommendation for an independent treasury and a hard money currency.

While these States-Rights men, in the several States of the South, denied the constitutionality of a national bank, it is a matter of history that their great leader was in favor of a United States bank in 1816, and that he supported and mainly carried through the charter under which it was incorporated by Congress; aiding his colleague LOWNDES in a speech of great ability. In that speech he admitted the constitutionality of such a bank, although reserving an expression of opinion as to how far its powers might constitutionally extend. During the twenty years of its continuance, he had never denied the power of Congress to create it; and in 1834, when the charter was about to expire, he advocated the renewal of its term for twelve years longer.

The States-Rights party, from 1832, had acted upon the idea that they held the balance of power between the two national parties, and by throwing their weight into this or that scale, as their interests were best subserved, they could modify the views of both parties and thus better protect the people of the South. Their course, however, was marked by an inconsistency which paralyzed them as an independent organization. As between General Harrison and Mr. Van Buren, in 1836, it would seem that their animosity towards the Federalism of the Jackson Democrats should have induced them to sustain General Harrison, who was a strict-construction Whig. Not so, however; they threw their ballots for Judge HUGH L. WHITE, of Tennessee, who carried the electoral votes of Georgia and his own State. Had the States-Rights party of Alabama voted for General Harrison he would have carried that State. They voted for Mr. WHITE, and thus Mr. VAN BUREN succeeded in Alabama by a majority of but three thousand four hundred in a popular vote of nearly thirty-five thousand. Among the revenges of time it is interesting to remember that the sage of Kinderhook, who was thus elevated to power, by the retiring of the States-Rights party to their tents, was destined to consolidate and lead the Abolition ranks at a later day, and by holding the balance of power in New York was able to defeat the party which had honored him with the highest office in the land.

Immediately upon the election of Van Buren, Congress was called together in special session to take into consideration the finances of the country, and the

Governor of Alabama called the General Assembly together to co-operate with Congress. CALHOUN having allied himself with Van Buren, his followers immediately united their forces with the Jackson Democrats, throughout the South. In the Alabama General Assembly, the two bodies thus remained united for ten years.

Analyzing the several political parties of the South, we find them with distinct characteristics, although the lines of demarcation merge here and there upon theoretical questions. The Whigs and the Democrats were so equally balanced that in nearly all of the Southern States the few thousand independent States-Rights men were able to turn the scale.

1. The DEMOCRATS believed in the least government necessary for the preservation of public peace. They denied all incidental powers of Government, except when such incidents were absolutely necessary to carry into effect expressed grants. They opposed a national bank system, a protective tariff, and internal improvements by the General as well as by the State government. They likewise opposed the distribution of the proceeds of the sale of public lands among the States, and the assumption of the State debt by the Federal Government. It is difficult to say what portion of the party at this time believed in the right of nullification and secession. The policy of the party was to express no opinion upon those questions, since none of the States except South Carolina believed that an occasion had yet arisen for the exercise of that reserved right even if it existed. There was, however, a large body of the people who stood by the anti-nullification proclamation of General Jackson. While

Georgia and South Carolina and even Tennessee repudiated the Unionism of JACKSON by voting for MANGUM and WHITE, the Democrats of Alabama sustained VAN BUREN, who was known to represent the sentiments of his predecessor. There were large numbers of the Democracy however, who while assenting to the reserved right of secession and recognizing the danger to the South from the incessant anti-slavery agitation, believed it best to abide by a national organization until oppression was unendurable. The tendency of the party, however, was to deny that the right of secession had been reserved by the State upon her accession to the Union.

2. On the other hand, the WHIGS gave a more liberal construction to the powers of the Federal Government. They advocated internal improvements by both the Federal and State Governments, the establishment of a national banking system, a protective tariff, and the assumption of State debts by the General Government, with a distribution among the States of the proceeds of public lands. So far as the question of slavery was concerned, they were content to abide by the Missouri Compromise. This compromise they considered an equivalent for the settlement of a disturbing question, and productive of no practical hardship to the slave owners. Fully understanding the grave prejudices which existed against slavery in all civilized countries, and appreciating the fact that there was no security for the property of the South except under the flag of the Union, the Whigs never hesitated to accept a compromise upon questions relating to negro slavery, when the South thereby suffered no material loss, and the North thereby admitted that it had no disposition nor

power to disturb slavery where it existed in the States. The little band of outright Abolitionists in Congress, led by John Q. Adams, who were intent on using the Federal authority to abolish slavery even in the States, had no terrors for the Whigs. They held that the patriotism of the whole people would sustain the rights of the South, and that by the use of compromises which affected no material interests of that section, she could be saved from an agitation which imperiled the Union. There were very many Whigs who believed in the reserved right of secession, but the great body of the party stood by Clay and Webster in repudiating such a remedy, for even the grossest oppression, as anything more or less than the inalienable right of revolution. Even those who acknowledged the existence of the right saw the futility of advancing it or of acting upon it except when prepared to enforce it by arms. To them, such a right, when denied by the opponent, could amount to nothing but the right of revolution.

3. The States-Rights party were the advocates of nullification, in 1832, and the defenders of the right of peaceable secession at any time the sovereign State might judge such action to be necessary. If New England had believed that the embargo and non-intercourse law justified it, she had a perfect right to secede; and so had Pennsylvania under the excise law; and Virginia under the carriage tax law; Georgia under the abrogation of the Indian Springs treaty; Alabama on the non-removal of the Creeks; and South Carolina under the tariff of 1824. From setting up the remedy in extreme cases, this party, grown familiar with the argument, fell into the habit of threatening secession in supposititious cases. Beholding the gradual expansion

of the Union and the formidable power which, by numbers and wealth, was being concentrated at Washington, the rapid development of fortune at the North and the shifting of political power from the agricultural regions south of the Potomac to the manufacturing regions north of that river, the States-Rights party watched the growth of the anti-slavery idea with increasing jealousy and distrust. Patriotism became tainted with doubt, and clouded with suspicion. Doubt and suspicion frowned at conciliation and compromise. With them a right was an absolute right, not a thing to be met with conciliation or cut in two by the cautious sword of compromise. While they were able to do so with dignity they would stand as a separate political body and throw their influence in that scale which inclined to their favor. When they could no longer assert their rights within one or the other political organizations, they would seize the first occasion to assert them by separation from the Union. Being strict-constructionists of the extreme school, the States-Rights men could not, except in a few cases, act with the Whigs. After 1840, although now and then carrying on a guerilla warfare, they were generally to be found in the Democratic ranks. With a single idea kept full in view, and with a tenacity which betokened courage, endurance, fidelity and honesty of purpose, they finally obtained a controlling influence within the ranks of their allies.

Even with the aid of the States-Rights men, the Democrats barely succeeded in endorsing the policy of Van Buren. At Tuscaloosa, then capital of Alabama, the House of Representatives stood fifty-one for payment of Government dues in specie, and forty against it.

Having cemented an alliance upon the financial questions of the day, the Democrats and States-Rights men fought under one banner in the autumn of 1840. Van Buren was their candidate for re-election. The manufacturers of the North had succeeded in thrusting CLAY aside because of his tariff compromise, and had compelled the Whigs to nominate General HARRISON. The nomination of that veteran officer was received with the wildest enthusiasm among the Whigs all over the country. Never was there such a series of electioneering expedients. The Van Buren men were thrown upon the defensive. The financial disorders, which were most severely felt in the southwestern States, were all laid at the door of Jackson and his successor. The President was charged with being an aristocrat. He was said to have purchased gold spoons for the White House, with the executive contingent fund. The chief magistrate who could use gold spoons when the poor farmers were suffering from a depreciated, and oftentimes worthless paper currency, was a tyrant, an aristocrat, a nabob and a monster. General HARRISON, on the contrary, was the friend of the people. He had lived in a log cabin. He had been a frontier-man and had worn a hat made of a raccoon skin. He was a temperate and humble man who drank nothing stronger than hard cider, and who would scorn to take soup with a gold spoon. He had been a brave and successful general, and had fought the battle of Tippecanoe. Hard cider, raccoon skins and log cabins, became the order of the day. Public meetings were held all over the South, and party excitement ran to the highest pitch.

The fact that the nullifiers, as they were called, were

acting unitedly with the Democrats, gave occasion to the Whigs to claim for themselves the distinction of being Unionists. So strong was the sentiment of unionism among the Whigs of that day, that a huge ball was rolled from the Mississippi river to the Atlantic, through all the Gulf States, bearing among its inscriptions—"South Carolina! Hemp for traitors!" "Massachusetts, ever faithful!" This ball was received at Montgomery with a grand ovation, and was conducted by one of the leading Whig politicians, JAMES ABERCROMBIE, one of the foremost men of that section.

The devotion to the Union which marked the Alabama Whigs of 1840, even to a denunciation of a sister State of the South, and an undeserved eulogium upon a sister State of the North, became intensified during the Presidential canvass of 1844. The people of Texas, an independent government, had applied for admission into the Union. This application was to become the prolific source of a new agitation of the slavery question. The friends of Mr. POLK throughout the South were ardent for annexation. Throughout the North, however, a large part of the Democratic party opposed annexation, because of the certainty that Texas would enter the Union as a slave State. Although the opposing WHIG candidate, Mr. CLAY, favored annexation with certain restrictions, his northern followers cherished the hope that the restrictions would be such as to defeat the project. Their position was that annexation should not be accomplished except by negotiation with Mexico; and as Mexico would certainly never give her consent, they could be held as positive and unqualified opponents of a measure which appealed most strongly to the pride and heroism of the country and most directly to the pecuniary interests of the people of the South. The wider the area of the Southwest, the more surely would slave property recede from the Potomac towards the Gulf, and the wider would become the belt of friendly territory between the mass of slave property and the personal liberty laws of the free States. The WHIGS of the South were as earnest for annexation as were the southern Democrats. On this question there could be no dispute between the parties in Alabama; but there was a grave and fundamental difference between them as to the important question of Union or disunion, which now grew out of the Texas matter.

The Legislature of Massachusetts, in its session of 1843, with a Democratic Governor in the chair, and a majority of Democrats in both branches of the Assembly, resolved: "that under no circumstances what-"ever can the people of Massachusetts regard the pro-"position to admit Texas into the Union in any other "light than as *dangerous to its continuance in peace*, in "prosperity, and in the enjoyment of those blessings "which it is the object of a free government to secure."

The danger to the peace of the Union, contemplated by this resolution, could exist only in the determination of the New England States to forcibly resist the annexation of Texas, or to secede from the Union at the happening of that event. The resolution was forwarded to Congress and to the several States. Naturally it called forth an indignant response from the South. It was a menace on the part of Massachusetts that no matter under what circumstances Texas might be acquired by the Union, there should be no peace between the sections. The succeeding Legislature, containing a majority of Whigs, left in no doubt the intention of their predecessors. That body, directing that their proceedings should be sent to Congress and to the States, solemnly resolved "that the project "for the annexation of Texas, unless arrested on the "threshold, may tend *to drive these States into a disso-"lution of the Union.*" Cotemporaneously with this resolution, the inaugural address of the Governor announced for the first time in the history of the Union a proposition which culminated finally in general abolition of slavery. He said:

"Indeed, there is reason to believe that before the "existence of our Constitution, our highest court held "the opinion that the Declaration of Independence put "an end to slavery in this State."

From this fact, he asked whether it was unreasonable that they should strive "to hasten the time when every "human being in this republic shall enjoy the inalien-"able right of life, liberty and the pursuit of happi-"ness." Here then was a distinct proclamation sent to every State in the Union, by Massachusetts, as the head of the New England States, that slavery in her opinion was abolished by the Declaration of Independence in every State of the Union, that it would be her duty to strive to enforce a perfect political equality of all the races, and that the introduction of another slave State would endanger the peace of the country and drive the New England States into a dissolution of the Union. When this resolution was presented to Congress, Senator KING, from Alabama, one of the most moderate and conservative Southern statesmen, as we have already seen, expressed his regret that a proposition should thus come from Massachusetts to dissolve the Union. What was a source of regret to Mr. KING, was a source of indignation to the mass of Southern people who had been constantly denounced as dis-Unionists by those who had goaded them almost to desperation, and who were now calmly considering the value of the Union when about to be defeated in their desire to obtain, upon geographical lines and for partisan purposes, control of the Senate of the United States.

Finally, Massachusetts passed another series of resolutions, and transmitted them to Congress and to all the States, in which she resolved, that as, in her opinion, Congress had no right, under the Constitution, to admit Texas by legislation into the Union, "such an "act of admission *would have no binding force whatever* "*on the people of Massachusetts.*" Here was a definite and distinct re-affirmation of the principles enunciated by the Hartford Convention. Massachusetts was to judge for herself of a violation of the Constitution. Any act passed by Congress for the admission of Texas was to be treated as a nullity. The fact that practically no occasion could arise under which Massachusetts could put her nullification resolutions into operation could not palliate such language. The wish, the words, the intent, the principle of nullification were all as clearly revealed, understood and adopted, as though a regiment of militia stood drawn up at Boston common to resist the collection of imports by the officers of the custom house.

To leave no doubt of the violent intentions of New England, JOHN QUINCY ADAMS, in his address to his constituents, made use of language calculated to arouse a warlike spirit in the breast of his followers, and to inflame still more the spirit of the South. Said he:

"Texas and Slavery are interwoven in every banner "floating to the Democratic breeze. Freedom or "Death should be inscribed on ours. A war for "slavery! Can you enlist under such a standard? "May the Ruler of the Universe preserve you from "such degradation. 'Freedom, Peace, Union,' be this "the watchword of your camp, and if ATE, hot from "hell, will come and cry 'Havock'—fight—fight and "conquer, under the banner of universal freedom!"

As the Federal party of New England sympathized with Great Britain in 1812, so now they so far sympathized with Mexico, in their desire to curb the South and restrict its free-trade power, that through the voice of one of their leaders they expressed the hope that a foreign government would welcome our patriotic troops "with bloody hands to hospitable graves."

While Massachusetts was thus heading the Abolition disunion movement, flooding Congress and the States with menacing resolutions, sending agents to the southern ports under the pretense of looking after the interests of negro sailors, denouncing the spirit of compromise, advocating equal political rights for all men under the Declaration of Independence, destroying peace between the sections, and nullifying an act of Congress, the State of South Carolina was not slow to meet her half way. At the head of the States-Rights party she replied, to all menaces, that Texas had as much right to join the Union as though she had been a part of our territory; that her annexation was material to the commercial prosperity of the whole Union, and especially of the Gulf States; that it was not certain that her admission would accrue to the power of the slave States, in as much as her territory was so great and so sparsely settled that two or three free States might yet be carved from her, and that whether she applied for admission with slavery or without, was a matter entirely with herself, and in no event could be a violation of the Constitution. Finally, wrought up to the highest pitch of indignation, South Carolina and the States-Rights party declared that a refusal to admit Texas upon the grounds stated in the Massachusetts resolutions would be good cause for a dissolution of the Union.

Those who in their public writings have placed the origin of the spirit of disunion in the breast of the South, have not ceased to allege that at that day the agitation for disunion began in South Carolina. Senator BENTON in his "Thirty years' view," says that so soon as Mr. POLK was nominated, "the disunion aspect manifested itself over many of the Southern States—beginning, of course, with South Carolina." This is so far from being the truth that it was as late as May, 1844, when the first meeting was held in South Carolina. It was a meeting to retaliate against Massachusetts, who had passed her disunion resolutions in the autumn of 1843. It was held at ASHLEY, in the Barnwell district, and its intention was to combine the slave States in a convention, to unite the Southern States to Texas, if Texas should not be received into the Union, and to invite the President to convene Congress to arrange terms for a dissolution of the Union. Another large meeting was held at BEAUFORT, another at Charleston, and another at the Williamsburg district, at which resolutions looking to the same end were adopted.

During this controversy the State of Alabama was ardently in favor of the annexation of Texas; but it is certain that a majority of her people would not have favored disunion in the event of a refusal of Congress to admit that State. She was emphatic in her reply to the resolutions and conduct of Massachusetts. Her General Assembly decided unanimously that the abrogation of the twenty-first rule, by which Congress had refused to consider abolition petitions, was a hostile act on the part of the North, and that South Carolina had a right to protect the peace and happiness of her people, by sending back the agent of Massachusetts, who had been delegated as an attorney to look after the interest of negro sailors who might be citizens of Massachusetts. Still the Whig party of Alabama, and very many of the Democratic party, denied the right of a State to disunite itself from the Union except in the last resort, and they believed that the acceptance or rejection of Texas by Congress was not adequate cause for secession. The Democratic party, embracing the States-Rights party, and receiving a large coloring of its principles from that wing of its army, were charged by its opponents with being disunionists. The banner of "Texas or Disunion," which was being flaunted throughout the South, was almost invariably in Democratic hands, and hence the Whig party took advantage of the acts and words of the States-Rights men to stamp the Democratic as the Disunion party, and to claim for themselves the distinction of being the Union party. Nor was it possible for the Democrats to retaliate upon the Whigs by saying that if the disunion element at the South were the allies of the former, the disunion element at the North were the allies of the latter, since it was a matter of record that the disunion sentiments of Massachusetts were expressed by both Whig and Democratic Legislatures, and that the Abolition press were intent upon breaking up the Whig party at the North as the great barrier in their way to disunion. If the Whig Governor of Massachusetts, in 1844, had embraced the Abolitionists, he only followed in the footsteps of the Democratic Governor of 1843. If the Northern Whigs voted to repeal the 21st rule, so did forty-seven Northern Democrats. And in the Presidential election which followed, the WHIGS could point triumphantly to the fact that Mr. POLK had been elected President by the Disunion element of the North. The candidacy of Mr. BIRNEY by the Anti-slavery party drew away enough votes in New York to have elected Mr. CLAY, just as the candidacy of Mr. VANBUREN in 1848 drew away enough votes to have elected General CASS. They could also point to the fact that Mr. BIRNEY, while Abolition candidate for the Presidency, was at the same time the regular Democratic nominee for the Michigan Legislature. The truth is, the Abolition party acted with either or neither of the regular parties, as its interests suggested, struggling to consolidate the anti-slavery sentiments of both Whigs and Democrats into a new geographical party which, while pretending the amelioration of the human race upon high humanitarian principles, was actually intending to revert the Government to the views, hopes and wishes of General HAMILTON and the Federalists.

When at last the Whig party of the North passed away, it is difficult to say whether the major portion, or what portion, of that party, went to form the new Republican party. If leading Whigs like SEWARD, GREE-

LEY and LINCOLN were to be found within its ranks, so also among its leaders were to be found Democrats like BIRNEY, CHASE, HAMLIN and CAMERON. The Republican party professed to be built upon the ruins of *both* the Whig and Democratic parties of the North, and it would not be far from the mark to say that as many Whigs went into the Democratic ranks after the defeat of General SCOTT as into the Republican ranks; and that the latter party drew its followers as largely from the one old party as the other. However this may be, the Whigs of the South were not to be deterred from their zealous advocacy of the Union by the charge, on the one hand, that their brother Whigs of the North were allied with the Abolition party; nor by the charge, on the other hand, that the cry of "Union" was now become synonymous with that of "submission."

The Whigs of Alabama in their protest against the cry of "Texas or disunion,', which had thundered forth from the States-Rights men in response to the New England threat of "rejection of Texas or dis-"union," were joined in sentiment and sympathy by hosts of Southern Democrats. The movement in New England took no positive form beyond words. The movement in South Carolina assumed an active form. A convention of the Southern States was called for, to meet at Nashville, to lay down the *ultimatum*. The resolutions of the South Carolina meeting met a response in several of the Southern States. A meeting held in Alabama suggested that the convention meet at Richmond. In reply to this suggestion, Mr. RITCHIE, editor of the *Enquirer*, said: "There is not a Dem-"ocrat in Virginia who will encourage any plot to dis-"solve the Union." The Richmond *Whig*, on the part of the Whigs, repudiated the suggestion with indignation. Nashville was not behind Richmond in declining the honor of being the seat of the disunion convention. A meeting of her citizens protested against "the desecration of the soil of Tennessee, by having any convention held there to hatch treason against the Union." The resolutions adopted by the Nashville meeting were those which marked the councils of the Whigs throughout the South. They condemned every attempt to bring into issue the preservation of the Union, or to bring its value into calculation. While entertaining for the people of South Carolina and for the States-Rights party everywhere, the most fraternal regard and the highest respect for the sincerity of their opinions, they lamented the exhibition by any portion of them of disloyalty to the Union, or a disposition to urge its dissolution with a view to annexation with Texas, and the construction of a Southwestern republic such as was contemplated by Aaron Burr.

The proposition for the Nashville convention met such powerful opposition that the hopes and prospects of the Whigs brightened throughout the South. The plan was discarded; Mr. Polk was elected; the tact and promptness of President TYLER hastened and secured the admission of Texas, to the confusion of New England and the satisfaction of the entire South.

The vote in the State of Alabama was for Mr. POLK, 36,740; for Mr. Clay, 26,084. The States-Rights party had grown in strength since 1840, and had taken two thousand voters from the Whigs and added them to their allies. Apart from this defection which was more than made good at the next Presidential election, the Whigs were as earnest and enthusiastic for

Clay as they had been for Harrison. The same old leaders who guided the party in 1840, were at its head in 1844.

The action of President Tyler in securing the admission of Texas in the last days of his Presidency, was followed by the war with Mexico and the ultimate capture of the capital of that nation. The first troops within the fortifications of Mexico were a South Carolina regiment, and the first flag that floated over the city was that of "the Palmettoes." General Quitman, the gallant son of Mississippi, was designated as the officer to receive the surrender of the city and to hoist the flag of the United States over a conquered nation.

The war with Mexico exerted a great influence in many respects upon the mind of the whole country. By extending the southwestern frontier it opened the slavery agitation anew, and more painfully than ever at the North; and at the South it aroused closer attention from those leading spirits who had participated in the war, to a more thorough consideration of what would be the condition of the Gulf States if the Free Soil party should succeed in accomplishing emancipation, and in bringing about that political equality which has invariably followed emancipation.

Mexico, in less than a quarter of a century, had followed all the routes that lead a republic to anarchy. Her weakness was not in her situation, her material resources, nor in her climate. All of these were admirable. She possessed as magnificent a land as the God of nature ever smiled upon—a land which claimed the flora of both continents, and which reveled in every plant that could be grown on the habitable globe; grand forests of every description of timber, numberless droves of wild cattle, birds of the brightest plumage and most ravishing song; a climate offering every degree of temperature, and mines of precious metal which for centuries had sustained the tottering thrones of Spain. Possessing every natural advantage which a government might wish, the American army found the Mexican nation rotten to the core. The people were overshadowed by a church, whose vast wealth gave them a temporal power even greater than the spiritual power. The religious corporations which controlled the monasteries and nunneries, and the secular corporations which controlled the mines, had added riches to riches, while the mass of people grew poorer and poorer.

The power of the corporations gave preferment in the army, and hence ambitious Mexicans, leaning to the money influence in order to rise in office rapidly and to reap an early fortune, regarded as little the letter of constitutions as they did the wants and necessities of the people. Hence in twenty years there had been forty revolutions. The rise and fall of parties, the overthrow and resurrection of Presidents, Emperors and Dictators followed each other in such rapid succession that the events and even the names of leaders have perished from memory.

The church and the army combined, possessing the purse and the sword, leaned constantly towards centralism. To preserve the independence of the States, or even the form of a Federal Republic, under such circumstances, was an impossibility. An ignorant country people cared nothing for the rights of the States so long as they could get offices in the army or employment at the mines; even at the capital the people saw their city surrendered as the battle-field of all the political aspirants who had won reputation in the camp.

This country of seven millions of people, twice as prosperous as were the colonies of Anglo-Saxons when they threw off the yoke of Great Britain, was now invaded by an army which assaulted their capital with less than six thousand men. This handful of invaders had landed under the walls of a strong sea fortification, had marched through almost impassable defiles and over easily obstructed mountains, had broken through a triple line of defences bristling with the most approved artillery and defended by an army of forty thousand Mexicans, and had finally fought its way along narrow causeways into a city so populous that had the people been possessed of half the spirit of the women of Salamanca, they could have annihilated the enemy by hurling hand grenades from the house tops.

The Anglo-Saxon, when overthrown or conquered, never fawns at the feet of the conqueror. The descendants of ALFRED and HAROLD preserved their dignity and their customs under the Norman invader, and the Saxons of HOLSTEIN and SCHLESWIG brooked the Danish yoke with such impatience that they readily rallied to the banner of Prussia. JULIUS CÆSAR, with the legions of imperial Rome, could not subdue those stalwart, blue-eyed, flaxen-haired warriors of the wilderness. But the mongrel population of Mexico threw themselves at the feet of the conqueror and offered him a crown. On taking possession of the city of Mexico, such was the order and security for life and property established by the American General that at least two-fifths of all the branches of government, including very nearly a majority of the members of Congress and the Executive, were anxious for annexation to the United States. Men in and out of office, of great influence, approached General Scott privately and offered to place at his disposal one million of dollars if he would remain in and govern Mexico. They knew that upon the ratification of the treaty of peace nineteen out of twenty of the army would be disbanded and would be free to enlist under any banner. It was expected that a large portion of the troops would be eager to serve as the favored guards of an American dynasty. One-third more was to be added to the pay of those officers and men who would engage in the proposed movement. New regiments of volunteers were arriving daily, and these, more readily than the others, were expected to be carried away by the novel project. Ten thousand Americans were counted upon as a nucleus, and this force could be greatly increased by recruits from New Orleans and Mobile. A salary of $250,000 per annum was offered General Scott. All the fortresses, all the armies of the country, all the custom-houses were already in his hands. A distribution of a little money, or the arrest of those who were opposed to the scheme, would easily secure a favorable vote of the Mexican Congress; and then nothing was left to obstruct the mounting of the American General to the Mexican throne, with as much ease as BERNADOTTE ascended the throne of SWEDEN. This offer, so shameful to the Mexicans, was rejected for two reasons, as given by General SCOTT himself. The first reason was, that he could not honorably resign from under his own flag except to add to the glory of his country by immediate annexation of Mexico to the United States. Such a reason, as clear as the sunlight to an Anglo-Saxon, could not be appreciated by the average Mexican. The second reason was that, as there were but one million of pure-blooded white men in Mexico, and six millions of Indians and mixed Indians, Negroes and Spaniards, the American General believed that the annexation of such a free population to the United States would be an injury to his country.

The soldiers mingled with the people, and soon discovered the intrigues into which their shameless enemy was entering. They repelled the proposition as earnestly as did their commander. If General Scott, who was no peculiar friend of the South, could discountenance a brilliant offer of empire because of the character of the population, the volunteers of the South who composed two-thirds of the army, could not for a moment consider a scheme by which six millions of people of debased blood and debased ideas were to be incorporated into a Republican Government which owed all of its vigor and glory to the unsullied and untainted blood of the Anglo-Saxon.

Of the seven millions of Mexicans only one million were white men. Three millions were Indians; and three millions were Mulattoes, Mestizoes and Samboes. The Samboes were a cross of the white man and the Negro, the white man and the Indian, and the Negro and the Indian, with all the intermediate shades and degrees of debased blood resulting from a union of the Mestizo with the Sambo, and the Mulatto with both. Many millions of white men had come and gone in the lapse of three centuries; many hundreds of thousands of Negro slaves had been imported and had perished; many millions of Indians had been swept away by the brutality of Cortez and his successors, and now the Republic of Mexico exhibited to the young Southerner who stood guard before the halls of the Montezuma the singular spectacle of a nation composed mainly of half-breeds, whose color was gradually year by year assuming a darker shade, until it must eventually go back to the copper complexion of the aborigines. This Republic of half-breeds, although generaled in the Senate, in the army, and in the church, by pure-blooded white men, was the miserable thing which taught the high-spirited Southerner that the strength of a nation depends more upon the race than upon the government.

The Government of Mexico is modeled after that of the United States; but what the pure-blooded Anglo-Saxon could accomplish, the mind of the dark races of Central America could not even compass. While the former advanced with the tread of a giant, driving the copper-colored race towards the Rocky Mountains, and holding the black race in servitude, Mexico surrendered to the optimistic ideas of natural race equality, which were sweeping over France and the Iberian peninsular. While the United States, with a homogeneous population of citizens, bounded to the front rank of nations, her mongrel sister Republic fell to the earth before a single feeble blow from a handful of brave and intelligent white men, under the lead of General Scott..

The gallant troops of South Carolina, Georgia, Alabama and Mississippi, which followed the banner of John A. Quitman and Jefferson Davis, on the bloody field of Buena Vista, and at the Belan Gate of Mexico, understood even at that early day that in a Republic there could be no intermediate station between the slave and the freeman. A freedman, without civil and political rights, without ultimate incorporation into the body politic, was a being unknown to the history of Republics. So soon as emancipation was accomplished, the tendency would inevitably be towards the retention of the freedman by the land owner, and his permanent fixture to the soil. What would happen then in a State like South Carolina, Mississippi or Louisiana, where the Negro race predominated, would be what had happened in Mexico. Even in the States of Georgia, Alabama and Florida, where mercenary white men might unite their fortunes with the black race it was possible that the whites would lose their ascendancy. The movement of the emancipated Negroes would be towards the Gulf States. White immigrants would loathe a line of march in which they would be doomed to such fellowship: and thus the fairest part of the South would be given up to the political power of the Negro. This political power would step by step acquire social power, and whether within or without the bond of wedlock, would finally blast the cotton producing region with a race of hybrids. How many years would be necessary for such a result to be reached could only be surmised; but certain it was that in less than half a century the Castilian Vice Kingdom of New Spain had cut loose from its typical white man's Government, and had become a Republic incapable of self-protection.

To the soldiers of the South, it appeared that in this beautiful but accursed land Nature had vindicated her physiological law of race. It was said by HORACE —"*Naturam expellas furca, tamen usque recurret.*" You may turn nature out of doors with violence, but she will still return. The diminution of the whites removed the source from which the Mulatto received his light shade, and the whole array of colors, Mulatto, Mestizo, Quadroon, Creole, Sambo, and Chino, were now reverting to the prevailing color, the copper of the Indian.

When Mr. CANNING made his celebrated boast in Parliament that he had created the Republics of Mexico and Peru, Columbia, Bolivia, and the Argentine, he did not consider that it was beyond his power to create races, and that he was simply giving the inhabitants an opportunity to return to the Indian type. The incorporation of all races into the body politic of these republics, and the breaking down of all social barriers, simply turned back the hand of time three hundred years on the dial. The recognition by England of those mongrel nations should have been styled—"a recognition "of the return of the New World to the aboriginal "Indian population, from whom no good have ever "come, and from whom nothing but evil could be ex-"pected." Would not the same physiological law hold good in the Gulf States? When the negro shall have prevailed in the cotton section, and familiarity shall have broken down the social barriers between the races; when the half-breeds shall have become so numerous as to absorb every vestige of political power; and when the pure whites shall have removed to States in which they may be ruled and taxed by men of their own color and race, will not the hybrids revert rapidly to the purer negro type, and thus through successive generations the last drop of Anglo-Saxon blood be swallowed up in the African? Such has been the history of Mexico; why might such not be the history of South Carolina?

Was it to be hoped that the danger would be averted by the supply of new material furnished the Anglo-

Saxon by the more Northern States? On the contrary, the negroes would become massed in the cotton-growing region, and their numbers would increase far more by concentration than the whites could increase by infiltration from the North. After a few generations, it was reasonable to believe, nay, absolutely certain, that the hybrids of the Gulf States would exhibit qualities identical with those of the mixed races of Mexico.

Impoverished, haughty, uneducated, defiant, bigoted, disputatious, without financial credit, beaten in arms, far behind the age in mechanical progress or social civilization, and loaded with debt, Mexico presented the miserable spectacle of a nation without nationality, of no distinct race, and reposing honor and confidence in worthless military leaders. The people found themselves oppressed by those whom they caressed, a republic with all the essential features of a military despotism, a lawless nation which would be more serviceable to the human race were it to revert once more to that aboriginal race which at least built the halls of the Montezumas.

Would not such be the fate of the fairest territory of her Anglo-Saxon sister, when four millions of uneducated negroes and mulattoes, incapable of reading the ballots which they cast for military chieftains, assume to legislate for the Anglo-Saxon race, to hold the balance of power in Presidential elections, and to guide the civilization of the 19th century as PHÆTON attempted to guide the chariot of the sun when he was wrecked on the deserts of Africa?

CHAPTER XI.

William L. Yancey and the Montgomery District—The Alabama Democratic Resolutions of 1848—General Cass and the States-Rights Party—The Nashville Convention and Defeat of the Secessionists—The Compromise Measures of Clay—Triumph of the Union Party all over the South—Defeat of Governors Seabrook and Quitman—The Georgia Resolutions—Union Leaders and Sentiment in Alabama, &c., &c.

"Two great powers that will not live together are in our midst, tugging at each other's throats. They will search each other out though you separate them a hundred times. And if by an insane blindness you shall contrive to put off the issue and send their unsettled dispute down to your children, it will go down gathering volume and strength at every step, to waste and desolate their heritage. Let it be settled now. Clear the place. Bring in the champions. Let them put their lances in rest for the charge. Sound the trumpet, and God save the right!"

HENRY WARD BEECHER.

"We confess that we intend to trample under foot the Constitution of this country. Daniel Webster says 'you are a law-abiding people,' that the glory of New England is 'that it is a law-abiding community.' Shame on it if this be true; if even the religion of New England sinks as low as its statute book. But I say we are not a law-abiding community. God be thanked for it."

WENDELL PHILLIPS, March, 1849.

The conquest of Mexico, and the eagerness with which the notables of that country embraced the idea of annexation to the United States, led to the hope in the Southern mind, that not only Texas and a part of Mexican territory, but the entire republic, might be acquired as a result of the war. General QUITMAN hastened to Washington and laid before the President a plan for permanent occupation of the country. The plan was rejected; it was very difficult to annex any portion of Mexico. The enemies of Southern expansion had fought hard against Texas. They would fight still harder to make free territory of the Mexican acquisition. They would listen to no scheme for more territory. The treaty of GUADALOUPE HIDALGO was signed and ratified, and the American army disbanded.

At the close of the Mexican war, the Alabama Congressional District, of which Montgomery was the principal town, was one of the most flourishing regions upon earth. The people were possessed of luxuriant cotton lands and of innumerable slaves. They were for the most part wealthy, educated and accomplished. The art of agriculture was carried to the highest point of success, and the theory of government was the universal study of the citizens. The city of Montgomery, the birth-place of the Confederacy, had been for years the residence of a man whose brilliant genius had been laboriously trained and who was destined to be a leader in those movements which were to make Montgomery famous in history for all time to come. WILLIAM LOWNDES YANCEY, a logician of a high order of intellect and an orator of most captivating address, was then in the meridian of his powers. He was a States-Rights man of the most extreme school, a devoted follower of CALHOUN. Believing that the anti-slavery movement would not cease until it invaded and destroyed the South, not only politically, but socially and commercially, he opposed at every step all efforts at compromise. He demanded the full measure of constitutional justice to the South. The North had no right to put a collar of shame upon the neck of the South by her Missouri compromise lines, by her denial of equal protection to all kinds of property in the common territory. With YANCEY it was not enough to say that slavery could never go north of thirty-six degrees thirty minutes, and that it was immaterial to debate about slavery extension when there were not enough slaves to thoroughly develop the slave States. With him, the denial of a right, however abstract, was an act of injustice and oppression. The injustice must be remedied or there could be no peace. A denial of justice was a badge of superiority, and he would never consent to live in union with a people who would refuse him any muniment of right given him by law. Impulsive as a mountain torrent dashing over rocks, his eloquence had a boldness, a coolness, a transparency which challenged admiration. There was nothing of the froth of declamation in his speech, but every leap of the torrent struck a resounding blow, bearing away all opposition and sweeping the debris before it, until it spread out into a broad, placid, irresistible current. What PATRICK HENRY was to the first American Revolution, WILLIAM L. YANCEY was to the second. But YANCEY possessed that which PATRICK HENRY did not have—cultivation, a thorough acquaintance with governmental law, and a wonderful command of vigorous English.

HENRY S. FOOTE, who played so conspicuous a part as Governor of Mississippi and United States Senator from that State during the Union contest of 1849-50, and who was subsequently a member of the Confederate Congress with Mr. Yancey, has given a very just description of this remarkable leader and orator. He says: "There was, in Mr. Yancey's person, at least in "his latter days, but little to impress the casual behold- "er, or to enkindle the sympathies of those who had no "special intercourse with him. In stature he was rather "below than above the height of ordinary men. His "face was well shaped, but neither strikingly handsome "or the reverse. His vestments were quite remarkable "for their plainness and simplicity, and did not always "fit him as well as they might have done. His aspect "was in general somewhat lacking in animation, and "often betrayed tokens of nervous exhaustion. His "manners were decidedly reserved, with a percepti- "ble approximation of moroseness. He made no at- "tempt to shine in ordinary converse. It is known "that he had studied men closely, and had looked "deeply into the motives and purposes of those with "whom he had held intercourse, or whose movements "in public life had specially attracted his attention. In "general he was able to keep the tempestuous feelings "of his soul in a state of stoical suppression; but occa- "sions sometimes arose when, either having lost his "accustomed power of self-control, or deeming it expe- "dient to make some display of the stormier energies "with which he was endowed, he unloosed all the furies "under his command upon some noted antagonist, and "did and said things which those who witnessed his "sublime ravings never again forgot. * *

"In my judgment, the South has contained within "her limits no such eloquent and effective political "speaker as Wm. L. Yancey since the death of George "McDuffie. When rising to discuss a question of "special dignity and importance, his aspect and man- "ner were marked with mingled earnestness and solem- "nity. His exordium was always uttered with an "imposing slowness and formality. He enunciated "every word and syllable distinctly. His voice was "clear, strong and sonorous. He commonly spoke in "the conversational tone, a little elevated. His ges-"tures were few, but these were most apt and impres-"sive. He never addressed either a deliberative body "or a popular audience without having previously mas-"tered the subject, upon which he was expected to "dilate, in all its parts. His acute and well-balanced "intellect, supplied as it was with vast stores of informa-"tion of almost every kind, generally enabled him to "anticipate and respond effectually to whatever might "be said by his adversaries in debate. His powers of "sarcasm were tremendous, and he sometimes indulged "in a bitter and sneerful ridicule which was very diffi-"cult to tolerate patiently. The greatest of his speeches "in Richmond was that which he delivered upon what "was known as the Judiciary question, in which he "took strong ground against conferring appellate juris-"diction upon the Confederate Supreme Court in cases "originating in the State courts. I had the satisfaction "of hearing the whole of his elaborate argument on "this occasion, and can declare that it seemed to me to "be nearly equal in vigor, brilliancy and classic orna-"ment to some of the best speeches of Webster or "Pinckney. Arthur F. Hopkins sat by my side on "this interesting occasion, and exclaimed to me more "than once that he was now thoroughly convinced that "Mr. Yancey was by far the ablest of living speakers.

"I have already said that Mr. Yancey had much "hand in the origination of the late civil war, and such "was certainly the case; but in regard to his conduct "in this respect, I have long since ceased to censure "him with bitterness. Trained in the days of his open-"ing manhood in the extreme States-Rights school of

" the South, he very naturally adopted certain plausible " dogmas, to the support of which he afterwards devoted " the best energies of his splendid and gigantic intel- " lect. He really believed that, under our system of " government, the States are absolutely sovereign, " bound together only by a league which they may at " any moment dissolve, and that the Federal Govern- " ernment, owing its origin to States, as such, is a mere " agency established by them for purposes of conveni- " ence, and has no powers whatever save those which " have been formally and specifically conceded to it. " He devoutly believed, with Mr. Calhoun, that African " slavery was a vital and indispensable ingredient of the " system of polity established by our fathers; that, " without it, no freedom, worthy of the name, could be " enjoyed by the white race of this continent, and that " the more widely diffused it might become, the more " prosperous and happy would be the whole republic.

" Entertaining these views, it is not at all wonderful " that Mr. Yancey should have sought to engraft upon " the Democratic political platform of 1848 a resolu- " tion affirmatively protective of slavery in the terri- " tories. It as little surprising that he and those agree- " ing with him in sentiment should advocate disunion " in 1851, because of the admission of California as a " free State; that they should have made an attempt " in 1860 to persuade the Democratic party to take " an 'aggressive attitude' in behalf of slavery; that, " failing in this, he and they should have attempted to " disintegrate that party; and that when, by these pro- " ceedings, the election of a Republican President was " brought about, secession was at once resolved on as "the only means left, in their opinion, of saving African slavery from ultimate extermination.

"I repeat that, far as I am, and have ever been, "from coinciding with Mr. Yancey and his States-"Rights adherents as to these matters, I am not at all "inclined, at this moment, to heap opprobrium upon his "memory. His sincerity in utterance of his opinions "I do not at all question, and it is due to him to say "that his conduct in Richmond as a legislator, during "the trying years of the war of the Rebellion, was in "the highest degree marked with consistency, firmness "and manly independence. Whatever else may be "justly said by enemies of Wm. L. Yancey, these "truths may be safely asserted of him; he never "sought to make money by the war; he ever opposed "the suspension of habeas corpus—a measure so bane-"ful to individual freedom; he never gave his assent "to the displacement of able and gallant military com-"manders, in order to make way for the incompetent "favorites of a prejudiced and self-willed executive "chief; he never proposed to murder in cold blood all "the prisoners taken in war [nor did any other Confed-"erate leader propose such a thing.—Author]; he never "introduced a bill providing for the permanent establish-"ment of martial law; he never united in a scheme for "the coercing of one of the States deemed by him sover-"eign, and constraining it to remain in a confederacy "after it had become heartily disgusted with it, and "wished to return to the Federal Union; he never voted "for a bill providing for the payment of the salary of "the Confederate President in gold, whilst the Con-"federate soldiers, in rags and barefoot, were refused "the wretched pittance of depreciated paper which they "had been allowed by law; he had no hand in the "unpardonable burning of Richmond, and, had he sur- "vived so long as the month of December, 1864— "seeing the ruin then impending over the Confederate "cause—he would, I feel perfectly assured, have urged, "with all the eloquence at his command, the making of "peace with the Federal Government, on the honorable "and advantageous terms at that time offered by Mr. "Lincoln, as all intelligent men now know.

"Future generations will undoubtedly recognize "Wm. L. Yancey as one of the ablest, most far-seeing, "and most statesmanlike personages that took part in "the Confederate struggle, as he was undeniably one of "the most profound jurists and most eloquent advo- "cates that have ever adorned the bar of the South "and Southwest."

Upon the appointment of Senator Wm. R. King to the French mission, and the election of Dixon H. Lewis to succeed him in the Senate, the seat vacated by Mr. Lewis in the Lower House was filled by the election of Mr. Yancey. At the next election Mr. Yancey was again elected to Congress, but in consequence of poverty, resigned the seat before the expiration of his term. At the present day when we see poor men entering Congress and amassing great wealth in a few years, it may astonish many that a man of Yancey's transcendant eloquence and ability should find no means of acquiring money at Washington, apart from his meagre salary. The astonishment of such persons would be increased when they are told that in that day no one dared to make presents, or give money or offer bribes in the shape of large dividends on nominal investments, to a representative from the South.

Mr. Yancey was the acknowledged leader of the States-Rights wing of the Democratic party. The States-Rights men had gradually grown in strength, just as the aggressions of the Abolitionists became bolder, more insulting and more harassing; and after the Mexican war there was but little difference between them and their allies, except as to the proper remedy for grievances. One point of difference however, which afterwards was swept away by the violence of sectional passion, was well defined towards the close of Mr. Polk's administration. It was as to the power of Congress, in establishing rules and regulations for the government of a territory, to exclude slavery therefrom or to empower the territorial legislature, its own agent, to enact such exclusion.

Mr. Calhoun, Mr. Yancey and the States-Rights men, after 1847, denied this power in Congress. A large, perhaps the greater portion of the Democratic party, before that date and for several years after, admitted the power. It is certain that the Whig party of the South generally admitted it down to the decision in the Dred Scott ca e. What is known as the Missouri Compromise, the act by which Congress forbid slavery in all the territory north of thirty-six degrees thirty minutes, was secured by Southern votes. Lowndes of South Carolina, King and Walker of Alabama, Pinckney of Maryland, Macon of North Carolina, Barbour and Pleasants of Virginia, Smith of South Carolina, Elliott and Walker of Georgia, all voted for its retention. Had it not been supported by the South it could never have prevailed. It is true, that without it Missouri might not have been admitted as a slave State; but an inconvenience like that would not have persuaded such men to sustain the measure if they had believed it to be unconstitutional. Mr. MONROE held it to be a constitutional measure. His Cabinet, according to his own recollection, and according to the diary of Mr. JOHN QUINCY ADAMS, gave it as their unanimous opinion that the act was constitutional. It was held to be constitutional by the large bulk of both the Whig and Democratic parties, who pointed to it as a sacred compact for more than thirty years. Had they believed it to be unconstitutional they would never have regarded it as sacred.

No question was made as to this power in Congress as late as the admission of Texas into the Union. The joint resolution by which Texas was admitted, provided that "in such States as might be formed out of said "territory north of said Missouri Compromise line "slavery or involuntary servitude, except for crime, "shall be prohibited." This measure received the votes of all the States-Rights men of the House. The whole South, Whig and Democrat alike, voted for it. When it went to the Senate, Mr. BUCHANAN said that he was pleased with it because "these resolutions went to re-es-"tablish the Missouri Compromise, by fixing a line "within which slavery was in future to be confined." As the joint resolution could not become operative for the prohibition of slavery in any part of her territory until Texas had actually become a State in the Union, it would appear that this act of Congress went further than the Wilmot Proviso, and actually effected the abolition of slavery in a portion of a sovereign State. No part of Texas had ever become or would ever become a territory of the United States. Again, when the bill for organizing the territory of Oregon was before Congress in 1847, Mr. BURT, of South Carolina, moved the recognition of the Missouri Compromise line, and every Southern member voted for it. Subsequently, in the Senate, in 1848, upon a motion to extend the Missouri line to the Pacific, the South voted for it unanimously. The Nashville Convention of 1851 favored the Missouri Compromise, and the caucus of Southern Congressmen, through their committee of fifteen, accepted this line, and adopted it as a settlement of disputes. CALHOUN, as a member of President MONROE's cabinet, did not object to, even if he questioned, the constitutionality of the power of Congress to preclude slavery from the territories. And so, as late as 1848, although opposed to the principle of the Missouri Compromise, he gave it his support in the case of Oregon. For nearly thirty years neither he nor any other States-Rights leader questioned the constitutionality of the act. Mr. YANCEY was among those Southern members of Congress who voted to apply the Missouri Compromise to the northern portion of Texas. By this vote he distinctly recognized the power of Congress to prohibit the existence of slavery in a future State which might be constructed from that of Texas, whether that State should apply with a constitution recognizing slavery or not.

ALEXANDER H. STEPHENS, one of the most pronounced of the States-Rights school, as late as 1854, said from his seat in Congress—"I say nothing of the constitu-"tional view of the question. When I have been asked "if Congress does not possess the power to impose re-"strictions, or to pass the Wilmot Proviso, I have "waived that issue; I never discuss it. On that point

"I have told my constituents, and I tell you, I treat it "as Chatham treated it in the British Parliament when "the question of power to tax the colonies without rep- "resentation was raised there. That question Chatham "would not discuss; but he told those who were so "unjustly exercising it, that if he were an American "he would resist it. The question of power is not the "question; the question is, is it right to exercise it?"

It was as late as February, 1847, when CALHOUN first denied the constitutional power of Congress to prohibit of itself or by its delegated agent, the territorial legislature, the introduction or holding of slave property in any of the territories. This denial was presented to the public in the shape of a series of resolutions introduced to the Senate. Although the Senate did not act upon them, they were taken up and acted upon by several of the Southern States. YANCEY presented the question to the Democratic State Convention which assembled at Montgomery, 1848, in a series of resolutions, which declared:

1. That the opinion advanced and maintained by some that the people of a territory, in other event than in the formation of a constitution preparatory to admittance as a State, can prevent the introduction or holding of any property, be it slave or otherwise, is a restriction as indefensible in principle and as dangerous in practice as if such restriction had been imposed by Congress.

2. That those who hold that such restrictions may be enforced, should not be recognized as Democrats.

3. That the Democratic party of Alabama are pledged, under any stress of political necessity, not to

vote for any one for President or Vice-Presldent who holds to such restrictions.

Yancey advocated these resolutions in a speech as concisely logical as that delivered by Mr. Calhoun, and with all the fervor and enthusiasm of Henry Clay. They were adopted by the Convention. Yancey was appointed one of the delegates to the Baltimore Convention. He wrote to the several gentlemen whose names had been spoken of in connection with the nomination, asking a response to the Alabama resolutions. Mr. Buchanan evasively replied that he favored the application of the Missouri Compromise line to the newly acquired territory. This was a rejection of the resolutions so far as more than half the common territory was concerned. General Cass replied that he considered the duty of Congress to be limited to the creation of a proper government for the territories, leaving to the people inhabiting them to regulate their internal concerns in their own way. This was a complete rejection of the resolutions.

Yancey was sent as a delegate from Alabama to the National Democratic Convention, which was to assemble at Baltimore. Foote, in his "Bench and Bar of the Southwest," says:

"I saw Wm. L. Yancey, for the first time, in the sum-
"mer of 1848. He had an interview with Mr. Calhoun,
"in the hall of the National Senate, when he was on his
"way to Baltimore, where the National Convention of
"the Democratic party were about assembling. Of
"what occurred at this interview, I received authentic
"and satisfactory information at the time. Mr. Cal-
"houn and Mr. Yancey, as well as many other pro-
"slavery men in the South, were not content with the

"protection understood to be given by the Federal "Constitution to slavery in the States where it then "existed, but desired to obtain for this institution additional organic guarantees. This they hoped to secure "through the instrumentality of the Democratic party, "and, with a view to this end, resolved to get, if they "could, a new plank in the accustomed political platform of that party, committing its members to the "adoption of a distinct *intervention* policy, and allowing slavery to be introduced into all the vacant territory of the Union. Mr. Yancey is well known to "have proceeded to Baltimore on the occasion referred "to, and to have made an effort to have such a resolution as has been described adopted by that body. "Failing in this, he withdrew from the convention in "disgust, returned to his own home in Alabama, and, "for some years thereafter, confined himself exclusively to the practice of his profession, in which he "had already become not a little distinguished. His "devotion to the study of law books was such as is not "often seen. Meanwhile, he read scientific and literary "works of acknowledged merit, and labored with a "most unremitting zeal to perfect himself in the art of "oratory. In a few years his fame as a jurist and "as a forensic advocate was widely diffused, and he attained such a degree of intellectual culture as placed "him far beyond the reach of all local rivalry."

When the National Democratic Convention met, YANCEY offered the Alabama resolutions, and they were rejected by a vote of 216 nays to only 36 ayes; so fixed at that day was the opinion of the Democratic party that Congress had the power, of itself or by its agent, to exclude slavery from the territories. The question with them was not one of power, but of justice. That the Democracy of Alabama were not wedded to the new doctrine, although they had declared in convention that under no stress of political necessity would they support a man who did not hold it, appears from the fact that they ratified the nomination of CASS, and when YANCEY declared that under the resolutions he could not support the nominee of the party, he was virtually ostracised. Although banished, but a few years elapsed before the party sought him in retirement and accepted his leadership.

While it is difficult to understand with what consistency YANCEY, who, by voting to apply the Missouri prohibition line to a part of Texas, had recognized the power of Congress to refuse admittance to a State applying with a constitution admitting slavery, could now lay down the counter-theory as the test of loyalty to the Constitution, it is not difficult to understand the reasons why the new position was taken. CALHOUN, in a letter to a member of the Alabama Legislature at this time, said that "instead of shunning we ought to court "the issue with the North on the slavery question"; that he would go one step farther and "force the issue "on the North." "We are now stronger, relatively," said Mr. Calhoun, "than we shall be hereafter politi-"cally and morally." From this day the action of the States-Rights party in Alabama and elsewhere became aggressive. The policy was no longer to find compromises by which grave and ever recurring questions could be evaded. It was now to hold the Free Soil element—the commercial States of New England—to the full measure of the Constitution. Whenever they forced an issue, the South was to meet it and force another.

The Free Soilers had constantly refused to abide by the Missouri Compromise. They would take nothing less than the abolition of slavery in all the territories by act of Congress. They would permit no master to take his slave servant in temporary travel through the North. They would permit no fugitive slave to be arrested. They would abolish the slave trade in the District. They would abolish slavery itself in the District. They would forbid the sale of slaves from one State to another. They would forbid slavery in all places belonging to the Government, even within the limits of slave States. At last they were beginning to contend that slavery was abolished in all the States by the Declaration of Independence.

In Alabama the contest of 1848, the period at which the aggressions of the Northern extremists were met by counter-aggressions from Southern extremists, was most violent. The States-Rights Whigs, who had joined the Democrats four years before, now returned to their ranks, and the Democracy threatened a rupture between the friends of YANCEY and that wing of the party which was led by BENJAMIN FITZPATRICK. The FITZPATRICK Democrats held with General CASS, and afterwards with Mr. DOUGLAS, that the honor and the interests of the South would be subserved by permitting the people of a territory to decide for themselves whether they would have slavery or not. They opposed breaking up the Union in the event Congress should refuse to enact a Territorial Code of laws recognizing and protecting slavery. The YANCEY Democrats denounced the CASS doctrine as "squatter sovereignty"; refused to accede to it, and threatened secession unless Congress protected slavery from the unfriendly legislation of the squatters.

They were ready and anxious to force the issue upon the North. The agitations and quarrels of half a century between the commercial and agricultural sections of the country had produced their fruit. The States-Rights men believed that now was the time for action, to organize their clubs, to inflame the people, and to precipitate at least the cotton States into revolution.

The Free Soilers of the North felt the fever of excitement which was being engendered at the South, fanned the flame, and held out to their excited brethren a wish that the Union might be dissolved. Senator HALE, of New Hampshire, presented a petition to the United States Senate to dissolve the Union. Senators SEWARD, CHASE and HALE voted to receive it. The apparent willingness with which the agitators of the North looked upon the idea of dissolution, and the often repeated threats and clamors for disunion, deceived the mass of Southern people into the delusion that secession might be peaceably accomplished. Thus both sections were learning to question coolly the value of the Union, and to look upon its dissolution as an escape from a disagreeable partnership. The idea of fighting to preserve such a partnership was gradually being banished farther and farther from the public mind.

While FANEUIL HALL, associated with so many delightful memories of the struggle for independence, was being thrown open to the meetings of the Boston Abolitionists, who had inscribed upon their banners—"The "Constitution, a covenant with death, an agreement with hell," and while its doors were being closed against DANIEL WEBSTER, the States-Rights men of the South were busily at work. CALHOUN had announced that now was the time for action. To wait longer would be to weaken the Southern cause. The issue must be forced upon the North. To wait until the North forced it upon the South by the purse and sword of a sectional administration would be suicidal. The course of President TAYLOR favored his schemes. The President had thrown himself into the arms of Mr. SEWARD. He disapproved the plan of adjustment proposed by Mr. CLAY, and pronounced in favor of the immediate admission of CALIFORNIA and in favor of the WILMOT PROVISO. The Southern WHIGS met in council and delegated Mr. C. M. CONRAD of Louisiana, Mr. HUMPHREY MARSHALL of Kentucky, and Mr. ROBERT TOOMBS of Georgia, to wait upon him and inform him that his Southern friends would be driven into opposition if he persisted in his course. His reply indicated that he would adhere to the Free Soil Whigs rather than to the Southern Whigs. The breaking up of the Whig party at that day would have thrown almost the entire population of the South into the ranks of the States Rights men, and would have precipitated in 1850 the revolution which the death of General TAYLOR postponed until 1860.

The violation on the part of the North of the rule agreed upon in the Missouri Compromise; by pressing the WILMOT PROVISO upon the South; by excluding Southern property from entrance into that territory which had been acquired by Southern blood and valor; by denying to the South an equal participation under the Constitution of the benefit of the common territories, plunged the people of the South into profound agitation. States-Rights men of all parties, Whigs, as well as Democrats, claimed that the Constitution which permitted and tolerated slavery in the States must likewise permit, tolerate and protect it in the territories so long as they belonged to all the States alike. It was difficult to deny this reasoning. To those who had inherited slaves and had grown familiar with the institution of slavery, it appeared as clear as the noon-day sun. Men like BENTON, who leaned to the Free Soilers, contended that under the Mexican law, forbidding slavery, California and New Mexico came to the Union with free territory, and must remain free unless some power inaugurated slavery there. This he claimed could not be done by Congress, as the Constitution could not establish slavery, however much it might protect it where it already existed. Men like WEBSTER contended that the Constitution was made for the States and not for the territories; that the territories were governed by rules and regulations made by Congress, and not by the articles of the Constitution; and that among those rules Congress might provide one, although Mr. Webster denied the policy of such action, against the introduction or continuance of slavery. To the first argument, Mr. CALHOUN replied that as soon as the treaty between Mexico and the United States was ratified, the sovereighty and authority of Mexico became extinct, and the Constitution took the place of Mexican law. To the second he replied that the rules and regulations adopted by Congress for the government of the territories must be constitutional and could not be arbitrary, and that in framing them the right of the people of the South to enjoy their property in the common territory must be observed.

Resistance to the several measures before Congress became the cry of the States-Rights party. In Mississippi, a county meeting proposed a convention at

NASHVILLE of all the Southern States, to take steps for a redress of grievances. In South Carolina, in Georgia and in Alabama, mass meetings were held in almost every county, denouncing the bills, and counseling resistance in the event they should become law. These meetings were participated in by States Rights Whigs as well as Democrats, although the great bulk of the protestants were from the Democratic ranks. The Whigs for the most part were content to remain quiet and await the issue. The members of the General Assembly of Alabama, at an informal meeting, nominated delegates to the proposed Nashville convention. They were selected from both of the political parties. Among those who attended, were BENJAMIN FITZPATRICK, WM. COOPER, JOHN A. CAMPBELL, THOS. J. JUDGE, JOHN A. WINSTON, L. P. WALKER, WM. M. MURPHY, NICH DAVIS, REUBEN C. SHORTER, THOS. A. WALKER, REUBEN CHAPMAN, JAMES ABERCROMBIE, WM. M. BYRD—men of the highest position in the State, of enlarged views, and of the strictest integrity. Many of those who attended the convention did so with a view to prevent extreme action.

The convention met June 3, 1850. The compromise measures proposed by Mr. CLAY were then pending, but the impression prevailed that they would be rejected. WM. L. SHARKEY, Whig, was made President of the convention. In his introductory speech he took occasion to say that they met, not to dissolve the Union, but to preserve it. The views of Mr. SHARKEY, however, were not the views of the convention. While the majority of the Virginia, Alabama and Tennessee delegations opposed the whole design of the meeting, the delegates from South Carolina, Mississippi, Texas and other States favored a clear declaration of resistance. JOHN A. CAMPBELL, of Alabama, afterwards a Justice of the Supreme Court of the United States, prepared and read the resolutions. They were cautious and prudent, condemning the Wilmot Proviso and the other proposed hostile legislation, but concluding not to advise a method of resistance, in the confident expectation that Congress would not adjourn without a final settlement of the questions in dispute. These resolutions were a substantial defeat of the South Carolina programme; but to show the sentiment of the convention an address was prepared to accompany the resolutions. This address not only denounced the several independent propositions before Congress, but also denounced the pending compromise of Mr. CLAY. THOMAS J. JUDGE, of Alabama, moved to strike out that part of the address condemnatory of the compromise. The Alabama delegation sustained Mr. Judge, as did portions of other delegations, but the motion failed. Mr. ABERCROMBIE, of Alabama, moved that the vote of each individual be recorded; and thus it was seen that the Whigs of the convention generally voted to accept the compromise, and the Democrats generally voted against its acceptance. Mr. SHARKEY declined to vote upon the proposition to strike out. He spoke in favor of it, but was induced, because of his position as President, to refrain from recording his vote. The convention adjourned to be called together by President SHARKEY after the action of Congress on the compromise measures. He declined to call them together again, and thus the movement for concerted resistance fell still-born.

Upon the return of the Alabama delegates from Nashville, a meeting was held at Montgomery to ratify the action of the convention. Mr. YANCEY addressed the meeting with his usual ability and earnestness. He said that it was his belief that the North would not do the South justice, that it was "time to set our house "in order," and to sustain Texas if need be with the bayonet. This appeal of Mr. YANCEY tended to arouse the spirit of especially the young men. It operated powerfully upon those who had volunteered in defence of the rights of Texas and had fought the battles of Mexico. When Texas won her independence the Rio Grande from its mouth to the source was yielded up by Mexico as her western boundary. But now the Free Soilers were intent upon carving out a territory, to be called New Mexico, from the soil of Texas, with the sole object of making it a free State. This was so flagrant a violation of the rights of Texas that the eloquence of YANCEY, in denunciation of the scheme, aroused a spirit of injury and resentment in the breast of thousands of those who still hoped for a satisfactory adjustment of the dispute.

From the meeting of the Nashville Convention in June to the passage by the Senate of Mr. Clay's compromise measures in August, political excitement was intense. The Abolitionists denounced the proposed fugitive slave law as violative of morality. The Free Soilers rejected by repeated votes in Congress every proposition to apply the Missouri Compromise line to the new territory. The obstinacy of the anti-slavery men was met by an equal obstinacy at the South. The Democratic press were almost unanimous in repudiation of Mr. Clay's measures. The Southern Rights associations denounced the compromise. The Montgomery *Advertiser and Gazette*, one of the leading journals of

Alabama, made incessant assaults upon the several measures of compromise and called for their rejection, although it was very evident that their rejection would be followed instantly by the secession of South Carolina. In South Carolina, and among the States-Rights men, especially in Mississippi, Alabama and Georgia, it was hoped that the plan of adjustment would fail, the secessionists being confident that now was the hour to strike.

On the other hand the dominant, but for awhile suppressed, sentiment of the people was in favor of the plan. The undercurrent of patriotism hoped that the compromise might succeed. In the language of CLAIBORNE, writing before the late war a memoir of QUITMAN: "But as the boldest tremble on the verge of eter-"nity, and shrink from the dark abyss beyond which "all is uncertain, so they were willing to postpone for "posterity this dread solution. Not one of them but "would have shed his blood freely for his country, and "now they clung to this compromise as the mariner "clings to the last plank in the surging seas. Let "those who feel themselves infallible sit in inexorable "judgment on the motives of their fellows, and con-"demn CLAY, BENTON, WEBSTER and CALHOUN, the lead-"ing advocates of the plan of reconciliation. Such "judgment is not for me. Had these four men pro-"nounced the words 'No Compromise,' war would most "probably have ensued—fratricidal war! And who "knows but that the God of vengeance and of right-"eousness would have stamped upon us the brand of "CAIN, and sent us to wander over the earth vagabonds "among the nations?"

Upon the passage of the compromise measures Governor SEABROOK, of South Carolina, wrote to Governor QUITMAN, of Mississippi, to know whether he would call the Legislature together to consider grievances. QUITMAN replied that he had issued his proclamation convening that body November 18th. SEABROOK expressed his gratification, and said that it was policy for South Carolina not to take the initiative, but that "she is "ready and anxious for immediate separation from the "Union." The General Assembly of South Carolina voted resolutions suggesting a Southern Congress, to meet at Montgomery, June 2d, 1852. They voted also the sum of $350,000 to arm the State. The feeling in Texas was apparently as deep as that in Mississippi. That State earnestly protested against that portion of the compromise which cut away her territory north of thirty-six degrees thirty minutes and added it to New Mexico. She denied the right of Congress to dismember a State for any purpose, and she denied the policy of doing so simply to appease the Free Soil professed regard for the sanctity of the Missouri Compromise line. Governor BELL convoked the Texas Legislature and called for one thousand volunteers to defend the unity of Texas. General QUITMAN, writing to General PINCKNEY HENDERSON, said that he was willing to draw his sword for Texas, and that so soon as a collision of arms appeared inevitable he would convene the Mississippi Legislature. Soon after, he issued his proclamation, basing the call upon outrages imposed upon the South by the compromise legislation. Upon the meeting of the Legislature he advised a call for a State Convention to act in concert with other States, or separately, in changing the relations of the State with the Federal Government. The Legislature decided to call a convention for September, 1851. [For the period of one year, therefore, the people of Mississippi were greatly agitated upon the question of acceptance or rejection of the compromise.] The Whigs, led by Sharkey, aided by a strong detachment of Democrats, formed a Union party, aroused the people, returned a majority of the State Convention, and elected Senator HENRY S. FOOTE Governor over Col. JEFFERSON DAVIS. Governor QUITMAN had been the original candidate against Mr. FOOTE, but had retired from the canvass when the people pronounced against secession in the election of members of the convention. Mr. DAVIS was nominated towards the close of the canvass. The issue of secession, being presented clearly and distinctly to the people of Mississippi, it was clearly and distinctly repudiated.

In Georgia the public excitement was quite as intense as in Mississippi, South Carolina and Texas. There a State convention was also called to consider the measure and remedy for grievances. In the election of members a large majority of Union men were returned. The resolutions of that convention, known as the "Georgia Platform of 1850," were reported by CHARLES J. JENKINS, a Whig, and an eminent lawyer. ALEXANDER H. STEPHENS was one of the committee who reported them. It was resolved, that as our fathers yielded to compromise to frame the Constitution, they should yield somewhat for its continuance; that while not approving all the measures of adjustment, they accepted and abided by them: and that Georgia should resist to the utmost any effort to interfere with the rights of the people of the South under the compromise. Nothing was said as to the right of secession; Mr. STEPHENS and other Whigs upon the committee believing in that right.

In the election for Governor, HOWELL COBB, the candidate of the Union party, was elected by an overwhelming majority.

Even in South Carolina the Union party, uniting their forces with the Co-operation party, exhibited such unexpected strength, that it was clear that an attempt at separate secession would meet resistance within her own borders; that the call of a Federal marshal to sustain a mandate of a Federal Court, would have rallied to his support a vast number of determined citizens, and precipitated civil war in every district.

General QUITMAN, to whom an appeal had been made to take the leadership in the secession movement, saw that even the Gulf States would refuse to act in concert. Writing to Colonel JOHN S. PRESTON of South Carolina, he said that the only way to arouse the South was for one State to secede, that the South would be startled, and the people be compelled to take sides upon a plain issue of coercion. Said he: "Should the Federal "Government attempt to employ force, an active and "cordial union of the whole South would be instantly "effected, and a complete Southern Confederacy organ-"ized." Believing this to be true the convention of Southern Rights Associations met at Charleston and arrived at the conclusion with but few dissenting voices, that although co-operation was in every respect desirable, still, resistance alone by South Carolina was to be preferred to obedience to the compromise laws. Men like BUTLER, BARNWELL, and ORR, opposed separate action, while men like PETTIGRU, opposing secession in either way, threw their numbers on the side of co-operation. The people of South Carolina met in convention, May, 1851. The two-thirds majority necessary to pass the ordinance for separate secession was wanting; the minority report recommending co-operation was ably advocated by Mr. ORR, and finally commanded the support of more than one-third of the convention.

In Alabama the contest waged as warmly as in the other States, and it was now that the Union principles, taught the people by the Whigs and Jackson Democrats in the campaign of 1840, became their guide. Brave, impetuous, spirited and defiant, it was difficult for her citizens to regard the aggressions of New England with patience. They saw their friends reviled as inhuman; their own fathers, as slave holders, read from the church by the anti-slavery party of the North; they saw the post offices teeming with incendiary publications; the United States flag displaced by the State flag on the Massachusetts State House; and the Constitution nullified by the passage of what was called personal liberty bills. Not only nullification, but they heard disunion openly proclaimed by the "Emancipa-"tor," and other kindred newspapers; they saw the leading Free Soil journal publishing an ode addressed to the flag of the United States—"Tear down that flaunt-"ing lie." They saw the Abolitionist, GARRISON, admitted to Faneuil Hall, and its doors closed against DANIEL WEBSTER, because of his opposition to the Wilmot Proviso. In spite of all these outrages, spurning the flag, trampling on the Constitution, nullifying laws, and rending the very churches in twain, the Union men of Alabama did not despond nor despair. They saw that the outcry against "the slave power" was simply an electioneering scheme of politicians at the North, that the South had not the slaves with which to populate territories as fast as the North could populate them with European immigrants, and with their own drifting anti-slavery people; that the preservation of the balance of power in the Lower House of Congress was an impossibility, and that its preservation in the Senate was doomed by the inability of the South to keep pace with the North in point of numbers; that the preservation of the rights of the South was only possible by a union of right thinking men North and South; and that slavery could be protected only under the flag of the Union. Above all, they saw the greatness and glory of our infant Republic; the freedom of thought, speech and action permitted in this, the last and only refuge of freemen; the light burden of Government; and the opportunities for fortune, peace, contentment and happiness. "Honor and praise," said RUFUS CHOATE "to the eminent men of all parties who rose "that day to the measure of a true greatness; who "remembered that they had a country to preserve as "well as a local constituency to gratify; who laid all "the wealth and all the hopes of illustrious lives on the "altar of a hazardous patriotism; who reckoned all the "sweets of a present popularity for nothing in comparison with that more exceeding weight of glory which "follows him who seeks to compose an agitated and "to save a sinking land."

For the purpose of calling out the Union sentiment of the State, a mass meeting was held at Montgomery soon after the passage of the compromise measures. It was presided over by judge BENAJAH S. BIBB, brother of the first two Governors of Alabama, and cousin of one of the colleagues of HENRY CLAY, in the United States Senate. Among the orators of the occasion was JAMES ABERCROMBIE, who had served many years in both houses of the Alabama Legislature, was afterwards a member of Congress from the Montgomery district, and who had headed the CLAY electoral ticket in 1844; THOMAS J. JUDGE, a promising lawyer of Lowndes county, who had also served with distinction in the Legislature, and who had striven, but unsuccessfully, to strike from the Nashville address the denunciation of the compromise; HENRY W. HILLIARD, an eloquent and cultivated orator, who had long adorned the Whig cause, had served in Congress and represented the country abroad; and THOMAS H. WATTS, a young lawyer of growing reputation, of large practice, unbounded personal popularity, and who was destined subsequently to become a Governor of his State, and the Attorney General of the Southern Confederacy.

The resolutions of the meeting in which these men participated expressed a warm and confident attachment to the Union and denounced as unnecessary and dangerous the systematic and formidable organization, in progress in South Carolina, aided and abetted in certain portions of other States, especially Georgia and Mississippi, having for its object violent resistance to the compromise acts. A letter was read from Senator WILLIAM R. KING, in which he said that he could see no justifiable ground for resorting to these revolutionary measures, which he regretted to find were openly advocated by some of our worthiest citizens; with such men he had no sympathy; he was no disunionist. Letters of a similar character were read from other distinguished Alabamians. CHARLES J. JENKINS, of Georgia, wrote that at present he could see "no cause for "the revolutionary right of secession." Evidently a formidable fraction of the Democratic party were favorable to acceptance of the compromise.

Cotemporaneously with this meeting, States-Rights associations sprung up all over the State of Alabama. They breathed hostility to the compromise and threatened resistance; without, however, naming the method of resistance. They stigmatised the Union men as submissionists. The Montgomery States-Rights Association took issue with the Union meeting and sent a written challenge to the Unionists to meet them in public debate. The *Advertiser and Gazette* daily assailed the compromise, applauded the followers of YANCEY, and denounced the Union men by name. Yet all this time, the editor of that journal, Col. J. J. SEIBELS, a gentleman who had commanded a regiment in the Mexican war and stood high as a citizen and a lawyer, submitted to the people no plan of resistance. He was a member of the States-Rights Association. If his remedy was not by going out of the Union, it must have been by repealing the compromise legislation Yet that legislation could not be repealed, for California was already admitted; and the compromise gave the South and North equal rights in all the territory acquired from Mexico. It also gave the South protection for her fugitives. It is, therefore, fair to infer that Colonel SEIBELS was in favor of secession by the most direct means. While YANCEY and SEIBELS were actuated by identical principles, the clubs with which they acted were divided as to the proper redress for grievances—whether secession should be accomplished by separate State action, or by co-operative action after deliberation in a Southern Congress. At this point it must be borne in mind that while men like SEIBELS, of Alabama, and BARNWELL, of South Carolina, favored co-operation of the slave States as the best and most certain step to secession, others favored co-operation because, unwilling to be ranked as submissionists, but yet firmly opposed to disunion in any shape, they looked upon co-operation as a bungling and cumbersome machine which must invariably prevent secession, as it had recently done at Nashville. One branch of the co-operationists were secessionists; another, and by far the larger, branch were Union men. It was the timidity of this last branch, who advocated co-operative resistance while seeking to prevent resistance, that ten years later placed them in a false position and gave the control of the State into the hands of the separate secessionists.

To settle the question as to the mode of redress, the Pleasant Hill, Dallas county, Club resolved that whereas there was a difference of opinion about the mode of resistance, a State Convention should meet and decide the matter. The *Advertiser and Gazette* joined in this call, declaring that the great object and the inevitable end of the Union movement "is and will be the abolition of slavery throughout the United States, and the people had as well prepare to resist, or make up their minds to submit to it *now*." The State Convention of States-Rights clubs met at Montgomery, February 10, 1851. THOMAS WILLIAMS, of Montgomery, a native of South Carolina, was made President. ADAM C. FELDER, also a native of South Carolina, was made Secretary. Among the prominent gentlemen who participated in the meeting were W. L. YANCEY, SAMUEL J. RICE, JOEL E. MATTHEWS, JOHN A. ELMORE, DAVID CLOPTON, GEORGE GOLDTHWAITE, J. J. SEIBELS, ABRAM MARTIN, A. P. BAGBY and B. F. SAFFOLD.

The Convention, after rehearsing the grievances of the South and the unsatisfactory character of the compromise legislation, resolved "that a tame submission "to or a patient acquiescence in this hostile and uncon-"stitutional legislation would not in our [their] opinion "be conducive to the peace, happiness, prosperity and honor of the Southern States." They resolved, further, that all old parties should be suspended, that a new Southern party should be formed, that the Governor should call the Legislature together for the passage of an act enabling the people to elect delegates to a Southern Congress; that if the Governor should fail to do so, the people are advised to open polls and hold an election for such purpose, and that should such Southern Congress, when assembled, decide that the Southern States should secede from the Union, and if one or more States, in accordance with that decision, should actually secede, it would be the duty and the interest of Alabama also to secede, and to aid in the formation of a Southern Confederacy.

This action of the Convention did not satisfy the separate secession wing of the party, nor did it satisfy the opposing party. The separate action men looked upon the election of a Southern Congress by all the Southern States as a virtual abandonment of resistance, for it was evident that a majority of such a Congress would never decide for secession. Virginia, Tennessee, Kentucky and Missouri would be a unit against it, and the other States would be more or less divided. To the Union men it appeared that the Convention were resolving that "I dare not" should wait upon "I would." Thereupon the Union leaders used every exertion to force the States-Rights associations to a more definite declaration of their intentions. To all these efforts Col. SEIBELS, in his journal, replied: "If Mr. WATTS and his "Federal Consolidation Fillmore friends could get us to "make this issue before the people, he is confident of "success—for he is satisfied that the Secessionists are "in a great minority in the State. * * * * "Now, so far as we are concerned, we shall not present "the issue of secession, whatever our individual opinion "on the subject may be, but we shall unite and go with "the States-Rights men of the State who are opposed to "your absolute, unconditional-submission doctrines with "the old obnoxious doctrine of Federal Whiggery "combined."

MR. YANCEY was not satisfied with this half-aggressive, half-defensive movement. He was not one of those who rode like the Mexican lancers at Contreras, starting at a charge with ribbons and pennants dancing to the wind, and as they near the point of concussion subsiding to a gallop, then to a trot, then to a walk, and finally to a halt. His policy was to charge with accelerated velocity, with lance in rest and helmet down, striking for the centre of the enemy's line. The movement which Mr. YANCEY favored was that of the leading statesmen of South Carolina—separate State action. It is true that in December, 1850, the South Carolina Legislature resolved to suggest and to send delegates to a Southern Congress to be held at MONTGOMERY, and to call a State Convention for consideration of the action of the proposed Congress, but it is also true that the people were in advance of their representatives. The idea of a co-operative movement was seen to be futile. The Nashville Convention had met with delegates regularly appointed from only two States, South Carolina and Mississippi; and the latter of these had provided that the action of the Congress should be submitted to a vote of the people. It had proven a *fiasco*, which had retarded rather than advanced the secession movement. During the winter session of 1850 of the South Carolina Legislature the separate-action party grew in strength daily, until in the following May Governor MEANS wrote to General QUITMAN that "there is now "not the slightest doubt but that the next Legislature "will call the Convention (State) together at a period "during the ensuing year and when that convention "meets the State will secede." Governor MEANS also said: "We are anxious for co-operation, and also anx-"ious that some other State should take the lead; but "from recent developments we are satisfied that South "Carolina is the only State in which sufficient unanim-"ity exists to commence the movement."

The Resistance party in Mississippi were as hesitating as that in Alabama. Col. MAXEY GREGG, writing to General QUITMAN urged him to hoist the banner of secession. He said: "I believe that if the resistance "party in Mississippi will now abandon all temporizing "and come out boldly for secession, they will greatly in-"crease the chance of success in the struggles with the "submissionists. But if they flinch from the issue of "disunion, they will suffer at once from all the odium "of the measures of South Carolina and all the weak-"ness of a false position. Let them contend manfully "for secession, and, even if beaten in the elections, they "will form a minority so powerful in moral influence, "that when South Carolina secedes, the first drop of "blood that is shed will cause an irresistible popular "impulse in their favor, and the submissionists will be "crushed." This was the plan finally adopted by South Carolina leaders. This was the plan urged by QUITMAN in Mississippi, and by YANCEY in Alabama. Neither of these men were strategists, nor temporizers. They put no value on victory apart from principles; they preferred defeat to equivocation; and hence it was that General QUITMAN after calling the State Convention in Mississippi, and seeing a majority of Union men returned to it, retired in disgust from the canvass; and hence it was that Mr. YANCEY not satisfied with the half-way movement of the States-Rights Convention at Montgomery made an issue with that body and hoisted the banner of separate secession. From that moment his labor was to gain over to his views the different clubs, then to press his views upon the States-Rights party in county meetings, and finally to imprint them upon the Democratic party banner.

Mr. WATTS, although a believer in the right of the State to secede from the Union, and an ardent States-Rights man, was opposed, as has been said, to the policy of secession, and was a most efficient leader of the Union element. He vainly endeavored to draw from the States-Rights associations an admission that they favored secession. But while the admission was wanting, the people thoroughly understood that an unqualified admission was not necessary to prove their design. However much the one or the other party might evade or shirk the issue, the contest in Alabama in 1851 was undoubtedly between Union and Secession.

In a controversy such as this, which so fearfully agitated the South, it was not possible to conceal or keep out of view the main question, whether a State has a right to secede from the Union peaceably. That question necessarily played a conspicuous part in the discussions. The friends of the compromise in the Alabama Legislature called a State Union Convention. It met January 19th, 1851, at Montgomery. JAMES E. BELSER, a prominent lawyer of Montgomery and recently a member of Congress, was made President. Among the delegates were THOMAS B. COOPER, R. M. PATTON, W. M. BYRD, B. S. BIBB, J. M. TARLETON, W. B. MOSS, JAMES H. CLANTON, LEWIS E. PARSONS, ROBERT J. JEMISON, H. W. HILLIARD, R. W. WALKER, THOMAS H. WATTS, NICH. DAVIS, JR., B. M. WOOLSEY, C. M. WILCOX, and W. A. ASHLEY. This Convention accepted the compromise legislation. They went further and denied the right of secession. They resolved that when governments become too grievous to be borne it is the right and duty of a people to "boldly defy its authority "by asserting in the spirit of the Revolution their "purpose to be free and independent." The remedy here set forth against tyranny, was clearly intended to present an issue with the Secessionists. That remedy was in their opinion not a reserved right of secession but such a right as our fathers exercised when they threw off the yoke of Great Britain. The spirit of the Revolution was the spirit of rebellion—an appeal to arms and not to law. To leave no doubt that the convention recognized no other mode of redress for grievances except that set forth in the Declaration of Independence, they resolved further: "That the asserted "right of secession of a State from the Union is un-"authorized by the Federal Constitution." Had they stopped here their declaration would have been pointless, for no one contended that the Federal Constitution either asserted or denied the right of secession; the

Secessionists holding that the right was reserved to the States among the residuary powers not granted to the Federal Constitution. But the resolution continued as follows: "But we claim it as a paramount right which "belongs to every free people to overthrow their gov- "ernment when it fails to answer the ends for which it "was established." There can be no dispute as to the meaning of this clause of the resolution. It means simply such revolution as our fathers waged against Great Britain—nothing more nor less. Had the Convention said that they claim it as a paramount right which belongs to every State of the Union to overthrow the government, their meaning might possibly have admitted of doubt, although the act of secession as recognized by the States-Rights men could not properly be spoken of as an overthrow of the government, being simply a retiring from a government which would still have actual force and effect among the States which remained confederated. But the claim of the Convention was that redress of tyranny could be effected only by means of that paramount right which belongs to every free people. The paramount right which belongs to every free people is simply the right of rebellion—the right to be styled patriot if successful like WASHINGTON—the right to be called traitor if unsuccessful like WILLIAM WALLACE or KOSSUTH, KOSCIUSKO or LOPEZ.

There were doubtless individuals in the Union Convention like Mr. WATTS and others, educated in the law school of the University of Virginia, who recognized the right of secession as claimed by HAYNE and CALHOUN. To such persons it must have appeared that an abstract right on the part of seceding States, which the non-seceding States denied, was in substance nothing but the natural right of revolution which every people possessed, and over which it was needless to waste words or raise an issue.

While these States-Rights Whigs remained silent over the anti-secession resolution, the vast body of the Union party, Whigs and Democrats, undoubtedly endorsed the resolution in its plain meaning most heartily. In evidence of this fact it is well to notice the cotemporaneous expressions of leading members and representatives of the party.

The WHIG newspaper at Montgomery, the JOURNAL, hoisted at the head of its columns the name of BENJAMIN GLOVER SHIELDS as the Union candidate for Governor. Mr. SHIELDS was a native of ABBEVILLE, South Carolina; had been a member of the Alabama General Assembly several years, was a member of Congress in 1841, and Minister to VENEZUELA under Mr. POLK. He was an active member of the Democratic party. So devoted and unqualified was his attachment to the Union that in a published card in reply to those who had nominated him for Governor, he said: "I am for "this Federal Union of ours under all circumstances "and at all hazards; right or wrong, I am for the "Union."

Not so unqualifiedly, but with equal distinctness, the several Union candidates for Congress uttered their repudiation of secession. C. C. LANGDON, of the First District, denied the right of secession. JAMES ABERCROMBIE, of the Second District, denounced the proposed action of South Caroliua, and spoke of walling her in with Federal authority in the event of secession, and of starving her to death on rice. Judge MUDD, of the

Third District, acknowledged the right of a State to secede, but at the same time admitted the right of the Federal Government to enforce its laws within her limits. W. R. SMITH, of the Fourth District, spoke at Tuskaloosa, and was thus reported by the *Monitor:* "He "denied the right of peaceable secession as it is called, "in all its phases, and sustained his position most tri-"umphantly." The *Monitor* added: "This thing "they call the right of peaceable secession is in our "view too preposterous to spend words about. We "acknowledge no such right." WILLIAMSON R. W. COBB, in the Fifth District, denied the right of secession *in toto.* GEORGE S. HOUSTON, in the Sixth District, also denied the right. In the Seventh District, ALEXANDER WHITE likewise denied the right of a State to secede.

In the County of LAUDERDALE, one of the richest of the Tennessee Valley, a number of questions were propounded to the candidates for the General Assembly. ROBERT M. PATTON, one of the candidates for the Senate, and afterwards Governor of the State, replied to the questions in these words:

"I do not believe that any State has the Constitu-"tional or reserved right to secede from the Union.

"All laws passed by Congress in pursuance of the "Constitution are the supreme laws of the land as well "in a State attempting secession as in any other State. "So I say that I believe that the President of the "United States has the Constitutional right to execute "all the laws of Congress within the limits of any "seceding State.

"My matured opinion is that the Legislature of Ala-"bama should refuse positively to give countenance to "any State attempting to resist with force the execution "of the laws of Congress within her limits; and as a "loyal citizen, and as a true patriot, I hold it to be my "duty to aid, if necessary, the supremacy of the Con-"stitution and laws."

So answered the other candidates, RICHARD W. WALKER, V. M. BENHAM, and S. C. SHEFFIELD.

The CONSTITUTIONAL UNION Club of Montgomery had frequent meetings, at which prominent citizens delivered addresses. At one of these meetings, THOMAS J. JUDGE spoke, denying the right of South Carolina to secede, and sustaining the right of the Federal Government to enforce its laws within her limits if she should do so. The *Advertiser* charged Mr. JUDGE with having advocated the right of coercion. This brought out a communication from him in which he said: "I contended "that if she seceded I would not be in favor of the "General Government 'subjugating' her, or making "her a 'subjugated province,' that I did not believe "the General Government had such power, nor had I "ever heard such power claimed; but I insisted it "would be the duty of the General Government to en-"force its Constitution and laws; that the Constitution "and laws had been enforced in South Carolina ever "since she had been a member of the Union, and if that "had not made her a 'subjugated province' the con-"tinuing to enforce the same Constitution and laws "would not make her so."

So clear was the sentiment of the UNION party against the right of secession that the *Advertiser* published the following summary of their views without denial from the opposing press:

"As deducible from their party presses, their great

" leaders and public speakers generally in this city and " elsewhere, they deny the right of peaceable secession " by a sovereign State. In case a sovereign State does " secede they look upon it as rebellion and contend for " the right of the General Government to, coerce and " subjugate her ; or, which is the same thing, they in- " sist that the General Government should enforce its " laws within the limits of the seceding State, after she " had seceded ; and to this end should apply whatever " force may be necessary for the purpose. They de- " fend the late compromise against the opposition and " resistance of the States-Rights men, and therefore ap- " prove of the admission of California, of the abolition of " the slave trade, and slavery too under some circum- " stances in the District of Columbia, and the dismem- " berment of Texas."

Apart from the unfairness of saying that acquiescence in the compromise was equivalent to approval of all its features, this summary very justly expresses the views and opinions of the Union party of 1850–'51—that party which in the subsequent election filled the General Assembly with men, who unlike those of Georgia, South Carolina and Mississippi, refused to call a State Convention, a party which forced the re-election of a Union Governor, returned four out of the seven Congressmen and carried the popular vote by a large majority. So strong was Alabama fixed in the Union faith that not the sound of a cannon would have shaken her then from her moorings.

CHAPTER XII.

The Montgomery District—Contest of States-Rights and Union Men over Yancey—The Georgia Platform—Yancey Retires and Cochran Takes His Place—Report of the Southern Rights Association—Defeat of the Yancey Party—Scheme to Acquire Cuba—Lopez and Quitman—Federal Arrest of a Governor—Reorganization of Parties—The Southern Whigs—The Whig Convention at Baltimore—Reply of Scott and Pierce to the States-Rights Associations, Etc., Etc.

"But the indissoluble link of Union between the people of the several States of this confederated nation is, after all, not in the right, but in the heart. If the day should ever come (may Heaven avert it!) when the affections of the people of these States shall be alienated from each other, when the fraternal spirit shall give way to cold indifference or collisions of interest shall fester into hatred, the bands of political association will not long hold together parties no longer attracted by the magnetism of conciliated interests and kindly sympathies; and far better will it be for the people of the disunited States to part in friendship from each other, than to be held together by constraint."

ADDRESS OF J. Q. ADAMS BEFORE THE N. Y. HIST. SOC., 1839.

The MONTGOMERY Congressional District, composed of some of the largest slave counties of the State, inhabited by descendents of Georgians, Virginians and Carolinians, occupied a most prominent position in the politics of Alabama. It was nearly divided between the two great political parties. Containing the capitol, it enjoyed a legal bar equal to that of any other portion of the State; and her mass meetings were therefore frequently addressed by the ablest men of the State. At that time Montgomery was upon the most direct highway from New Orleans to New York. The energy and intellect of the whole country became familiar with her people, and aided to impart to them that intelligence and independence of character which is the result to so large a degree of contact with the world. This district had been ably represented in Congress for a number of years. DIXON H. LEWIS had won for himself a national reputation. HENRY W. HILLIARD was also well known throughout the Union. WILLIAM L. YANCEY had also made for himself a national reputation. These gentlemen, better known, were not however superior in point of character and ability to many others who had not yet played a part upon the national arena. With the States-Rights men it was a matter not only of ambition, but almost of necessity to wrest this district from the hands of the Whigs, who had held it but by an uncertain tenure for some years. On the other hand it was a matter of pride for the Whigs to continue to hold it, and for the Union man to defeat at his own door the plan of Mr. YANCEY for precipitating secession.

In April, 1851, the District Convention of the Southern Rights party met at CLAYTON and nominated Mr YANCEY for Congress. In May, a Union Convention met at the same place and nominated JAMES ABERCROMBIE. The resolutions of this latter convention presented an earnest "appeal to all quiet and law-abiding citizens "to aid with their influence and votes in arresting the "wild and fiery spirit of disunion." The Convention also adopted the Georgia Platform, which accepted the compromise measures as a permanent adjustment of sectional controversy. That platform after accepting the compromise measures provided that the South should, even to a disruption of the Union, resist certain measures if attempted by Congress. The measures to be resisted were these: Abolition by Congress of slavery in the district without the consent of the owners; abolition of slavery at places owned by the United States in the slave States; suppression of slave trade between the States; refusal to admit as a State any territory applying for admission because of the existence of slavery therein; any act prohibiting the introduction of slaves into the territories of Utah and New Mexico; any act repealing or materially modifying the fugitive slave law. This enumeration of acts of Congress which would justify resistance does not include an act of Congress prohibiting the introduction of slavery into other territory than that acquired from Mexico. The reason for this omission may be found in the fact that the compromise measures of 1850 were held to deal only with the Mexican territory. The Missouri Compromise dealt only with the territory acquired with Louisiana. The latter act was held by the Whigs generally not to have been repealed by the former. They argued that it did not follow, because a part of the Mexican acquisition extended above 36 degrees 30 minutes, and any part even above that line, might come into the Union with slavery, therefore an act forbidding slavery above 36 degrees 30 minutes in the Louisiana acquisition was null and void. The Georgia platform therefore, holding to the compromise of 1850 as a final adjustment declared that the exclusion by Congress of slavery from any of the Mexican acquisition justified resistance, and was silent as to a similar exclusion from other territory. In the opinion of the friends of that platform the whole question of slavery in the territories was settled so far as the Mexican territory was concerned by the compromise of 1850; and so far as the rest of the territories was concerned, by the Missouri Compromise. If this had not been their opinion they would have announced in their platform that the prohibition by Congress of the introduction of slaves into *any* of the territories would justify resistance.

The Union Convention of the Montgomery District, adopting the Georgia platform, held that the Missouri Compromise was not repealed by the compromise of 1850. Mr. STEPHENS, in his "History of the United States for schools," says that the compromise for 1850 established the principle of non-intervention for all the territories in lieu of the Missouri Compromise. As he was one of the committee who drafted the Georgia platform it is strange that he provided for resistance as to Utah and New Mexico, and not as to other territory. The argument set forth at a much later day than 1850 that the Missouri restriction was removed by the adoption of the new compromise which omitted such a restriction in the case of the newly acquired territory (a restriction to which the first compromise, of course, could not apply), did not meet the approval of the Whigs and Union Democrats of 1851. They held that in these compromises there was no question of principle; and that the Missouri restriction over territory of the Louisiana purchase was no more inconsistent with non-restriction over territory of the Mexican purchase, than restriction above the line of 36 degrees, 30 minutes, was inconsistent with non-restriction below the line.

Immediately following the Union Convention, the Southern Rights Association met at Montgomery and was addressed by Mr. YANCEY in one of his brilliant and captivating speeches. He declared that the only issue before the people was secession, and that he would make no false issue; that his principles were founded on the Constitution and must ultimately prevail; that he wore them as a frontlet between his eyes that all the world might see them. He thereupon proposed a series of resolutions urging separate secession. He stated that he had private advices to the effect that South Carolina would secede the next spring; that she had one hundred pieces of artillery ready, more than twenty thousand small arms, and a large quantity of military stores. Mr. YANCEY declined the nomination for Congress. He fully understood that the people were not ready for his extreme movement, and hence determined not to let defeat dim the lustre of his shield. In his letter declining the nomination he said that there were but two parties, the Secession party and the Submission party. Rehearsing the perils of the South and the difficulty of co-operation, he closed by saying "In this "view I am decidedly in favor of preparing the State "by all proper means for exerting the right of "secession."

In marked contrast with Mr. YANCEY's letter was that of Mr. ABERCROMBIE accepting the Union nomination. He stood by the measures of 1850, and planted himself firmly on the Georgia platform. He would battle for the Union, with the slavery question settled as to the territories and not to be disturbed, but he would not submit to further encroachments at the hands of the North.

JOHN COCHRAN, of Eufaula, a lawyer of great ability, was nominated in place of Mr. YANCEY. This gentleman after the passage of the compromise measures had written a letter to Mr. RITCHIE, editor of the Washington

Union, in which he said that "they perfect the degra-"dation of the South in the Union, and nothing can "redeem her but secession." Further on, he said: "I pray God that the South may tear herself from the "power of the monster which does not conceal its pur-"pose. I do not think the Union will be dissolved "immediately, but I believe, and rejoice in the belief, "that at this moment there is amongst us here a leaven "of disunion, which by a more or less rapid, but per-"ceptibly certain, process will leaven the whole lump. "We feel that in the confederacy we are degraded, and "have now no remedy but secession." The author of these sentiments was sustained in the canvass by Mr. YANCEY, the States-Rights associations, and by almost the entire Democratic party. On the other hand Mr. ABERCROMBIE was sustained by Mr. HILLIARD, the entire Whig party, and a few hundred Union Democrats. It may be said that the contest in this district was one between the Whig party as representing submission to the Compromise Acts, and the Democratic party as representing secession from the Union.

Mr. COCHRAN was a member of the Southern Rights Association of Eufaula. That association had adopted a report on "Southern wrongs and remedies" made by the chairman of a committee, JAMES L. PUGH, Esq., afterward member of Congress, which set forth the views of the States-Rights party upon the questions at issue and left no doubt as to the position held by Mr. COCHRAN.

I. The report reviewed the compromise measures at length. It declared that the admission of California, without the formality of a preceding territorial enabling act, was an outrage on the South because half of the

State lay south of 36 degrees 30 minutes, and the people of the South should have been given time in which to introduce their slaves and compete for the plan of the constitution. It declared that, by a convention of the Southern States making the demand, "California may "yet be divided, and the Southern people allowed an "opportunity of establishing therein the institution of "slavery."

To this declaration, it was replied that California was properly admitted; that the Constitution gave Congress the power to admit new States and was silent as to the manner of admission. The mode and manner were left entirely to the discretion of Congress. While injustice was shown the South in the haste with which that State was admitted without an enabling act; no practical nor constitutional injustice was done his people. There was no probability of slavery being carried to California, if she remained a territory for ten years. The rapid influx of a mining population from all over the world, hostile to slavery, made it necessary that a State government should be speedily formed, and rendered it impossible for the institution of slavery to have more than a handful of supporters. The fact that half of California lay south of 36 degrees 30 minutes did not give the South any more rights in the southern portion than in the northern. The Missouri Compromise line did not apply to the Mexican acquisition; and if it had applied thereto, it would simply have excluded slavery north of 36 degrees 30 minutes, and left the people south of that line to exclude it or not as they might see proper. The people of California had seen proper to exclude slavery, and the Union party was ready to vindicate the right of that people to have slaves or not as they saw proper. It was contended that such demands as this for the division of California, after she had been admitted as a State, when it was certain that slavery could by no possibility be voted into any one of the proposed divisions, tended to damage the South by putting her in a false position. By preferring unreasonable demands she would not be listened to with respect and consideration when her demands were just and proper. They were ready to be aggressive at all times when the power of the people was illegally shorn away, but they were not willing to be aggressive simply for the purpose of preserving what was called a balance of power in the United States Senate between the free and slave States. If a State wished to be a free State it had a right to be so, whether the so-called balance of power was affected or not. They had no fault to find with the two Senators from Alabama for voting against the admission of California, since a delay in her admission might have developed a fairer and fuller expression of the opinion of her people; they were to be commended for refusing to join in the protest made by the ten Southern Senators. Senators CLEMENS and KING deserved the thanks of the State for refusing to sign a paper protesting against the admission of a State and threatening dissolution of the Union because of such admission, simply because half of it was not made a slave State without regard to the wish of the people.

II. The Southern Rights report objected to the compromise, in the next place, because Congress had not repealed the local law which abolished slavery in Utah and New Mexico when they were a part of Mexico. "Now," we ask, say the committee in their report, "if the refusal to repeal the Mexican law, upon the "ground stated, does not indicate the same hostility by "the Federal Government to the institution of slavery "as the passage directly of the Wilmot Proviso. Since "the passage of the great 'peace measures,' and in the "midst of the 'patriotic rejoicings' over the prostra-"tion of Southern rights and honor, insult has been "added to injury by the introduction of bills to apply "this odious Proviso to the territories of Utah and "New Mexico. Then, what security is there in carry-"ing slaves to these territories?" To these questions it was replied that the compromise acts, so far as the territories acquired from Mexico were concerned, did ample justice to the South. They might come into the Union with or without slavery. So the act provided; and not even the Missouri restriction had been applied to them. The local law of Mexico no longer existed. The constitution, and the rules and regulations made by Congress for the territories, had abrogated it; and the slave owner could take his property to New Mexico just as he could take it to Missouri and Arkansas before their admission as States. To say that the Union should be dissolved because the Wilmot Proviso could be made to apply to a territory at some future day, was to anticipate ills which might never happen. There was always risk in taking slaves to a territory, because, on the formation of a State constitution, slavery might be abolished; but that was a risk attendant on the nature of the property. The Wilmot Proviso had been invariably defeated; and now, if the people of the South showed a determination to stand by the compromise measures as a final settlement of the slavery question, we need have no apprehension that the Wilmot Proviso will gain the victory in Congress. There will always be agitators and fanatics who will press it forward, but the conservative sentiment of the whole country will always defeat it. Let us not then rush into disunion because of apprehensions which have no solid basis.

III. The report objected to the settlement of the Texas boundary question, under which a portion of Texas was added to New Mexico in consideration of ten millions of dollars to be paid Texas by the United States. The objection was that enough territory was taken from a slave State to form two States thereafter, and that these two States might be brought into the Union under the operation of the Wilmot Proviso. To this it was replied that there were grave doubts as to whether the territory in question properly belonged to Texas, but that if Texas chose to part with it for ten millions of dollars, there certainly could be no objection raised by any one else; and that so far as the danger of having the Wilmot Proviso applied to that section was involved, the same proviso could, by the same power, be applied to the identical territory were it to remain a part of Texas, and at some future day, by the permission of that State, apply for admission to the Union. If the provisions of the New Mexican act were to be invalidated hereafter by application of the Wilmot Proviso, the provisions of the act admitting Texas could be as easily invalidated. This objection then must fall to the ground. It was simply a general objection that the people of the North would not unite with those of the South in standing by Clay, Webster, Fillmore, and Cass, and their compeers, in abiding by the compromise. Let us see whether they would not, before we prefer extravagant demands, however just and constitutional, and before we declare ourselves ready for disunion, and even before we know whether our demands are accepted or rejected. The Union men were opposed to this constant drawing of heavy drafts on the patriotism of the great conservative masses of the North. Those masses were disposed to give us all our rights under the Constitution, but they were opposed to slavery, and we must not expect them to legislate with a view of preserving what we call a balance of power.

IV. The report next objected to the abolition of the slave trade in the District of Columbia. "If Congress "has a right to say that a slave shall be free when "brought into the District for sale, it can also say that "he shall be free when brought there to labor." To this it was replied that Congress undoubtedly had the right not only to stop the slave trade in the District, but even to abolish it there. It was thought that the latter step should not be taken except upon a vote of the people of the District; but so far as the prohibition of the slave markets in the District was concerned the Union men were willing to yield so much at the seat of Government to the prejudices of that large portion of mankind who were sensitive as to the slave trade. It was not necessary to keep up a slave auction under the very windows of the Capitol. If any one in the District desired to purchase a slave he could do so in ten or twenty minutes by crossing the river. The continuance of the slave auctions in the District did more than all else to keep up the agitation against slavery at the North. It might be well for the South that they were discontinued.

V. In conclusion the report declared that the South should meet in convention and demand that California be divided, and the southern portion be allowed to establish slavery. If the north should not acquiesce, then the South should make immediate preparations to secede. "Discard all past political differences"—"Turn aside from the Submissionist as your worst "enemy"—"Starve out the National Submission press "at the South"—"Exclude all Northern newspapers "from our midst"—"Patronize Southern Ministers and "Churches" — "Cease visiting Northern watering "places"—were among the suggestions of the States-Rights pronunciamento.

To the general argument that the South would be shorn of her rights in the Uuion, it was answered that the only protection for slavery was in the Union; that the South could not expect the people of the North to vote slavery into the territories or aid in making constitutions recognizing slavery; that all efforts to continue to bring in a slave State whenever a free State was introduced must in the end prove futile; that the South had neither the population nor the slaves to spread over vast territories. The question was simply reduced to this: Shall Alabama secede from the Union because possibly after a series of years three-fourths of the States may be free States and may amend the Constitution so as to abolish slavery? That event may happen. If it should, it would be a Constitutional proceeding. But certainly there would be no emancipation without compensation to masters. The alternative then arises: Is it better for Alabama to await gradual emancipation at some far distant day under a compensatory system, than to break up the Union, rush into civil war, and lose in disaster all that we are contending for? Most of the Alabama Unionists did not believe in peaceable secession. No government in the world had ever broken to pieces except with civil war. They would not stop to argue the question of secession. That was a question they never argued. If the right of peaceable secession existed, it was no peaceable right if denied by the other side. All the North denied it to be a right. All the border States denied it. Even Virginia had held that the Supreme Court was the common arbiter between the States and the General Government. A large and perhaps controlling portion of the South denied the right at heart. If they were willing to break up the Union, they would go into the movement with the expectation of doing what our grandfathers did at Lexington and not of reading the resolutions of 1798 at the mouth of a cannon. The right of peaceable secession was being urged by Mr. YANCEY they said for the purpose of deluding the people into the belief that there would be no war in case of disunion. By removing the idea of danger it is hoped that converts may be more rapidly made. Let not the people be blinded to the truth! There can be no such thing as peaceable disunion. When secession is once entered upon, the country will be deluged in blood. If we win we will be called patriots. If we lose we will be called traitors. That is the sum and substance of the right of peaceable secession. It is nothing more than the natural right of revolution, which all would be ready to assert when our grievances were too great to be borne. At present they did not believe our grievances were so serious as to justify secession. They had watched with alarm the growing spirit of hostility to the South and her rights—but were satisfied that the conservative element of the country would always rally to our defence in an emergency, as it had done in the recent adjustment. That compromise was not all they wished, but it was more than they expected. They were willing to stand by it as a final settlement of the slavery dispute between the North and the South.

The contest between COCHRAN and ABERCROMBIE raged bitterly throughout the District, but at the election, ABERCROMBIE was returned with an unprecedented majority. From one end of the State to the other, and in the largest slave-holding counties, the advocates of secession were routed horse, foot, and dragoons. Mr. YANCEY was mortified to see the Gulf States ratifying the compromise and denouncing disunion—the very strongholds of the secession party giving unusual large majorities for the Union candidates—and even South Carolina failing to give the requisite vote for secession.

The acquisition of Texas was undoubtedly a movement by Southern leaders for the purpose of preserving the balance between the slave and free States. But the Mexican war had accomplished more than they intended. It had given Texas to the South; but it had also given California and Utah, and possibly New Mexico, to the North. All of the five States into which Texas was expected to be divided eventually, might or might not be admitted as slave States; all the other larger territory was almost certain to become free States. The balance of power must be secured in some other way. The Southern leaders cast their eyes on CUBA. NARCISSO LOPEZ, a native of Venezuela, a veteran soldier of Spain, and for some years a resident of Cuba, visited the United States in 1849 for the purpose of enlisting sympathy in behalf of Cuban independence, and of organizing a military expedition for the invasion of that island. On his arrival at Washington, Mr. CALHOUN called upon him, and upon the following day repeated his visit. The policy which had urged the distinguished South Carolinian to secure Texas to the South, now urged him to secure Cuba. If the South remained in the Union, the accession of Cuba would give several more slave States. If the South seceded, the possession of the island would add greatly to the resources of a Southern Confederacy. In either event, therefore, it became the policy of the South to aid and encourage the attempt of LOPEZ. The leading States-Rights men immediately enlisted themselves in the enterprise. LOPEZ visited Gen. QUITMAN, and proposed that they divide the civil and military leadership of the enterprise between them. LOPEZ was to be President of Cuba, and QUITMAN was to be Commanding General in the field. Had the offer been accepted, there can be no doubt that an immense force would have rallied to the call of QUITMAN. The soldiers of his old Division were scattered from Charleston to New Orleans. Each one of them would have become a recruiting officer; for the name of their old leader would give confidence and dignity to an enterprise which, under the lead of a stranger, would be open to suspicion and distrust. QUITMAN was then Governor of Mississippi. He was ardently in favor of secession, and fully expected that disunion would occur during his administration. A State convention had been called, and he could not find it consistent with his duty to lead a military movement, however promising of glory and renown, against a foreign people, when his services as a leader were now demanded by the States-Rights party in a movement at home which promised no less renown and military glory.

Soon after the decision of Gen. QUITMAN, LOPEZ embarked for CUBA with a small volunteer force under O'Hara, Wheat, Pickett, Hawkins and Bell. His men were chiefly from Kentucky. Landing at Cardenas, he repulsed an attacking force of Spanish troops, but meeting no encouragement from the people, re-embarked intending to make another landing. The Spanish steamer PIZARRO giving him chase, he was compelled to run into Key West, where his force was disbanded. Not disheartened by his first failure, he proceeded to effect a new organization, visiting New Orleans and several places in Mississippi. Everywhere he was received with enthusiasm. At GAINESVILLE, Miss., he spoke to a large meeting, and with singular address aroused a warlike feeling. Though born in another land, and speaking a different language, he was not ignorant, he said, of the history of Mississippi. He knew what she had achieved in 1815 on the plains of CHALMETTE, where the gallant HINDS at the head of her dragoons braved the fire of the whole British line, and became the pride of one army and the admiration of another. He remembered the deadly execution of her rifles at the storming of Monterey - the flashing sword of DAVIS on the field of Buena Vista—her battle-riven banner when it was planted on the walls of Mexico by the heroic QUITMAN. With these memories of brilliant events, he came from a kindred and friendly State—from noble-hearted Louisiana—to breathe for a few days the pure air of your forests and to tread a soil consecrated to Liberty. He desired to know and to mingle with his brother republicans, anxious to see and to study their practical exemplifications of free government, and to witness the phenomenon of a whole people engaged in trade, agriculture and mechanics, comprehending and practicing the political problems that Europe, with all its philosophy, refinement and learning has never been able to solve.

The compromise measures had passed, and the prospect for Southern secession was less favorable than ever. At least QUITMAN believed so, and thinking that his sword would not be demanded by his own State, he now inclined more favorably towards the proposition of LOPEZ. It was generally believed that he would head the Cuban movement. The Grand Jury of the United States Court at New Orleans found a bill against Gen. QUITMAN, JOHN HENDERSON, and others, for setting on foot the invasion of Cuba. The question arose, could the Governor of a sovereign State be carried away to another State by the General Government to answer a criminal charge? General QUITMAN was disposed to resist the attempt. If such a power rested with the General Government, the sovereignty of the State was gone. At any moment her officers might be abducted and the wheels of government either stopped or left in the hands of subordinates, who might be the tools of the arresting power. Suppose a case in which the Governor, elected by the people, was opposed to the party in power at Washington, and the Lieut. Governor, elected by the Senate, was friendly to that party, and to any schemes which it might favor, the arrest and abduction of the Governor on any pretended charge, would defeat the will and safety of the people. Suppose a new-elected General Assembly about to convene, should be almost divided between the friends and opponents of the Administration at Washington, how easy could the will of the people be defeated by the arrest and abduction of enough of the majority party to leave the organization of the Legislature in the hands of the minority party! Gen. QUITMAN denied the power of the United States to arrest him. Hon. JACOB THOMPSON wrote to him from Washington: "If they can arrest, they can refuse bail; if they can "refuse bail, they can, without trial, take him away "from his duty, incarcerate him, and by rendering it "impossible for him to perform his official duties, vir- "tually vacate the office of Governor and leave the "State without a Chief Executive. This is an absurd- "ity. The consequence of the power claimed annihi- "lates State sovereignty, and soon we may expect to "see Governors of States, like Roman satraps, brought "to the capital in chains if the power claimed is tamely "submitted to." Hon. R. BARNEWELL RHETT called upon the Governor to resist, and thus bring about a collision between the State and Federal forces, which must ultimately involve the whole South.

Gen. QUITMAN was wiser than his counsellors. He saw that if the South would not resist the Compromise Acts, they would not enter into a war with the General Government because of an indictment found by a Grand Jury against a citizen who happened to be Governor. The people sympathized with QUITMAN, but they held that every citizen, however high his position, was amenable to the laws, and that the Governor of a State should be arrested for counterfeiting the coin, robbing the mail, piracy, or breaking the neutrality laws, as though he were a private citizen. The argument which would apply to the Governor, would apply equally to every Executive and Legislative officer of a State. If none of these could be arrested by the United States, then we would see the strange spectacle of thousands of citizens, shielded by the possession of an office, violating the laws of the Federal Government with impunity. There were inconveniences connected with this power to arrest State officers; but no system of government could be devised in which such inconveniences would not occur. Politics was not one of the exact sciences. So fallible was human nature that all the wisdom of all the ages was not adequate to foresee the various problems which would arise.

QUITMAN determined to resign the office of Governor and to stand his trial. The jury made a mistrial in the case of HENDERSON, and thereupon the case against QUITMAN was dismissed. When he left the court-room there was a great manifestation of popular sentiment in his favor. Deputations from Mississippi, Louisiana, Alabama and South Carolina waited upon him, offering congratulations. This display of feeling arose from the profound impression on the Southern mind that QUITMAN was actually enlisted in the Cuban enterprise, and was destined to be the liberator of that fair island. The whole South sympathized in the movement; the States-Rights party, because in the event of Southern secession they contemplated a magnificent Confederacy of slave-holding States, including Cuba, Mexico and Central America—the old dream of AARON BURR; the Union party, because in the annexation of CUBA the preservation of the balance of power would postpone that dreaded day when three-fourths of the States would be anti-slavery.

A mass meeting was called at Montgomery, August

5, 1851, to express sympathy for and proffer aid to the Cuban independence movement. Gen. WM. TAYLOR was called to the chair, and JAMES H. CLANTON, a young and active Whig, was invited to address the people. Taking the stand, he made a most eloquent appeal in behalf of Cuba, avowing the deepest sympathy in the struggle of the patriots and offering his personal services in their behalf. He concluded by offering a resolution, which was unanimously adopted, calling upon the Government to recognize the independence of the island. JUDGE BIBB offered a resolution soliciting contributions for the cause. At the close of CLANTON'S speech many wealthy citizens came forward with liberal subscriptions, and a number of young men enrolled themselves in a company for the purpose of joining the expeditionary force of Lopez. That force had sailed for New Orleans a few days before. The Montgomery company elected CLANTON Captain, and proceeded to New Orleans. There they found not less than two thousand volunteers awaiting transportation. A regiment was organized with WHEAT as Colonel and CLANTON as Lieutenant Colonel. The troops received every attention from the hospitable citizens of New Orleans, but they were eager and impatient to embark. They longed to set foot on the beautiful island, and to see at last the stars and stripes floating over MORO CASTLE. While chafing at the delay of embarking, one morning came the startling news of the defeat of LOPEZ, his capture and execution. He had separated himself from the command of CRITTENDEN, had relied too much upon the co-operation of the Cubans, and had departed from New Orleans without waiting for the troops which were now pouring in from all quarters. Had he taken the advice of QUITMAN, kept his force united, debarked at a more distant port, secured the arrival of an army of five thousand men at one time, his expedition would have doubtless been crowned with victory. He failed, and thus added another to the many proofs that no great enterprises can be pressed to success under the lead of the dark and hybrid races of Central America. LOPEZ was executed by the garote, and Col. CRITTENDEN and his men were shot. When ordered to his knees, CRITTENDEN replied: "*Americans kneel only to their God.*"

The Union party having achieved a signal victory all over the South, the States-Rights associations resolved in their several meetings to adjourn the question of secession. It was not to be dismissed, but to remain in abeyance. Mr. YANCEY's policy was to keep his forces well organized and to seize the next pretext for an advance movement. To strengthen their position, which had been considerably weakened by the repulse on the Compromise questions, a majority of the States-Rights leaders deemed it best to withdraw under shelter of the Democratic organization. By drawing back to the Democratic party those who had been acting with the Union party, they forced the residue of the Unionists to return to the Whig organization. It was a piece of masterly generalship to load the Anti-Secession party of Alabama with the sins of the free-soil wing of the Whig party of the North; to attack them as partisans of SEWARD rather than as supporters of the Union. The Union men understood the tactics of the Secessionists, and struggled to preserve the Union organization. A Union meeting was held at Montgomery in December, 1857. The call for it was signed by all the leading Whigs of the General Assembly and several leading Democrats, but when it met no Democrat of prominence participated in its session. They determined to send delegates to a National Union Convention, and to urge upon their approaching State Convention the duty of joining a national organization which would abide by the Compromise, and alike battle against the Secessionists on the one hand and the Abolitionists on the other. It was their hope that the friends of the Compromise all over the Union would unite upon this as a final settlement of the slavery question, and nominate Mr. FILLMORE for the Presidency.

Before the State Union Convention could meet, however, there were developments of public opinion which divided the Union ranks. The Union Democrats, finding that the Democratic party would sustain the Compromise unequivocally as a final settlement, deserted the Union organization in mass and rallied under their old colors. Of the Whigs who were left, there were a large majority who saw the futility of attempting to make a National organization of Whigs alone, under a new name at the South, so long as the Whigs at the North retained their old designation and were preparing to go into a National Convention. They argued that, without some of the Southern States, the Whig party could not carry the Presidential election, and that rather than lose the support of Southern Whigs, the National Convention would endorse the Compromise; that if the Compromise was not endorsed, it would then be time to separate from the party; and that rather than establish a sectional party, as would be a Union party composed of Southern Whigs alone, it would be preferable to repose confidence in the National Whig organization. So thought Mr. HILLIARD.

A portion of the Alabama Whigs thought differently. They believed that a return to the Whig party would be a surrender of their organization into the hands of the Free-Soilers. Mr. Watts published a letter in May, in which he advocated a continuance of the Union organization. "Look," said he, "at the vote of the "Democratic caucus assembled at the commencement "of the present Congress, repudiating the Compromise "as a finality. Look at the vote in Congress on the "resolution of Mr. JACKSON, of Ga., as amended by Mr. "HILLYER, showing that Northern members of Congress, "as well as many Southern members, are not in favor "of standing firmly by the Compromise. And, above "all, look on the decision of the Whig Congressional "caucus recently assembled in Washington City." Not to unite with the National Whig Convention was a duty, insisted Mr. WATTS, which we owed "to the "Southern Whigs who withdrew from the Congressional "caucus, and to the other noble Whigs who refused to "go into it after the announcement of the chairman of "the caucus that he would entertain no resolutions "looking to the finality of the Compromise measures." The vote upon the resolution of Mr. JACKSON, to which Mr. WATTS here referred—a resolution to recognize the binding efficiency of the Compromises of the Constitution and to abide by such Compromises and to sustain the laws to carry them out—was as follows:

YEAS.		NAYS.	
Northern Democrats	35	Northern Democrats	22
Southern Democrats	39	Southern Democrats	11
Southern Whigs	20	Southern Whigs	1
Northern Whigs	7	Northern Whigs	30
Total	101	Total	64

Mr. WATTS, from this vote, drew the conclusion that the Northern Democrats were dangerously divided as to making the Compromise a conclusion of the slavery agitation; that the Southern Democrats were materially divided as shown by the vote, and were known to be far more dangerously divided than the vote shows; that the Northern Whigs were also dangerously divided, with the preponderance largely in favor of renewed agitation; and that the Southern Whigs were alone united. From this conclusion he argued that the Southern Whigs should maintain the Union organization, and gradually draw to its support all those elements which voted yea upon Mr. JACKSON's resolution. To do so would be to settle the slavery question now and forever, by depriving it of material upon which to operate. Not to do so would be to leave the question an element of discord in both the Whig and Democratic organizations until it should rend both in twain and plunge the country into civil war. To confirm this view of WATTS, CLANTON, JUDGE and other far-seeing and patriotic Southern Whigs, the New York *Tribune*, representing the SEWARD Whigs, replied to the protest of the Southern Whigs at the Congressional caucus:

"Oh green and verdant gentlemen of the House of "Representatives, ye who vainly fancy that carrying "the Compromise measures through your illustrious "body is a great political stroke, even a triumph over "an ever-active principle in the heart of man, it is time "you were resolving that the sun shall stand still on "Gideon. It is time that you were erecting a stage "under the ends of the rainbow in order to spike it on "to the sky. It is time you had resolved that the "ocean should cease to surge, the streams to flow or "the seasons to return. You cannot 'compromise' a "question of human freedom."

When the State UNION Convention met, those who believed that the Whig party would endorse the Compromise and that the Democratic party would not, proved to be in the ascendant; and the Convention, after a faint and feeble recommendation for a National Union Convention, dissolved, with the general understanding that the Whig party was restored. Mr. HILLIARD, who had been favored with exalted trusts under the HARRISON, and again under the TAYLOR Administration, ever eager for a wide national theatre of action, and ambitious of the power which success would give the leaders of a national party, led off, at a Macon county meeting, in favor of sending delegates to the Whig Convention. The Pickens county WHIGS replied with a similar movement, and forthwith the blows of the Democratic party shattered to utter dissolution the remaining walls of the Union party. Nothing was now left of the organization which defeated secession in 1850. The Whigs had cast everything upon the chances of the Baltimore Convention. If they lost, what would follow?

If the Whig Convention did not fully and fairly accept the Compromise, it would follow that the Southern WHIGS, constituting a large minority of the Southern people, and one which by the aid of Union Democrats could always arrest an attempt at secession, would be left powerless. If slavery agitation was to continue, they must take the side of their people and their property, and demand for their protection every guaranty of the Constitution. If the North would not accept a compromise in which the Free-State party received every advantage and the South gave up more than half of her constitutional rights, then the Whigs of the South would also hoist the banner of States-Rights and abide the issue.

"Let us go and demand the Compromise," said the Whig papers of Alabama.

The evening before the meeting of the Whig National Convention at Baltimore, a caucus of Southern Whigs adopted and resolved to submit to the Convention the following resolution:

"That the series of measures commonly known as "the Compromise, including the Fugitive Slave Law, "are received and acquiesced in by the Whig party of "the United States, as a settlement in principle and "substance—a *final* settlement—of the dangerous and "exciting questions which they embrace; and, so far as "the Fugitive Slave Law is concerned, we will main-"tain the same, and insist on a strict enforcement, "until time and experience shall demonstrate the "necessity of further legislation, to guard against "evasion or abuse, not impairing its present efficiency; "and we deprecate all further agitation of the slavery "question as dangerous to our peace, and will discoun-"tenance all efforts at the renewal or continuance of "such agitation in Congress or out of it, *whenever*, "*wherever* and *however* the attempt may be made; "and we will maintain the system of measures as a "policy *essential to the nationality of the Whig party* "*and the integrity of the Union.*"

If this resolution were not adopted substantially, the Southern Whigs were to withdraw. It will be observed that it embraced—

"1st. A distinct recognition of and acquiescence in "a *compromise* or *settlement*, embracing a series of mea-

"sures known by that name and including the Fugitive "law.

"2d. A declaration that said *settlement* shall be *final.*

"3d. A declaration that the Fugitive law, as a part "of such *settlement*, shall be maintained and enforced "until further legislation is required to guard against "abuse or evasion.

"4th. A declaration against the further agitation of "the Slavery question, in Congress or out of it; and a "further declaration that the policy thus set forth in "the various averments of the resolution is *essential* to "the nationality of the Whig party."

Such was the Southern Whig demand, presented as containing no one point which could be spared, if the Whig party was to be a national and not a sectional party. This resolution was emasculated by the Committee of the Convention and adopted by that body in the following language:

"3. That the series of acts of the Thirty-first Con-"gress, the act known as the Fugitive Slave Law "included, are received and acquiesced in by the Whig "party of the United States as a settlement, in principle "and substance, of the dangerous and exciting ques-"tions which they embrace; and, so far as they are "concerned, we will maintain them, and insist upon "their strict enforcement, until time and experience "shall demonstrate the necessity of further legisla-"tion to guard against the evasion of the laws on "the one hand, and the abuse of their powers on the "other—not impairing their present efficiency; and "we deprecate all further agitation of the questions "thus settled as dangerous to our peace, and will dis-"countenance all efforts to continue or renew such "agitation, *whenever*, *wherever* or *however* the attempt "may be made; and we will maintain this system as "*essential to the nationality of the Whig party and the* "*integrity of the Union.*"

It will be observed that this resolution differs from the other in these respects:

"1st. It contains no sort of recognition of the fact "that there has been *any compromise at all.* No such "term, no such fact, no such idea appears in it.

"2d. Still less does it recognize, or in any way "allude to any *final settlement.*

"3d. The resolution, so far from recognizing any "special covenant obligation in the compromise "measures, puts them all upon precisely the same "footing with *every other law* enacted by the Thirty-"first Congress"

As soon as the report was read, Mr. Rufus Choate sprang at once to his feet to interpose the dazzling shield of his eloquence between the ruins of their resolution and the objections of the Southern Whigs. Adroitly reminding his audience that he had not heard the exact terms of the last resolution, he proceeded at once to claim for it a merit and a character to which its exact terms present a marked contrast. He understood, *in general, that it affirmed the finality of the Compromise*, and that it deprecated any further political agitation on the subject of slavery. *And, if he rightly understood it*, he made haste to rise and thank God that the doctrine for which he had contended in his measure and place, though circumstances were unpropitious, in Faneuil Hall, when Faneuil Hall was opened—if he might judge by the cheering indications—*seemed to be sustained* by the highest authority which, as a party man and Whig, he could recognise in the Convention of Union Whigs of the United States.

But, on the contrary, Mr. CHARLES ANDERSON, of Ohio, rose sturdily up to tell the plain truth about the whole business, and he spoke out the Whig creed bluntly. He said: "This Compromise was, after all, "nothing but a *law like all others on the statute book.* "The first Compromise of Mr. Clay was nothing more "than an act regulating the duties on imports. So with "this Compromise—it is nothing more than any other "law on the statute book. Those who are opposed to "it at the North are men who do so, not from any "passion on the subject, *but from sectional pride.* "The Whigs of the free States have witnessed the "diminution of their numbers—have seen their friends "go off by scores—*on account of forcing this Compro-* "*mise upon them.*"

The resolution of the Southern Whigs, in order to soothe the Northern animosity to certain features of the Fugitive Slave Law, provided that the law was to be maintained until experience should demonstrate the necessity of further legislation to guard against evasion of its provisions or an abuse of its powers. The other laws were to be maintained as final. But the Convention provided that experience was to be the test of all the Compromise laws. This change in the wording of the resolution, taken in connection with the repeated declaration of members that the Compromise laws were no more final and fixed than other laws, and with the nomination of Gen. SCOTT over Mr. FILLMORE and Mr. WEBSTER, satisfied many leading Whigs of the South that as between the two National parties, it was their duty to cast themselves with the Democratic, which, to the surprise of Alabama Whigs, had endorsed the Compromise, with a declaration that they would resist all attempts at renewing in Congress or out the agitation of the slavery question. Upon this platform, all that the Union party of Alabama had ever asked, they had placed as their candidate for Vice-President a distinguished son of Alabama who had, two years before, denounced the secession movement in spirited, prompt, and unequivocal terms.

Immediately upon the nomination of Gen. SCOTT, ALEXANDER H. STEPHENS, ROBERT TOOMBS, and JAMES JOHNSON, of Ga., CHARLES JAMES FAULKNER, of Va., WALTER BROOKE, of Miss., ALEXANDER WHITE and JAMES ABERCROMBIE, of Ala., published a card in the Washington papers withholding their support from the Whig nominees. The defection of these leading Southern Whigs created quite a commotion in the ranks of the party. Mr. ABERCROMBIE wielded a great influence in the Montgomery District, and Mr. WHITE was scarcely less potent in the Talladega District. Still Messrs. HILLIARD, LANGDON, WATTS, BELSER and the bulk of the party in Alabama, placed upon the Whig resolution relating to the Compromise Acts the construction which Mr. CHOATE had placed upon it, and which its plausible language might be made to bear. They resolutely shut their eyes to the construction placed upon it by the Seward Whigs of the North, as well as to the position claimed for Gen. SCOTT by the New York *Tribune* as the ally of free-soil and emancipation.

A SCOTT and GRAHAM ratification meeting was held at Montgomery, July 7, and speeches were made by MOSS, BELSER, and CLANTON. The Whig State Convention met Sept. 1 and ratified the action of the Baltimore Convention.

The States-Rights party found themselves *in* a

difficult position. They had denounced the Compromise measures, and now they were to vote to accept them as the least of evils. Their Convention, which had assembled at Montgomery in February, had appointed a committee to draw up a report and address to the people of the State. Upon this committee were such distinguished lawyers and eminent citizens as W. L. YANCEY, JOHN A. ELMORE, SAM'L F. RICE, H. M. ELMORE, and G. W. GAYLE. The address was published during the spring, disseminated over the State, and was fresh in the recollection of the people when the two National Conventions took action. It said that the States-Rights associations were "composed of men "who believe that the tendency of old party organi-"zations has been to lead their members to avoid any "decisive action on the great slavery question, and to "wink at and acquiesce in aggressions on the South "rather than endanger party success by opposition to "them, and who have determined to stand aloof from "those parties until the wrongs done to the South, "while each of those parties have administered the "government, shall be amply redressed and the rights "of the South fully guaranteed against future aggres-"sion; or in the event of failure of such just demands, "until 'new safeguards' have been provided for the "maintenance of our liberties." The address then argued at length the failure of the Compromise Acts to do the South full justice, and concluded by advising the people of Alabama to secede at once. It said:

"In view of our condition, the question forces itself "upon us--'What policy does our interest and our "duty alike dictate shall be pursued by us?' In the "opinion of the Convention, the only issue which can "be made in answer to that question is—Submission "or Secession.

"The first is recommended to you under the more "honeyed term, 'acquiescence.' It implies that past "aggressions afford no ground for resistance, and that "your safety is not endangered by submission.

"Fellow-citizens! The Abolitionist recommends to "you to submit! The Federalist says it is your "duty! The North desires you to interpose no "obstacle to the success of its designs! In what "consists the difference between such advice from "such quarters, and the same advice from some of "your own brethren? Simply in this: the advice of "the first is dictated by a selfish desire to be unmo- "lested in their operations against you; that of the "latter is dictated from a selfish desire, on the part of "the leaders, to preserve unimpaired that old party "organization which tends to elevate them to power "and place in this government—and on the part of "the masses who follow them, by that feeling of timidity "and love of ease, which in ages past has permitted "many a tyrant to rule millions of his fellow men. "Tories were found in the days of the Revolution to "denounce our fathers as 'agitators,' and to preach up "'acquiescence' in the action of the parent govern- "ment, and to portray the horrors of war to the excited "imaginations of the weak. Men are found now to do "the same thing.

"'Acquiescence' is the policy which the wisest free- "soiler may well advocate. A 'masterly inactivity "now, will accomplish all his aims. Time, acting as "the friend of his scheme, will ripen his measures into "a profuse fruition. Free soil State after free soil

"State will come into the Union. The free soil majority "now in the Senate will increase with each accession. "The free soil majority in the House will continue to "enlarge its gigantic proportions. The Executive will "be but the reflex of a dominant free soil power in "the government; while the South, with no hope of "corresponding territorial expansion, will be struggling "with the very plethora of slavery. Our public men "seduced from the thorny, self-denying path of duty, "will be found struggling for place in the affections of "some Northern President. And when Time shall "have ruthlessly produced these effects, and the sunny "South has become the Ireland of the Union, the spirit "of 'Acquiescence' may complacently claim them to "be the fruits of her policy—a policy but occasionally "and feebly disturbed by some Emmett whom the "sufferings of our land may induce to attempt its "rescue, and whose blood will quench the feeble fire of "patriotism, which his eloquence may serve to kindle "in the bosoms of his abject, 'acquiescing' coun- "trymen."

The language of this address stigmatized as Tories and Federalists those who advocated acquiescence in the Compromise. But the Democratic party had now acquiesced in it, and even more plainly and unequivocally than those who had just composed the Union party. What was to be done? Mr. WILLIAMS, who was President of the Association, and Mr. ELMORE, of the Committee on the Address, wrote to Gen. PIERCE and Gen. SCOTT asking them to define their position on the question of slavery. Gen. SCOTT replied that his letter of acceptance was his only reply to the numerous letters he received relative to his political views. Gen.

PIERCE made no reply. Gen. QUITMAN was also written to. The reply of this distinguished gentleman was satisfactory to the association. He rejoiced to learn that the Southern-Rights party of Alabama still retained its organization. The policy whether they should go into the Presidential contest as an organized party, was one which they alone could decide. If the people of the whole South finally settle down into quiet acquiescence in this precedent set and the encroachments made by the aggressive measures in question, they will soon have nothing worth contending for.

Upon the receipt of these letters, the States-Rights party were called together in Convention at Montgomery Sept. 13, and unanimously adopted a report declaring that, whereas Messrs. PIERCE and SCOTT had failed to answer the interrogatories propounded to them, they could not consistently vote for either. They therefore recommended the nomination of Ex-Gov. GEO. M. TROUP, of Ga., and Gen. JOHN A. QUITMAN, of Mississippi, for the Presidency and Vice-Presidency.

Immediately after the Democratic nomination Gen. QUITMAN had said in a published letter:

" It was but a short time since we regarded some of " the compromise measures as unjust, destructive of the " equality of the Southern States, against the spirit, if " not the letter, of the Constitution, and evidence of a " fixed design to abolish slavery everywhere. If our " opinions are changed—we have found ourselves mis- " taken; if these measures are so benign as to deserve a " place in our political creed, let us honestly make " proclamation to that effect, and raise altars to their " authors, Clay, Cass, and Foote. But if not, let us " not write ourselves down as asses or rogues. How " would Colonel Davis, Governor Brown, or I appear, " vindicating, defending, and approving such a platform?

"Why, those political chameleons, Foote and Sharkey, "could not beat it. But I must conclude by summing "up: My present opinion then, is, that if Pierce be "nominated without any indorsement of the compro- "mise measures, and if he assume no other objectional "positions, States-Rights men should give him their "support. If, on the other hand, the Convention have "placed him on that ebony and topaz platform, I "think it will become our duty to stand aloof, or, what "would be better, if we can muster spirit, use our exer- "tions to rouse up and rally the old State-Rights Guard, "form societies, hold conventions, nominate a separate "ticket, and declare war to the knife.

"But it may be said that such action on our part "might, perhaps, result in the defeat of the Democratic "ticket and success of the Whig All the answer I "have to this is, that if Democracy is to retain power "by striding this centaur hobby, with Abolition head "and Southern tail, it had better be unhorsed. If "reorganized Democracy admits the absolute doctrines "of the existence and sovereignty of a supreme "national government, possessing power to coerce the "States, nothing will be lost by its defeat and de- "struction."

The outspoken sentiments of Gen. QUITMAN were endorsed by the entire States-Rights party, yet one branch of it supported Gen. PIERCE and the other repudiated him. Of the latter class, was Mr. FISHER, editor of the *Southern Press*. Writing from Washington, he said:

"I can not concur in the support of Pierce at all "with such a platform, and I can not isolate him from "it when he says it is in accordance with his judgment. "If a Southern-Rights party had resolved to support "him with a distinct repudiation of the platform, and "with a power, from its own separate organization, of "resisting his administration in any attempt to pursue "the compromise policy, I could have co-operated. "But you must forgive me for saying that I consider "it one of the most disastrous signs of the times that "men of the two extremes, Free Soilers and Fire-"eaters, hasten into parties and yet repudiate the "platforms. It looks like a love of party for the sake "of party. The consequence is, the success of the "Democratic party will be the complete ascendency of "Compromise faction, and the continual defection "of Southern-Rights men in order to obtain place."

Of the former class was Hon. E. C. WILKINSON, of Miss., one of the PIERCE electors, who, writing to QUITMAN, said:

"It would doubtless have been better for the party "with which I am now acting, if you had not pursued "this course, but I can not say that I see anything "in what you have published inconsistent with your "own antecedents. Yours is a position somewhat dif-"ferent from that of any other States-Rights man in "Mississippi. You are expected to carry out your "creed in all its severity, and not to flinch in the least "from its conclusions. The time may come, and I do "not doubt it will, when you will find your advantage "in it; for when the States-Rights party is formed "again (and who can tell how soon it may be reorgan-"ized?) it will naturally turn at once to you, who have "stood, and stand now, like old Torquil in the romance "of Scott, all alone, battered, but not beaten, while "every living soul has fallen around you."

Mr. YANCEY was of that class, who as bold as QUITMAN, were as cautious as WILKINSON. He well knew that the Compromise could not be depended upon as a settlement of the slavery question. His own resolutions, rejected in 1848, denying the power of the people of a territory to drive out slavery before the adoption of a constitution for State government, would renew the strife again whenever presented in a National Convention or in Congress. The question whether the Compromise of 1850 had not overthrown that of 1820 and opened up all the territories to slavery, was another entering wedge which at any time could be driven to the heart of the Union and rend it in twain. The success of the Democratic party would give the South the control of it. Let him once become the power behind the throne, and he would show himself greater than the throne! Let the deluded people North and South accept the Compromise as a finality, there were a hundred ways of renewing the agitation, and at the same time protesting that the Compromise justified it! There was no estoppel in politics. The States-Rights men were determined that the agitation should be renewed, and they knew very well that the Free Soil party were intent upon something more radical than building a platform under the end of a rainbow and attempting to fasten it to the sky with a spike.

At the Presidential election in November, the vote of Alabama was for Pierce, 26,881; for Scott, 15,038; for Troup, 2,174. The vote for Polk in 1847, had been 37,740, and for Cass in 1848, 31,363. Not less than 15,000 Democrats failed to vote for Pierce, and not less than 15,000 Whigs failed to vote for Scott. Here was a mass of thirty thousand reflecting men who had been driven from the Whig party by the agitation of the Abolitionists, or led away from the Democrats by the agitation of the States-Rights party. This formidable array of malcontents were ready for an advance movement.

CHAPTER XIII.

The Kansas-Nebraska Bill—Preparing for Battle Over the Outpost—Sharpe Rifles—Emigrant Societies—Rise of the American Party—Fillmore and Buchanan in the Southwest—Political Elements of the Elections of 1856, Etc., Etc.

"At the coming election I cannot doubt that the free States * * will take possession of this government, restore to the Constitution the proportions of power established by Washington, reinstate in full force that barrier against the extension of slavery called the Missouri Compromise, make Kansas a free State, and put an end forever to the addition of any more slave States to this Union—duties to be fulfilled *at any hazard—even to the dissolution of the Union itself.*"—[JOSIAH QUINCEY, SR., June 5, 1856.]

"Your estate is gracious that keeps you out of hearing of our politics. Anything more low, obscene, purulent, the manifold bearings of history have not cast up. We shall come to the worship of onions, cats and things vermiculate. 'Renown and grace are dead.' 'There is nothing serious in mortality.' If any wiser saw or instance ancient or modern occurred to me to express the enormous, impossible inanity of American things, I should utter it."—[RUFUS CHOATE, 1855.]

When the House Territorial Committee reported in 1853, a bill to organize the Territory of NEBRASKA, no question was raised as to the Missouri Compromise having been repealed by the compromise of 1850. The bill was adopted by a vote of 98 to 43. It was silent as to slavery; the whole territory, including what was afterwards Kansas, lying north of 36 deg. 30 min. Those who voted for it were alike Democrats, Whigs, and Free Soilers. This bill was reported back to the Senate by Mr. DOUGLAS, Chairman of the Senate Territorial Committee, without amendment, on the last day of the session, March 3, 1853. The debate upon it barely alluded to the question of slavery. It was laid upon the table because of objections to the manner in which it dealt with the Indians. A year later Mr. DOUGLAS, against the remonstrance of President PIERCE, it is said, and apparently looking to the Presidential succession by means of the Southern vote, brought forward an amendment to a bill introduced by a Senator from Iowa—to organize the Territory of Kansas, and which, like the preceding Nebraska bill, was silent as to slavery—declaring that "when admitted as a State "or States, the said Territory, or any portion of the "same, shall be received into the Union with or without "slavery, as their Constitution may provide at the "time of their admission." This amendment, referring in express terms to the Missouri Compromise, declared that, being inconsistent with the principles of non-intervention laid down by the compromise of 1850, it was inoperative and void. From that day began the renewed slavery agitation which was not to rest until the Continent was drenched in blood.

The Free Soilers, who had been quiet since the election of President PIERCE in 1852, now rejoiced to find food upon which to strengthen their fortunes. The amendment of Mr. DOUGLAS was denounced by SUMNER, SEWARD and CHASE in unmeasured terms. The sanctity of the Missouri Compromise (never voted for by the Free Soilers, and always rejected by them whenever advanced by the South), was held up to the North as violated by slave propagandists. Resolutions against the passage of the bill were forwarded to Congress by New York and Massachusetts. Memorials flowed in against it from every portion of the North, East and West. Three thousand and fifty New

England ministers, in a petition, protested against it. Mrs. STOWE and eleven hundred women of Andover, Mass., joined the memorialists, who were now stirring up the worst blood of the people. The anti-slavery sentiment of the North had been intensified during the past year by the unprecedented circulation of Mrs. STOWE's novel against slavery. "Uncle Tom's Cabin" had drawn tears from the eyes of hundreds of thousands, and given birth to a horror against slavery in the Northern mind which all the politicians could never have created or allayed. Of that remarkable work, which did more than all else to array the North and South in compact masses against each other, 400,000 copies were sold in the United States. One edition was published in the German language and circulated among the Germans of the West. Over 500,000 were sold in England. It was translated into every language of Europe, and into several of those of Asia, including Arabic and Armenian. In many of these languages, as in the German, French, Italian, Welsh, Wallachian, and Russian, there were from two to twelve different translations.

The Whigs of the South could not understand why DOUGLAS should renew the slavery agitation by his inauspicious amendment. When TEXAS was about to be annexed, Mr. ALEX. H. STEPHENS had well expressed their sentiments when he said of slavery: "I have no "wish to see it extended to other countries; and if "the annexation of Texas were for the sole purpose of "extending slavery where it does not now, and would "not otherwise exist, I would oppose it"—and when at a later day he had said of the measures of 1850: "Whatever abstract rights of extension and expansion "we may have secured in the settlement of that policy, "you may not expect to see many of the territories "come into the Union as slave States unless we have "an increase of African stock. The law of population "will prevent. We have not the people." More than half of the Whigs of Alabama had refused to vote for Gen. SCOTT because they believed his administration would not abide by the Compromises as a final settlement. A large body of them had, since the adoption of the PIERCE platform, given in their adhesion to the Democracy, in the vain hope that the policy of the new administration would be to let the question of slavery alone.

If the citizen had a right to carry his slave to any territory north of 36 deg. 30 min., why not let the courts, they asked, decide the question? Why incorporate a declaration as to his power to do so in an Act of Congress—especially when there was little or no probability that any citizen would thus defy the laws of nature and the dictates of prudence? Whenever Kansas should apply, with a constitution recognizing slavery, it would be time enough for Congress to express their opinion; but there was no more necessity nor occasion to declare in advance of the fact that she should be received as a State recognizing slaves as property, than to declare that she should be received with a constitution recognizing property in buffaloes or saw-mills. It was a mere trick of politicians to pander to the sentiments of States-Rights men who controlled the Democratic party South. Grant the abstract principle to be true, it was equally true when the first compromise was adopted. If we were to fall back on abstract principle, why had not the Southern man a right to have his property protected in a Northern State as well as in a Territory? But while the Southern WHIGS were preparing to organize themselves anew in opposition to the Kansas-Nebraska Bill, the tornado from the anti-slavery party, now forming itself into the REPUBLICAN party, swept down from the North with its whirlwind of angry passion, its derisive and abusive epithets, its threats of violence and disunion, and its actual nullification and obstruction of law.

HILLIARD, WATTS and other Whig leaders had already announced themselves against the policy of the repeal of the Missouri line. But what mortal could brook the assaults which New England hurled at all the South indiscriminately, and live? Before the passage of the bill, an event occurred which silenced any protest which the Southern Whigs might have been disposed to make, and which drove them away from all consideration of compromises to an assertion of constitutional principle. Previous to the passage of the Compromises they had held that the Southern citizen had a right to carry his slave property to a common territory, as the citizen of Georgia had carried his slaves to Alabama and Mississippi. The opposition of the Free Soilers to the Missouri Compromise, so repeatedly expressed; their constant demand for a Congressional Act forbidding slavery in the Territories; their Personal Liberty Laws, designed to nullify the act for the rendition of fugitive slaves—all tended to drive the Whigs, in common with other slaveholders, to the further position that Congress should not by its agent, the Territorial Legislature, do that indirectly which it could not do directly. The Missouri line being removed by the common consent of the Free Soil North and the States-

Rights South, nothing was left for the Southern Whigs except to adhere to the principle adopted by Mr. CLAY and his compeers in 1850 for the government of New Mexico.

The event which destroyed any effort at a restoration of the Compromise of 1820, and drove the Southern Whigs to a clear enunciation of abstract rights, was the passage by the Legislature of Massachusetts of an Act incorporating "The Massachusetts "Emigrant Aid Company." The incorporators were leading Free Soil politicians. Their capital stock was to be five millions of dollars. The men who directed the company, and the large amount of money to be expended, proved to the South that it was a scheme to acquire political control of the new Territory—to interfere with the natural laws of immigration, and to thrust out the property of legitimate Southern emigrants by seizing and misusing the powers of the Territorial Legislature. This company was followed by another with a similar capital of five millions, and styled "Emigrant Aid Society." An Association of Free Soil Congressmen was at the same time secretly formed at Washington, under the name of the "Kansas "Aid Society," whose object was to send persons to Kansas to "prevent the introduction of slavery." These associations were undoubtedly violative of the letter of no law; the emigration of citizens opposed to slavery was a legal right not to be disputed; but to the Southern people it appeared a great moral wrong, and contrary to the peaceful spirit of Republican government, that the political control of a Territory or State should be secured by the use of vast sums of money, and the employment of vagabond mercenaries as against a fair and free expression of the will of resident and permanent citizens. If such a system of crusade were admissable, what was to prevent a similar inroad of immigrants into Missouri, Kentucky, or Virginia, and the overthrow and destruction of valuable property by the votes of paid persons who had no interest in the soil? Ten millions of dollars could give sustenance for twelve months to one hundred thousand voters. This army of crusaders thrown from Territory to State, and from State to State, would be so powerful as to carry Free Soilism wherever it might go. The forces sent out by the Emigrant Aid Societies were well armed with breech-loading rifles of approved army pattern—not fowling pieces for game, nor the ordinary huntsman's rifle—but short and rifled breech-loaders, suitable only for warfare. These rifles were often presented by churches. The Free Soil newspapers sportingly alluded to "the Sharpe's rifle argument."

Down to this moment a majority of Southern people had not entertained a thought of forcing slavery into Kansas. The few settlers from Missouri were more than outnumbered by those from Iowa. They knew that the South had not the white population nor the slaves to indulge in such a rash experiment. A large minority of the South were at that very time protesting against the removal of the Missouri Compromise. But when the march of a Northern army and the gleam of Northern arms announced that the war had begun, it was useless for them to talk further of conciliation and compromise. The largest slave-holding counties of the South had been invariably Whig. Their overtures to the North had been rejected; their compromise of rights had been certainly spurned; their property was now being warred against. Still they yearned for and expected peace and Union. Their only hope now was in the boldest position—in the declaration and maintenance of the abstract principle on the part of the South, and a solemn determination to meet force with force on the fields of Kansas. Opposed as they were to the repeal of the Missouri Compromise, now that it was removed, they would obey the new law and see to it that its principle of peaceable non-intervention should be carried out. It had always been their opinion that a law of Congress should be obeyed until it was repealed. They were for the Union, the Constitution and the enforcement of the laws in spirit as well as letter.

Far different was the sentiment of the Free Soil agitators. At a public meeting held in his church in the interest of the "Emigrant Aid Society, Rev. HENRY WARD BEECHER said that "he believed that the "Sharpe rifle was truly a moral agency, and there was "more moral power in those instruments, so far as the "slaveholders of Kansas were concerned, than in a "hundred Bibles." Such was the blasphemy of the Abolition Church. Mr. LLOYD GARRISON said: "Massachusetts has already made it a penal offence to help "to execute a law of the Union. I want to see the "officers of the State brought into collision with those "of the Union." Such was the treason of Abolition legislation. Again said Mr. GARRISON: "No Union "with slave-holders. Up with the flag of disunion, that "we may have a free and glorious Union of our own." Such was the cry and the hope of the Northern Secession party. Said Mr. JOSHUA R. GIDDINGS: "I would "not be understood as desiring a servile insurrection; "but I say to Southern gentlemen, that there are hun-

"dreds of thousands of honest and patriotic men who "will laugh at your calamity and mock when your fear "cometh." Such was the humanity of the Abolition heart.

That, at the outset, the abrogation of the Missouri line was not intended to carry slavery North of it, and that the South entertained no hope or expectation of such a result, is evidenced by a speech of Mr. YANCEY, in which he said:

"The South had done its duty in using all its "exertions to bring Kansas into the Union 'in accord- "ance with the p inciples of the Constitution.' She did "it knowing that the new State would be represented "by Free Soil Senators and Representatives. She had "nobly performed her duty without counting the cost."

It was in May, 1854, that the Free Soil party took up arms, by its Emigrant Aid organization, to "prevent "the introduction of slavery into" a territory where the laws of the United States had decreed that it might go. It was two years later that an appeal was made by States-Rights leaders of Alabama in behalf of emigration to Kansas. All parties now stood shoulder to shoulder against the armed invasion of that territory by New England. Mr. YANCEY was appointed to receive contributions. JEFFERSON BUFORD, a lawyer of respectability and social standing, and a member of the Southern Rights Association of Eufaula, proceeded to organize a company of emigrants.

During the first week in April, 1856, a body of emigrants under command of BUFORD, to the number of five hundred, arrived at Montgomery on their journey to Kansas by way of New Orleans and the Mississippi River. An impromptu reception of the emigrants by the citizens was held at Estelle Hall. An eloquent address was delivered by ALPHEUS BAKER, of Barbour county, who had followed and animated by his soul-stirring addresses at all resting points since leaving Eufaula, this body of emigrants, to whose care was confided the interests of the South in the new Territory of Kansas. Mr. Baker's speech occupied at least one hour and a half in its delivery, and was listened to with profound attention. He dwelt upon the constant assaults made upon the South by the Abolitionists of the North, and the insidious means which they employed to deprive Southerners of their property; he took a cursory glance at the course of injustice and partiality which had fallen to the lot of the South. He considered Kansas the battle-ground on which Southern Rights were to be triumphantly maintained or ingloriously relinquished. He counseled no hasty or unconstitutional movements on the part of the South, but urged a firm, determined spirit to "commit no wrong "and relinquish no right." He said the South had borne, long and patiently, the aggressions, encroachments, and haughtiness of the North, not because she was tremulous for the result should she meet these—but for the sake of Union. He now considered it meet and proper that the South should show her determination to suffer persecution no longer. He called upon the proverbial chivalry of her sons, and appealed to their dearest interests to come up *now*, manfully to the rescue, to stand by their constitutional rights, and to maintain in all vigor the institutions to which they were accustomed from their infancy. He wished to oppose no spirit of dictation or haughtiness to the North, but he wished to see the entire South united on the question, as to whether the South should maintain its rights or surrender them at the beck and call of rampant fanaticism. At the conclusion of his eloquent speech, Mr. Baker was loudly applauded.

On Saturday, April 5, the emigrants were formed in line before the Madison House on Market street, when Maj. Buford addressed them, recommending an abstinence from intoxicating drinks, and a general bearing such as becomes good citizens. At two o'clock P. M., they marched to the Agricultural Fair Grounds, where an election for officers was held, and the emigrants were divided into companies—Maj. Buford being elected *General* of the battalion.

A large and enthusiastic meeting of the citizens of Montgomery was held the same night at Estelle Hall, to express their approval of and to aid the Kansas Emigration movement. Calls were made on several distinguished gentlemen to address the meeting. Major BUFORD delivered a dignified and stirring appeal, explaining the patriotic motives which had induced him to engage in the undertaking. His address was received with great expressions of applause from the assembly. He expressly declared that the intention of the emigrating party under his charge was peaceably to settle Kansas with true-hearted Southern men; that they intended no acts of lawlessness, or force, or fraud; but in the event of an interference with their rights by the hired minions of Northern Freesolism and Fanaticism, they would, to the last extremity, defend themselves and the institutions of their choice. He said that Kansas was the "outpost" which should be now defended by the South if the South intends to preserve her institutions and her character.

Judge William P. Chilton said that it was well known that he had always been a "Union man," that he was still a Union man, but the crisis had arrived in which he felt it his duty not to falter, but to maintain strictly every right of the South, in the Union if possible; if not, then out of the Union! He said that the great fault of the South heretofore had been in compromising their rights for the sake of peace and harmony. Such compromises had only urged the North to new acts of aggression; henceforth he deemed it the duty of the Southern States to suffer no infringement of their guaranteed privileges, but to contend to the last extremity for a full and complete equality with their Northern sister States.

The following resolutions were read by the Secretary and unanimously adopted by the meeting:

"*Resolved*, That our grateful thanks are tendered "to the noble band of emigrants who have so promptly "responded to the call made upon them to march forth "and throw themselves in the breach in defence of "Southern Rights and the constitutional privileges of "the South, and though we hope their mission may be "a peaceful one, and not involve them in an appeal to "arms, yet should Abolition fanaticism force such an "issue, we wish them to consider themselves as but "the vanguard of the mighty hosts of their brethren of "the South who are ready to march to their relief and "stand with them in the struggle.

"*Resolved*, That we are satisfied their conduct will "be governed by a strict observance of all the consti-"tutional laws of the Federal Government, and that we "deem it unnecessary to exhort them to oppose, by "all the means placed in their hands by the God who "made them, the least aggression on their rights and "privileges by the base hirelings of Northern fanat-"icism.

"*Resolved*, That the South has made sacrifices and "compromises to promote the harmony, peace, and "union of these States on divers occasions, and all such "efforts have only tended to encourage our adversa-"ries in their lawless and fanatical proceedings, and to "urge them on to repeated outrages against our char-"acter and standing as equals in the confederacy; "therefore, henceforth let there be inscribed on our "banners, 'No Compromise of our Rights,' but a full, "ample and entire equality with all our sister States, "even at the hazard of Disunion and War!"

On Sunday the entire battalion of Emigrants repaired to the Baptist Church, where they listened to an eloquent sermon from the pastor of that congregation, Rev. Dr. I. T. Tichenor. At the conclusion of the services the Reverend gentleman remarked that, inasmuch as several ministers at the North had been prominent in urging the necessity of sanctifying and civilizing the Territory of Kansas by the aid of Sharpe's rifles, he hoped his congregation would aid him in presenting each of the emigrants in Maj. Buford's battalion with a more potent weapon, and one much better calculated to bring about brotherly love and christian charity—a Bible. The congregation acted on the suggestion, and an adequate collection was immediately taken up for this object.

On Monday the battalion formed in line, and under the command of their officers marched to the Baptist Church. The entire side-galleries, and a large portion of the body of the Church, were occupied by the emigrants, while the remaining space was filled by spectators, among whom were many ladies. Rev. Mr. Dorman, of the Methodist Episcopal Church, offered up a prayer, asking that the blessings of the Almighty might descend on Maj. Buford and his command, and that the enterprise in which they were engaged might meet with the approbation of Heaven.

Rev. Mr. TICHENOR, in behalf of his congregation, then presented BUFORD with a large-sized elegant Bible, bearing an appropriate inscription; accompanying the presentation with an eloquent appeal to the feelings, patriotism, and the moral sense of the emigrants to walk in the paths of virtue, and to practice with assiduity the teachings contained in the Holy Word. He stated that it had been the intention of the congregation to present each individual of them with a copy of the Scriptures, but that a sufficient number of copies could not be found in the city. The sum sufficient to make the purchases had been raised, which he would confide to Major BUFORD's care, in order that he might, at some convenient point on his route, procure the necessary copies and present them to his command on behalf of the church. The Rev. gentleman closed by wishing them all life, happiness and prosperity, and hoped that the blessing of God would crown their endeavors to perpetuate the institutions of the South—which were fully in accordance with the law of God.

BUFORD received the Bible from the hands of the Rev. speaker, and, after reverently kissing it, replied on behalf of the emigrants that all their hopes of success were founded on the firm conviction that they were *right*, and that they were animated by motives of pure patriotism and a hearty desire for the welfare of the South and her institutions.

Benediction was then pronounced by Rev. Mr. DORMAN, and the emigrants marched to the wharf, where the steamer *Messenger* was lying to take them to Mobile. The crowd of spectators in attendance at the wharf could not have been less than five thousand in number, a large portion of them ladies. A band of colored musicians discoursed exhilirating music.

Arriving at the wharf they halted, and Hon. H. W. HILLIARD addressed them briefly, setting forth the right of the Southerners, relying for protection on the Constitution of the country, to enter the Territory of Kansas with their institutions and property, and to claim protection therefor from the Federal Government. He counseled a spirit of peace and conciliation, to act on the defensive—and remarked that he was glad to see them go armed with the Word of Truth and the Constitution, rather than with Sharpe's rifles. He avowed his confidence in the success of their mission, and felt satisfied that by no act of theirs would the South have cause to blush for those who had taken upon themselves the defence of her interests. Mr. HILLIARD spoke from a cotton-bale. He said it was typical of the supremacy of the white race. Said he: "Providence may change "our relations to the inferior race, but the principle is "eternal—the supremacy of the white race." Mr. ALPHEUS BAKER again spoke in his usual eloquent language. The bell of the steamer rang, and the expedition departed amid the huzzas of a united people, and to the sound of cannon booming along the bluffs.

The National WHIG party having been broken to pieces by the incessant agitation of the question of slavery by its Northern wing, the conservative portion of it, North and South, and a portion of the Democratic party, which was wearied with the "forcing issue" policy of the States-Rights men who controlled the PIERCE administration, now united under cover of secrecy in an organization which they hoped would issue from its cloak, fully panoplied, and grapple successfully with the grave problems of the day. Mr. JOHN M. CLAYTON, who had been Secretary of State under President TAYLOR, had announced in 1854 that this "Know Nothing" party would refuse "to test "the suitableness of any man for public office by the "question whether he is for or against the mere exten- "sion of slavery in some territory of the United States." This was satisfactory to the South. It was acquiescence in the principle of non-intervention in the territories. In June, 1855, the party met in National Council at Philadelphia, and laid down its platform. Forthwith the Whigs of the South gave in their adhesion to the organization, which now assumed the name "American Party.". In Alabama the old Whig leaders, BIBB, HILLIARD, CHILTON, WATTS, JUDGE, CLANTON, JEMISON, WHITE, LANGDON, and SHORTRIDGE arrayed themselves under the new banner. It may be asked why these citizens were not content to abide by the Democratic party upon their platform of 1852? They recognized the justice of the principles of the States-Rights men; why not join their organization? Why maintain separate organizations with parallel principles? The answer may be found in the June, 1856, platform of the National American Party:

1. The Southern Whigs, while admitting the principles of the Kansas Bill, charged the Democrats, in the

language of the first American resolution, with "having "elevated sectional hostility into a positive element of "political power and brought our institutions into "peril." For this reason they could not repose confidence in a party whose policy, under the leadership of QUITMAN, RHETT, DAVIS, and YANCEY, was to follow Mr. CALHOUN and to force the issue on the North.

2. The American party declared that it would abide by and maintain the existing laws upon the subject of slavery as a final and conclusive settlement of that subject. The Kansas Bill was then a law. It also declared that Congress *ought not* to legislate upon the subject of slavery within a territory of the United States.

3. The doctrine that the naturalization laws should be more strict, and that foreigners should not be allowed to vote until naturalized, would curtail the Free Soil vote and curb in the West the growing power of a class of citizens whose language, ideas, and habits were foreign to our own. The Whigs of the South were ready to seize upon this as a policy advantageous to the South, which had not a handful of foreign-born citizens.

4. So far as opposition to the Roman Catholic Church entered into the party, the Southern WHIGS everywhere rejected it, as pandering to the lowest prejudices of bigotry and unworthy of the dignity of a true republican, with whom liberty of conscience should be as sacred as life itself. But in those large cities of the North wherever the Romish Church interfered with secular affairs, they held that it was a proper subject for political opposition.

The Alabama State Council of Americans met at

Montgomery, Nov. 13, 1855. The rapid growth throughout the country, and wonderful success in many of the States, of their new party, as also the conservative platform laid down by the National Council in June, had delighted the more moderate people of the South. They saw in the AMERICAN party a worthy successor of the Whig. But while the Grand Council of Alabama was rejoicing over a new national party which appeared to be actually desirous of quieting the slavery agitation, the grand councils of many of the Northern States were also in session resolving that the Missouri Compromise should be restored, and that unless it were restored Congress should refuse to admit into the Union any State above that line which might apply for admission. The Free Soil element had gained access to the American party North, and was now ready to force the party to apply the Wilmot Proviso to Kansas and Nebraska. To the Southern Whigs the repeal of the Missouri Compromise was one thing. Its restoration at the mouth of Sharpe rifles was quite another thing. Therefore it was that the Alabama AMERICAN Convention resolved that the people of all the States have an equal right to enter and occupy any territory with their property, and that they are protected in the enjoyment of their property there by the Constitution of the United States, until such time as the people may frame a constitution preparatory to admission as a State. This was the principle set out by the resolutions of Mr. YANCEY adopted by the Democratic Convention of Alabama in 1848, and rejected by the National Democratic Convention of that year. By breaking down the barrier of the Compromises which separated them, Mr. YANCEY now saw the Democratic party and his old opponents of the Whig party occupying the same intrenchment, with ranks almost touching. The AMERICAN party North had not as yet fully indicated that it was being controlled by the Free Soilers, when the AMERICANS of Alabama once more met in convention, Feb. 4th, '56, and re-endorsed the position assumed by their Grand Council in November.

HENRY C. JONES, of Franklin county, was President of this Convention. Among its delegates were BIBB, CLANTON, BELSER, PARSONS, WHITE, JEMISON, JOS. W. TAYLOR, J. J. HOOPER, BENJ. GARDNER, W. A. ASHLEY, R. F. INGE, W. B. H. HOWARD, JEROME CLANTON, E. A. POWELL, and other distinguished members of the old Whig party, besides a number of those who had heretofore acted with the Democratic party. The overthrow of the American party in Virginia by the vigorous canvass of HENRY A. WISE, had alarmed the greater portion of the Democrats who had entered the Know Nothing lodges, and they had beat a hasty retreat; but quite a number still remained, and it appeared quite probable that the AMERICANS might carry the State of Alabama. The Convention announced the following principles:

1. That the people of all the States have a constitutional right to enter and occupy any of the territories, as well with their slaves as with any other species of property, and are protected in the enjoyment of the same by the Constitution and the flag of the country; and that neither Congress nor a territorial Legislature can legislate slavery into or out of a territory, but must protect the citizens in the enjoyment of their property of whatever description.

2. That the power to exclude slavery from a territory resides only in a convention of the people when assembled under an Act of Congress to frame a constitution preparatory to admission as a State.

3. That the opposite doctrine of squatter sovereignty is repudiated.

4. That neither Congress nor a Territorial Legislature can enable unnaturalized foreigners to vote within a territory; and that no foreign-born resident should vote within a State unless legally naturalized.

Addressing the Convention in support of these principles, Mr. HILLIARD argued that the Kansas-Nebraska Bill authorized the squatters in a territory to exclude slave property whenever they chose to do so, and that this doctrine of squatter sovereignty was worse than the Wilmot Proviso. By the exercise of the Wilmot Proviso the people would know at the outset that they could not remove with their slaves to a territory, but by being subjected to squatter sovereignty the tenure of their property would be left to the accidents of the hour, and to the whims of political hirelings who might be sent to the territory, not as actual residents and permanent citizens, but to accomplish the success of a certain political party. He charged the Kansas-Nebraska Act with containing this monstrous principle, so unworthy of dignified government, and the Democratic party with having accepted it. It was intended, he said, to please both sections; the South, because it removed the Missouri line and enabled the slave-holder to take his slave to any of the territories; the North, because the Free Soil settlers, without impediment, could first rush in and seize the territorial government. The fact that the Democrats of Alabama had resolved that they were opposed to squatter sovereignty, was immaterial. They had so resolved in 1848, and their resolutions being rejected by the National Convention, they had acquiesced, accepted Mr. CASS and repudiated Mr. YANCEY. Notwithstanding their late State Convention had reaffirmed Mr. YANCEY's resolutions of 1848, it would be seen that the Democratic party would nominate Mr. BUCHANAN, whom Mr. YANCEY then denounced, and that Mr. BUCHANAN would substantially endorse the doctrine of Mr. DOUGLAS. The AMERICAN party deplored the removal of the Missouri line as unnecessary and provocative of renewed sectional agitation; but being removed, nothing was left except to plant themselves upon the clear abstract right of holding slaves as other property until the Territory, when admitted as a State, should prohibit it. This, he felt satisfied, was sound constitutional law, and would be so held by the Supreme Court of the United States in the case then pending before it.

The State American Convention had sent delegates to a National American Convention which was to convene at Philadelphia Feb. 22. It was the hope of the Southern members of that party that the National Convention to nominate for the Presidency would be postponed to July. But the Northern members insisted upon an earlier day. The Southern States had but few representatives present, and the controlling sentiment was for free soil. The Convention repudiated the policy of the preceding Convention of June, took the ground of the newly-organized Republican party by declaring opposition to the reckless and unwise policy of the existing administration, and announced a free and open discussion of the question of slavery. So plain was the meaning of their new platform, that a despatch was forwarded to a "Republican" Convention, sitting at Pittsburg, in this language:

"The American party is no longer united. Raise "the Republican banner. Let there be no further "extension of slavery. The Americans are with you."

ALEXANDER WHITE and GEO. D. SHORTRIDGE, two of the delegates who had been appointed from Alabama, published a letter protesting that the Philadelphia Convention was not a representative body, that it had been assembled in unseemly haste and for the purpose of excluding the South; that it had planted itself on sectional ground and abandoned the conservative position of the former convention. There was a moral sublimity in the June platform; there was debasement for the South in that of February. Can we follow them? asked the letter. The Alabama party in their resolutions had declared that they would not support for the Presidency any one who would not publicly avow the correctness of their views. It was now time for the South to take her destiny in her own hands. Messrs. WHITE and SHORTRIDGE could not follow men or a party who would not avow the justice and maintain the principles of the Alabama American platform. Their only hope was that the party would hold a National Convention in July and return to the sound and constitutional position of the National Council of 1855.

Notwithstanding the fusion of the Free Soilers of the American party North with the Republican party, there was still a large body of conservative citizens at the North who were anxious for a cessation of sectional controversy. These, added to the anti-administration vote of the South, constituted one-fourth of the entire popular vote of the Union. It was hoped and believed that this body of citizens, always devoted to the Union, always anxious and willing to compromise questions which involved no practical interest, always moderate and conservative in action and expression, would form a nucleus around which would concentrate a dominant national party. These men met at Baltimore in July. It was a large assemblage, representing all parts of the Union and composed of persons of the highest intellectual attainments and moral worth. With great unanimity they nominated Mr. FILLMORE for the Presidency.

In August, 1855, the Gubernatorial election in Alabama had shown 30,639 votes for Judge SHORTRIDGE, the American candidate for Governor, and 42,238 for WINSTON, his Democratic opponent. The vote for SHORTRIDGE was twice that for SCOTT in 1851. The vote for WINSTON was but four thousand more than was cast for POLK eleven years before. The American vote for SHORTRIDGE was the largest opposition vote that had been cast in the State of Alabama. It appeared from this that the dissolution of the Whig party in 1852 had not discouraged nor disheartened the conservatives of the South. They were more compact than ever against the agitation policy of Mr. YANCEY and the States-Rights party. Had the American party remained a national one, abided by the platform of June, 1855, and had not its Northern wing thrown itself into the arms of the Free Soilers in February, '56, it is probable that the vote between Mr. BUCHANAN and Mr. FILLMORE in Alabama would have been as closely contested as that between Gen. CASS and Gen. TAYLOR.

Notwithstanding the cloud that was cast over the

party South by the action of the Philadelphia Convention of February, the Alabama Americans resolved to accept Mr. FILLMORE upon the strength of his administration and the principle involved in the Compromise of 1850, as announced in the resolutions of the several Alabama American Conventions.

Mr. YANCEY, at the BUCHANAN ratification meeting held at Montgomery, had said that every generous and just-minded man present would admit that the Democrats of Alabama had a right to congratulate themselves on the complete justification of the resolutions proposed by him and adopted by the State Convention of 1848. The striking truth then announced was so palpably true as to admit of no dispute. It was a matter which had so forced itself on the attention of Southern Whigs as to compel such men as TOOMBS and STEPHENS, of Ga., BENJAMIN, of La., CARUTHERS, of Mo., PRESTON, of Ky., and the WALKERS, PATTONS, PUGHS, and hosts of other true and gallant men of Alabama and elsewhere, to dissever their old party associations in obedience to the impulses of patriotic duty, and ally themselves with the Democracy as the only National party possessing the power and the will to protect the South and assure the continuance of the Union upon a constitutional basis. There can be no question but that Mr. YANCEY had consistently adhered to the CALHOUN resolutions of 1848, and that in the spirit of CALHOUN, he had steadily forced upon the Democratic party the doctrine of non-intervention by a territorial legislature with the institution of slavery. But a large portion of the Democratic party denied that Mr. YANCEY's construction of the Cincinnati non-intervention resolution was correct. Recognizing the difference of opinion which existed as to the duty and powers of a territorial government, Mr. BUCHANAN, in his letter accepting the nomination for the Presidency, said "that the people of a territory, *like those of a State,* shall decide for themselves" as to the existence of slavery. This letter was doubtless intended to meet the demands of both sections. At the North it was construed to mean that the people of a territory might legislate as to property like those of a State. By the Southern Democracy it was construed to mean that the people of a territory could decree what was to be property in the same manner the people of a State could make such decree, namely: by a properly assembled convention.

Seizing this expression of Mr. BUCHANAN, the American speakers in Alabama contended that Mr. YANCEY'S construction was wrong, and that the Northern Democracy were intent upon leaving to the will of the first squatters of a territory the exclusion of Southern property. If, said they, this is the conclusion of the whole matter, why was the Missouri line disturbed, and why was sectional agitation once more renewed? They maintained that the AMERICAN resolutions of the National Council of June, 1855, and the Alabama resolutions of the February following, expressed the true position of the American party. They held that, as between the Free Soil Whig party of the North, and the States-Rights Secession party of the South, the American party stood, the only national one which could give peace to the country and perpetuity to the Union. The American party had decided to abide by the existing laws. It had declared that Congress could not exclude a State from admission to the Union because of the existence of slavery. It is true the

National Council had pretermitted any expression of opinion as to the power of Congress to establish or prohibit slavery in any territory, but they had declared that Congress *ought not* to legislate upon that subject. Thus while Mr. YANCEY and his friends denied the power of Congress, the AMERICANS held that the higher motive of moral obligation should induce Congress to refrain from all attempts to exercise the power. The constitutional obligation might be in doubt, as thought one wing of the Democracy; but with the Americans there was no doubt as to the moral obligation.

The political elements which entered into the Presidential contest, were as follows:

1. The Republican party, solid and compact, in favor of the power and duty of Congress to prohibit slavery in the Territories. This party lacked only the vote of Pennsylvania to carry FREMONT into the Presidency.

2. The Northern Democracy, giving a squatter sovereignty construction to Mr. Buchanan's letter of acceptance, just as Mr. YANCEY, in 1848, had given a similar construction to his Berk's county letter. This element, while unable to give an electoral vote in proportion to its numbers, constituted two-thirds of the entire Democratic population.

3. The Southern Democracy, now controlled by the successors of Mr. CALHOUN, and construing the acceptance of Mr. BUCHANAN and the Cincinnati platform to mean non-intervention both by Congress and its agent, the territorial legislature. This element, while constituting but one-third of the Democratic popular strength, was able to control four-fifths of the probable Democratic electoral votes.

4. The American party, which, in the North, evaded

the question of slavery, and which, in the South was divided between those who, while not denying the power of Congress to prohibit slavery in the Territories, contended that the existing legislation on the subject should be abided by as a final settlement, and those who denied such a power to Congress and insisted on congressional protection to slaves until the territory became a State. Both sections of the party, South, agreed that the present laws should be carried out, and that the constitutionality of the question should be left to the decision of the Supreme Court. This party at the South was able to poll against the Democracy more than one hundred thousand more votes than were cast for Gen. SCOTT, and nearly fifty thousand more than were cast for Gen. TAYLOR.

CHAPTER XIV.

The Dred Scott Decision—Condition of Parties in 1858—The Irrepressible Conflict—The John Brown Raid—Leagues of United Southerners—The Southern Commercial Convention—Debate between Yancey and Pryor—Precipitating the Cotton States into Revolution, &c., &c.

"Free labor and slave labor, these antagonistic systems, are continually coming into close contact, and collision results. Shall I tell you what this collision means? They who think it is accidental, unnecessary, the work of interested or fanatical agitators, and therefore ephemeral, mistake the case altogether. It is an irrepressible conflict between opposing and enduring forces, and it means that the United States must and will, sooner or later, become either entirely a slave-holding nation or entirely a free-labor nation."

W. H. SEWARD, IN 1858.

"Our own banner is inscribed: 'No co-operation with slave-holders in politics: no fellowship with them in religion: no affiliation with them in society: no recognition of pro-slavery men, except as ruffians, outlaws and criminals.'" IMPENDING CRISIS.

"As long as the blood-stained Union exists, there is but little hope for the slave."

W. L. GARRISON, AT NEW YORK, 1857.

At the time when the Whigs of Alabama in their support of Mr. FILLMORE, had asserted the right of the people of any State to remove to and hold within a territory any species of property, subject to the decision of the people of the territory, through a constitution framed as preliminary to their admittance as a State, the Supreme Court of the United States had pending before them a case (Dred Scott vs. Sandford, 19 Howard's Reports, p. 393,) involving all the contested questions in regard to slavery. Two days after

Mr. Buchanan's inauguration, a decision was announced upon this case which affirmed the correctness of the Alabama American platform. It established the proposition that the Federal Government could not interfere with the possession of slave property in a slave territory, and could not authorize the local government to do so, and that it was the duty of the Government to protect such property there. The Republican party denied the binding force of this decision. Although composed principally of Northern Whigs who applauded Mr. Webster when he named the Supreme Court as the arbiter in disputes concerning constructions of the Constitution, they now found it convenient to reject that arbitration. They, together with the adherents of Mr. Douglas, held that the Court could pass simply upon each case as it came before them, and could not lay down a general principle which would bind the political department of the Government. The Douglas Democracy in thus rejecting the umpirage of the Supreme Court were undoubtedly in accord with the views of Hayne, Van Buren, Calhoun and other leaders of the Democratic party of the preceding generation. The Buchanan Democracy could not, with consistency, claim the Dred Scott decision as strengthening their case. They had, theretofore, uniformly declared that the dignity of the States would not permit the decision of constitutional questions to rest with a Federal Court. For the purpose of advancing their party interests, the Northern Whigs and Southern Democrats, the extreme Free Soilers and the extreme States-Rights men, at this point reversed their positions. The party that had once spurned the idea of listening to the Supreme Court upon political questions, now emblazoned the Dred Scott decision upon its flag, and the party which had invariably appealed to the Court in the days of MARSHALL now rejected it with loathing and hate in the days of YANCEY. The Whig party of the South alone maintained its ancient land-marks. Inheriting the traditions of 1830 and of 1840, it still adhered to the faith of Webster and Clay, and bowed to the decision of the Court. They still held that the Constitution, and the laws made in pursuance thereof, were the supreme laws of the land, and that the Supreme Court could alone decide whether a law was made in pursuance to the Constitution.

All of the Compromises of the Constitution having been rejected, and the Supreme Tribunal having now announced its decision upon the grave question of the day, the Whigs of Alabama had no further point of dispute with their adversaries upon matters growing out of slavery. They still, however, held themselves in solid array against the Democracy upon the ground that the Territorial question was an impracticable one, upon which the continuance of the Union should not be staked, and that the States-Rights leaders who now held unbounded sway in the Democratic ranks, had come to the conclusion that secession should be resorted to without awaiting any further overt act than the Conference Bill, under which Kansas was virtually refused admittance with her Lecompton Constitution. So determined was this array that in the election for Congressman in the Montgomery District, as late as November, 1858, Mr. JUDGE, who has been already alluded to as a prominent leader of the Whigs, failed of an election by only two hundred and fourteen votes in a poll of more than thirteen thousand. Referring to this election, it is worthy of note that the large slave-holding counties of the District gave majorities for Mr. JUDGE, notwithstanding the newspapers charged him with want of fealty to the institution of slavery in voting at the Nashville Convention to accept the Compromise of 1850, and in publishing the card relative to the right of secession, to which reference has already been made in a preceding chapter. The charge of disloyalty to the South thus preferred against Mr. JUDGE by the Montgomery *Advertiser* and other Democratic newspapers, did not prevent the people from casting for him 6,666 votes, against 6,880 votes for Mr. CLOPTON, his competitor. The counties most largely interested in slavery, and possibly in the extension of slavery to Kansas and Nebraska, voted for Mr. JUDGE. He was defeated by the votes of those counties which were the least interested in that subject. Thus firm and unbroken was the front maintained against the Democratic party around the home of YANCEY and the cradle of the Confederacy. Such was the conflict, not of principle, but of sentiment and temper, in one of the largest slave-holding Districts of the South, inhabited by a population wealthy, high-spirited, and intelligent—a conflict which would, by nicely balancing the power of the disputants, have preserved the Union for an indefinite period—when suddenly occurred a series of events which paralyzed the labors of men like WATTS, JUDGE, LANGDON, and CLANTON, and struck the South with such alarm and indignation as to add intensity to the secession movement which had now once more assumed definite shape.

These events were: 1. The announcement by Senator SEWARD, the leader of the Republican party, that an irrepressible conflict existed between the North and South, a conflict which must eventually give free labor to the South; 2. The endorsement by Mr. GREELEY, Mr. SEWARD, and all the Republican leaders, of a book published by a charlatan, entitled "Impending Crisis," which advised the opponents of slavery "to land military "forces in the Southern States who shall raise the "standard of freedom and call the slaves to it," and to "teach the slaves to burn their masters' buildings, to "kill their cattle and hogs, to conceal and destroy "farming utensils, to abandon labor in seed-time and "harvest and let the crops perish"; 3. The invasion of Virginia and the *emeute* at Harper's Ferry by JOHN BROWN and his Abolition force.

Cotemporaneously with these events, which did more to fire the Southern heart than all the speeches of States-Rights leaders, was the meeting of the Southern Commercial Convention at Montgomery, and the organization of Leagues of united Southerners to take the place of the old States-Rights Associations.

A Southern Commercial Convention held at Knoxville, in August, 1857, had appointed a committee, of which L. W. SPRATT, of S. C., was chairman, to prepare business for the next meeting, covering these questions: 1. The African slave trade; 2. The political relations of the South to the Union; and, 3. The foreign policy the South should advocate.

The next meeting of the Convention was held at Montgomery, May 10, 1858. The welcoming address was made by Mr. YANCEY on behalf of the Mayor and Council of Montgomery. He said:

"I must be allowed, at least on my own behalf, to "welcome you, too, as but the foreshadowing of that "far more important body, important as you evidently "will be, that, if injustice and wrong shall still continue "to rule the hour and councils of the dominant section "of this country, must, ere long, assemble upon "Southern soil, for the purpose of devising some "measures by which not only your industrial, but your "social and your political relations shall be placed upon "the basis of an independent sovereignty, which will "have within itself a unity of climate, a unity of soil, a "unity of production, and a unity of social relations; "that unity which alone can be the basis of a successful "and permanent government." [Loud applause.]

Among the members of the Convention were men whose names had been long familiar to the public, some of the leading intellects of the South. There were CALHOUN and HAYNE, of S. C., able representatives of their distinguished kinsmen who had passed away; PRESTON and PRYOR, of Va.; HILL and LAMAR, of Ga.; BRECKINRIDGE and WHITE, of La.; MCRAE and DUNN, of Miss.; CHASE and BREVARD, of Fla. From Alabama were seen the faces of YANCEY, HILLIARD, CLANTON, COCHRAN, LEA, WALKER, BELSER, BETHEA, and many others of distinction. A. P. CALHOUN, of S. C., was elected President. Mr. SPRATT submitted to the Convention an elaborate report touching the questions submitted at the last session of the Convention, and recommended the adoption of the following resolutions:

"1. That slavery is right, and that being right, there "can be no wrong in the natural means to its formation.

"2. That it is expedient and proper the Foreign "Slave Trade should be re-opened, and that this Con-"vention will lend its influence to any legitimate "measure to that end.

"3. That a committee, consisting of one from each

"slave State, be appointed to consider of the means, "consistent with the duty and obligations of these "States, for re-opening the Foreign Slave Trade, and "that they report their plan to the next meeting of "this Convention."

Mr. ROGER A. PRYOR, of Virginia, stated that although a member of the committee from whence this report purports to come, yet he had not seen it, nor had he heard any of its arguments or conclusions until it was read to the convention. He therefore hoped the convention would indulge him by giving him an opportunity to prepare and present to the convention the arguments founded upon considerations of high State policy, of eminently high Southern policy, which would forbid this convention, which purports to represent the interests of the South, from embarking in so serious an enterprise as that of proclaiming before Christendom that they now intend to insist upon re-opening the trade in African slaves.

Mr. YANCEY, of Alabama, said he, also was a member of the committee from which this report comes, and from circumstances beyond his control, he had not seen it. But from what he had heard of it, as it was read, he was free to confess that he gave it his most hearty concurrence. There might be some things in it to which he could not give his consent.

The question recurring on the following day, Mr. PRYOR addressed the convention at length. He differed from the gentleman from South Carolina (Mr. Spratt) in his argument that the diffusion of slavery strengthened it. Diffusion is not strength; but, on the contrary, concentration is strength. It was not the opinion of Thomas Jefferson that diffusing slavery strengthened it. While he admired the genius and patriotism of Jefferson, he must, at the same time, confess, with humiliation and shame, that he was the most intelligent adversary of slavery that the world has ever produced. But he offered the Missouri restriction because, by using his own words, "by diffusing the "institution of slavery you weakened it." Look at Missouri, where slavery is very much diffused, and then at South Carolina, where it is more concentrated than in any other State in this Confederacy, and then say where the institution of slavery has the most strength.

The policy advocated in this report is and ought to be impracticable. We are committed by the action of our forefathers to give the Federal Government unconditional and absolute control over the African slave trade. The gentleman from South Carolina cannot expect to get the Federal Government to open that trade. No sensible man here believes that that will ever be done under any circumstances, for the North has complete control of the legislative and executive departments of the Government. Does the gentleman propose to open the trade by action of the several Southern States? That would be an act of bad faith, for we have agreed to the Constitution of this country, and as long as we remain in the Union, we must uphold that Constitution. It is what we require of others, and let us, like honorable men, do the same thing ourselves.

Another objection to the agitation of this subject, said Mr. Pryor, is that by committing ourselves to this policy we sacrifice our friends at the North, and the National Democratic party in the North. It was that

Democratic party which affected an amelioration in the financial system of this Government; which redeemed the country from the oppression of a National Bank; which has extended the area of the Union by the acquisition of Florida, Texas, and California. His memories of that party appealed to his heart not rudely and ruthlessly to sacrifice it. There are members of that party in the North that he was unwilling to consign to irretrievable perdition and destruction by imposing upon them a test they cannot be expected to stand. He would rather, in an excess of generosity and magnanimity, sacrifice some of his own feelings and rights than to sacrifice those who have stood by us in our hour of need. It was utterly impossible for any Northern man, however faithful to the interests of the South, to advocate the revival of the African slave trade. There were exceptional cases, anomalies in nature, *lusus naturæ*, like the editor of the *Day Book*, but he was but an exception. The gentleman from Alabama (Mr. YANCEY) said yesterday—whether he intended it as a compliment or a reproach—said that the National Democratic party was the only ligament that united the North and South, and he was unwilling to sacrifice it.

This proposition, if endorsed, would shock the moral sentiment of Christendom. Some may say that they do not care for that. But we of the South who profess to be Christians should endeavor, if possible, without sacrificing rights, to seek rather to propitiate the moral sentiment of Christendom. He was not willing to throw the gauntlet in the face of the Christian world. He was very much governed by considerations of policy. And the sentiment of the Christian world was gradually coming around to one standpoint.

Look at England with her Coolies, and France with her apprentices. The despatch from our Minister to France shows a gradual amelioration in sentiment upon this subject. We should bide our time, and not, by this public action, give our institutions an irretrievable recoil. *Quieta non movere.* Allow things to go along smoothly.

He objected to the introduction of a horde of barbarians from Africa among us. That was incompatible with the present status of slavery here. Ours is a patriarchal institution now, founded in pity and protection on the one side, and dependence and gratitude on the other. It would become under this policy like slavery in Cuba, where the master is forced to be cruel and stern in his government and control of slavery. It would create a new grade of slavery, and create in the slaves we already have a feeling of superiority that we should avoid.

In short, this proposition to revive the African Slave Trade was purely and simply a proposition to dissolve the Union, because it cannot be carried out while the Union lasts. When that proposition is boldly and openly made, Virginia, though a border State, would not shrink from her duty. But Virginia was unwilling to put the perpetuity of this Union upon any such issue as this proposition to kidnap cannibals upon the coast of Congo and contend with the King of Dahomey in the marts of wild Africa for the purchase of slaves there. If you intend dissolution, declare it boldly and manfully. [Applause.] Present your proposition with your preamble and resolutions, and we will meet you upon it, and either acquiesce and go with you heartily and zealously, or give our reasons for not doing so.

Mr. JOHN A. JONES, of Georgia—Will the gentleman go, go now, to-day, for a dissolution of the Union? [Applause.]

Mr. PRYOR—I am not going to take a position outside of the Union until I can go with a united South. Give me a case of oppression and tyranny sufficient to justify a dissolution of the Union, and give me a united South, and then I am willing to go out of the Union. [Applause.]

Mr. JONES—If the gentleman waits for an undivided South he never will go out of the Union.

Mr. PRYOR—I will not so stigmatize any State or any class of my fellow citizens by believing that when a case arises sufficient to justify a dissolution of the Union, any State of the South will stand back. In no crisis has the Old Dominion ever been recreant to her duty. When the ball of the revolution was set in motion in 1774, Virginia was not behind. When Jackson desired to send the Federal troops to crush out South Carolina, Virginia was not recreant to her duty. [Applause.] But recollect that the first onset, in case of revolution, must be met by Virginia, and gentlemen must not expect of her an inordinate enthusiasm that may be felt by others not situated as she is. But take my word for it, Virginia will not disparage the memory of her illustrious heroes, and abdicate the proud position she now occupies in the annals of our country. The true position of the South was the position of defence. We claim nothing but our rights, nothing more than our forefathers guaranteed to us, and so help us God, Virginia will never take less than that. If there is to be a disseverance of the Union, let there be no disseverance of the South. Believe the border States true and loyal; recollect that suspicion begets resentment. Let us collect our energies for the final struggle, so that when it comes, the entire South may precipitate herself upon the foe, like a thunderbolt from Heaven, with irresistible effect.

This speech of Mr. PRYOR was received with great favor by that portion of the immense audience which was opposed to a disruption of the Democratic party and to forcing issues upon the people of the North. The applause which greeted his resistance to the new proposition of the States-Rights leaders, the opening of the African slave trade had barely died away when Mr. YANCEY obtained the floor. He said that he had, under the circumstances, considered it advisable to prepare a report embodying his views, which he would submit to the Convention. He then proceeded to read his report, which concluded with the following resolution:

"*Resolved*, That the laws of Congress prohibiting "the foreign slave trade ought to be repealed."

Mr. YANCEY said that he supposed that the gist of the remarks of the gentleman from Virginia (Mr. Pryor) was to be found, like the important part of a lady's letter, in the postscript. He supposed the true reason for his opposition to the report of the committee was to be found in the latter part of his speech, the effect that it would have upon our friends at the North. God save us from such friends. Have their fidelity and friendship been exhibited in the recent passage of the Conference Bill concerning Kansas? And yet we are told in a Southern Convention to reflect before we assert our undoubted right, upon the effect it will have upon our Northern allies. Are we never to give an open, manly, frank avowal of our constitutional position in the Union, or must we depend upon a mere subterfuge, in regard to the meaning of which there are a half a dozen different opinions? Then, unlike the gentleman from Virginia, he was for disunion now. [Applause.] He would shed his blood to save the Union as our fathers left it, but not the Union which has been reared upon its ruins. The Union of our fathers has already been dissolved by oppression and fraud, and there was no drop of blood in his heart that he was not ready to shed in defence of Southern rights against that Union. [Applause.]

What was the measure recommended to the Convention? The repeal of a law which discriminates against the labor of the South. Is there an Alabamian here who does not endorse that sentiment? Is there a Virginian here who does not endorse it? The General Government has no right to discriminate against us. The Constitution does not authorize it. It says: "Congress shall enact no law prohibiting the emigra-"tion or importation of such persons as the States now "allow before the year 1808." That very clause was a constitutional guarantee of slavery and the slave trade, because it forbid Congress to interfere with it before 1808. In 1807 a law was passed that after 1808 no slaves should be imported into this Union, which law was unconstitutional in its discrimination against the South.

In 1807 the slave trade was declared a misdemeanor. In 1820 it was declared piracy. And yet we must not demand the repeal of these discriminating laws for fear we may offend our Northern allies, and perchance defeat some aspirant for the Presidency. The gentleman from Virginia refers to the opinions of Christendom upon this subject—they are rather the opinions of devildom. The great advocates of what is called Christendom have met in convention in the Northern States and voted if the Bible recognized slavery, it was the work of the devil rather than of God. And New England male and female teachers and parents have endeavored to impress upon the minds of the youth there that God himself should be dethroned if he recognized African slavery.

Now, if it is wrong to hold slaves and to buy them and sell them, it is right in morals and under the Constitution which guarantees the institution, that we should buy them in whatever place we may choose to select. He did not wish to be compelled to go to Virginia and buy slaves for $1,500 each, when he could get them in Cuba for $600, or upon the coast of Guinea for one-sixth of that sum.

As to the reduction in the value of land by the re-opening of the slave trade, he would ask why the land in the South, though as rich and fertile as any in the world, brought less in the market than the comparatively sterile lands of New England and New York? It was because the South lacked the supply of labor necessary to cultivate her land, while in the North the land was not enough for the supply of labor.

There is no amount of ingenious reasoning, no claptrap of words, no trick in language that can do away with the great law that if you increase the number of slave owners you increase the basis of the institution. There is no denying that there is a large emancipating interest in Virginia, and Kentucky, and Maryland, and Missouri, the fruits of which we see in Henry Winter Davis, Cassius M. Clay, and Thomas H. Benton. We need to strengthen this institution; and how better can we do that than by showing the non-slave-holding class of our citizens that they can buy a negro for $200 which, in a few years, by his care and instruction, will become worth a thousand dollars? Teach the poor white man who cannot now buy a negro, that by this means he can buy one, you secure him to the interests of the South.

But it is said to us—*cui bono?* What good in this? The North has the power, and will not repeal these laws. That is no reason why we should not resist. Nations should be actuated by the same high sense of honor as individuals. If a man spits in my face I will strike him, though he may thrash me. I know we cannot wrest this justice from the dominant North. They have fastened the shackles upon us, and will not loose them. But let us stand up and resist them like men. If the principle of submission is to sway the councils of the South, it will not be long before will be fulfilled the boast of Seward that the whole American Continent would soon be under the flag of this Union, and there would not be upon it the foot of a slave. He is a calm, cool man, not given to imaginative speculation, but he spoke this in the fullness of his heart as what he believed. He said this when goaded by his thick-headed associate, Hale, for voting for the increase of the army, which he expected to command himself in 1860, that he had not designed us to get a glimpse of.

There are elements entering into the opinions of gentlemen upon this question that ought not to enter here—elements of national party, opinions of Christendom, etc. Public sentiment needs some corrective upon this subject; and that corrective can only be made by directing the public attention to this subject. We can agitate our wrongs; we have no rights I fear to agitate; we can agitate our injuries; we have no favors to talk about.

We are told that we should not assert the rights of the South upon this issue. Will the gentleman from Virginia say what is the issue upon which the South should contest their rights?

Mr. PRYOR said he was not willing to assert the rights of the South upon the proposition to kidnap cannibals from Africa, or buy slaves of the King of Dahomey. But should a Black Republican President be installed in the Executive chair in Washington, and the power of the government be palpably in his hands —whenever the gentleman can satisfy the intelligence of the people of the South in sufficient numbers to justify the movement, then he was willing to make the issue, and he could pledge Virginia not to be behind Alabama. And he would say further, that when the issue was presented, and he was convinced that a majority even of the people of Alabama were, upon mature consideration, willing to leave the Union, they of Virginia would be ready to go with them. [Applause.]

Mr. YANCEY said he was unfeignedly happy that he had been able to draw from the gentleman from Virginia such a declaration. This morning he was for waiting for a united South; now he would join with Alabama alone. The speaker had great hopes in agitating this question; he trusted that the attention of the people of the South would be aroused to the assertion of their rights. If this demand should be refused by the North, it would be one other evidence that injustice is the ruling spirit of the hour in our national legislature. There would be one link more between Southern men and Southern men—one link more snapped between Southern men and Northern men.

The speech of Mr. YANCEY on this occasion is said to have been one of his best. From the imperfect reports of it, we can only gather the fact that he and his friends, in advocating such a preposterous measure as an agitation for a repeal of the laws prohibiting the African slave trade and declaring it to be piracy, were simply attempting, by advocating extreme propositions, to snap the last feeble links which held together the Democratic party. Such was his plain declaration. He wanted disunion now. But Mr. PRYOR, and those who thought with him, were not then for disunion. Fearing that his answer to Mr. YANCEY's last question might be misunderstood, Mr. PRYOR explained that what he had intended to say was that he did not suppose that Alabama would undertake to leave the Union without sufficient cause as would justify every other Southern State in the Confederacy from following her.

Mr. HILLIARD, who had now left his old Whig friends and had become a partisan of the Buchanan Administration, replied to the speech of Mr. YANCEY: He contended that the power granted to Congress to regulate commerce with foreign nations, gave them power to regulate the African Slave Trade; and the clause in the Constitution referred to by Mr. YANCEY, merely restricted them from exercising that power before 1808, expressly conceding to Congress the power to do so after that time. Such had been the opinion of the framers of the Constitution; such the opinion of Jefferson, Madison and Monroe, and also of John C. Calhoun, who was a member of Monroe's Cabinet when the act of 1820 was passed declaring the slave trade to be piracy.

He was not prepared to go for a dissolution now upon existing causes, and upon mere abstractions and questions of doubtful policy. He believed that the time had come, however, when the South must resist all aggression upon her institutions, or give them up, and he believed that she would do so. He believed when there should be made or attempted a palpable infringement of the rights of the South, she would be united in her resistance. He admitted that there had been improper legislation, and that South Carolina was right in the stand she took, and he believed she had brought the General Government back again to the right track, and he preferred to-day, if we could bring the government to the right track and preserve the integrity of the Constitution, to remain in the Union and preserve our rights there. He thought the present indications were such as to lead us to believe that such will be the case. He alluded to the decision of the Supreme Court in the Dred Scott case—to the known opinions of the present Chief Magistrate as evidence. And he said that he believed if the case should be carried to the Supreme Court, the decision would be that slaveholders have the constitutional right to pass through any State in this Union with his slaves. He thought the progress of this Government was onward in the right direction, and not backward.

He thought there would be a disposition on the part of the North now to yield us all our rights. And he was not for disunion upon the present issues with the Federal Government.

As for the fears expressed by gentlemen here that the North will triumph hereafter over the South, he could not join with them. Now that the South was fully aroused, he thought she would be able to defeat the North in the future. He thought the aspect of affairs at present was hopeful, and with the present prospect he was not prepared to-day to abandon the Union for existing causes of complaint. But he would say that in his judgment the election of a Black Republican to the Presidency would result in the subversion of the Government. The people of the South would not wait to see him clothed with the insignia of office; would not wait for any overt act; the end will then have come. But he did not desire to see the South divided upon such a question as this; we are now one people—a united people. Let us remain in the Union, one and undivided, or let us go out of it, if go we must, a united people.

Mr. WM. BALLARD PRESTON, of Virginia, representing that conservative Whig element which Mr. HILLIARD had parted from, obtained the floor.

In regard to the constitutionality of the laws sought to be repealed, he would ask the Convention if they would not be compelled to go with him against this policy, if he should succeed in showing to them that these laws were constitutional? The doctrine of the States-Rights school was to uphold the Constitution, and not from any motive of interest, gain or ambition, to surrender one jot or tittle of that revered instrument. He read from the Madison Papers containing the debates on the Constitution of the United States, to show that the Constitution as at first reported contained a provision that no navigation act should be passed by Congress except by a two-third vote of all the members present; and no law should be passed prohibiting the importation of African slaves. Upon that a conflict arose between the North and the South. The matter was recommitted to the committee of detail to endeavor to frame some provision which should reconcile the conflicting interests of the two sections, and the result was the provision in the present Constitution under which these prohibitory laws had been passed.

Mr. P. read from the remarks of Mr. Pinckney, of South Carolina, to show that at the time this clause was reported he and others from the South, in the Convention, understood it to grant the power to prohibit the importation of African slaves after the year 1808. It was considered a bargain struck, a contract made by the patriotic framers of the Constitution, in order to unite the two conflicting interests of the North and South, and enable them to form this Federal Union.

The gentleman from Alabama (Mr. Yancey) argues in his report that these laws are discriminating against the South, and constitute a degrading badge, a dishonorable mark upon the South. By whom was the law of 1808 passed? By a Democratic Congress, sanctioned by the administration of Thomas Jefferson, in which was James Madison, one of the original framers of the Constitution. Was it to be believed that those men who framed the resolutions of '98 and '99, and inaugurated and established the doctrine of States-Rights, could in eight years have so changed, or have become so far forgetful of the rights of the South as to have sanctioned a law that places the brand of Cain upon her forehead, and stamps her with dishonor before the civilized world? Who passed the law of 1812 authorizing the employment of a naval force upon the coast of Africa, to suppress the traffic in African slaves? A Democratic Congress, and James Monroe was in the executive chair. He had Wm. H. Crawford and John C. Calhoun in his cabinet to advise and counsel him. Shall we now say that our ancestors were dull, obtuse, incomprehensive, and negligent of the rights of the South, insensible to degradation and willing to bear the brand of dishonor before Christendom? Not so. He stood there to preserve the inheritance of glory and honor which had descended to him and to all of the South from these men. These laws were constitutional, the power to pass them having been freely yielded by the South, and which power had also been exercised by Southern men. He was not in favor of taking any equivocal position, in which the honor, integrity and fairness of the South can in any manner be questioned. Should we do so, we will lose all that, should it become necessary for us to go out of the Union, would take us out with honor, a sense of justice and right that could not be gainsaid.

The South should be united, should be able to go up to the Federal Government with a united array, whenever it was deemed necessary to demand redress for wrongs inflicted, or the granting of rights refused. How stands the South upon this question? But two States had had the question brought before them, Louisiana and South Carolina, and they had taken no action. Your entire representation in the popular branch of Congress, at the session before the last, had, with the exception of eight or ten, solemnly resolved that it was inexpedient, unwise, and contrary to the settled policy of the country, to re-open the African Slave Trade. To accomplish the object here recommended, you must first attack and overthrow all your public men who had expressed their opinions upon this subject. We should act like wise statesmen, and not seek to do that which is impracticable and impossible; to do that for the South which the South herself, speaking through her representatives, has declared to be unwise and inexpedient.

Mr. YANCEY closed the debate in a speech of even greater force than that with which he opened it. He had been assailed on all sides, and it was the hot battle of argument which invariably called forth his closest logic and most brilliant rhetoric.

He believed that the laws prohibiting the African slave trade were in spirit unconstitutional. He admitted that gentlemen upon the other side had produced authorities to show that when these laws were passed, they might not have been in opposition to the letter of the Constitution, and were not intended by those who passed them to work injuriously to the South. Yet they might well have become in their effects repugnant to the spirit of the Constitution. It was no sound argument against his position, to say that the constitutionality of these laws had not been questioned until within a very brief period. The Missouri Compromise, approved by Mr. James Monroe, had been considered constitutional for more than 30 years. And yet in 1857 the Supreme Court of the United States had declared it to be unconstitutional.

It had been urged against the proposition before the Convention that it would produce division among the people of the South. He would ask, upon what is the South now united? The South was not even united upon the question whether she was right or wrong in asserting that her rights had been trampled upon by the North to such an extent as to justify her breaking the bonds of this Union. The Convention had been addressed by eloquent gentlemen, to the effect that nothing had yet been done to justify such a course upon the part of the South. All admit that we have suffered wrongs and injuries. And the only thing that the South are united upon is that we are submitting to these wrongs. And the proposition now before the Convention cannot destroy a unity which does not exist among the Southern people.

It was argued against this measure that the South would not unite upon it. He knew there would be opposition to it. He never expected to see the day when a Southern convention met upon Southern issues would be superior to that band of patriots that met in the convention that framed the Declaration of Independence, for even there were some in that body who proposed for a little time longer to trust to the clemency of the British Crown before extreme measures were resorted to. It was human nature that there should ever be found some such men in every body that should assemble to discuss so mighty a question as one in which life, fortune and sacred honor were involved. He therefore never expected a unity of action on the part of the South on any one issue. But one thing would influence one mind ; another thing would influence still another mind, till at last all these influences would produce sufficient effect to enable the South to move forward from a Lexington to a Bunker Hill, and so go until the foe had been driven from the land.

It was said that this was an inferior issue. A tax of three cents a pound on tea was practically an inferior issue. But, as his colleague (Mr. Scott) had said, that involved a great principle. A great principle was involved here, the principle of equality, the principle that our government should not be permitted to brand our institutions as unworthy of extension, even if the letter of the Constitution gave it the power to do so.

He could produce a proposition—if it would not be considered presumption in him to do so—let us meet and consult together upon this question of the duty of the South now, and if the assembled sovereignty of the South should say, wait, we are not ready to move now, he would respect that voice. But perhaps that Convention might say, we do not wish to move alone—in Alabama, for instance—but would prefer to have all the other States with us. He would go to Virginia, and though she cannot move on account of her peculiar border position, she might say in a spirit of true sisterhood to the Gulf States—move on, form your Confederacy, and we will see that you are not molested by a foe that should reach you across our territory. And if Virginia should give that response, he would take her by the hand and bid her farewell and turn Southwards and ask South Carolina, Georgia, Alabama, Mississippi, Texas, Florida, Arkansas, and Louisiana, to form a confederacy of right and equality and justice, with a unity of clime, production and brotherly love. And when they had thus done, there would be room enough upon our shield to inscribe the "*Sic Semper Tyrannis*" of Virginia. North Carolina, Tennessee, Kentucky, and Missouri could come in, and there would soon be produced such a retrograde movement in the opinions of the North that there would not be a Yankee within a hundred miles of the border of the slave confederacy who would not become a slave catcher if we would let him trade with us. This was but a faint foreshadowing of an idea that was at the bottom of his heart, but which he had kept down, because he had not been shown the proper time to give it shape.

It was in the course of this address that Mr. YANCEY alluded to the position assumed by Mr. HILLIARD, that nothing had yet occured to justify secession, but that the election of a Republican President in 1860 would justify it. The language of Mr. YANCEY, as taken down at the moment by a short-hand reporter, was this :

"I say with all deference to my colleague (Mr. Hil- "liard) that no more inferior issue could be tendered to "the South, upon which we should dissolve the Union, "than the loss of an election. If, in the contest of "1860 for the Presidency, Seward should receive the "legal number of votes necessary to elect him accord- "ing to the Constitution and the law, gentlemen say "that then will be the time to dissolve the Union. If "that is made the cause of disunion, I say to them I "will go with them, but I am going in the wake of an "inferior issue; that there was a banner over me that "is not of the kind I would wish. When I am asked "to raise the flag of revolution against the Constitution, "I am asked to do an unconstitutional thing, according "to the Constitution as it now exists; I am asked to "put myself in the position of a rebel, of a traitor; in "in a position where, if the Government should succeed and put me down in the revolution, I and my friends can be arraigned before the Supreme Court of the United States—which would be the creature of Seward, as he has already given notice in the Senate—and there sentenced to be hanged for violating the Constitution and the laws of my country. And if I should be asked why sentence should not be passed on me, I could not then, as I can now in reference to past issues—I could not say then, even to the bloody judges who would sit upon the bench—my hands are guiltless of wrong against the Constitution of my country, and I appeal to an enlightened posterity, to the judgment of the world, to vindicate my name and memory, when, as Emmett said, my country shall have taken her place once more an equal among the nations of the earth. Why am I ready to go with you? (for disunion.) Because, in my judgment, the Union is now dissolved; because we have a Government, but not the Union which the Constitution made."

Subsequently, when the Alabama Legislature resolved that the election of a Republican President would justify secession, Mr. Yancey explained this language by saying that with him and men of his way of thinking, the justification had already existed for thirty years, but with those who had thus far found no justification for such a movement, the election of Lincoln simply could not furnish the excuse.

No action was taken by the Commercial Convention upon the several reports and sets of resolutions. The proceedings derive importance simply from the glimpse they give of the opinions and temper of the leading minds of the South relative to the question of disunion.

Congress had virtually refused Kansas admittance to the Union with a Constitution recognizing slavery. So now, as in 1850, the States-Rights leaders commenced an agitation for secession. Soon after the adjournment of the Southern Commercial Convention, Mr. Slaughter wrote to Mr. Yancey suggesting that the South resolve itself(itself) into a great States-Rights party, and that the old National Democratic party be abandoned. To this letter Mr. Yancey replied as follows :

"Montgomery, June 15, 1858.

"*Dear Sir:* Your kind favor of the 15th is re-"ceived.

"I hardly agree with you that a general movement "can be made that will clear out the Augean stable. "If the Democracy were overthrown, it would result in "giving place to a greater and hungrier swarm of flies.

"The remedy of the South is not in such a process. "It is in a diligent organization of her true men for "prompt resistance to the next aggression. It must "come in the nature of things. No national party can "save us; no sectional party can ever do it. But if "we could do as our fathers did—organize 'commit-"tees of safety' all over the cotton States (and it is "only in them that we can hope for any effective "movement,) we shall fire the Southern heart, instruct "the Southern mind, give courage to each other, and "at the proper moment, by one organized concerted "action, we can precipitate the cotton States into revo-"lution."

"The idea has been shadowed forth in the South by "Mr. Ruffin; has been taken up and recommended in "the *Advertiser*, under the name of 'League of United "Southerners,' who, keeping up their old party relations "on all other questions, will hold the Southern issue "paramount, and will influence parties, Legislatures

" and statesmen. I have no time to enlarge, but to " suggest merely. In haste, yours, &c.,

" W. L. YANCEY.

" *To James S. Slaughter, Esq.*"

On the 10th of July, at a barbecue given at Bethel Church, near Montgomery, Mr. YANCEY spoke in favor of the " League," saying that he " bided the time when " the people would throw off the shackles, both of party " and of the Government, and assert their independence " in a Southern Confederacy." At another barbecue given at Benton, July 17, he again recommended the formation of local and State Leagues, and a Central Southern Congress of the Leagues. At Montgomery, July 20th, he again urged the establishment of the the Leagues. He said that in this matter the people were not without a great precedent. Long before the Declaration of Independence, long before it was dreamed (save by a few) that the colonies would be compelled to withdraw from the British Empire—while the provincial Congress were even yet discussing the phraseology of their petitions to the King to redress their grievances, the colonists acting upon the wise practical principle of " Pray to God and keep your " powder dry," formed committees of safety all over the country. These committees were active in forming a public opinion and giving voice to that opinion, in gathering up munitions of war, and in every conceivable way organizing our ancestry into such an array that when independence was declared they were able to crown it with the triumph of Yorktown. The lesson and the example, said Mr. YANCEY, are eminently suggestive.

Never was there such an agitator as WILLIAM L. YANCEY. His person was imposing, his eloquence was always attractive, forcible and captivating, at times almost supernatural. He was fully imbued with the policy of the leading minds of his native State, South Carolina, and he lost no occasion upon which to enforce that policy. With the language of DEMOSTHENES against PHILIP, he had the will which urged CÆSAR across the Rubicon, and the persistence which placed the crown upon the brow of ROBERT BRUCE. But, although the rejection of the Lecompton Constitution by Congress, the denunciation of the Supreme Court by the dominant party at the North, and the declaration of the "irrepressible conflict" by Mr. SEWARD aided him in his efforts at agitation, still the views of Mr. YANCEY met a strong opposition at his own door and far stronger resistance in the border States. Mr. PRYOR, with his brilliant pen, assailed the Leagues vigorously, and indulged in an acrimonious debate with Mr. YANCEY. In reply to one of Mr. PRYOR's most forcible articles, Mr. YANCEY published an elaborate defence of his course. His letter to Mr. PRYOR reveals the prevalent sentiment of the States-Rights men of the Gulf States, the position of the border States, and the facts and expectations upon which they based the ultimate independence of the South. He said:

"You take exception to these expressions; 'Let us "form these leagues all over the cotton States, as it is "only in them we can hope for any effective movement.' "'At the proper moment, by one organized, concen- "trated action, we can precipitate the cotton States into "a revolution.' Commenting on this, you say, 'the "leading States of the South are specifically excluded "from his plan of concerted operations; and that is "done on the avowed pretence of a lack of Southern "spirit in Virginia and the other border States!'

"To be candid, I place but little trust in such States "as Delaware, Maryland, Tennessee, Kentucky, and "Missouri. In the first, slavery is but a nominal insti- "tution; and anti-slavery ideas prevail to a large extent. "In Maryland, a freesoiler is an honored representative "in Congress; and, in the great issue in 1856, that "State separated herself from her sisters and voted for "Fillmore. Tennessee has long maintained a Free Soil "Senator in Congress, and a large minority now sustain "him there. In the Methodist Conference her dele- "gates voted against striking out the anti-slavery "clause in its discipline—while she maintains on her "Supreme Court bench, and in the chair of law pro- "fessorship in her University, one who openly declares "'slavery to be a moral, social and political evil.' In "Missouri, Benton was upheld when unsound on this "issue—was sent to the House of Representatives "when ousted from the Senate, because of his anti- "slavery ideas; and now the St. Louis District is "represented by a Free Soiler, who is a candidate for "re-election upon the emancipation platform. Sur- "rounded, as she almost is, by free soil territory, her "slave owners are emigrating in large numbers to "Texas, and will soon leave her a prey to Seward's "abolition system of legislation.

"In Kentucky Mr. Clay's emancipation and coloni- "zation ideas are bearing legitimate fruit, and Mr. "Crittenden holds powerful sway over the affections of "its people; and it is hardly to be doubted but that "Mr. Crittenden, conjoined with the Anti-Slavery

"American party of the North, would carry Kentucky. "I may well be excused, then, if I said, in private cor- "respondence (what I frankly confess I would have "hesitated to make a matter of public discussion) that "I only hoped for an effective movement in the cotton "States. There is much in the way in which an idea "is put. I said this much, and no more. I did not "write, as you have charged, either in words or in "spirit, that I acted on an *avowed* pretence of a lack "of Southern spirit *in Virginia* and the other border "States. That is your own language and idea—and I "repudiate both. I did not name Virginia. It is true "I did not discriminate between Virginia and the "other border States. My purposes did not call for it. "In a hastily written private note, it would have been "out of place, as between Mr. Slaughter and myself.

"It is equally true that I do not expect Virginia to "take any initiative steps towards a dissolution of the "Union, when that exigency shall be forced upon the "South. Her position as a border State, and a well "considered Southern policy—(a policy which has "been digested and understood and approved by some "of the ablest men in Virginia, as you yourself must "be aware)—would seem to demand that, when such "movement takes place by any considerable number of "Southern States, Virginia and the other border States "should remain in the Union, where, by their position "and their counsels, they could prove move effective "friends than by moving out of the Union, and thus "giving to the Southern Confederacy a long abolition, "hostile border to watch. In the event of the move- "ment being successful, in time, Virginia, and the "other border States that desired it, could join the

"Southern Confederacy, and be protected by the "power of its arms and its diplomacy.

"Your charge, that I designed to, and did impeach "the fidelity of Virginia, is untrue, however much of "truth there may be in it with reference to those border "States that I have named.

"The article in your issue of the 21st also assailed "me as having opened 'a new school of Southern "statesmanship,' and having abandoned the old and "wisely considered policy of Southern unity, and 'sub-"stituted a system of mutual suspicion and isolated "action.'

"I cheerfully accept the position assigned me as a "member of 'A New School of Southern Statesman-"ship,' however far you may consider it from being "complimentary. In my opinion the South stands "greatly in need of such a school. The benefits of that "old school of statesmanship, which you applaud so "much, are few, while its aggregate results have been, "in a high degree, disastrous to the South. Under the "influence of that 'old school,' that magnificent pro-"slavery domain, now covered by the anti-slavery "States of Ohio, Indiana, Illinois, Michigan, Wisconsin, "and Iowa, was excluded from the march of Southern "progress, and devoted forever to free soil; under the "same 'old school' influence, four-fifths of the vast "pro-slavery territory of Louisiana was wrested from "us, and the South forever excluded from settling it "with her institutions; under the same influence, the "black line of 36 deg. 30 min. was run through the "pro-slavery State of Texas; under the same influ-"ence, the slave trade with Africa was prohibited, and "afterwards an entangling and most mischievous alli-

"ance made with England to send men and ships to "blockade the coast of Africa; under the same influ-"ence, the internal slave trade between Virginia and "the District of Columbia was abolished; and, under "the same old school influence, has the haughty de-"mand of the Free Soiler been submitted to—that "Kansas should not be admitted as a State under its "pro-slavery constitution, unless that constitution shall "substantially and practically receive the approval of "the Free Soil majority in Kansas.

"That 'old school of Southern statesmanship' found "the South an equal in the Senate, and the owner of "nearly all the territories. It has left the South in a "minority of two States in the Senate, with five vast "Territories, out of which no sane man in the South "expects ever to see another pro-slavery State added "to the Union!

"The policy of that 'old school of Southern states-"manship' has been to ignore as 'wicked and foolish,' "and as 'mischievous,' a persistent demand of all our "rights in the Union, and to yield a part for 'harmo-"ny's' sake. It has been a policy based upon the "maintenance of the harmony of administrations and "of parties, upon the advancement of the chances of "Presidential aspirants; and he who has ever become "alarmed at the disastrous results to the South, and "has not considered them as at all counterbalanced by "the splendid success of parties, and of our great men, "in controlling and leading those parties, has invariably "been denounced by the partisan editors attached to "that 'old school' as 'factionists' and 'extremists,' "and as 'disaffected' and 'disappointed politicians.'"

CHAPTER XV.

Instructions to Alabama Delegates—Action of the Alabama Legislature—Views of Forsyth, White and Others—Meeting of the Charleston Convention—Yancey's Great Address—Withdrawal of Southern Delegates—Position of Political Parties—Yancey at Baltimore—He is Offered the Vice-Presidency—Nomination of Breckinridge, Etc., Etc.

"The Republican party is a conspiracy, under the forms, but in violation of the spirit of the Constitution of the United States to exclude the citizens of the slave-holding States from all share in the government of the country, and to compel them to adapt their institutions to the opinions of citizens of free States."—[*Speech of Judge Wm. Duer, of N. Y., at Oswego, Aug.* 6, 1860.

"Remember, in addition to this, that the leading Abolitionists acknowledged no law which might stand in the way of their interests or their passions. Against anybody else the Constitution of the country would have been a protection. But they disregarded its limitations, and had no scruples about swearing to support it with a predetermination to violate it. We had been well warned by all the men best entitled to our confidence—particularly and eloquently warned by Mr. Clay and Mr. Webster—that if ever the Abolitionists got a hold upon the organized physical force of the country, they would govern without law, scoff at the authority of the courts, and throw down all the defences of civil liberty." [Judge JERE S. BLACK.]

On the eleventh day of January, 1860, the Democratic party of Alabama met in Convention at Montgomery and adopted, with singular unanimity, a series of resolutions declaring that the principles recognized by the Supreme Court in the Dred Scott case, should be maintained by the South; that their delegates to the approaching National Democratic Convention at Charleston, should present these resolutions for the adoption of that body: that they insist upon the adoption of the resolutions in substance; and that if they should not be adopted the delegates must withdraw. It was provided that in case of the withdrawal of the delegates, the Executive Committee should call the State Convention together to take action as to their next step. Mr. YANCEY was a leading spirit in this Convention. After twelve years he had succeeded in bringing his party firmly to the support of the Calhoun resolutions of 1848. Gen. CASS had evaded the issue then. Gen. PIERCE, in 1852, had been elected upon the Compromise measures, and the Calhoun pronunciamento at that time seemed almost forgotten. In 1856 Mr. BUCHANAN had also evaded the issue, under the doubtful language of the Cincinnati Convention; but now in 1860 the Supreme Court had recognized the justice of Mr. CALHOUN's position; had vindicated the principles of Mr. YANCEY; and the people of the South, irrespective of party, however great the difference among them upon mere questions of policy, acknowledged the justice of the claims preferred by the Democratic State Convention of Alabama.

On the 24th of February, 1860, the Alabama Legislature, with but two dissenting voices, adopted joint resolutions declaring that, whereas, a sectional party calling itself Republican, committed alike by its own acts and antecedents, and the public avowals and secret machinations of its leaders to a deadly hostility to the rights of the Southern people, has acquired the ascendency in nearly every Northern State, and hopes by success in the approaching Presidential election to seize the Government itself, therefore it shall be the duty of the Governor, upon the success of that party in the election, to call together a State Convention to consider, determine, and do whatever, in the opinion of said Convention, the rights, interests and honor of Alabama may require to be done for her protection. The resolutions also declared that it was the solemn duty of the people not "to permit such seizure (of the "Government) by those whose unmistakable aim is to "pervert its whole machinery to the destruction of a "portion of its members," but "to provide in advance "the means by which they may escape such peril and "dishonor, and devise new securities for perpetuating "the blessings of liberty to themselves and posterity."

At a later day in their session, the General Assembly replied to resolutions forwarded from South Carolina, that Alabama had declared that under no circumstances would she submit to the foul domination of a sectional Northern party, and had called for a State Convention, and had provided money for military contingencies in the event of the triumph of the Republican party in the Presidential election.

The unanimity with which these resolutions were adopted was not due to a unanimous purpose to break up the Union in the event of a constitutional election of a Republican to the Presidency, for during the ensuing campaign many leading speakers from the hustings advised against disunion until the commission of an unconstitutional act, or, as it was called by some, an *overt* act, by a Republican administration; and very many others, constituting it was claimed a majority of the people of Alabama, contended that disunion should not be attempted by separate State action, but that the question should be submitted to a Congress of all the Southern States, a majority of which Congress Mr. Yancey, in his letter to Mr. Pryor, had clearly shown would be opposed to secession in any form. The instructions to the Democratic delegates to withdraw from the Charleston Convention unless the construction given by the Supreme Court to the territorial question was recognized, were voted for by many simply as a threat, and with the purpose of intimidating the National Convention. It was supposed that a proposition coming in the shape of a demand from a united South, and coupled with a threat of ruin in the event of its refusal, would so operate upon the fears of those who could not afford to lose the electoral votes of the Southern States, as to secure its recognition. The same threat was made by the Democratic State Convention of Alabama in 1848, at the instigation of Mr. YANCEY, but the party had not considered itself bound by the threat after the nomination of Gen. CASS. So now, many of the surging mass who composed the State Convention, in voting for the resolution of withdrawal, were more intent upon terrifying their Northern associates than upon actually breaking up the only national party in existence. As there were many who voted for the withdrawal with no expectation or desire that it would take place, so there were many who, while willing for the withdrawal in the event contemplated, were honestly of the opinion that such withdrawal would neither break up the Democratic party nor the Union. Men of this latter class argued that the nominee of the withdrawing States, comprising three-fourths or more of those which would certainly cast their electoral votes for a Democratic candidate, might be finally recognized as the legitimate candidate by the controlling voice of the Democracy of New York, Pennsylvania, New Jersey, California, and Oregon, and thus be successful; or, failing in this, they believed that, with three or four candidates for the Presidency, there would be no election by the people, and the decision would then rest with Congress, as a majority of the Representatives in the House, from a majority of the States, was Democratic, but opposed to Mr. DOUGLAS, they believed the election of their own candidate to be certain, if in the end it should have to be determined by that body. If the House should fail to elect by the 4th day of March, then the Senate, in which the Democratic opponents of Mr. DOUGLAS had a clear majority, would elect a Vice-President, and he would become President by default. So argued many of the most intelligent leaders of the people, and thus—some actuated by a hope that intimidation would prevail, others that withdrawal would not materially affect the party vote, and still others because of popular clamor—all joined in the instructions which rent the Democratic party in twain. ALABAMA was the first name on the list of States. Mr. YANCEY was the most prominent man. It was generally conceded that to him should belong the honor of presenting to the Convention the claims of the South. At that day he was the foremost man in importance in the whole Union. His eloquent voice was to lay down to the United States the *ultimatum* of the South.

The unanimity of the General Assembly in the passage of the resolutions calling a State Convention in the event of Republican victory, was likewise more an apparent than an actual unity of sentiment. Many who voted for the call were ready to deny that occasion existed for extreme action, and in the event of the meeting of a convention, would be ready to resort to any delay by which the passions of the hour could be assuaged and the dreaded spectre of disunion be exorcised. JOHN FORSYTH, late Minister to Mexico, then a member from Mobile, spoke and voted against the resolutions. His remarks proved to be prophetic. Mr. Forsyth, in a letter dated Sept. 13, 1859, to WM. F. SAMFORD, had said:

"But to come to your *ultimatum;* for your inability "to grasp this bit of moonshine, you will go out of the "Union! break up the Government! Well, sir, you "will find a larger majority against you in such a prop-"osition in Alabama than you did a few weeks ago, "when without the backing of that 'party' at which "you sneer, you sought to be elected Governor of the "Commonwealth on the naked strength of your political "theories. Sir, the Union cannot be dissolved upon "such issue, and the sin of your course, and that of those "who, with you, are agitating this firebrand of abstrac-"tion in the Democratic party on the eve of a vital con-"flict with the combined hosts of Black Republicanism, is, "that in the pursuit of a fallacious hope and an impossi-"ble dream, you are paving the way for the defeat of the "South; for bringing it to the footstool of an Aboli-"tion President, and for draining a deeper cup of "humiliation and disgrace than it has yet touched with "its lips. I charge that you are no friend of the "South in the counsels you give it; I arraign not your "sound heart but your hot head; I charge that you "advise it to risk its controlling influence in the Gov-"ernment and disastrous defeat in the forthcoming "battle with the Lucifer of fanaticism and his devilish "array of Black Republicans. I charge that you "propose to break up the Democratic party, and sweep "from existence the only obstacle that stands between "the Constitution and the Federal ravisher—to give "over the Government to centralism, to protective "tariffs, to the bottomless abyss of expenditure for "internal improvements, to the upheaving and toppling "down the mighty structure of Democratic policy "which Jefferson founded, and Madison, Jackson, Polk "and Pierce have built upon, to the subversion of the "form and the spirit of States-Rights as vital elements "in our Federative system, to the undoing of all that "Democratic statesmen have tired and toiled for during "three-quarters of a century. And for what? For a "vague theory of constitutional right as devoid of "value, form and substance as the 'baseless fabric of a "vision.'"

In the same vein Mr. FORSYTH addressed the General Assembly on the 2d of February, 1860, declaring that there was no occasion for the adoption of the resolutions reported by the Committee on Federal Relations. He said that no friend of the Democracy could consistently go with the late Democratic State Convention, because they send to Charleston a platform "which it "is known beforehand cannot be granted without scat- "tering the Democracy of the Union to the winds." Said he: "I am in the minority now, perhaps; I was "two months since, but I have seen cheering evidences "to show that my little party is growing apace, and "that even on this floor my cause has many a friend "that gentlemen 'wot not of.' But whether I am or "not, I am right, and time will prove it."

A few weeks later ALEXANDER WHITE, who had been elected to Congress by the Whig party upon the Compromise of 1850, and who had at a later day joined the Democracy, a gentleman who generally represented correctly the changes in the popular pulse, published a letter in which he opposed the policy of disunion. By resorting to a Southern Union, he argued, we brought Canada to our own door. The institution of slavery being restricted to the Southern Confederacy, it would gradually retire from the border to the Gulf States, and soon the same elements of discord which existed in the old Union would be found rife in the new. Mr. FORSYTH and Mr. WHITE represented a very respectable portion of the Democratic party.

Besides what was afterwards known as the Douglas Democracy, the entire Whig party at the beginning of this eventful year, was in opposition to the spirit of the resolutions of the General Assembly. It was as late as September 21 before Mr. WATTS, the generally recognized leader of the Whigs, announced that the election of Mr. Lincoln would justify secession. Gen. CLANTON, who was an elector for BELL and EVERETT, denounced the policy of secession in a hundred speeches, and down to the day of Mr. LINCOLN's election, contended that neither forcible resistance to his administration nor disruption of the Union, should be resorted to until some unconstitutional act was perpetrated.

The National Democratic Convention met at Charleston, April 23, 1860. On the following day a committee was appointed, consisting of a delegate from each State, selected by the respective State delegations, to report resolutions as a platform for the party. On the 27th majority and minority reports were made; the majority report accepting the Cincinnati platform with a clause explaining the doctrine of non-intervention as the South desired and as the Dred Scott decision declared it. The minority report, after also reaffirming the Cincinnati platform, proceeds: "Inas-"much as differences of opinion exist in the Demo-"cratic party as to the nature and extent of the "powers of a territorial legislature, and as to the powers "and duties of Congress, under the Constitution of the "United States, over the institution of slavery in the "Territories, *Resolved,* That the Democratic party will "abide by the decisions of the Supreme Court of the "United States upon questions of constitutional law."

The Southern delegates held that this minority resolution was too vague and indefinite to meet the case. It failed to recognize that a decision had already been rendered by the Court. If the Northern delegates intended to stand by that decision, it was impossible to say that "differences of opinion" existed among the Democracy as to the nature and extent of the powers of Congress and of the Territorial Legislature over the institution of slavery. It was moved that the minority report be substituted for the majority. It was upon this motion that Mr. YANCEY addressed the Convention. His reputation as an orator had preceded him. On the preceding night an immense crowd, with banners and music, had waited upon him. To their shouts and huzzas he responded only with an excuse for not speaking. He was at the chief city of his native State. Around him were the abodes of a proud, intelligent, high-spirited people, and from the galleries looked down an immense concourse of fair ladies and gallant gentlemen who sympathized with his past history and his present labors. The occasion and the scene were enough to inspire one of far less enthusiasm and nobility than YANCEY. The hour and the man had met.

Ascending the stand, the orator had pronounced but

a few of his well-weighed, rounded and musical sentences before he had quieted the noise and confusion which invariably attends the collection of a large multitude of men, and had riveted the attention of every eye and mind. Those who had heard of him as an agitator, yielded their objection to his consuming more than one hour of time when they looked upon his pleasant, mild and benignant face. Those who were disposed to clamor against the disunionist, became silent when they gazed upon his noble presence. The angry glance which followed him from those who had regarded him as a plotter of treason, was softened to tears by the pathos of the most perfect voice that ever aroused a friendly audience to a frenzy of enthusiasm, or curbed to silence the tumults of the most inimical.

With closely woven statements of fact and logical deduction, with graceful gesture and melodious tones, he advanced, vindicated and defended the cause of the South. He asked for nothing but the recognition of those rights which the highest tribunal had declared to belong to the people of the South. Ever and anon the audience would break forth in the wildest applause, and as the speaker became warm in his subject, and the keen reasoning and brilliant illustrations leaped to his lips, the responsive shouts of approbation and the thunders of the excited multitude became so frequent that it was moved by a delegate that the galleries be cleared. "No, no," was cried out from all around, "there is as much noise upon the floor." Captain RYNDERS, of New York, arose and shouted that if they wished to prevent applause on the floor, they must stop Mr. YANCEY from speaking; a piece of truthful wit that was received with great cheering and laughter.

The peroration of his magnificent address was worthy of the man, the cause, and the occasion. Said he:

"Gentlemen of the Convention, that venerable, that "able, that revered jurist, the honorable Chief Justice "of the United States, trembling upon the very verge "of the grave, for years kept merely alive by the pure "spirit of patriotic duty that burns within his breast— "a spirit that will not permit him to succumb to the "gnawings of disease and the weaknesses of mortality— "which hold him, as it were, suspended between two "worlds, with his spotless ermine around him, standing "upon the very altar of Justice, has given to us the "utterance of the Supreme Court of the United States "upon this very question. [Applause.]

"Let the murmur of the hustings be stilled—let the "voices of individual citizens, no matter how great and "respected in their appropriate spheres, be hushed, "while the law, as expounded by the constituted "authority of the country, emotionless, passionless and "just, rolls in its silvery cadence over the entire realm, "from the Atlantic to the Pacific, and from the ice-"bound regions of the North to the glittering waters of "the Gulf. [Loud cheering.] What says that deci-"sion? That decision tells you, gentlemen, that the "Territorial Legislature has no power to interfere with "the rights of the slave-owner in the Territory while "in a Territorial condition. [Cheers.] That decision "tells that this Government is a union of sovereign "States; which States are co-equal, and in trust for "which co-equal States the Government holds the Ter-"ritories. It tells you that the people of those co-equal "States have a right to go into these Territories, thus "held in trust, with every species of property which is "recognized as property by the State in which they "live or by the Constitution of the United States. The "venerable Magistrate—the Court concurring with "him—decided that it is the duty of this Government to "afford some government for the Territories which shall "be in accordance with this trust, with this delegated "trust power held for the States and for the people of "the States. That decision goes still further; it tells "you that if Congress has seen fit, for its own conven-"ience, and somewhat in accordance with the sympa-"thies and instincts and genius of our institutions, to "accord a form of government to the people of the Ter-"ritories, it is to be administered precisely as Congress "can administer it, and to be administered as a trust "for the co-equal States of the Union, and the citizens "of those States who choose to emigrate to those Ter-"ritories. That decision goes on to tell you this: that "as Congress itself is bound to protect the property "which is recognized as such of the citizens of any of "the States—as Congress itself not only has no power, "but is expressly forbidden to exercise the power to "deprive any owner of his property in the Territories; "therefore, says that venerable, that passionless repre-"sentative of Justice, who yet hovers on the confines "of the grave—therefore, no government formed by "that Congress can have any more power than the "Congress that created it.

"But, we are met right here with the assertion: we "are told by the distinguished advocate of this doctrine "of popular sovereignty, that this opinion is not a "*decision* of the Supreme Court, but merely the opinion "of citizen Taney. He does not tell you, my coun-

" trymen, that it is not the *opinion* of the great majority " of the Supreme Court bench. Oh, no ; but he tells " you that it is a matter that is *obiter dicta* outside the " jurisdiction of the Court ; in other words, extra-judi- " cial—that it is simply the opinion of Chief Justice " Taney, as an individual, and not the decision of the " Court, because it was the subject-matter before the " Court. Now, Mr. Douglas and all others who make " that assertion and undertake to get rid of the moral, " the constitutional, the intellectual power of argument, " put themselves directly in conflict with the venerable " Chief Justice of the Supreme Court of the United " States, and with the recorded decision of the Court " itself—because Chief Justice Taney, after disposing " of the demurrer in that case, undertook to decide the " question upon the facts and the merits of the case ; " and," said he, "in doing that, we are met with the objec- " tion 'that anything we may say upon that part of " the case will be extra-judicial and mere *obiter dicta.*' " This is a manifest mistake," etc., " and the Court—not " Chief Justice Taney, but the whole Court, with but " two dissenting voices—decided that it was not *obiter* " *dicta ;* that it was exactly in point, within the juris- " diction of the Court, and that it was the duty of the " Court to decide it. Now then, who shall the Democracy " recognize as authority on this point—a statesman, no " matter how brilliant, and able and powerful in intel- " lect, in the very meridian of life—animated by an " ardent and consuming ambition—struggling as no " other man has ever done for the high and brilliant " position of candidate for the Presidency of the United " States, at the hand of his great party—or that old " and venerable jurist who, having filled his years with

" honor, leaves you his last great decision before step-" ping from the high place of earthly power into the " grave to appear before his Maker, in whose presence " deception is impossible, and earthly position as dust in " the balance ?" [Loud and continued cheering.]

Had the States all voted as units, or had the delegates all voted as individuals, the majority report would have been sustained, but the friends of Mr. DOUGLAS, in the Pennsylvania delegation, succeeded in obtaining a rule by which the vote of each individual should be expressed. That State instead, therefore, of casting twenty-seven votes for the majority resolutions, cast only three. The minority report was substituted for the majority, and when the vote was taken upon the vague explanatory resolution accompanying the report, it was rejected by almost a unanimous vote, both elements of the party looking upon it as a subterfuge and evasion.

When the final vote on the last clause of the minority report was announced, and the Chair declared that it was carried, the dropping of a pin might have been heard in the Convention. Every man, woman and child within the vast hall in which the delegates assembled seemed aware that a great crisis had arrived, and that events were about to occur in which the dearest interests of American citizens were involved. That great and hitherto tumultuous assemblage seemed awed into silence and intent suspense. The silence was broken by Mr. LEROY POPE WALKER, of Alabama. In a few terse and eloquent remarks he gave his reasons why he and his colleagues could not accept the platform just adopted in behalf of the people of his State, and why, under these circumstances, the Alabama delegation deemed it their imperative duty to withdraw from the Convention. No sooner had Mr. WALKER resumed his seat, having discharged this solemn task, than Mr. BARRY, of Mississippi, rose to his feet, and read a paper setting forth the reasons why the delegation of his State had also resolved to withdraw. When the reading of this grave act of secession was finished, the gallant and eloquent Colonel GLENN, of Mississippi, in terms of simple eloquence, intense feeling, and conscious dignity, which touched the heart of every one of the thousands who heard him, explained why the Mississippi delegation had reluctantly taken so serious a step. Then arose the venerable ex-Governor MOUTON, of Louisiana, who declared that he and his co-delegates had resolved to withdraw from a Convention which had refused to acknowledge the great fundamental principle of the Democratic party, equality of the States. The respective chairmen of the delegations from South Carolina, Florida, Arkansas, and Texas, then announced that they too, would withdraw, and caused to be inserted in the minutes of the Convention their several protocols containing the reasons which impelled them to do so. There was no swagger, no bluster. There were no threats, no denunciations. The language employed by the representatives of these seven independent sovereignties was as dignified and courteous as it was feeling. As one followed the other in quick succession, one could see the entire crowd quiver as under a heavy blow. Every man seemed to look anxiously at his neighbor as if enquiring what is going to happen next. Down many a manly cheek flowed tears of heartfelt sorrow. A pause of a few moments ensued after Arkansas had withdrawn, and people were beginning to resume their composure, when the Senator from Delaware, Mr. Bayard, was observed to enter the hall and proceed rapidly up the central aisle towards the platform. When he uttered the words, "Mr. Chairman," in a voice not devoid of agitation, although resolute in tone, and when the Chairman responded, "The gentleman "from Delaware, Mr. Bayard," the Convention again held their breath, not knowing what course that high-minded statesman was going to pursue in so great a crisis. He spoke but a few minutes. His language betrayed the deep emotion which filled his patriotic breast. He represented what were the views and sentiments of his constituents; stated that they accorded with those of the delegations which had withdrawn; that he had been sent by his people to represent them in a great National Democratic Convention wherein delegates from all the States of the Union could sit in harmony and equality; and that as the Convention no longer possessed that character, he and his colleague, Mr. Whitely would withdraw, confident that their action would be sustained at home.

When all the seceding delegations had retired, it is impossible to portray the dismay of those by whose conduct that grave event had been occasioned, and when a motion to adjourn was made it was readily assented to.

The excitement outside was intense. Everybody asked "how many delegations will withdraw to-morrow? "What will the seceding delegations do?" The whole town was on foot, and unqualified approval of the action of the retiring delegates expressed to applauding crowds at every street corner. An informal meeting of the seceders for consultation was held at St. Andrew's Hall the next day, when it was resolved that they should assemble at the Military Hall and organize, and then await the action of the Convention before they determined on their future proceedings. An immense mass meeting was held in front of the City Hall, which was addressed by the Hon. L. Q. C. LAMAR, of Mississippi, Mr. YANCEY, and other prominent Democrats, in able and stirring speeches.

On the tenth day of its session, after ineffectual balloting, the Convention adjourned to meet at Baltimore June 18th.

Before adjourning, the Virginia delegation had conferred with the Southern delegates as to the best mode of restoring harmony. In consequence, Mr. HOWARD, of Tennessee, stated to the Convention that "he had a "proposition to present in behalf of the delegates from "Tennessee, whenever, under parliamentary rules, it "would be proper to present it." He should propose the following: *Resolved*, That the citizens of the United States have an equal right to settle with their property in the Territories of the United States; and that under the decision of the Supreme Court of the United States, which we recognize as the correct exposition of the Constitution of the United States, neither the rights of persons or property can be destroyed or impaired by Congressional or Territorial Legislation. Mr. RUSSELL, of Virginia, informed the Convention that this resolution, he believed, received the approbation of all the delegations from the Southern States which remained in the Convention, and also the approbation of the delegation from New York. He was informed that there was strength enough to pass it when in order. Mr. HOWARD in vain attempted to get a vote upon it.

The friends of Mr. DOUGLAS interposed objections of order, and no vote was ever taken upon it, either at Charleston or Baltimore.

That portion of the old WHIG party which had preserved a show of organization, and had steadily refused to yield to the policy of the Republican party on the one hand, and that of the Democratic on the other, met in Convention at Baltimore May 9th, assumed the name of "Constitutional Union" party, and nominated JOHN BELL, for President, and EDWARD EVERETT, for Vice-President. They adopted no platform of principles, presenting their candidates to the people in the spirit of Whig Conservatism, and simply upon their records as lovers of the Union and respecters of the rights of the States.

The opponents of the Democratic party in Alabama believed that, as in 1858, when Mr. YANCEY advanced the demand for and a repeal of the law making the African slave trade piracy, on the ground that in pressing it as an issue there would be one more link between the Southern man and the Southern man, and one more link broken between the Southern man and the Northern man, so now in aiding thus materially to break up the Democratic party upon the Territorial abstraction, by advising and urging the withdrawal of the Alabama delegation, the object of the States-Rights leaders was to let the administration pass into the hands of the Republican party as the final step towards dissolution. They believed that the States-Rights party wanted disunion, not because of any practical restriction of the rights of the Southern citizen, but because the desire for a Southern Confederacy, growing out of an accumulation of petty defeats upon immaterial and disputed questions of public policy, had become so cherished, intensified and attractive as to shut from their view the weakness of such a Confederacy, the dangers of civil war and the horrors of defeat.

An "Opposition" meeting, in which most of the old Whigs participated, was held at Montgomery, June 19. It endorsed the principles of the Dred Scott Decision, and appointed delegates to a State Convention to assemble July 2. Meantime various counties of the State had appointed delegates to a "Constitutional "Union" Convention to meet at SELMA, June 21, for the ratification of the nomination of BELL and EVERETT. In this latter Convention appeared the rank and file of the old Whig party. This Convention ratified the action of the Constitutional Union Convention at Baltimore, endorsed the principles of the Dred Scott Decision, accepted Mr. BELL upon his record in the Senate, and endorsed Mr. EVERETT upon his action with reference to the Compromise of 1850.

A "States-Rights Opposition" Convention assembled at Montgomery, July 2. Delegates were present from but seven counties, and among them but few men of prominence. They adopted resolutions stating that the question of protecting slave property in the Territories was the paramount question before the country, and that no other party in Alabama except their own had avowed in their platform, until a recent day, the duty of Congress to afford such protection. Many delegates to this Convention believed the time had come for the establishment of a party representing a united South, and were disposed to act with the seceders from the Charleston Convention. The Douglas party having preserved the forms and organization of the National

Democracy, it was hoped that the seceders would now unite with the States-Rights opposition in a sectional party. Following out the line of the argument they had maintained for four years, it was now mooted whether this portion of the "States-Rights Opposition" should not pronounce for the candidates of the seceders; and so we find them declaring it their duty, "not as "Democrats, but merely as determined friends of "Southern equality and Southern institutions, and as "allies of those who, by placing their nominees upon a "platform substantially asserting our own long-cher-"ished principles of protection to slave property in the "Territories, have given signal proof of their devotion to "Southern equality and Southern institutions, to support "BRECKINRIDGE and LANE, if in their letters of acceptance "of their nomination, or otherwise, they give their "unqualified sanction to the platform upon which they "have been nominated." Mr. WATTS moved to amend the resolution by a proposition to write to Messrs. BELL and EVERETT, and to support the Constitutional Union candidates if they abide by the principles expressed in the platform. Upon a vote by counties, Montgomery county voted for Mr. WATTS' amendment, and the remaining counties against it. In no sense was this a representative vote. Its effect, however, was to draw from Mr. BELL a fraction of the old Whigs led by men of strength like JUDGE, CHILTON, and RICE. The majority of Mr. BRECKINRIDGE over his two competitors in Alabama was but seven thousand. Had the Whigs remained united upon Mr. BELL, it is more than probable that a majority of votes in the State would have been cast against Mr. BRECKINRIDGE. It might be difficult to understand how this Opposition Convention could, upon principle, arrive at the conclusion to support Mr. BRECKINRIDGE to the exclusion of Mr. BELL. On all other questions than that of slavery in the Territories, their associations and traditions had been with the latter rather than the former. Why, then, upon "the "paramount question" could they not give Mr. BELL an opportunity to claim their votes by defining his position? The only solution of the movement must be found in the profound conviction which had seized upon the minds of many hitherto devoted Whigs, that any attempt to keep alive a separate organization, under whatever name, must prove futile and could only embarrass the position of the South. Such a party could expect no electoral votes except at the South. It was, therefore, in the opinion of the Convention, powerless for good, and might be productive of injury. Mr. WATTS thought differently. In his opinion there would probably be no election by the people, and Mr. BELL would receive electoral votes sufficient to make him one of the three candidates before the House. As neither DOUGLAS nor BRECKINRIDGE could control the House, it was his hope and belief that the discordant elements adverse to Mr. LINCOLN would finally concentrate upon Mr. BELL. In reply to a letter addressed to him by Mr. WATTS, Mr. Bell enclosed for his inspection certain of his speeches with paragraphs marked, stating that these speeches were full and explicit answers to the questions asked him. Mr. WATTS published a letter, July 30, in which he said:

"Mr. Bell thus distinctly announces, in my judg-"ment, the following propositions—

"1. A distinct repudiation of Wilmot Provisoism.

"2. A distinct repudiation of squatter sovereignty "as long ago as 1848.

"3. A distinct announcement that the Territories "are common property of the States composing the "Union, and that the citizens of each State have the "right to go into such Territories with their property "of every description, and while there to have protec- "tion to property and person."

The Democratic Executive Committee having called a convention, that body assemblad at Montgomery early in June. On the same day, and at the same place, assembled a DOUGLAS Convention. Both bodies nominated full electoral tickets, the one endorsing the action of its delegates to Charleston and authorizing them to meet the seceders at Richmond; the other condemning the secession at Charleston, recognizing the Douglas wing as the proper organized National Convention, and appointing delegates to act with that Convention at Baltimore.

On the 18th of June the Douglas fragment of the Democratic Convention met at Baltimore. The State of New York was now ready to adopt the resolution of Mr. HOWARD, and had the seceders taken their seats the Convention and party might have harmonized. The seceders adjourned from Richmond to Baltimore, but the first act of the Douglas men was to declare the seats of the seceders vacant, and to admit the new delegates who had been lately appointed by Douglas Conventions. Thereupon Virginia, North Carolina, Tennessee, Kentucky, Maryland, California, Oregon, and Arkansas withdrew from the Convention and joined the seceders. They were accompanied by Mr. CUSHING, President of the Convention, and five more of the

Massachusetts delegates. The seceders now represented twenty States—and all that were certain to give Democratic majorities.

After the adoption by the seceders of the majority report which had been presented at Charleston, and the nomination of Mr. BRECKINRIDGE, loud calls were made for Mr. YANCEY. Amidst great applause that gentleman ascended the platform and addressed the Convention with his usual force and fire. Rehearsing the events which had transpired, and defending the principles of the majority report as the only basis of a Constitutional Union founded on the equality of the States, he said:

"I congratulate you, Mr. President, the representa-"tive of the National States-Rights Democracy, and "you, venerable gentlemen, who sit here as the repre-"sentatives of your several sovereign States, and "gentlemen, who are the delegates of the Democracy—"you, who are the stern and true friends of the old-"fashioned National Democracy, that there is yet in "existence an organization pledged to uphold and "revere our beloved Constitution, and through it to "uphold the Union. [Applause.] Accept these con-"gratulations at the hands of one who has, through the "assiduous and wily influence of our common enemies, "acquired a reputation for being factious and disrup-"tionary—for being a disunionist. Accept that "congratulation at the hands of one who, some nine or "ten years ago, desired and endeavored to obtain a "disruption of this Union, because he believed then, as "he believes now, that there was a then existing cause "why that Union should have been dissolved—because "the Constitution had been violated in the admission of

"California into the Union upon the principle of "'squatter sovereignty,' and because the internal slave "trade between the District of Columbia and the "States had been destroyed by Congressional legisla- "tion, by that act initiating the great policy of abolition.

"I went before the people of the State of Alabama, "and asked of them if they would secede from a "Union that had thus forgotten to observe its pledges. "She thought it fit in her wisdom to decline, and voted "down the seceding party. From that day to this I "have urged no measure of dissolution, but I have "bowed in submission to the will of the State, to which "I owe my allegiance. From that day to this, under "all these wrongs, I have not urged them as a sufficient "cause why the Union shall be dissolved—and though "injustice and wrong has since been done to my "section, yet they are not of that character which, of "themselves, call for disunion. And when it has been "stated, for the purpose of injuring the cause with "which I am connected, that I am urging my friends "to disunion, and to the disruption of the Democratic "party, that has been stated that is utterly false as an "inference and false in itself. [Applause.] There is "nothing that I have done or said in the progress of "measures leading to organization for this canvass, "nothing that actuates me, no motive of mine that can, "with fairness, be so construed. Whenever the time "comes in which a wrong shall be done to the section "in which I live; which is palpably and clearly done "with a view of wronging that section—a wrong that "shall effect its honor and equality, I shall endeavor to "be, as I was in 1851, among the first to raise the "banner of State secession. Until cause for that event "occurs, I here and elsewhere, shall rally under the "banner of the Democracy and of the Constitution." [Applause.]

It is interesting in this connection to recall an incident as illustrating how utterly careless were illustrious politicians as to the question over which they were dividing parties and imperiling the country In passing through Washington Mr. YANCEY was the guest of Mr. PUGH, a member of Congress from Alabama. While at Mr. PUGH's house he was visited by Mr. S. S. BAXTER, of Tenn., and H. W. FISHER, of Virginia, both of whom in published letters afterwards, testified to the correctness of the conversation which occured between themselves and Mr. GEO. N. SANDERS, of New York, who stepped in during their visit. Mr. SANDERS was a shrewd politician of some note, and had held the important position of Consul to London under President PIERCE. Mr. YANCEY said the Vice-Presidency had been offered him by the friends of Mr. DOUGLAS if he would bring about a reconciliation between the factions. Mr. SANDERS had made the offer, it was said, with the knowledge and consent of Mr. DOUGLAS. During this conversation Mr. SANDERS urged Mr. YANCEY to accept, and suggested that Mr. DOUGLAS would die in six months after his inauguration, when the whole question would be solved. Mr. FISHER repeated this conversation in a public speech at Baltimore, and his statement was not denied.

CHAPTER XVI.

The Canvass in Alabama—Assaults upon Yancey—Position of the Three Contestants—Yancey's Canvass of the West and North—His Arrival at Memphis—Reception at Knoxville—Speech at Washington—Attempted Fusion in New York—His Speech in Faneuil Hall—At Lexington—At New Orleans—Return of Yancey and Visit of Douglas to Montgomery, Etc., Etc.

Mr. President: "If you wish to put a stop to cheering and applause upon this floor, you must stop Mr. Yancey from speaking."—[Rynders in the Charleston Convention.

"Your policy in this great crisis of a final struggle between the South and its foes is mad and suicidal in the last degree. It is to risk everything for nothing. It is to annihilate the only living power that can defend us, and to consummate a ruin of Southern hopes and prospects, under which your own favorite abstraction of 'protection' will be the first and deepest buried. Do you expect to obtain congressional protection for slavery in the Territories by electing William H. Seward President?"—[Public Letter of John Forsyth.

The political campaign was now opened. The WHIG candidates for Presidential Electors attacked the DOUGLAS Democracy because of their squatter sovereignty principles, and the BRECKINRIDGE Democracy because of their disunion tendencies. In Alabama the opinions and declarations of Mr. YANCEY became the special target for the opposition. It was argued that Mr. YANCEY was a pronounced secessionist in 1851, and that he was still a disunionist. It was true he now denied that he was a disunionist; but he made the same denial then. Then it was that he organized and harangued the States-Rights Associations; but yesterday he was organizing and harangueing the Leagues of

United Southerners. Ten years ago he was for instructing the South in the principles of States-Rights, and admonishing them not to be trammelled by ties of parties. Two years ago he was for instructing the Southern mind in the same direction, for firing the Southern heart and precipitating the cotton States into revolution. This being precipitated into revolution could mean nothing more nor less than separate State secession upon the election of a Republican President. In his speech at the Commercial Convention, Mr. YANCEY had said that the election of a President under the forms of the Constitution by the Republican party, would not of itself justify secession; and he had said in his Baltimore speech that there had been no injustice and wrong since 1850 which would justify disunion. The principles of the States-Rights party were those of the Virginia resolutions of '98, which declared that the injustice and wrong which authorized secession on the part of a State, must be "a deliberate, palpable and "dangerous exercise of powers not granted by the "compact." The power of electing such a President as they prefer, is one of those undisputed powers which could not be denied to the States. Alabama, therefore, had no justification to secede simply upon the election of a Republican President, and well had Mr. YANCEY spoken of such a purpose as "revolution." She, together with the entire South, declared by large majorities that the injustice and wrong of the Compromise Measures of 1850 were not sufficient cause, and Mr. YANCEY had publicly declared that since that day the injustice and wrong done his section was not sufficient to justify disunion. Such being the case, said the Unionists, it would seem the duty of patriots, the interest of men who yearn for continued peace and prosperity, that the State should not be dragged into the suicidal policy of South Carolina, that the people of Alabama were in danger, was evidenced by the actions and schemes of Mr. YANCEY and his peculiar friends. He had brought about the disruption of the Charleston Convention by procuring from the Alabama Democratic Convention instructions that delegates should withdraw in a certain contingency. He had been largely instrumental in obtaining from the General Assembly a call for a State Convention in the event of LINCOLN's election, and a declaration that his administration would be resisted. He had fired the Southern heart by obtaining this declaration for disunion from the representatives of the people, and he was now for precipitating the State into secession. He wanted no delay, no reflection, no waiting for co-operative action. Co-operation would bring delay, and delay would cool the passions and fortify reason. Success for his schemes depended upon precipitation, and precipitation would result in ruin.

The old Whig leaders believed that there was a possibility of the election of Mr. BELL by the people. There was certainly no hope for the election of Mr. Douglas or Mr. Breckinridge. It was probable that the names of LINCOLN, BELL, and BRECKINRIDGE would go to the House. In that event Mr. BELL had an excellent chance of being put into the Presidency as a compromise man, since the DOUGLAS and LINCOLN Representatives would prefer to elect him before the 4th of March rather than see the President of the Senate assume the Presidency of the United States after that day. Gen. CLANTON, everywhere throughout the District, the same old District which had so often witnessed the defeat of the States-Rights party, held that, should Mr. LINCOLN be elected, his administration ought to be submitted to until it committed some unconstitutional act. He showed that the President could do nothing unless backed by Congress, that the Senate would be against him, and in all probability the House also, and that the Supreme Court were against his political views. LINCOLN would be utterly powerless if elected. Any appointment he might make must be confirmed by a Democratic Senate; why, then, need we apprehend any danger from a President who would have the support of neither a majority of the voters of the Union nor of any of the Departments of the Government? Was this the powerless object before which the Union must be rent in twain? This was not submission to Black Republican rule, as it was termed. It was obedience to the Constitution and submission to the Government of the United States, which would still be, for all practical purposes, in the hands of the South, through the preponderance of Southern Senators among those who would be in opposition to Mr. LINCOLN.

MR. JOHN F. CONOLEY, the Douglas elector for the Third District, maintained that the nomination of Mr. DOUGLAS was the only regular Democratic nomination. Why, he argued, had the opponents of Mr. DOUGLAS insisted upon an explanatory clause to the Cincinnati platform? Had not the Supreme Court sufficiently explained what the Cincinnati platform meant by non-intervention? Mr. YANCEY, in his powerful argument at Charleston, had proved beyond the power of refutation, that "squatter sovereignty" was not in the Kansas Bill. By reference to the Dred Scott case, he had also proved that it could not by any possibility be in any other Territorial Bill. By the same argument he had showed that it could not be in the Cincinnati platform. Then why had he insisted upon a change of platform even to the disruption of the party and the Union? Was it because a fraction of the party denied the construction of the Court? That faction could hardly cast a Democratic electoral vote. It was too weak and impotent to justify alarm. But granting that the election of DOUGLAS would enure to the success of what is known as squatter sovereignty, was there anything alarming in that doctrine? Under it, it was admitted, slavery had an unrestricted right of expansion and would go wherever the people wanted it. Squatters had carried it to Tennessee, Kentucky, Missouri, Alabama, Mississippi, and Arkansas, without any law to protect it, and to Texas against a law prohibiting it. Under this doctrine it could and would be carried to all countries where climate, soil, productions and population would allow. Non-intervention is thus regulated by natural laws, and no Act of Congress could carry it into any Territory against those laws. If we have not the population to compete with the North in the colonization of Territories, no Act of Congress could cure the difficulty. What was the objection to DOUGLAS? Was it that the nomination was not by a two-thirds vote? Mr. DOUGLAS received more than two thirds of those who voted. Never in the history of Democratic Conventions had it been held that the candidate should receive a number equal to two-thirds of all the electoral votes. Two-thirds of a House means two-thirds of the voting members, and not two-thirds of all the members. Was the objection to the platform?

The platform was the same that was considered broad enough in 1856 for the whole Union. Was the objection to the man who led the ticket? If Mr. DOUGLAS had offended, it was alone upon the question how far a territorial legislature may constitutionally impair the right or usefulness of any kind of property by any system of laws they may enact. This point of difference between Mr. DOUGLAS and others did not involve a question of the equality of the States in the Union or any principle essential to our security. The people of the Territory were the ultimate disposers of the whole question. They could manage it better than Congress could. Mr. DOUGLAS was for removing the slavery agitation from the halls of Congress. His opponents were for continuing and increasing the agitation by calling upon those in Congress whose prejudices were all against slavery, to enable them in enacting slave codes. Could there be peace when such demands were made by the South? The seceders knew that such demands would be rejected, and that the rejection would be made the pretence for disunion. There was no mode of quieting the slavery question or securing peace to the country except by the policy of Mr. DOUGLAS. So spoke the candidates for the Electoral College.

During the progress of the canvass it became apparent that Mr. LINCOLN would be elected unless the States of New York and Pennsylvania could be carried against him by a fusion of all the Conservative elements. The Republicans, in order to prevent such fusion, and to weaken the strength of Mr. BRECKINRIDGE, made free use of the name, opinions and published sentiments of Mr. YANCEY. The newspapers had published what purported to be a copy of the constitution of the "League "of United Southerners," which declared that its object was to break up the Union. Mr. YANCEY thereupon wrote a letter to the Democracy of Tennessee, July 19, presenting a true copy of the League Constitution, and stating that its declared object was to preserve the rights of the South in the Union, or failing in that, "a prompt resistance on the next aggression." He stated that the establishment of the LEAGUE had been first recommended by the *Advertiser* newspaper of Montgomery, that its first meeting had been organized by himself, CHAS. G. GUNTER, and J. C. B. MITCHELL of that place, that but three chapters had ever been formed; that its sessions were open, and that the people, not approving, it had long since been discontinued. The notable part of this letter is the admission by Mr. YANCEY that, while not favoring disunion in 1858, he was for prompt resistance on the next aggression; and yet at Baltimore he had asserted that nothing had occurred since 1858 to justify secession, and at the Commercial Convention he had declared that the election of a Republican President would not alone justify it.

The important part which YANCEY had played at the Convention which had nominated Mr. BRECKINRIDGE, and the wide-spread denunciations of him as a disunionist at the North, induced his party friends to urge upon him the duty of making addresses at as many of the prominent cities as time would permit. After several addresses in Alabama among those who had been accustomed to hear him, his first speech outside of the State was made at Memphis. During the day, upon the evening of which he was to address the people there, the railroad trains and country road wagons and carriages poured into the city a host of people, some to applaud as a patriot, some to hiss as a traitor, the most widely criticised man in the Union. The excitement was intense. Threats to mob him was indulged in openly by heated partisans, and the audience appeared so largely his enemy that many of his friends advised him not to speak. There never was a braver man than YANCEY. There never was a crowd which could silence or intimidate him. There never was a passion-tossed audience which he could not curb or control. On this occasion the immense audience, supposed to be greatly against him, cheered and jeered, swayed to and fro and interrupted his first sentences with impertinent and insolent interjections. The orator not for a moment lost temper or countenance. He would not notice that the confusion was anything unusual for a large audience. Soon his musical voice attracted attention, and then his graceful gesticulation; then a rounded period brought applause from those nearest him. Then silence and attention spread a little farther, and a little farther, until before he had been speaking fifteen minutes the vast concourse was perfectly silent, and following breathless his rapid flights of declamation and irresistible rush of argument. At the close of each sentence a ripple of cheers would follow, and ever and anon a roar of applause would make the welkin ring. For four hours he held that audience spell-bound, and at last when his magnificent peroration struck the blood of every listener with the chill of pleasure and admiration, and the orator had closed, a universal shout broke out—"Go on! Go on! "We can listen to you until the sun rises!"

Mr. YANCEY left Montgomery about the middle of

September upon a tour to the North. After speaking at KINGSTON, Ga., with his usual power, he proceeded to Knoxville, the hot-bed of Unionism in East Tennessee. There he addressed an audience of not less than three thousand people, defending his cause with such signal ability as to deeply impress all who heard him, of whatever shade of opinion. To break the force of his argument, and just before he appeared ready to conclude, an incident occurred which well illustrates the temper of the times. The Knoxville *Register*, describing the events of the day, says:

At this stage (of Mr. Yancey's speech) a voice, Mr. Manley, asked, what would you do if Lincoln was elected President?

Yancey—Come upon the stand.

Mr. Manley went up and took his seat.

Mr. Yancey said he received twelve years of his education in New England, and there learned the Yankee mode of answering questions, and said to Mr. M. I'll answer your question by asking another.

Manley--Ask it.

Yancey—Who are you in favor of for President?

Manley—John Bell.

Yancey—Will you endorse what John Bell has said on breaking up the Union?

Manley—Said he had propounded the question at the request of others.

Mr. Yancey asked their names. A note was handed to him signed S. R. Rogers, Wm. Rogers, Jno. M. Fleming, W. G. Brownlow, and O. P. Temple. He called out the names of these gentlemen and requested them to come on the stand with him. After some little delay they appeared on the stand as requested.

Mr. Yancey asked them who they were in favor of for President. All answered—John Bell. He then repeated the question he had propounded to Mr. Manley, and requested an answer from each.

Col. Temple—Said Bell had always been a Union man; though some Breckinridge men had, by garbled extracts from his speeches, sought to create a different impression. Thus recognizing Mr. Bell, he was prepared to endorse his position properly entrusted. He did not mean to charge Mr. Yancey with garbling, etc.

Yancey—Said he did not suppose any gentleman would try to insult him on the stand, and he did not regard Mr. Temple's remarks as applying to him, or he would have replied in a different manner.

Mr. Brownlow, in answer to the question, said yes, and added—I propose when the Secessionists go to Washington to dethrone Lincoln, I am for seizing a bayonet and forming an army to resist such attack, and they shall walk over my dead body on their way.

S. R. Rogers endorses Mr. Brownlow's position.

J. M. Fleming—If Mr. Bell had been interrogated on this point, he would endorse his answer.

When the question was asked Wm. Rogers, Mr. Brownlow said, we all answer in the affirmative.

Yancey—I asked him. I suppose he knows better than you, unless you have agreed on a stereotyped answer.

Brownlow—No, we have not been initiated into your League.

Yancey—No, or you would have been a better Southern man.

Mr. Yancey then read an extract from John Bell's speech (the extract published a short time since in the

Register), and said, now, gentlemen, I will answer your question, and answered it in the following words:

I now proceed to answer this question, although unable to perceive in what manner my future act in Alabama can, in the least degree, affect your votes here, on the question of the election of a President.

By an act of the General Assembly in Alabama, passed last winter, it is made the duty of the Governor, in the event a Black Republican shall be elected President, in a certain period after he ascertains it, (thirty days I believe) to make proclamation of the fact—and that an election shall then be held by the people to elect delegates to a Convention of the people of the State, which Convention will consider what the sovereignty and wrongs done the State require at its hands.

As I said to you in the earlier part of my speech, I am a States-Rights man—believing in the right of a State to command the allegiance and obedience of its citizens, and therefore that my allegiance is first due to my State. I do not believe in exercising the individual natural right of rebellion, until both States as well as Federal Constitutions are broken, and my rights are destroyed. If the Federal Constitution shall be broken and destroyed by the usurpation of a Higher Law faction, my right to resist is subordinate to my allegiance to my State Constitution. *As an individual, therefore, I shall not rebel against such an election, for that would be rebellion also against my own State authority.* But whatever course Alabama may take, that course I shall be bound by as a citizen, and if it is to acquiesce, I shall do so—if it is to secede, I shall cast my fortunes with that of the State. If the Convention shall see fit to go into a consultation with the other Southern States, and act as they agree, I shall abide by that action. If it shall decide to demand new guaranties for its rights, before it will remain longer in the Union, I shall acquiesce in that. In fine, as I am bound by, so shall I acquiesce in all that my State may decide to do.

If my State resists, I shall go with her; and if I meet this gentleman (pointing to Mr. Brownlow), marshaled with his bayonet to oppose us, I'll plunge my bayonet to the hilt through and through his heart and feel no compunctions for the act, and thank my God my country has been freed from such a foe. This man, forgetful of his nativity, had uttered fratricidal sentiments of hostility towards men of the South who differ with him upon their views of their rights and the time and manner in which they should be asserted and supported, but who, if they err in judgment, err on the side of patriotism and through devotion to their native land. If Providence, in pity, refrain sending its thunderbolt, crushing this old oak tree, whose boughs now shelter us, and which has lifted its head to heaven since the days of Washington, and our revolutionary sires—he, but one individual of the South, might safely leave the author of such sentiments to the reproaches of his own conscience and the retributive justice which, sooner or later, ever overtakes those who oppose their country's weal. He rocognized those who came on the stand as gentlemen, and he bore no personal malice towards them. He hoped no militia office would be conferred on this gentleman (pointing to Mr. Brownlow.) He had better preach.

He regretted that he had been diverted from words

of peace through interruption. He called it an interruption, but in one sense, and that not an offensive one. He expressed his thanks to the people for their kindness and courtesy. He also thanked the Bell men who were gentlemen, and those not gentlemen.

He knew the power of the press, the base slanders it had uttered against him, and between now and the end of the canvass, they would still go where his voice could not reach. Their lies were like a scrubby quarter nag, while Truth was a thorough bred four-mile horse. On a short race the quarter nag was always successful, but thorough bred Truth was always victorious in a long race.

A few other eloquent and complimentary remarks to the ladies, Mr. Yancey closed. At the conclusion of his remarks Mr. Brownlow took the stand, and said in substance that the gentleman had spoken of him as a parson, and suggested his duty in that capacity. He had read some Scripture, and he would say to the gentleman, get thee behind me, Satan. He had heard the gentleman in a whisper ask a gentleman on the stand if that was not the parson, referring to the speaker. The gentleman said yes. While he was on the subject of parsons, the gentleman should have referred to the fact that the gentleman of whom he asked the question (Rev. Isaac Lewis) was a Federal office-holder, as was another parson present, and that the Democrats had on their State ticket, and as an Elector for this District, two more parsons, who only differed with him in the fact that they had been silenced for lying.

He declined speaking any more, but would speak out through his paper.

Mr. Yancey said, if you have anything to say, say it here before me like a man.

The crowd called again for Mr. Yancey. He said, gentlemen, you cannot expect me to dignify such a speech with a reply.

The State of Virginia, while generally Democratic, had been so uncertain at all times, that now it was believed that the DOUGLAS party would take sufficient votes from the regular Democratic Electoral ticket to give her to Mr. BELL. It was deemed advisable that Mr. YANCEY should speak at Richmond. Remaining there one night he spoke to an immense audience with his usual effect. Declining invitations which came to him from all parts of Virginia—a State which remembered the brilliant words he uttered when he received at its Capitol the field-glass of GEORGE WASHINGTON, presented to him by the ladies of the Mount Vernon Association a few years before—he hastened to Washington. Wherever he went the crowds which poured forth to meet him increased in numbers. So great had become the fame of his eloquence and power, that the largest buildings could not contain those that flocked to hear him. To one of these mighty hosts at the Capital of the Union, he spoke as follows:

"I say to you, then, though we deprecate disun-
"ion, we will have the Union of our fathers. It has
"been said that the South has aggressed upon the
"North. When and where has my people ever
"aggressed upon the people of any other section?
"When and where has any Southern statesman pro-
"posed a wrong to be done to the West, the North-
"west, the East, or the Northeast?"

A voice—"Never."

Mr. Yancey—" Never. History will proclaim it. " This age proclaims it. Our enemies will proclaim it " by their silence when we defy them to answer the " question.

" Ours, then, is a position of defence within the " limits of the Constitution. We uphold its banner. " We intend to defend its principles. We ask only " equal rights in our common Government. We ask " protection for these rights in our common Govern- " ment. Nothing more, and, so help me God, we will " submit to nothing less." [Applause.]

" Now, my fellow-citizens, I do not intend to address " you at length to-night. I am wearied, having trav- " eled all night, and having been detained on the way " by an accident on the railroad. I have spoken four " times this week, and once I had the modesty to " address an audience four hours. [A voice—' Give " us four hours more to-night.'] I, therefore, have no " physical ability to detain you any longer to-night. " I conceive that you have met here to-night not from " any special respect to an individual, but that you " have recognized me as one earnestly striving to " advance the cause of the Constitution ; and in that " spirit, and in that only, have shown your respect for " the cause of Democracy—something that is deserv- " ing of that respect—for that I most sincerely thank " you. I trust that I shall never deserve a want of " respect at your hands, or at those of any one else, by " proposing aggression on any, or by proposing any " measure not in accordance with a strict construction " of the Constitution."

A voice—" What will the South do in the event of " Lincoln's election ?"

Mr. Yancey—"I don't know what she will do; but "I will say to you—I put it to you, my friend. Now "if you live in a slave-holding State—"

The same voice—"I do, sir."

Mr. Yancey—"Well, then, if John Brown commits "a raid on that State while in the peace of God, and "while in the peace of the country, under the peace of "the Constitution that is supposed to protect it—if he "comes with pike, with musket, and bayonet, and "cannon; if he slaughter an inoffensive people; if his "myrmidons are scattered all over our country, where "it is supposed rests this institution which is so unpal-"atable, inciting our slaves to midnight arson, to mid-"night murder, and to midnight insurrection against "the sparsely scattered white people; if the brother-"hood of this nation shall be broken up, and the com-"mon citizenship shall be ignored; if the protection "that is due from every citizen to every other citizen "shall be no longer afforded; if, in the place of it, a "wild and bloodthirsty spirit—not of revenge, for "we have done no wrong to be revenged—but a "bloodthirsty spirit of assassination, of murder, and "of wrong takes its place, and we find scattered "throughout all our borders these people, and we find "the midnight skies lighted up by the fires of our "dwellings, and the wells from which we hourly drink "poisoned by strychnine; and our wives and our "children, when we are away at our business, are found "murdered by our hearthstones, my answer, my friend, "is in these words: What would *you* do?" [Loud applause.]

A voice—"I would stop him before he got that far."

Mr. Yancey—"I believe that the God of liberty, to

"whom it is our duty at all times to pray; He who "holds in his hands the very destinies of nations—"will so turn the hearts of our people that such an "event shall not happen."

A voice—"Amen."

Mr. Yancey—"For myself, I do hope that in the "Northern States, which hold this question in their "hands, in some way a feeling of justice will be aroused "in the minds of the people, and they will consider "this matter, and prevent this dire result. As for the "South, we are in a minority. We cannot prevent it, "however much we may desire to do so. The North "is now the dominant section of this country. It has "183 electoral votes to our 120. It is for them to "say what is to be our destiny within this Govern-"ment. It is not, thank God, for the North to say "what shall be the destiny of Southern freemen. "['Good,' and applause.] That we hold in our own "hands. Our prosperity, our safety, our institutions "do not depend upon any vote the North may give in "this matter as long as we are true to ourselves. They "are safe, though the Constitution may be rent asunder. "We prefer our protection and our defence within the "lines of the Government of Washington and Jefferson "and of Hancock, but if it is not given to us, we know "that we have freedom within our own breasts. But "within this Union, this Union must be preserved by "Northern votes.

"The issue is now left with the North, and it is ten-"dered her to save the Union and the Constitution by "putting down the Black Republican party." [Good.]

The October elections had taken place in PENNSYLVANIA, and that great State had pronounced for the

Republican party. There was now no hope of preventing the election of Mr. LINCOLN except by bringing about a fusion between the DOUGLAS and BRECKINRIDGE parties of New York. To that end Mr. YANCEY visited New York, and approved of the fusion, which was successfully accomplished. The State of New York cast thirty-five electoral votes. The entire electoral vote by which Mr. LINCOLN was elected was 180; the vote for all the other candidates was 123. Had New York voted for DOUGLAS instead of for LINCOLN, the vote would have been 158 against the latter, and only 145 in his favor. The decision would have gone to Congress, and either Mr. BELL or Gen. LANE would have become President. The vote of New York was 362,000 for LINCOLN and 312,000 for the fusion ticket. Had the compromise been effected at an earlier day, there can be no doubt that New York would never have cast her vote for LINCOLN. Just here, the reviewer of the events of that day pauses to enquire how it was possible to bring about a fusion at New York when the damage was already done, and it was not possible to bring it about at Charleston or Baltimore. How could Mr. YANCEY succumb to policy in October when he had scorned to listen to it in April and June?

It was the purpose of the Republicans to drive Mr. YANCEY to the wall upon the question whether he favored disunion in the event of Mr. Lincoln's election. His position upon that question would materially affect the floating vote in the city of New York. If he should say that he would favor disunion in that event, the Republicans would denounce the fusion ticket as composed partly of disunionists, and would appeal to the pride of the Union men to defy such threats. If he should say he would not favor such a movement he would repudiate the declaration of the General Assembly of his State and his own present wishes and intentions. Speaking in the grand hall of COOPERS Institute to such a mass of men as only New York can present to a popular public orator, he said:

"I have been asked here to-night certain questions, "which I deem it right to answer now, at the present. "One of these questions is, 'Would you consider the "election of Abraham Lincoln as President a sufficient "cause to warrant the South in seceding from the "Union?' The second is, 'Whether, in the case of "Mr. Lincoln being elected, and any of the States "attempted to secede, would you support the General "Government and the other States in maintaining the "integrity of the Union?' The first question is a "speculation—a political speculation, at that. It has "nothing to do with the canvass. I am here, however, "aiding you to prevent such a calamity. I am hon-"estly endeavoring to maintain the integrity of the "Government and the safety of the Union at the ballot-"box. [Applause.] I am here to aid you in trying "to prevent the election of Abraham Lincoln, the "author of the irrepressible conflict; and if others as "faithfully do their duty, he will never be elected. "[Applause.] I am asked, and have been asked "before, whether I consider the election of Lincoln "would be a just cause for the secession of the South-"ern States? That is a matter to come after the ballot-"box. [Cheers and derisive laughter, and cries of "'Answer the question.'] Be quiet, gentlemen. Hear "me, hear me. [Great excitement and tumult—cries "of 'Order, order,' from the platform.] Don't be im-"patient, gentlemen. [Increasing disorder.] Don't "be impatient, and above all things keep your temper. [Laughter and applause.] This is not the time to fight, "certainly. [Laughter.] This is a time to vote, and "to consider how to vote."

A voice—"Let us have an answer to the question."

Mr. Yancey—"You are impatient, my friend. What "is the matter with you?"

An excited individual on the platform—"Put him "out."

Mr. Yancey—"If gentlemen are so desirous of know-"ing my opinions, they ought to abide by my decisions "when they are uttered. [Cheers.] This thing of "asking advice of a man and then not taking his "advice, is a monstrous poor way of getting along. "Now, I am going to say this about it. This question "that is put to me is a speculation on the future. It is "what I consider would happen in the event of some-"thing else happening. I hope to God that that will "never happen, and that the speculation will never "come to a head. [Applause.] I am no candidate "for the Presidency, my friends who wrote these ques-"tions, though some of you seem to have thought so, "judging from the manner in which you have treated "me and Mr. Breckinridge. I am no candidate for "any office, and I do not want your vote. But I would "like to advise with you and get you to vote for a "good man—for any man, I do not care who it is, "excepting one of the irrepressible conflict men. [Up-"roarous applause.] In the first place, there is no "such thing as the South seceding. I do not know "how she would go about it. [Cries of 'Good,' and

" loud cheers.] There is such a thing as a State sece-" ding; but the South seceding is a thing which I " cannot comprehend. I do not know how the South " would go about it. I do not think it could ever " happen; and, therefore, I have no answer to give as " to what the South should do. Now, then, I am a " citizen of the State of Alabama. I am what is called " a States-Rights man. [Cheers.] I believe in the " rights of my State. The Constitution of my country " tells me that certain powers were given to the General " Government, and that all which were not expressly " given, or were not necessary to carry out the powers " granted, were reserved to the States and to the people " of the States. My State has reserved powers and " reserved rights, and I believe in the right of seces-" sion. [Excited cries of 'Good.'] Virginia and New " York were parties to that compact. When the ques-" tion was presented, the State of Virginia expressed " her willingness to join under the compact. The " State of New York also did so through her con-" vention.

" It was provided that if nine States assented, it " would be a government for those nine, and for all the " States that would sign the compact. Therefore, the " compact was a compact between the States mutually " assenting: willingly assenting. If any dissented there " was no proposition to force them into the Union. " Therefore, I believe in the right of a State to go out " of the Union if she thinks proper. The State of Ala-" bama, in her last General Assembly, passed a law " requiring the Governor, in the event of a Black Repub-" lican being elected President of the United States, to " convene, within so many days after he ascertained "that fact, a convention of the people of the State, for "the purpose of considering the question which is here "presented to me. It is a question for the decision of "my State—I cannot decide it. As one of the citizens "of Alabama, I shall abide by the decisions of my "State. If she goes out, I go with her. If she "remains in, I remain with her. I cannot do otherwise. "[Laughter and cheers.] It is a grave question, but "one which I hope God, in His Providence, will keep "me from considering, by the safety of this Govern-"ment in the election of some man opposed to the "'irrepressible conflict party. [Cheers.] But when "the time comes for me to make up my mind, I will "have deliberate consultation with my fellow-citizens in "Alabama. You in New York have nothing to do "with it; nothing. Whatever deliberations you choose "to have, as citizens of New York, on the fate of your "State, will be for yourselves. I have no interest in "that question except incidentally, and have no right "to advise with you or say anything to you about it. "But upon this Presidential question I have a common "interest with you, because it is the election of one to "administer the Government for the next four years— "for my State as well as yours. Therefore it is a "common question, about which I can consult with you. "But whether my State or any other State will go out "of the Union, is a question which it will be for that "State itself to determine. It is not to be determined "by arguing it before the election. It would be a grave "matter for me to commit myself here, to a crowd in "New York, to any policy that might be influenced by "after events, by surrounding circumstances, by the "expressed sympathies of large majorities of the people "of New York or other States with the South. For "me here, merely to gratify some political antagonist, "to express my opinion on that point would be folly; "it is the wildest folly to expect I will. That opinion "will be rendered to the people of my State whenever "they ask for it. [An individual on the platform— "'Three cheers for the answer.'] Now, I am asked "one other question. I am asked whether, if any "portion of the South secedes, I will aid the Govern-"ment in maintaining the integrity of the Union. Yes, "my friend, the integrity of the Union. [Cheers.] "I am now struggling for it; I shall struggle for it to "the day of election. The integrity of the Union I "shall struggle for with my life's blood if required. "[Enthusiastic cheers.] But if this question means by "the integrity of the Union the preservation of an ad-"ministration that shall trample on any portion of the "rights of the South, I tell him that I will aid my "State in resisting it to blood. [Great cheering.] "The common rights of resistance to wrong which "belong to the worm—those rights are not the rights "which were meant to be secured by our fathers in the "Declaration of Independence, when they cut them-"selves loose from despotism and the despotic ties of "the old world. The serf of Russia has got the right "of revolution. The hog has got the right to resist if "you try to put a knife to his throat. [Cheers and "laughter.] The right of revolution is only the poor "serf's right. It is no right at all. It is only the last "expiring throe of oppressed nationality." [Tumultuous cheering.]

Proceeding from New York to Boston, Mr. YANCEY spoke at FANEUIL Hall. Nowhere had he been misrepresented more than in New England; nowhere was his name more detested than at Boston. FANEUIL HALL had once been closed to Mr. WEBSTER, and now a fiercer States-Rights man than WEBSTER's old adversary, HAYNE, was about to address the constituents of SUMNER and BURLINGAME from a rostrum devoted to freedom. The hall was densely packed with an excited and hostile mass of men. At the outset of his remarks there was unmistakable tendency to designed confusion and deliberate interruption, but Mr. YANCEY refused to notice that the demonstrations were other than accidental. He alluded in a few terse words to that freedom of thought and speech for which Boston had been distinguished since the days of WARREN and REVERE. Appealing to the pride of a Boston audience he soon secured silence and attention. Then, once more, he repeated the argument which, in his hands, had become almost irresistible, demanding the equality of the States in the Union, and abating not one jot or tittle from the pretensions of the South. He asked:

"Do you shrink from an honest competition with "the slaveholder? ['No!'] Then take your hands "off of the slave labor, and let us fight it out with you "there in an honest way. [Loud applause.] I think "I know something about the character of the ancient "men of Massachusetts, if I know nothing about the "men of to-day; and I tell you that the men who "fought at Bunker Hill and Lexington, and fought all "over the Union for the common rights of all—those "men were men of too much pride, too much common "sense, and too much love of justice to ask that in any "race they tried with anybody else, their opponents "should be held fast and they let loose. [Cries of "'good.'] Now, if you think that your institutions "are better than ours, if you think yours are more "civilizing than ours, if you think they can carry on "the great cause of civilization better than we can, all "we ask is—hands off—fair play—and victory to him "who wins. [Loud cheering. A voice—'Do you "mean to withdraw from the Union?'] We will never "withdraw from the Union as long as the Constitution "exists in its integrity. I will tell you what the South "must do, what she inevitably will do, if you put your "heel on her, if you deny her equality, if you say she "shall not have the rights in the Union which your "fathers declared she should have. If you violate the "Constitution, I tell you, the South tells you, her "safety does not depend upon you, gentlemen. Her "safety does not depend upon you. The descendants "of the men who fought the battles of Eutaw, King's "Mountain, and Yorktown, and helped you fight your "battles here, can take care of themselves if you won't "take care of them. [Renewed cheering.] And, "mind you, I utter it in no vaunt, and as no threat. Why, "my countrymen, walk in a field, tread on a caterpil-"lar, and the poor creature will turn on your boot and "try to sting you. ['Do you think so?'] Yes, my "friend, I do think so, and you think so, too, if you "have an ounce of manhood in your weight of hundred "and fifty pounds. [Great applause and laughter.]

"And mind, I say, that in all this that I declare the "South will do, she does not mean to trespass upon "you. Thank God, I can say so for my section, that "she has never proposed a wrong upon you—she has "always resisted every proposition of wrong upon you "—she has been ready to fight. When the flag was

"'Free Trade and Sailor's Rights,' she helped to carry "forward the contest of the war of 1812, when some "men in fair New England shrank from that contest." [Loud cheers.]

The effect produced by this speech at FANEUIL HALL may be understood from the cotemporaneous comments of the newspapers. The Boston *Courier*, an advocate of the election of Mr. BELL, said:

"It is enough to say that Mr. Yancey's speech was "worthy of the famous hall in which it was spoken. "He was eloquent, logical, patriotic, and patient under "the taunts which were poured in upon him. The "speech will be remembered a long time by all who "heard it. Whether we agree or not with Mr. Yancey, "we are glad that he has given us an address which "will set our people thinking. When the men of Mas-"sachusetts begin to reason, we shall see day breaking."

The Boston *Post* said:

"He spoke as a son of Alabama, who loved his own "State the best, but who recognized co-equal rights in "the State in which he stood. Then he went on "frankly and boldly for over two hours with admirable "closeness of argument and richness of illustration.

"The lucid presentation of the historical argument; "the analysis of the commercial relations which bind "the North and the South; the development of the "importance of the cotton interest; the defence of "Southern institutions—were done with master ability. "Interspersed with the main lines of argument, was a "succession of questions put by unwilling listeners, "which, so far from embarrassing the orator, were met "with a promptness and directness of reply that now "drew forth shouts of laughter and now thunders of "applause. We hazard nothing in the remark, that "there has not been seen such an exhibition of the "power of oratory for a long time, if ever, in this hall— "and at quarter past ten, when Mr. Yancey intimated "that exhaustion would oblige him to close his speech, "the closely packed audience still remained and urged "him to go on—and his beautiful and noble peroration "was listened to in the profoundest silence!

"We spread the letter of this remarkable effort "before our readers, and they can read the words; but "no words can give an idea of the tones, the gesture, "the manly bearing, the ready wit and the conclusive "point of the orator; and the quick appreciation of the "excited audience. It was a succession of triumphs, "and at the conclusion the hall rang with the wildest "applause."

Returning South by way of the Western States, Mr. YANCEY spoke at CYNTHIANA and LEXINGTON, at CINCINNATI and at LOUISVILLE. Mr. GEO. D. PRENTICE, of the Louisville *Journal*, while decrying his speech through the press, had paid the orator the very highest compliment by listening to him four hours and in a standing posture. At New Orleans the distinguished speaker was received with the wildest enthusiasm. The audience which greeted him was the largest that had ever assembled in the Crescent City. Large numbers came in from the country. Opulent planters were seen upon the stand side by side with merchant princes of the city. It was said that no popular meeting had ever before been witnessed in New Orleans where the officers who presided represented so large an amount of the wealth of the State. Twenty thousand voices uprose to the heavens in long continued plaudits, while from the balconies and windows whicl overlooked the square, thousands of handkerchiefs wer waved by the ladies. When the meeting was dissolved the vast multitude formed into procession, the well-organized clubs taking the lead with lamps and transparencies, marched through the principal streets greeted by multitudes on the sidewalks with cheers and huzzas for BRECKINRIDGE, YANCEY and the South.

The week preceding the Presidential election witnessed the arrival, at MONTGOMERY, of Mr. DOUGLAS and the return of Mr. YANCEY. The reception of the former was comparatively tame and cold. His address to the people was a repetition of those which he had already made during a protracted canvass. As he had said at Norfolk in reply to a question what should be done in the event of the secession of a State, so now again he answered that the election of Mr. LINCOLN would not jstify a disruption of the Union, and no State should be permitted to set up an independent government against the United States. This declaration was received with cheers by the large audience which, partly from sympathy, partly from courtesy, but more especially from curiosity, had assembled to hear him. Although the cheering was by no means general, it was sufficiently widespread and distinct to exhibit an unmistakable Union spirit in the audience. The visit of Mr. DOUGLAS appeared to be ominous. As he left the city and spoke his farewell words to the people upon the bank of the river, the deck of the steamer upon which he stood gave way and precipitated him several feet below. Mrs. DOUGLAS, who was standing with Mrs. FITZPATRICK and a company of Montgomery ladies around them, barely escaped fatal injury.

The reception of Mr. YANCEY at his home was an event long to be remembered by the people of Montgomery. He was already endeared to his political followers by twenty years devotion to their principles. He was now looked upon with pride by even his opponents, who felt that their city and State were honored in one whose splendid oratory had thrilled the Union from centre to circumference. The little city of ten thousand inhabitants turned out *en masse* to welcome her distinguished son. As the evening shades fell upon the streets myriads of lights illumined the dwellings, the sidewalks and the public buildings. The political clubs emerged from their halls with transparencies and torches. Bonfires blazed at the corners of streets. As the mass of eager people followed the march of the clubs the procession lengthened out indefinitely, and with one accord, accompanied by music and banners, they marched to the residence of Mr. YANCEY. There the orator was received in an open carriage drawn by four splendid horses and conducted to the Theatre, which was already well filled with ladies. The men crowded upon the stage, filled the aisles and passages with a dense mass, and sought from the lobby, the vestibules and the stairways to secure a glimpse of the inspiring scene within. "Welcome to the Garibaldi of the South," "Yancey and States-Rights," "Equality in the Union "or independence out of it," were some of the significant mottoes which decked the stage. Boquets were showered around him as the speaker appeared, and the whole audience rose to their feet with cheer upon cheer. The multitude outside who could not obtain entrance, clamored for Mr. JUDGE to come out and address them. Thus the audience in the street who listened to Mr.

YANCEY by deputy was almost as great as that which filled the theatre.

The orator reviewed the canvass which was now to close upon the following day. Mr. LINCOLN would probably be elected, and it became the duty of all true Southern men to stand united in resistance to his domination. The die was cast; the argument was exhausted; would his friends stand to their arms? The answer of those friends was given in the motto over his head. They looked upon him as THE GARIBALDI OF THE SOUTH.

On the 6th of November, while Mr. LINCOLN was elected President under the forms of the Constitution and by the unrepresentative system of Electoral Colleges, the people had declared against him by a large majority. The majority of votes against him was nearly two hundred thousand. The Supreme Court and the Senate were already against him; and now the elections had increased the majority against the Republicans in the lower House of Congress. Of the twelve hundred and fifty-one thousand votes cast in the slave States, Mr. BELL and Mr. DOUGLAS, representing the UNION sentiment, as against the secession sentiment, received six hundred and and ninety thousand, a clear majority of the whole. In the State of Alabama there were 41,000 against Mr. BRECKINRIDGE to 48,000 in his favor. A larger vote had been polled in Mr. YANCEY'S own State for candidates who denounced both the right and policy of secession, than ever before in her annals. In Georgia the vote for BELL and DOUGLAS was larger than for BRECKINRIDGE. In Mississippi, the grave of QUITMAN and the home of DAVIS, the BRECKINRIDGE ticket stood to the others only as four to three. LOUISIANA threw five thousand majority against BRECKINRIDGE.

In the Gulf States, from the Atlantic to the Mississippi, there was, in a poll of 330,000 votes, a bare majority of 14,000 for Mr. BRECKINRIDGE. While 172,000 men stood by Mr. YANCEY, there were, 157,000 who stood with Mr. BELL for "the Constitution, the "Union and the enforcement of the law," or with Mr. DOUGLAS in denying the right and policy of secession in the event of Mr. LINCOLN's election.

CHAPTER XVII.

Election of Lincoln—Reception of the News—Mass Meeting at Montgomery—Yancey Declares for Secession—The People Taught that Secession will be Peaceable—Co-operationists and Secessionists — The Crittenden Compromise—Its Rejection and Defeat.

"Wayward sisters, depart in peace!"—[Gen. Winfield Scott.

"I have good reason to believe that the action of any State will be peaceable—will not be resisted—under the present or any probable prospective condition of Federal affairs."—[W. L. Yancey.

"Were the plan of the Convention adverse to the public happiness, my voice would be, REJECT THE PLAN. Were the Union itself inconsistent with the public happiness, it would be, ABOLISH THE UNION."—[Madison in the Federalist, No. XIV.

On the night of the eventful 6th of November, 1860, as the telegraph carried to every nook and corner of the Union the news of the election, the people of Montgomery thronged the streets and the newspaper offices to a late hour to learn the result. All depended upon New York; it was past midnight before definite returns could be received from that vast State. At last the result was announced. The administration of the United States had been consigned to the Free Soil party, the restrictionists of slavery. Mr. WATTS had already broken the Whig line by announcing, towards the close of the canvass, that in the event of LINCOLN'S election he should advise and advocate secession. He had been educated at the University of Virginia in the school of constitutional law presided over by DAVIS, afterwards by HOLCOMBE, and had steadfastly recognized the right of secession. As it was a right, so he believed that now it was the duty of Alabama to secede. The excited citizens who had been watching the returns asked, "Mr. WATTS, what will you do now?" His reply was, "Gentlemen, we ought not to stand it." CLANTON, whose views were moulded in a different school, walked the streets to a late hour, appealing to his party friends not to commit themselves—to wait for the cool second thought; but by noon of the next day so rapid appeared to be the defections from the Union ranks among the people of Montgomery and the adjacent country, and so unmistakable was their intention to vindicate the declaration of their General Assembly, that men of all parties at the Capital, with but a few exceptions, pronounced for instant and separate secession. (?)

It was the policy of those who advocated secession to strike while the iron was hot, to arouse the people to fury immediately upon the heels of the election, and to persuade them that immediate action while many friends of the South were still influential and powerful at Washington, would so concentrate and consolidate the strength and resources of seceding States as to render the movement entirely peaceable. On the morning of the 8th, while passions were still inflamed, the leading journal at Montgomery, in the confidence of Mr. YANCEY, published a leader entitled, "AND NOW." It said: "Organize! We can now enforce a peaceable "secession. The time may come, will come, must "come, if you delay when you can gain your freedom, "if at all, only as the colonies gained it when they "separated; only as our forefathers gained it when "they fought the battle of disunion, through toil and "bloodshed, through carnage and desolation." The burden of the cry from all quarters was—make haste and all can be done completely and peaceably; delay, and the enemy seeing you unprepared to prevent the coercion of South Carolina, will force you to battle and perhaps desolation! Between the two alternatives as here presented, there was but little hesitation in the cities and towns where the question was most thoroughly discussed.

In the midst of the highest excitement and popular indignation a mass meeting was called at ESTELLE HALL. At the request of TENNENT LOMAX, His Excellency Gov. A. B. MOORE took his stand upon the platform and addressed the vast audience amid tumultuous and long continued applause. The Governor said he saw no course left but to secede from the Union, resume sovereignty, and form a Southern Confederacy. He had no discretion with regard to calling the Convention—this he was forced to do by the resolutions of the Legislature, but if he had, he should most assuredly call it, for he felt that honor, liberty, and property were not safe under the rule of Abolitionism. The Governor took his seat after a short address, and was succeeded by Judge S. F. RICE.

Judge RICE said that he did not appear for the purpose of making a speech, but to introduce a resolution, which he read, as follows:

"*Resolved,* That the authority and control of the "Northern sectional Abolition party, calling itself Re-"publican, which has lately elected Abraham Lincoln "to the Presidency, over the institutions, rights, and "liberties of the people of Alabama, or any other slave-

"holding State of the South, would be ruinous; that "such ruinous authority and control is not to be sub- "mitted to, but can only be effectively resisted by "separate State action; that we are in favor of such "separate State action, and without any further delay "than may be necessary, by the most prompt available "means, to procure a free and fraternal consultation "among the peoples and authorities of the respective "slaveholding States, entered into and conducted under "the patriotic hope that such consultation will result in "the general conclusion on the part of the people of "the slaveholding States, that it is not fit or safe, that "they or any of them should be subject to the control "of any government, the destinies of which are in the "hands of said sectional Abolition party."

Judge Edward W. Pettus, of Cahaba, in obedience to the repeated calls of the audience, took the stand and made a few eloquent remarks in favor of the resolution. He was followed by N. H. R. Dawson, of Selma, whose earnest and thrilling address made an evident impression upon his hearers. Loud calls were made for Mr. Watts, who responded in a spirited appeal in behalf of his State and section. When Mr. Watts had concluded, Judge Goldthwaite was called for, and taking his place on the platform, vindicated the cause of the South and defended the right and policy of secession. His remarks were repeatedly interrupted by outbursts of applause. Mr. Yancey responded to the enthusiastic demands of the audience, and spoke as Yancey *always* spoke. It was his night of triumph. The first resolution ever passed by a public assemblage at the Capital of the State in favor of secession, had just been adopted. He said:

"This night two weeks ago, I was asked, while "speaking in New York, what course I would advise "Alabama to take in the event that Lincoln should be "elected President. Acting in perfect good faith to "the issues presented by the party, whose cause I ad-"vocated, and which issues contemplated a solution of "the political questions at the ballot-box only, within "the Union, I declined to give utterance to my indi-"vidual opinions, which could only tend to embarrass "my friends and to encourage their foes, but told the "people of New York that I should cheerfully give "that advice to my fellow-citizens of Alabama, when-"ever they should see fit to ask it; [applause] and I "redeem that pledge to-night, by saying that in my "opinion the election of Abraham Lincoln to the office "of President of the United States by the Black Re-"publican party, taken in connection with his own "political utterances, and the views and acts of his "party in Congress, and in the several Northern States, "is an overt act against the Constitution --[applause] "against the Constitution, and against the Union, [ap-"plause] and as such should be deemed sufficient cause "for a withdrawal of the State of Alabama, and a "resumption of all the powers she has granted to the "Union, by separate State secession. [Prolonged ap-"plause.] And while giving utterance to this advice, I "repudiate as utterly untrue, that in any just sense I "am a Disunionist. [Applause.] If always to have "advocated the right of all under the Constitution—if "never to have assailed any single provision of that "Constitution—if the advocacy of a policy of defense "against wrong done to Southern rights—equality and "honor within the Union, constitutes a friend to that

"'more perfect Union,' represented by the Constitu-
"tion, then by universal acclaim I should be held to
"be a Union man, [applause] and if to-night I advise
"my State to withdraw herself from this Federal Gov-
"ernment in order to protect her rights and the rights
"of her people from wrongs done to them by a viola-
"tion of that Constitution by a numerical power that
"controls the government, I have the judgment of the
"Constitution itself in my favor and against its viola-
"tors, and am no disunionist. But, I am not content
"with my own vindication. That with which we are
"falsely charged is true of our accusers. [Applause.]
"Look back at the history of our government. I will
"not enumerate the list of grievances of which the
"Spirit of the Constitution complains—and about
"which our patriotic Chief Magistrate spoke so clearly
"to-night, but I will refer for a moment to the acts of
"the now dominant party upon the fugitive slave law.
"The Constitution calls for the enactment of this law
"in plain terms. One of the very first acts of our
"patriot sires was to enact a fugitive slave law. The
"Constitution, it is well known, could not have been
"formed without the provision for the surrender of
"fugitive slaves. The Constitution, too, is a compact,
"not between the majority and the minority of the
"people of the United States, but between sovereign
"States. It was submitted to a Convention of each
"State for its adoption or rejection; and was for a long
"time in operation before two of the original thirteen
"States concluded to come into the Union. It is then
"a compact between the States. How has that com-
"pact been kept by the Black Republican States?
"Twelve of them have passed laws nullifying the fugi-

"tive slave law and provision in the Constitution, have "made it a crime in their citizens to aid in its execu- "tion, punishing such action by heavy fine and impris- "onment in the penitentiary. The compact, then, has "been broken—the Union has been dissolved—the "Constitution has been violated by this infamous "party; and now, when we, one of the parties to that "compact, propose to act on the well-established princi- "ple that a compact broken in part is broken as a "whole, if either party chooses to consider it, *the viola- "tors*—the breakers of that compact—those who have "themselves disrupted the bonds of Union, cry out "treason! disunion! [Applause.] Fellow-citizens, we "have long been released from any obligation to con- "tinue in association with these Northern States under "this broken, mutilated compact. And now, when the "real, true disunionists have, at last, elected a Presi- "dent—by a majority of electoral votes—by a majority "of the popular vote—by a purely sectional vote, and "propose to 'inaugurate the policy of the irrepressible "conflict into the government—which is the end of "slavery,' [in Mr. Seward's words,] we propose to "withdraw from beneath such usurpation and power, "and protect ourselves. [Applause.]

"There are other States, each and all having similar "wrongs to complain of, and similar rights and institu- "tions to save and protect. If any of those States "wish a consultation with us and each other, it is our "duty to afford a fair opportunity for a full, free, fra- "ternal interview. Should that take place, I hope, as "my friend Mr. Watts expressed it, that 'we may all go "together;' as Judge Goldthwaite expressed it, that 'we "will act together.' [Applause.] But there is a point "beyond that. In the contingency that consultation "shall not produce concert—that all will not 'act'—or "'go out together,' what then? Shall we, like them, "linger yet within the desecrated portals of the gov- "ernment—shall we remain and be all slaves—shall "we remain but to share with them the disgrace "of inequality and dishonor? God forbid! [Tremen- "dous applause.] Let us act in that event for our- "selves. [Applause.] I have good reason to believe "that the action of any State will be peaceable—will "not be resisted—under the present, or any probable "prospective condition of Federal affairs. I believe "there will not be power to direct a gun against a sov- "ereign State. [Applause.] Certainly there will be "no will to do so during the present Administration. "[Applause.] And if resisted, blood shed will appeal "to blood throbbing in Southern bosoms, and our "brethren from every Southern State will flock to "defend the soil of a State which may be threatened "by mercenary bayonets. [Applause.] It is not all "of life to live, nor all of death to die. To do one's "duty, is man's chief aim in life. Better far to close "our days by an act of duty—life's aims fulfilled, than "to prolong them for years—years filled with the cor- "roding remembrance that we had tamely yielded to "our ease and our fears that noble heritage, which was "transmitted to us through toil, suffering, battle and "victory, with the condition that we likewise should "transmit it unimpaired to our posterity. [Applause.] "As for myself, rather than live on, subject to a gov- "ernment which breaks the compact at will, and places "me in a position of inequality—of inferiority to the "Northern free negro—though that life might be illus-

"trated by gilded chains—by luxury and by ease, I "would in the cause of my State gather around me "some brave spirits who, however few in number, would "find a grave, which my countrymen—the world and "all future ages, should recognize as a modern Ther-"mopylæ! [Prolonged applause.]"

At the close or Mr. YANCEY's remarks, Gen. CLANTON was called for by the audience. He said that he had been always a devoted friend of the Union, that even in the late canvass he had declared himself in favor of waiting for an overt act, but that the immense majorities given to the Abolition ticket convinced him that we had nothing to hope for from the North, and he could not consider the liberty and property of Southern men safe in the Union. He was for immediate secession. Gen. CLANTON said that he had never heretofore agreed with Mr. YANCEY and those who thought with him, that one month ago he thought he never would agree with them, but that now he was willing to bury the hatchet and unite with all true Southern men in establishing a free and independent government of slaveholding States. The facts which had induced Gen. CLANTON to forego his intention of waiting for the commission of an unconstitutional act by the LINCOLN Administration before establishing a separate government, had arisen just before the close of the canvass and since the election. WENDELL PHILLIPS, the boldest and most philosophic leaderof the Lincoln party, had declared, and the declaration had been repeated bythe press and from the rostrum until it had become a party cry: "No man has a right to be surprised at this state of "things. It is just what we have attempted to bring "about. It is the first sectional party ever organized "in this country. It does not know its own face, and "calls itself national; but it is not national--it is sec- "tional. THE REPUBLICAN PARTY IS A PARTY OF THE "NORTH PLEDGED AGAINST THE SOUTH." It was now announced that Mr. SEWARD would be Secretary of State. In his "Irrepressible conflict" speech he had asserted that the "United States must and will, sooner or later, "become either entirely a slave-holding nation or "entirely a free-labor nation." These declarations of hostility to the South had been repeated oftener as the canvass approached a close, and on the 6th of November few persons, North or South, failed to understand that the election of LINCOLN was to be the restriction and ultimate dstruction of slavery without regard to law or courts. On that day the State governments at the North had passed into or had been retained in the hands of the Republican party by overwhelming majorities--a party which freely boasted that the Personal Liberty Laws should remain in force, and the Fugitive Slave Law remain nullified. Gen. CLANTON believed that nothing could be longer hoped for from the temper of the North--that, although the LINCOLN Administration might be trammelled for four years by a hostile Congress and Court, at the end of that time the power of all the Departments would pass into the hands of the Republican party, and the South, with her forts and arsenals guarded by large garrisons, and with her territory occupied by the troops of the Presidential Commander-in-Chief, would find herself unable to assert her independence when the *overt act* should be committed.

There was another incentive which urged him most powerfully to declare for instant secession. It was to preserve a Constitutional Union. He had come to believe that the secession of the Southern States would be peaceably acquiesced in by the North, that it would be followed by a call for a general Convention of the States at which the questions in dispute might be weighed and accommodated and the Union reconstructed upon the principles of the Constitution, well-defined and accepted. It may be a matter of wonder that a man of the political sagacity and general intelligence of Gen. CLANTON should have believed for a moment that the secession of the Cotton States would be acquiesced in by the General Government. He did not believe so until after the election, and then his belief was based upon the clear declaration of one of the leaders of the Republican party that secession ought not to be interfered with. That secession might be, and doubtless would be, a peaceable measure, was almost universally believed by the secession party of the South. The military preparations made by the States would barely have secured an efficient border and coast police. The money and supplies voted for military purposes would not have fed an army a month. So contemptible were the preparations for defence, so meagre the supplies for action, so few the muskets and accoutrements, that nothing could have relieved the Legislatures of the seceding States from a charge of insanity except a firm belief in their minds that there would be no necessity for armies—that there would be no coercion. As an illustration of the delusion upon this subject, even with prominent statesmen and military men, Gen. CLANTON was accustomed to tell how, when a few months later than the election, a cavalry regiment of militia, of which he was a field officer, was offered to President DAVIS, the reply was that the Confederacy would not need cavalry, that it would be an infantry war, and that a few regiments of infantry would be sufficient. This feeling of security was exhibited throughout the Southern press. "We can "now enforce a peaceable secession," exclaimed the *Advertiser*. Mr. YANCEY, fresh from his Northern tour, declared: "I have good reason to believe that "the action of any State will be peaceable—will not be "resisted—under the present or any probable prospec-"tive condition of Federal affairs." It was understood at the South that the views of Mr. SEWARD, the leading spirit of the Republican party, and of Mr. CHARLES FRANCIS ADAMS, who had been a candidate for the Vice-Presidency upon the Abolition ticket as early as 1848, were those of the illustrious JOHN QUINCEY ADAMS. That distinguished gentleman, in his "Discourse "delivered before the New York Historical Society," on the fiftieth anniversary of Gen. Washington's inauguration as President, had admitted the natural right of the people of a State to secede from the Union, whilst deprecating its exercise. He had said:

"But the indissoluble link of Union between the "people of the several States of this confederated nation "is, after all, not in the *right*, but in the *heart*. If the "day should ever come (may Heaven avert it) when "the affections of the people of these States shall be "alienated from each other; when the fraternal spirit "shall give way to cold indifference, or collision of "interest shall fester into hatred, the bands of political "association will not long hold together parties no "longer attracted by the magnetism of conciliated inter-"ests and kindly sympathies; and far better will it be "for the people of the disunited States to part in friend-"ship from each other, than to be held together by "constraint. Then will be the time for reverting to "the precedents which occurred at the formation and "adoption of the Constitution, to form again a more "perfect Union by deploring that which could no longer "bind, and to leave the separated parts to be re-united "by the law of political gravitation to the centre."

Such was the opinion of the younger ADAMS, and such, it was believed, was the opinion of the profounder thinkers of New England. To confirm the delusion engendered at the South by such admissions as these, appeared an editorial in the New York TRIBUNE, three days after the election, written by Mr. HORACE GREELEY, in which the following sentiments were announced:

"If the Cotton States shall become satisfied that they "can do better out of the Union than in it, we insist on "letting them go in peace. The right to secede may "be a revolutionary one, but it exists nevertheless. "* * * We must ever resist the right of any "State to remain in the Union and nullify or defy the "laws thereof. To withdraw from the Union is quite "another matter; and whenever a considerable section "of our Union shall deliberately resolve to go out, we "shall resist all coercive measures designed to keep "it in. We hope never to live in a Republic whereof "one section is pinned to another by bayonets."

This declaration of Mr. GREELEY, one of the founders of the Free Soil party, and its ablest advocate with the pen, was telegraphed all over the South. It threw into the ranks of the Secessionists thousands upon thousands of those who had heretofore wavered; and showed to many thousands more a door of escape by which a more perfect Union might be formed—in the language of Mr. ADAMS, "By dissolving that which could no "longer bind," and leaving "the separated parts to be "reunited by the law of political gravitation to the "centre." Mr. GREELEY continued his appeals in behalf of the right of the South to be let alone. On the 17th of December, three days before the secession of South Carolina, he said:

"If it [the Declaration of Independence] justifies "the secession from the British Empire of three millions "of colonists in 1776, we do not see why it would not "justify the secession of five millions of Southrons from "the Federal Union in 1861. If we are mistaken on "this point, why does not some one attempt to show "wherein and why? For our own part, while we deny "the right of slaveholders to hold slaves against the "will of the latter, we cannot see how twenty millions "of people can rightfully hold ten, or even five, in a "detested Union with them by military force. * * "If seven or eight contiguous States shall pre- "sent themselves authentically at Washington, "saying: 'We hate the Federal Union; we have "withdrawn from it; we give you the choice between "acquiescing in our secession and arranging amicably "all incidental questions on the one hand, and attempt- "ing to subdue us on the other;' we could not stand "up for coercion, for subjugation, for we do not think "it would be just. We hold the right of self-govern- "ment, even when invoked in behalf of those who "deny it to others. So much for the question of prin- "ciple."

In this course the *Tribune* persisted from the date of Mr. LINCOLN's election until after his inauguration, employing such remarks as the following: "Any "attempt to compel them by force to remain, would be "contrary to the principles enunciated in the immortal "Declaration of Independence, contrary to the funda-"mental ideas on which human liberty is based."

Even after the Cotton States had formed their Confederacy and adopted a provisional Constitution at Montgomery, it gave them encouragement to proceed in the following language: "We have repeatedly said, "and we once more insist, that the great principle em-"bodied by Jefferson in the Declaration of American "Independence, that governments derive their just "powers from consent of the governed, is sound and "just; and that if the Slave States, the Cotton States, "or the Gulf States only, choose to form an independ-"ent nation, they have a clear moral right to do so. "Whenever it shall be clear that the great body of "Southern people have become conclusively alienated "from the Union, and anxious to escape from it, we "will do our best to forward their views."

Mr. GREELEY was not alone in his opinion that the South should be let alone. The Cincinnati *Commercial*, a leading Western journal, said as late as March, 1861: "We are not in favor of blockading the Southern coast. "We are not in favor of retaking by force the property "of the United States now in possession of the seceders. "We would recognize the existence of a Government "formed of all the slaveholding States, and attempt to "cultivate amicable relations with it."

Mr. THURLOW WEED, who, if any one, represented the wishes of Mr. SEWARD, said in his newspaper, the Albany *Journal*: "The chief architects of the rebellion, before "it broke out, avowed that they were aided in their "infernal designs by the ultra-Abolitionists of the "North. This was too true, for *without such aid the "South could never have been united against the Union.*" In a published letter of Gen. F. P. BLAIR, he says: "When the rebellion broke out, Mr CHASE used this "language: '*The South is not worth fighting for!*' "Several gentlemen of high position in the country "heard him utter this sentiment substantially. He "was at that time Secretary of the Treasury. * * * "JEFF DAVIS said, '*Let us alone!*' CHASE said '*Let "them alone!*'"

"Let them alone," "Let them go," was the cry of nearly all the leading Republican journals and politicians. The New York press was almost a unit for permitting peaceable secession. The *Herald*, Harpers *Weekly*, the *Day Book*, the *Tribune*, all said, "Let "the South go." The General commanding the armies, the veteran SCOTT, also joined the cry and said: "*Wayward sisters, depart in peace!*" That these distinguished officers, statesmen and journalists afterwards yielded their views to the clamor of a mob, does not affect the fact that such views were widely entertained, were believed to be the views of the people of the North, and were accepted as such by a large body of Southern citizens who otherwise would probably have thrown their influence against secession. The editorial of Mr. GREELEY upon the heels of the election, and while Southern blood was hot, confirmed the announcement of Mr. YANCEY that the South would be let alone, and did more to secure the secession of Alabama, Georgia and other Gulf States than all else besides. The secession party had all along been in a minority in Alabama. The vote for Mr. BRECKINRIDGE was not composed entirely of secessionists; while the vote for Mr. BELL and Mr. DOUGLAS was composed almost entirely of Union men. Now, to the compact mass of secessionists was added a large element of the old Whig party, who believed that by the speedy secession of all the Southern States the Union could be reconstructed upon a stronger constitutional basis.

While men like CLANTON believed that the safest course at this juncture was to push forward boldly, form the new government, and amicably adjust terms for reunion; and while WATTS, JUDGE and other old-line Whigs believed that no adjustment was longer possible, and that secession should be resorted to without regard to whether it might be peaceable or otherwise, there was still a formidable body of citizens, away from the lines of railroads, on the hills and in the valleys of the mountain country, who put no faith in the promises of the Northern enemy, and no confidence in secession as a peaceful or revolutionary remedy for grievances. These men were, for the most part, engaged in agricultural pursuits, they were non-slaveholders. They had sustained JACKSON as a Union Democrat and CLAY as a Union Whig. They had no leaders of marked ability. If they had possessed a leader with the fire of YANCEY or the industry of WATTS, the honesty of PETTUS or the courage of JUDGE, the result in Alabama might have been different; NICHOLAS DAVIS was brave, JERE CLEMENS was eloquent, BULGER was firm as a rock, and JEMISON was discreet; but none of the Union leaders, if leaders they could now be called, possessed the power of YANCEY to breast the whirlwind and the tide until the passing of the storm.

The meeting at which CLANTON, JUDGE, GOLDTHWAITE,

and WATTS all took their stand by the side of YANCEY, appointed a committee to wait upon the Governor and learn his intentions with reference to calling a State Convention. Governor MOORE replied that in accordance with the resolutions of the last Legislature, he would issue his proclamation calling for the election of delegates to a State Convention so soon as the Electoral Colleges cast their votes. He appointed Dec. 24th as the day for the election, and Jan. 4th as the day for assembling. The Governor proceeded to say why, in his opinion, Alabama should secede:

"They [the Republicans] have now succeeded by "large majorities, in all the non-slaveholding States, "except New Jersey, and perhaps in Oregon and California, in electing Mr. LINCOLN, who is pledged to "carry out the principles of the party that elected him. "The course of events show clearly that this party will "in a short time have a majority in both branches of "Congress. It will then be in their power to change "the complexion of the Supreme Court so as to make "it harmonize with Congress and the President. When "that party gets possession of all the Departments of "the Government with the purse and the sword, he "must be blind indeed who does not see that slavery "will be abolished in the District of Columbia, in the "dock-yards and arsenals and wherever the Federal "Government has jurisdiction. It will be excluded "from the Territories, and other Free States will in hot "haste be admitted into the Union until they have a "majority to alter the Constitution. Then slavery will be "abolished by law in the States, and the 'irrepressible "conflict' will end; for we are notified that it shall "never cease until 'the foot of the slave shall cease to "tread the soil of the United States.' The state of "society that must exist in the Southern States with "four millions of free negroes and their increase turned "loose upon them, I will not discuss—it is too horrible "to contemplate."

The Governor then dismisses the dangerous part of the question with this dash of his pen:

"If a State withdraws from the Union, the Federal "Government has no power, under the Constitution, to "use the military force against her, for there is no law "to enforce the submission of a sovereign State, nor "would such a withdrawal be either an insurrection or "an invasion."

Now that the Governor had called an election for a State Convention, it was remembered and published that Mr. YANCEY, at the Commercial Convention two years before, had said that if he should go for disunion because of the election of Mr. SEWARD to the Presidency, he would be going in the wake of an inferior issue, he would be doing an unconstitutional thing, could be arraigned as a rebel and traitor, and be hanged for violating the laws and Constitution of his country. It became necessary for him to explain away that speech, and to do so he published a letter in which occurred the following paragraph:

"I remember well the views I then entertained "and then expressed. Mr. Hilliard, as I understood "him, had expressed the opinion that the South was "then on rising ground as to Federal affairs, and that "there was no just cause of complaint in the past; but "that if a Black Republican should be elected Presi- "dent in 1860, the South should resist. I contended "that there were causes in the past action of the anti-

"slavery party which would justify secession—and in "order to rebuke the tameness of spirit, as well as in- "consistency, involved in Mr. Hilliard's position, I "presented the argument that an election of a Black "Republican, under the form of law, was, *per se*, in "itself, constitutional, and if considered without refer- "ence to the past action and avowed aims of the party "electing him, was in my opinion no cause for disun- "ion, but if considered as an accumulative fact, the "culminating movement and grand success of a party, "which for near forty years had been warring on "slavery and the South, and had in several instances "(as to slave-trade in the District of Columbia, Mis- "souri Compromise, and nullifying the fugitive slave "law) violated the constitutional compact between the "States, it would overflow the cup of our wrongs, and "be the point beyond which forbearance would cease to "be a virtue. In other words, my position was as to "one occupying Mr. Hilliard's position; the election of "a Black Republican was an inferior issue. Whereas, "to one occupying my position, disunion could be jus- "tified before such an election, and such an election "would be but another incentive to it."

This satisfied his friends; and forthwith they had the weight of his name for separate State secession, and his assurance that he had reason to believe that there would be no attempt at coercion by the existing or the next administration.

A contest now commenced between the advocates of separate State secession and the advocates of co-operative secession. So high was public excitement that no one was willing to be spoken of as a submissionist. The secessionist and the co-operationist alike declared that they would not submit to a Republican Administration. But while the secessionist intended his declaration literally, the co-operationist intended it to mean that he would not submit to unconstitutional acts, such as would be acts of the administration as contradistinguished from legitimate acts of the Government. They would submit to the Government but would not submit to a tyrannical Administration. That the co-operation party stood pledged to some kind of secession, does not appear substantiated. It is true that before the election, the General Assembly, with but one or two dissenting voices, had passed the joint resolutions calling a State Convention to consider, determine and to do what was necessary for the safety of Alabama in the event of Republican success. But it is certain that the vote would not have been so nearly a unit had not the anti-secessionists believed that the resolutions were susceptible of two constructions. Upon examining those resolutions we find the Assembly declaring that whereas the Republican party "hopes by success in the approaching Presidential election to seize the government itself," and whereas, "to permit such seizure * * * would be an act of suicidal folly and madness," therefore, they "deem it their solemn duty to provide in advance the means by which they may escape such peril and dishonor, and devise new securities for perpetuating the blessings of liberty." This language, it must be readily seen, was such as might be adopted by either a secessionist or an anti-secessionist. If it was the design of the Republicans *to seize the government* in defiance of the Senate and Supreme Court, then the Union men and all were ready to provide means for escaping the peril. Those means might be provided, however, within the Union. "Let "us fight within the Union!" was the cry of a large body of the people, embracing statesmen of distinction, conspicuously among whom was HENRY A. WISE.

Nor was the Union man and Co-operationist in their opinion committed to *some* kind of secession by the resolution adopted unanimously on the first day of the session of the Alabama Convention. The resolution as offered by Mr. WHATLEY, of Calhoun, was as follows:

"Whereas, The only bond of Union between the "several States is the Constitution of the United States; "and, whereas, that Constitution has been *violated* both "by the Government of the United States and by a ma-"jority of Northern States, in their separate legislative "action, denying to the people of the Southern States "their constitutional rights;

"And, whereas, a sectional party known as the "Black Republican party, has in the recent election "elected Abraham Lincoln to the office of President, "and Hannibal Hamlin to the office of Vice-President "of these United States, upon the avowed *principle* "that the Constitution of the United States *does not* "*recognize property in slaves*, and that the Govern-"ment should *prevent its extension* into the common "territories of the United States, and that the power "of the Government should be so exercised that *slavery* "*in time should be exterminated*; Therefore, be it

"*Resolved*, By the people of Alabama, in solemn "Convention assembled, that these acts and designs "constitute such a violation of the compact between "the several States as absolves the people of Alabama "from all obligations to support a government of the

"United States to be administered upon such principles, and that the people of Alabama *will not submit* "to be parties to the *inauguration and administration* "of Abraham Lincoln as President, and Hannibal "Hamlin as Vice-President of the United States of "America."

This resolution was offered in the Alabama Convention, as was said by the mover, to test whether any delegates were in favor of submitting to LINCOLN's Administration. "I desire to ascertain," said he, "the "sense of this body upon the question of submission or "resistance." Mr. SMITH, of TUSCALOOSA, said: "Present a naked question of resistance to Black Republican rule, and you will doubtless receive a unanimous vote in favor of it. But do not so interlard it "with generalities and political abstractions that we "shall be forced to reject the good on account of its "too close association with the evil. I object particularly to make an intimation that I would oppose by "force the inauguration of LINCOLN. I would not have "anything to do with that in any way. I deprecate "the idea of intimating to the people, even remotely, "that the laws ought not to be respected." Mr. POSEY, of Lauderdale, said: "We intend to resist. It "is not our purpose to submit to the doctrines asserted "at Chicago, but our resistance is based upon consultation and in unity of action with the other slave "States." It was well understood on all sides that a resistance based upon consultation with the other Slave States, would be simply a peaceful resistance at the polls. The resolution as proposed by Mr. WHATLEY was finally amended and passed unanimously, in the following shape:

"*Resolved*, By the people of Alabama, in Convention assembled, that the State of Alabama cannot and will not submit to the administration of Lincoln and Hamlin as President and Vice-President of the United States upon the principles referred to in the preamble."

This resolution was a clear evasion of the whole question. It was simply a declaration that the people would not submit to LINCOLN's administration if certain things as expressed in Mr. WHATLEY's preamble were true. But Mr. POSEY had just denied that the matters set out in the preamble were true. He said: "I oppose the resolutions because the first recital in the preamble places resistance to Mr. LINCOLN's Administration upon the aggressions of the Federal Government as well as those of the Northern States. The last charge is true; the first is not true."

The passage of this conditional resolution unanimously has been held by those who are unwilling to acknowledge that a political adversary may evade a question as a declaration that the Co-operationists, as a party, favored secession in some shape. They forget that the opponents of secession in 1850 adopted similar tactics with success. While favoring co-operation, as at the Nashville Convention, they took care that the co-operation should be in favor of peace and Union. That the above resolution as adopted was not construed by them to mean necessarily some kind of secession or disunion, is satisfactorily shown by the sentiments of co-operation the members expressed throughout the proceedings, and finally upon the adoption of the ordinance of secession. Thus the minority report upon the question of secession laid down "a basis "for a settlement of the existing difficulties between "the Northern and the Southern States." This report, and the plan of a Convention for all the slave-holding States at Nashville, looked not to resistance, not to certain secession in some mode, but to a continued Union. This minority report was endorsed by all the co-operation members and received 45 votes as against 54. It was reported by Mr. CLEMENS, of Madison, and may be taken as the authoritative expression of the views of the Co-operation party. The basis for a settlement upon which the Union might be maintained was not presented as a *sine qua non;* the report provided that it was not to be regarded as "absolute and unaltera- "ble." The remarks of members also indicated that whatever might be the meaning of the resolution not to submit, it did not mean that they were not to make one more effort to preserve the Union. Said Mr. CLARKE, of Lawrence: "Is the great Constitution under "which we live—covering this whole country—is it to "be thawed and melted away by secession as the snows "on the mountains? No, sir! No, sir! I will not "state what might produce disruption of the Union; "but, sir, I see as plainly as I see the sun in heaven "what that disruption itself must produce." Again, speaking of the plan for a Convention at Nashville, Mr. CLARKE said: "If some plan of reconciliation were de- "vised by it which should satisfy the demands of the "Southern States, as I confidently believe would be "done, certainly every good patriot would hail it with "delight." Mr. POSEY said: "We would make one "more effort to preserve the Federal Government." Mr. WINSTON, of DeKalb, said: "I represent a constitu- "ency opposed to this hasty dissolution of the best "government the world ever knew." He said further, "that an effort should be made in the Union to adjust "our existing difficulties with the North."

Senator FITZPATRICK, whose residence was in AUTAUGA county, only a few miles from Montgomery, was one of the recognized leaders of the Co-operation party. As Mr. FITZPATRICK had so often defeated the policy of Mr. YANCEY, it was now a labor to which the advocates for secession devoted themselves most assiduously to defeat the wishes of the Senator. BOLLING HALL, a warm personal and party friend of Mr. FITZPATRICK, became the candidate of the Co-operationists for a seat in the Convention from Autauga county, and the contest between him and his opponent was one of the most bitter in the State. A correspondent of the *Advertiser*, writing from that county and describing a debate between the candidates, gives a fair idea of the political contest. He says:

"As the policy of co-operation was first inaugurated "in this county by Hall and Fitzpatrick, a great desire "was manifested on the part of our citizens to hear "what the Major [Hall] had to say in its defense. "Leading off in a debate, he consumed an hour and a "half in a vain attempt to explain the unfortunate polit-"ical position which he occupies before the people of "Autauga county. We have heard him often, and we "must confess that it was the most futile effort that we "have ever heard him make. His mind seemed alto-"gether clouded with the subject; and so desultory "were his remarks, that all their force was lost. He "was openly for co-operation, however, but said 'he "was afraid that even that would lead to secession at "last.' He was opposed to Alabama seceding without "a sufficient number of States would go with her; but "he refused to answer the question put to him by Dr. "Rives as to how many States he thought would be a "'sufficient number.' Major Hall, with his co-opera-"tion doctrine, met with cold comfort at this place, as "he took his seat without having received a single "applause."

Another correspondent writing from Autauga, said:

"In this county (Autauga) co-operation is, or has "terminated into *unionism*. Major Bolling Hall stated "in his speech at Milton, 'that he wanted to make one "more effort to save *this* glorious Union.' At Chest-"nut Creek the Hall men had a flag with thirty-three "stars, and one side in large letters '*Union*,' and they "marched in procession singing a song with the chorus "'Bolling Hall, and the *Union, too*.' Let the secession "men keep a lookout for the Union men. Major Hall "did not tell those Union men that he was in favor of "secession, but he depicted in the most vivid colors "the horrors of disunion, the weakness of Alabama, "and in fact everything that would or could deter them "from going for secession."

Such was the meaning of co-operation with FITZPATRICK and HALL. The vote of Autauga was 603 for HALL and 626 for his opponent. Thus only twelve votes decided that a county adjoining the home of Mr. YANCEY should not be represented by a delegate who would make one more effort to save the Union.

The resolutions adopted by primary meetings nominating candidates, also indicate the character of co-operation. LUKE PRYOR and THOS. J. MCCLELAND, distinguished lawyers, were nominated to represent Limestone county in the State Convention. The following resolution characterized the spirit of the nominating Convention:

"*Resolved,* That we favor a Convention of the fifteen "slaveholding States, to consider what is best to be "done, trusting that there is yet a reasonable ground 'for a peaceable solution of all differences between the "North and the South inside of the Union and the "Constitution."

TUSKALOOSA county adopted a similar resolution:

"*Resolved,* That we hold it to be our duty—*first,* "to use all honorable exertions to *secure* our rights in the "Union * *."

What was thought to be the tendency of the Co-operationists is shown by this extract from a leading article of the *Advertiser:*

"But they do not attempt at first to advocate open "submission. That may take with a few real estate "speculators in the town, who are afraid of a temporary "depreciation in the price of their lots, but the honest "countryman, who thinks himself a white man, and "the equal of any other white man, has a prejudice "against negro equality, and will never consent to be "ruled by an Abolitionist and a free negro. No, the "friends of Mr. Lincoln's Administration will not advo-"cate open submission, they will talk about acting with "the entire South, they will try to get Alabama to wait "until *all* the slave States are ready to go out."

The Northern press also understood that the contest being waged in Alabama was like that of 1850, between secession on the one side and Union on the other. The New York *Times* said:

"In truth, all the indications we are now receiving "from Alabama are to the effect that the sentiment "favorable to co-operation is decidedly in the ascend-"ant. This is a happy symptom. Co-operation "means delay—delay involves reflection, conciliation, "and possible satisfaction; and if those act with suffi-"cient vigor to prevent other States from following the "lead of South Carolina, it is impossible, in the nature "of things commercial, economical and political, for that "solitary republic to persist through six months in her "experimental independence. Before the energies of "coercion would be applied, she would be an eager "suppliant for re-admission. The more we hear of "co-operation, the less we have to fear from disunion."

The editor of the local paper describing the election in TALLAPOOSA county, said:

"The Separate State Actionists were defeated in this "county on the 24th Dec., by a decided majority, by "the Co-operationists. And since their victory, some "of the sub-Co-operationists have come out in their true "colors. Some talk about shouldering their muskets "and offering their services to the General Govern-"ment, in coercing South Carolina to remain in the "Union. Others say they prefer to live under Lin-"coln to Buchanan. Others glory in the idea that they "have lived in the Union all their lives thus far, and "wish to continue in it, no matter who is President. "And we have heard of another still, who exulted on "account of Lincoln's election, because, he said, it "would free all the negroes, and then poor white men "could get better wages."

In the Co-operation party could be found, as a matter of course, all those who were determined to maintain the Union in any event, and all those who were deterred from secession through cowardice; but these men did not give character to the party. The party were primarily in favor of saving the Union. All their hopes and efforts were fixed upon that end. But they were also intent upon presenting a united South and demanding guaranties from the North such as would pacify the apprehensions of the people. The conditions or their equivalent upon which the Co-operation party were willing to abide by the existing Union, as specified in the minority report of the Convention, were—1. A faithful execution of the Fugitive Slave Law; 2. A more effective provision for the surrender of criminals escaping from one State to another; 3. A guaranty that slavery shall not be abolished in the District of Columbia or in any place over which Congress has exclusive jurisdiction; 4. A guaranty that the inter-slave trade shall not be interfered with; 5. A protection to slavery in the Territories while they are Territories, and a guaranty that they may be admitted to the Union with or without slavery as they may wish; 6. The right of transit through free States with slave property; 7. The foregoing guaranties to be irrepealable.

It was provided in the report that this basis of settlement was not to be regarded as mandatory, but simply as an indication of the wishes of the Convention to which the proposed delegates should conform as nearly as possible. Evidently the views of the Co-operationists as here expressed were satisfactorily met by, and were probably based upon, the CRITTENDEN Compromise measures then pending in Congress.

On the 19th of December, but a few weeks before the Alabama Convention met, Mr. CRITTENDEN presented to the U. S. Senate a series of resolutions providing—1. A restoration of the Missouri Compromise line; 2. A prohibition against the abolition of slavery by Congress in places owned by the United States within the limits of slave-holding States; 3. That Congress shall not abolish slavery in the District of Columbia without the consent of Maryland and of the owner of the slaves; 4. That Congress shall not interdict the transportation of slaves from one slave State to another; 5. That the United States shall be responsible for the escape and loss of fugitive slaves; 6. That these provisions shall be unchangeable.

It is probable that the adoption of these resolutions would have sent a majority of anti-secessionists to the Alabama Convention; but the Restrictionists appeared determined to defeat them. At first the feeling among the politicians at the North was for a settlement upon the CRITTENDEN Compromise. Petitions flowed into Congress in unusual numbers from all parts of the North asking for its adoption. It was believed at the outset that Mr. SEWARD was favorable to it. Senator PUGH, of Ohio, declared his belief that it was approved by an overwhelming majority of the people of his State and of nearly every other State. Senator DOUGLAS endorsed it in a most eloquent appeal. Senators DAVIS and TOOMBS, and indeed all the Southern Senators, except IVERSON and WIGFALL, believed that the Compromise would be acceptable to the South, and were in favor of it. Senator BIGLER, after the defeat of the Compromise in the Committee of Thirteen, said:

" When the struggle was at its height in Georgia " between Robert Toombs for secession and A. H. Ste- " phens against it, had these men in the Committee of " Thirteen, who are now so blameless in their own estima-

"tion, given us their votes, or even three of them, Ste-"phens would have defeated Toombs and secession "would have been prostrated. I heard Toombs say to "Douglas that the result in Georgia was staked on the "action of the Committee of Thirteen. If it accepted "the Crittenden proposition, Stephens would defeat "him; if not, he would carry the State by 40,000 ma-"jority. The three votes from the Republican side "would have carried it at any time; but Union and "peace in the balance against the Chicago platform "were sure to be found wanting."

Mr. SEWARD gave the cue for the defeat of the Compromise in his speech at New York on the 22d of Dec. He treated the position of the South as simply a political threat which it was not worth while to notice. He said that, in his opinion, the secession of South Carolina would not be followed by many other States, and would not be persevered in long. Everything looked brighter than on the 6th of November, and "sixty days more suns will give you a much brighter "and more cheerful atmosphere." Forthwith the Republican party professed to treat the danger as a mere bagatelle. The New York *Tribune* wished to know whether the party was "to convict itself of having "either been a rank hypocrite before the election or of "being a skulking craven now." Mr. CHASE, in a letter from the Peace Congress, avowed the purpose of his party "to use the power while they had it, and "prevent a settlement." "Don't yield an inch," became the cry of the Republican press.

CHAPTER XVIII.

Effect of Seward's Speech—The Vote for Delegates to the Secession Convention—Meeting of the Alabama Convention—Caucus at Washington — Excitement in the Convention—Parties Nearly Equally Divided—Refusal to Submit the Ordinance to the People—Yancey's Threatening Speech—Counter Threats, etc., etc.

"I expressly said that now was not the occasion for the application of any doctrine of coercion; but by some strange misunderstanding I am represented as a determined and fierce advocate of coercion upon the seceding States."—[J. J. Crittenden, Senate Jan. 23, 1861.

"And should the Northern vote (which is not among the possibilities) reject so fair a compromise [the Crittenden Compromise] then the entire Middle States, whose sentiments you so nobly vindicate, would be amply justified before the world and posterity, in casting their lot with their more Southern brethren."—[Horatio Seymour's Letter to Crittenden, Jan. 18, 1861.

The speech of Mr. SEWARD was made Dec. 22d, and the election for members of the Alabama Convention was held Dec. 24th; but notwithstanding the hostile attitude of the Republicans in repelling all proffers for an amicable adjustment, the returns of the election showed that nearly, if not quite, a majority of the people, were favorable to continued efforts to preserve the Union before resorting to a separation. It is almost impossible to arrive at a correct knowledge of the meaning of the vote, or the relative strength of the parties. The separate secession journal at the capital computed the vote at 36,000 for secession and 27,000 for co-operation, whereas the opposition journal computed it at 24,000 for secession and 33,000 for co-operation. The difference in their estimates arises from the fact that in certain counties where two sets of candidates were before the people, it was assumed that one set was for separate secession and the other set were for co-operation—whereas, both sets might have been for secession or both for co-operation. In some counties it was known that one set of candidates was for co-operation and another for unqualified Union. In other counties it was known that votes cast for a third candidate against two secessionists was simply an expression of dislike for one of the candidates, and was not an expression for co-operation. In some of the counties, there being none but secession candidates, a small vote was polled. In other counties there was similarly a small vote polled for the co-operation candidates. In one or two counties which were undoubtedly opposed to separate secession, the parties compromised, as it was called, upon prominent citizens who were elected without pledges, but who at the meeting of the Convention were found to be for immediate and separate secession, when they were supposed by their constituents to be favorable to another effort to preserve the Union. Thus it was that the number of secessionists or of co-operationists who were elected to the Convention was not an accurate index of the sentiment of the people. Certain it is, however, that in this momentous election the highest number of votes claimed to have been polled for secession candidates was but 36,000 out of a population which at the preceding Presidential election had polled more than 90,000 votes.

The Convention met and organized on the 7th of January, 1861, in the Hall of the House of Representatives at the State Capitol at Montgomery. Of the one hundred delegates, not one was absent, so great was the anxiety to participate in the first action of the Convention, and so great was the doubt as to which party had secured the victory. On Sunday night it was believed that the Co-operation party was in the ascendancy, but on Monday, when the Convention met, it was known that there were 54 members for secession and 46 for co-operation. The first day was occupied with debating the resolution of resistance to the LINCOLN Administration, to which reference has already been made. While the co-operation members in their remarks upon Mr. WHATLEY's resolution did not withdraw their opinion that an effort should be made to preserve the Union by co-operation of the slave-holding States, they exhibited an uncertainty of expression and a confusion of purpose which bordered upon timidity. The clamor of the populace was in their ears. The young blood of the State was at fever heat. The CRITTENDEN Compromise had been insolently rejected by an unanimous vote of the Republicans. Only two days before, the compromise proposition agreed upon by the border States had received only one vote in the Republican caucus, and the door of reconciliation upon any plan whereby the rights of the South could be guaranteed, was closed, it seemed, forever. If the united Southern members of Congress, of the Peace Congress and of the border States Convention, would not be listened to, was there any hope that an appeal by a Congress of co-operative slave States would meet with a better reception ?

On the day before the Alabama Convention met the Senators from those of the Southern States which had called Conventions, met in caucus in Washington and adopted resolutions favoring immediate secession and recommending the holding of a Congress of all the seceding States at Montgomery on the 15th of February. These resolutions were telegraphed to the Conventions of Alabama, Mississippi and Florida. South Carolina had already seceded, and her Commissioner, ANDREW P. CALHOUN, was in waiting to address the Alabama Convention. To confuse the public mind still more, and to intricate the plain question of what was best to be done for the interest of the people of the State, the Governor had seized Fort MORGAN and Fort GAINES at the mouth of Mobile Bay, and the U. S. Arsenal at Mount Vernon, and had garrisoned them with Alabama troops, while the State was yet a member of the Union. Thus while the Co-operationists were earnestly desirous and constantly voted to secure a plan by which disunion might be averted, they were met by all the adverse weapons that ever assailed a patriotic body of men. As Southerners they were entreated to prevent the coercion of South Carolina. As Alabamians they could not witness their State authorities arraigned for treason in seizing the forts whose guns might have been turned at any time against their liberties. As men they could not brook the insolence of the Republican party, which contemptuously spurned every overture towards a settlement.

On the second day of the Convention, Jan. 8th, Mr. CALHOUN presented his credentials and delivered an effective address. He asked Alabama to unite with South Carolina and form a Union of the Cotton States. So confident was he of the strength of the Cotton States alone, that he said: "An Union at the earliest day "between them, will guarantee success. We cannot be "conquered; but united we will hurl defiance at our "assailants." Mr. WATTS laid before the Convention a telegraphic despatch from Messrs. MOORE and CLOPTON, members of Congress—"The Republicans in the House "to-day refused to consider the border States Compro- "mise, complimented Major ANDERSON, and pledged to "sustain the President," and another from Messrs. A. F. HOPKINS and F. M. GILMER, Commissioners to Virgina: "Legislature passed by 112 to 5 to resist any "attempt to coerce a seceding State by all the means "in her power. What has your Convention done? "Go out promptly, and all will be right." The excitement within the Convention was beginning to grow as intense as that upon the streets. The vestibule was crowded with an animated mass of citizens, eager to hear the latest bulletin from Washington or to catch an opinion from a member. The President laid before the Convention a despatch from Commissioner E. W. PETTUS: "Jackson, Miss., Jan. 7.—A resolution has "been passed to raise a committee of fifteen to draft "the ordinance of secession," and "The Convention "met at 12, Mr. Barry is President. The State will "probably secede to-morrow or next day;" also, a despatch from Commissioner E. C. BULLOCK: "Con- "vention (Florida) by a vote of 162 to 5 adopted res- "olutions in favor of immediate secession. Committee "appointed to prepare ordinance of secession." The Virginia Commissioners telegraphed: "Our friends "here think the immediate secession of Alabama, not "postponed to any future time, would exercise a favor- "able, perhaps a controlling effect, on the secession of "Virginia." Mr. WATTS presented a despatch from Pensacola: "Send us 500 men immediately"; and another, "Shall United States armed vessels be per-"mitted to enter harbor? If so, shall they be fired on "and destroyed?"

Mr. YANCEY offered a resolution that the Governor be instructed to send 500 volunteers to the Governor of Florida, with a view to taking possession of the forts at Pensacola. This resolution was opposed by the Co-operationists on the ground that both Florida and Alabama were still members of the Union. It was adopted by a vote of 52 to 45.

The third day of the Convention, Jan. 9th, opened with increased and growing excitement. Mr. DAVIS, of Madison, offered a resolution that the action of the Convention should be submitted to the people for ratification. It was rejected by a strict party vote. The argument of the minority was based upon the small vote cast for the secession delegates, and upon the uncertain character of the election. They asked how can the wishes and the views of the people of the State be clearly and satisfactorily ascertained? All parties contend that the election of delegates was not a satisfactory indication of the views of the people. Even if it was held to be so, it would not absolve them [the Convention] from the duty of submitting their action to the people for approval or disapproval. That is the only fair and satisfactory mode of arriving at the wishes and the views of the people. In the late canvass there was but little time afforded for discussion and investigation; no plans or details of plans were spread before the people; and in many counties the candidates occupied no definite and clear position. One man may have voted for one from personal friendship; another, under the impression that he was casting his vote for a co-operationist, while another may have voted for the same person as being a Secessionist. But the submission of their action to a direct vote of the people would leave no room to doubt the drift of the popular current, and would satisfy every one, both at home and abroad, what views the people of Alabama entertain as to her duty at this time. Such a course would not merely give great moral force to the position assumed by the State, but it would powerfully tend to harmonize and weld together our own people. It will conciliate and disarm the minority, to thus give them an undoubted demonstration that they are in a minority, and to have this all done fairly and openly, and without any legislative jugglery or political wire-drawing.

So much for the question of policy. As to the question of law, the Co-operationists argued that neither the General Assembly nor Gov. MOORE had the right to call a State Convention. The Legislature is not supreme. It is only one of the instruments of that absolute sovereignty which resides in the whole body of the people. Like other departments of the Government, it acts under delegated authority and cannot rightfully go beyond the limits assigned to it. This delegation of powers has been made by a fundamental law which no one department of the Government nor all the departments united have authority to change. That can only be done by the people themselves. A power was given to the Legislature to propose amendments to the Constitution which, when approved and ratified by the people, become a part of the fundamental law. But no power was given to the Legislature to call a Convention for any purpose whatever. That is a measure which must come from and be the act of the people themselves. Neither the calling of a Convention, nor a Convention itself, is a proceeding under the Constitution. Instead of acting under the forms and within the limits prescribed by that instrument, the very business of a Convention is to change those forms and boundaries as the public interests may seem to require. A Convention is not a government measure, but a movement of the people having for its object a change, either in whole or part, of the existing form of government. As the people had not only omitted to confer any power on the Legislature to call a Convention, but had prescribed another mode of amending the organic law, it was held by the Co-operationists that the call for the Convention was of no more binding force than if it had been made by a hundred private citizens. Nothing done by it could be of binding effect until ratified by the people. It would have been perfectly proper if the General Assembly had submitted at the outset to the people the question of "Convention" or "No Convention." Had the people voted for "Convention," then the present body would have been sovereign, and its acts need not be referred to the people for ratification. But as the people had not called the Convention, it occupied simply the position of an advisory body. The fact that a majority of the people voted at the election for delegates, did not validate the call made by the Legislature. In the Michigan case, Mr. CALHOUN had denied that the going to the polls of any number of people and the voting for delegates could constitute a legitimate Convention. A majority of those voting might be opposed to a Convention, but at the same time solicitous of proper representation should the Convention be held legal. The

New York Council of Revision, in 1820, composed of Justices KENT and SPENCER and Governor CLINTON, had vetoed a bill calling a State Convention without submitting to the people the question of expediency whether the Convention should be called or not, and from that day to the present it had been held most consonant to the principles of free government that the people should first vote upon a legislative act recommending a Convention. It was monstrous that a partisan majority in the Legislature should be conceded the power to call a sovereign Convention, designate the number of members and the districts to be represented, and that such Convention representing Districts framed with special reference to returning a partisan majority, should have unlimited power for any length of time it might choose to sit. The people of Alabama should have been permitted to say whether they wished a Convention; but now that the opportunity had passed, they should be allowed to say whether the acts of an improperly called Convention should be ratified and thus legalized. Thus argued the Co-operationists.

To this it was replied by the Secessionists that it had been established by precedents that in the silence of a Constitution as to the calling of a Convention, the General Assembly of a State was the legitimate authority for the issuance of such a call; that although the voting by the people of "Convention" or "No Convention" had often been made a *sine qua non* to the meeting of a Convention, many had assembled without such condition precedent and had exercised supreme power, and the ordinances adopted by such Conventions had been recognized by all the Courts as legitimate and binding. In the case of Alabama, a majority of her people had voted for delegates to this Convention. Of 90,000 voters more than 60,000 had voted at the election, and many thousands more would have voted had there been any opposition in their counties to the candidates. Certainly this was the voice of the sovereign people. As to submitting the ordinance of secession to the people for ratification, it was only necessary to say that the Constitution of Alabama under which they were then living had never been submitted to the people for ratification. Indeed, the Constitution of the United States itself was never submitted to the people. It was urged also, especially by Mr. YANCEY, that policy dictated that there should be no delay in completing the work. Said he: "We have gone too far to "recede with dignity and self-respect. Such submis-"sion involves delay dangerous to our safety. It "could not well be effected before the 4th of March." The argument from the inconvenience of delay decided the question. It is almost needless to say that what was a matter of doubt when the delegates were elected, was no longer so after Mississippi, Florida, Louisiana, Georgia and Texas had followed the steps of South Carolina. The martial spirit of the people had been aroused. The Republicans had rejected all overtures. The fife and the drum was being heard along the seaboard. The Northern press was saying "Let them "go!" Mr. SEWARD had declared at New York that for every old State which went out a new one was ready to come in, as though all that wished to go would be cheerfully and peaceably spared. Had the ordinance of secession under such circumstances been submitted to the people of Alabama, there is little doubt that it would have been ratified by a large majority.

After the Convention had voted against submitting its action to the people, a resolution was offered by Mr. COLEMAN, of Sumter, pledging the power of Alabama to aid in resisting any attempt upon the part of the United States to coerce a seceding State. In behalf of this resolution it was argued that a State has the right to secede, and if in her sovereign capacity she determines to resume her independence, the other States which have a common interest in the protection of this right, must come to her defence. Mr. MORGAN, of Dallas, said: "The effect of the resolution is, that South Carolina may recruit her armies in Alabama, and that our treasury shall stand open to her demands so long as she shall need the means of defence and protection." Mr. STONE, of Pickens, said: "The Convention which framed the Constitution expressly refused to grant to the General Government the power to employ force against a State." He declared his belief that the passage of the resolution would give strength to the Southern cause. "It may secure peace," said he, "if the government at Washington is informed that the coercive policy with which South Carolina is now threatened will be resisted, and that the first Federal gun fired against Charleston will summon to the field every Southern man who can bear arms. It may produce a peaceful solution of the pending difficulties."

Mr. YANCEY was urgent that the resolution should pass at once. It appeared to him that anti-coercion was a doctrine upon which every Southern man could stand. Hardly a prominent law writer from the earliest days of the Republic to within a few years past, but had denied the right of the Federal Government to coerce a State. He had looked for opposition at other points, but here he expected to see a united South. To his chagrin he found the co-operation party a unit against giving the pledge he wished to transmit with lightning speed to his native South Carolina. Mr. EARNEST, of Jefferson, said: "I fully recognize the "doctrine that a sovereign State, acting in her sover-"eign capacity, can withdraw or secede from the "Union; and that after that any acts she or her citi-"zens may do to protect her rights or to defend her "independence, even to bloody war, is not and cannot "be treason. But the State must act in her sovereign "capacity; no other act by any body or individuals "can withdraw her from the Union or relieve her citi-"zens from the laws of treason, if overt acts are com-"mitted by the citizen or the State against the Gen-"eral Government." Language equally as explicit was uttered by Mr. JONES, of Lauderdale. "Wait, at "least," he said, "until to-morrow, when it is "morally certain that the ordinance of secession will be "passed, and the members of this Convention ab-"solved by the sovereign authority of Alabama from "their allegiance to the Federal Government. Until the "State so absolved him he could not and would not "vote for resolutions proposing to declare war on the "Government of the United States." Mr. SMITH, of Tuskaloosa, said: "An assurance by a bare majority "of this Convention of aid to be given by the State of "Alabama, would be considered by South Carolina "almost an insult. She might be delighted at first to "hear and receive such an assurance; but when she "learned the fact that the resolution had been adopted "by a bare majority, she would be inspired with dis-

"gust; and she would swell with indignation if it "should appear (as it may upon a calm and thorough "examination, and a comparison of the facts and "figures) that the minority here were really the repre-"sentatives of a majority of the sovereigns of this "State."

The gentleman who used this language was the Hon. WM. R. SMITH, who had been a Circuit Judge, and had served three terms as a Representative in Congress, having been elected for his second term over two of the most prominent lawyers of the State and with every newspaper of the District against him. He thoroughly understood the people. Mr. YANCEY immediately leaped to his feet and demanded the authority upon which Judge SMITH had stated that the minority of the Convention represented a majority of the people. "I "receive my information," was the reply, "from tables "in the public prints; I do not assert them to be true, "but I believe that a popular majority of the State is "represented here by the minority." Mr. YANCEY had been restive under the powerful opposition which met him at every step. He now lost patience. One or the other party in this controversy, if the legitimacy of the Convention was to be brought in question, must go to the wall. If the powerful minority in the Convention believed that they represented the majority of the people, and that an ordinance of secession, passed by a Convention which had not been called together by a vote of the people, would have no binding effect in law or morals, the result might be that two governments would be established in the State, and all the horrors of civil war be burst upon the people. It was necessary for Mr. YANCEY and his friends to boldly and unflinchingly maintain that the Convention was sovereign, and that whatever it did by the smallest majority was supreme law for all the people. "If the ordinance "should pass by the meagre majority of *one*," said the impulsive and excited orator, "it will represent the "fullness and the power and the majesty of the sover-"eign people of Alabama. When it shall be the "supreme organic law of the people of Alabama, the "State upon that question will know no majority or "minority among her people, but will expect and "demand and secure unlimited and unquestioned obedi-"ence to that ordinance." Any one daring to array himself against the ordinance after its passage, would be a traitor to Alabama; he would occupy towards the true people of the State the relation which the Tories bore to the Whigs of the Revolution. However such men might be aided by Abolition forces, he believed that they and their unnatural allies would be defeated by the patriotic citizens of the State. Thus for an hour Mr. YANCEY proceeded in a torrent of invective against those who should doubt the supremacy of the proposed ordinance when adopted. His speech threw the Convention into the highest excitement.

Mr. WATTS, who saw the impolicy of the speech of his colleague, rose and expressed his regrets at its tone and apparent temper. This was no time for the exhibition of feeling or for the utterance of denunciations. He hoped the resolution would be postponed, so that on the morrow it might be passed by a unanimous vote of the Convention. But Mr. WATTS could not eradicate the sting of the preceding speech. Mr. JEMISON wished to know for whom and by what authority Mr. YANCEY spoke when he threatened to apply to those who might oppose the ordinance of secession the nomenclature of the Revolution. Nothing that the minority had said or done justified such sentiments. They were unprovoked and uncalled for, and unbecoming any gentleman on the floor. Here Mr. YANCEY arose and the President called Mr. JEMISON to order, whereupon he took his seat. There was great confusion throughout the hall, and Mr. YANCEY was also called to order by the President. When order was restored, Mr. JEMISON continued by saying that it was his earnest desire to see good feeling and harmony, "but, sir, when the great leader "of the majority shall call the minority party *tories*, "shall denounce us as *traitors*, and pronounce against "us a *traitor's doom*, were I to pass it in silence the "world would properly consider me worthy of the "denunciation and the doom." Mr. YANCEY explained that his remarks were not applicable to or intended for the minority of this Convention; they were intended for those in certain portions of the State where it was said the ordinance of secession, if passed, would be resisted. Mr. JEMISON continued—"I am glad, Mr. "President, to hear the gentleman disclaim any impu-"tation of disloyalty to the minority in this Convention. "But has he bettered it by transferring it to the great "popular masses in certain sections of the State, where "there is strong opposition to the ordinance of seces-"sion and where it is said it will be resisted? Will "the gentleman go into those sections of the State and "hang all who are opposed to secession? Will he "hang them by families, by neighborhoods, by towns, "by counties, by Congressional Districts? Who, sir, "will give the bloody order? Who will be your exe-"cutioner? Is this the spirit of Southern chivalry?

"Are these the sentiments of the boasted champions of "Southern rights? Are these to be the first fruits of "a Southern Republic? Ah! is this the bloody "charity of a party who seek to deliver our own "beloved sunny South from the galling yoke of a fanat-"ical and puritanical abolition majority? What a "commentary on the charity of party majorities! The "history of the Reign of Terror furnishes not a par-"allel to the bloody picture shadowed forth in the "remarks of the gentleman. I envy him not its con-"templation. For the interests of our common coun-"try I would drop the curtain over the scene, and "palsied be the hand that ever attempts to lift it."

Mr. NICHOLAS DAVIS, of Madison, followed Mr. JEMISON. The father of Mr. DAVIS had been the leader of the Whigs of North Alabama from the day when the State was admitted to the Union. Twice had he been an unsuccessful candidate for Governor. The son possessed the father's eloquence, spirit and devotion to the Union. He said: "Mr. President, I cannot allow "this occasion to pass without saying a word in reply "to what has fallen from the gentleman from Mont-"gomery (Mr. YANCEY.) Under other circumstances, "his remarks might pass unnoticed; but I feel I owe "it to those I represent, at least, to state correctly the "position they hold upon the question so unexpectedly "brought before this body. I claim, sir, to know their "views, and I say to this Convention that they have "not intended to resist its action when in conformity "to the wishes of the people of the State. The ques-"tion with them, sir, is, does the Convention represent "the will of the people? If it does, they will stand by "it, no matter what its decision may be. Now, sir, I "need scarcely say that the act of this Convention "will not be conclusive in this matter. And why? "Because, as every one knows, the popular vote of "this State may be one way, the Convention another, "and this resulting from the *manner* in which it was "called by those who are guilty of an usurpation of "power. In short, Mr. President, the sovereignty of "this body is denied, and its action will be sustained or "resisted as the popular will may be reflected through "it. The gentleman from Montgomery (Mr. YANCEY) "asserts upon the authority of a newspaper statement, "the vote to be one way; the gentleman from Tuska-"loosa, (Mr. SMITH,) upon like authority, claims it to "be another. I submit, sir, in deciding a question of "such moment, that the proof on either side is unsat-"isfactory. The people of the State will so regard it. "We have the means in our hands of ascertaining "their will by submitting our action for their ratifica-"tion or rejection; and should a course so manifestly "just be refused, a committee of this body, with the "evidence at the door, can arrive at a satisfactory con-"clusion. In either event, I pledge those I represent "to stand by the expressed will of the people. I repeat "that I know this to be the position of my constituents, "and such, so far as my knowledge extends, is the "position of the people in North Alabama." At this point Mr. YANCEY interrupted Mr. DAVIS by saying that he (YANCEY) had said nothing about the people of North Alabama. Mr. DAVIS continued: "No, sir, you "did not, but it is very well understood by every "member upon this floor to whom your remarks were "applicable. If it should turn out that the popular "vote is against the act of secession, should it pass, I "tell you, sir, that I believe it will and ought to be "resisted. The minority of this State ought not to "control the majority. But we are told that this is a "representative government—not a pure Democracy, "and in this form minorities may rule. If our State "Government be representative in this sense, who "made it so? The people, who in Convention framed "its Constitution and organic law. They set it on "foot, and whilst it moves in the orbit which they pre-"scribed, I grant that it is representative and has the "feature which it is claimed. Secession, however, "destroys that Constitution, and the people are muz-"zled in this Convention by a Legislature which derived "its existence from the instrument to be destroyed. "But I do not propose to discuss this matter. Judging "from the speech of the gentleman from Montgomery, "this is not the mode in which it is to be decided. We "are told, sir, by him, that resistance to the action of "this Convention is treason, and those who undertake "it traitors and rebels. The nomenclature of the Rev-"olution is to be revived, and the epithet of *Tory* in "future may ornament the names of Alabamians. I "cannot accept this as applicable to my constituents; "nor do I perceive the fitness or force of the intended "illustration. The Whigs of the Revolution were the "friends of this Government, the Tories its enemies. "If names shall hold the same relation to the Govern-"ment now as then, I shall have no objection to the "historical reminiscence. And not less odious in my "estimation than the name of *Tory*, is the doctrine "which is claimed of the right to coerce an unwilling "people. We must be dealt with as public enemies. "But yesterday this Convention condemned this doc-

"trine. With one voice you declared against it, and "expressed your determination to meet such an "invasion of your rights as it ought to be met, with "arms in your hands. It will be asserted as readily "against a tyrant at home as abroad; as readily by "the people of my section against usurpation and "outrage here as elsewhere. And when compelled to "take this course, they will cheerfully no doubt assume "all the responsibility that follows the act. I seek no "quarrel with the gentleman from Montgomery or his "friends. Towards them personally, I entertain none "other than the kindest feelings. But I tell him, "should he engage in that enterprise, that he will not "be allowed to boast the character of an invader. Com-"ing at the head of any force he can muster, aided and "assisted by the Executive of this State, we will meet "him at the foot of our mountains, and there with his "own selected weapons, hand to hand, and face to face, "settle the question of the sovereignty of the people."

In the midst of deep excitement the Convention adjourned without taking action upon the resolution. With such evidences of hostility to the manner in which the Convention was called, and to its refusal to submit its action to the people, what would happen on the morrow? Would the minority, claiming to represent a majority of the people, secede from the Convention and defy the Act of Secession? There were many sleepless eyes in Montgomery on the night of the 9th of January, 1861. What would the morrow bring forth?

CHAPTER XIX.

Adoption of the Ordinance of Secession—Popular Enthusiasm—Union of all Classes of the People—Assembling of the Southern Congress at Montgomery—Arrival of President Davis—Ratification by the Alabama Convention of the Confederate Constitution—Conclusion.

"The effect of this [Lincoln's Proclamation of April 15, 1861,] upon the public mind of the Southern States cannot be described or even estimated. * * Up to this time a majority, I think, of those who had favored the policy of secession, had done so under the belief and conviction that it was the surest way of securing a redress of grievances and of bringing the Federal Government back to constitutional principles. Many of them indulged hopes that a Re-formation or Re-construction of the Union would soon take place upon the basis of the new Montgomery Constitution; and that the Union under this would be continued and strengthened, or made more perfect, as it had been in 1789 after the withdrawal of nine States from the first Union, and the adoption of the Constitution of 1787. This proclamation dispelled all such hopes. It showed that the party in power intended nothing short of complete centralization. There was no longer any divisions amongst the people of the Confederate States."—[A. H. Stephens.

On the morning of Jan. 10, 1861, the Alabama Convention met at the Capitol. The President laid before them a despatch from the President of the Mississippi Convention announcing that they had adopted an ordinance of secession for their State by a vote approaching unanimity, and that Mississippi desires on the basis of the old Constitution a new Union with the seceding States. A despatch from Charleston was also read, announcing that a steamer with reinforcements for Fort Sumter was fired into by the forts, that she was disabled, had retreated and was lying at anchor. The despatch suggested, but did not vouch for the truth of the statement, that the disabled vessel had hauled down her colors. Another despatch said: "Anderson, it is said and believed, intends firing "upon our shipping and cutting off communication "with the fort." Another said: "Anderson writes to "the Governor he will fire into all ships. Governor "replies and justifies what we did. Now Anderson "replies his mind is changed, and refers the question "to Washington." All this was an exciting prelude to the grave business of the day.

Mr. YANCEY then, from the Committee of Thirteen, reported an ordinance of secession for Alabama, withdrawing "all the powers over the territory of said "State, and over the people thereof, heretofore delegated to the government of the United States of "America," and inviting the slave-holding States to meet the people of Alabama Feb. 4, 1861, at the city of Montgomery, for the purpose of consulting with each other as to the most effectual mode of securing concerted and harmonious action in whatever measures may be deemed most desirable "for our common peace "and security." Mr. JERE CLEMENS, from the minority of the same committee, made a report signed by six of the thirteen members. They said that they were unable to see in separate State secession the most effectual mode of guarding the honor and securing the rights of the State, but that it was becoming to make an effort to obtain the concurrence of all the States interested before deciding finally and conclusively upon a policy of their own. They contended that in so important a matter sound policy dictates that an ordinance of secession should be submitted for the ratification and approval of the people. The resolutions submitted with this minority report recommended a Convention of all the Southern States to meet at Nashville on the 22d of February, to consider the wrongs of the South and to devise appropriate remedies. A basis of settlement was suggested by the resolutions, but not to be regarded as absolute and unalterable. If the proposition for a conference should be rejected by any or all of the States, then Alabama should adopt such a plan of resistance as might seem best calculated to maintain her honor and rights. In the meantime Alabama would resist, by all means at her command, any attempt on the part of the General Government to coerce a seceding State.

Mr. CLEMENS moved that the minority report be substituted for the majority report. The ayes and noes were called upon this motion and resulted—ayes 45, noes 54. A change of five votes from the noes to the ayes would perhaps have changed the fate of Alabama and of the entire South. The Huntsville *Advocate* had said that, "but for the unexpected loss of Autauga and "Mobile by bad management, the Co-operationists "would have had a majority in the Convention." Autauga had one representative and Mobile had four. These five votes had it in their power to defeat the ordinance. Autauga was the home of FITZPATRICK, who had steadily opposed secession. Mobile was the home of FORSYTH, who in his speech at Hibernia Hall, Charleston, at the time of the withdrawal of the Southern delegations, had said that the proceedings there would force him against his will to be a "Union man;" that he despised Union shrieking, and had always thought that Unionism had gone far enough when a man was just and true to States Rights, but it was quite certain that the people of the South would meet Mr. YANCEY's attempt to "precipitate a revolution" with a counter revolution to save the country—that there were twenty-five thousand good citizens in Alabama who had never been Democrats who would take a hand to help prevent a dissolution of the Union. Writing to the journal of which he was then editor, Mr. FORSYTH had also said: "The Democratic party has "now a double sectional fight in hand North and "South. The Union depends on the issue. Heaven "defend the right." Mobile county had voted in November previous for Mr. BELL, 1,629 votes; for Mr. DOUGLAS, 1,828 votes; and for Mr. BRECKINRIDGE, only 1,541 votes. There were 3,452 votes cast for Union candidates against 1,541 for the candidate supported by Mr. YANCEY. From these and other facts, it was believed by many that the minority report would have been ratified in preference to Mr. YANCEY's ordinance of secession, had the Convention actually represented the voice of the people.

After the refusal of the Convention to substitute the minority for the majority report, Mr. CLEMENS offered a resolution providing that the ordinance of secession should not go into operation unless ratified by the people. The vote being taken on this proposition, it was rejected by the same vote which rejected the minority report. Mr. YANCEY then moved the adoption of the ordinance of secession. The Convention adjourned until next day, the 11th, and then occurred one of the most interesting and painful scenes ever witnessed by a deliberative body sitting upon measures involving the life or death of States. The members of the minority, before casting their votes, protested against the act about to be committed, and each in turn raised his warning voice.

Mr. CLARKE, of Lawrence, said: "I will not state "what might produce disruption of the Union; but, "sir, I see as plainly as I see the sun in Heaven, what "that disruption itself must produce. I see it must "produce war, and such a war I will not describe in its "two-fold character. Once more, therefore, in the "name of Liberty, of Peace, of happy hours—of the "aged, of the poor, of our mothers, of our sisters—of "helpless humanity throughout the borders of our "State, I implore you to concede something to the "counties of North Alabama." Mr. POSEY, of Lauderdale, said: "Division at home would be worse than "secession; this is the opinion of the minority on this "floor upon mature reflection." Mr. JONES, of Lauderdale, said: "This had been the most solemn hour of "his life; he expected to feel no more solemn when he "should stand in the presence of the King of Terrors." Mr. SMITH, of Tuskaloosa, said: "My opposition to the "ordinance of secession will be sufficiently indicated by "my vote; that vote will be recorded in the book; "and the day is not yet come that is to decide on "which part of the page of that book will be written "the glory or the shame of this day." Mr. KIMBALL, of Tallapoosa, said: "In all my intercourse with my "fellow-citizens, I found none who did not cordially "desire a united South: not a dissenting voice. In the "*Advertiser* of this morning I find a despatch express-"ing the opinion of Gen. Scott, who is said to be the "great war-spirit, who unhesitatingly says, that with a "certain unanimity of the Southern States, it would be "impolitic and improper to attempt coercion."

Mr. DAVIS, of Madison, said: "It cannot be denied "that circumstances have greatly changed since this "Convention met on last Monday. We have seen "State after State, in the exercise of its sovereign "powers, withdrawing from the Union in the past few "days. Florida has seceded; Mississippi has seceded "—each by overwhelming majorities. It is now no "longer a serious apprehension that Alabama will stand "alone in this movement of secession. It is confidently "asserted that Georgia and Louisiana and Texas will "follow. Under this aspect of the case, it is not re-"markable that a great change has come over the Con-"vention—a change clearly indicated by the speeches "that have been this day delivered in this hall. I "shall vote against the ordinance. But if Alabama "shall need the strong arm of her valorous sons to "sustain her in any emergency which, on account of "this ordinance of secession, may arise within her "borders, by which her honor or the rights of her citi-"zens are likely to be endangered, I say for myself "and for my constituents—and I dare say for all "North Alabama—that I and they will be cheerfully "ready to take our part in the conflict. We may not "endorse the wisdom of your resolves, but we will "stand by the State of Alabama under all circum-"stances."

Mr. CLEMENS, of Madison, said: "For the present it "is enough to say that I am a son of Alabama; her "destiny is mine; her people are mine; her enemies "are mine. I see plainly enough that clouds and "storms are gathering above us; but when the thunder "rolls and lightning flashes, I trust that I shall neither "shrink nor cower—neither murmur nor complain. "Acting upon the convictions of a life-time, calmly "and deliberately I walk with you into revolution. Be "its perils, be its privations, be its sufferings what they "may, I share them with you, although as a member "of this Convention I opposed your ordinance. Side "by side with yours, Mr. President, my name shall "stand upon the original roll; and side by side with "you I brave the consequences."

Mr. YANCEY closed the debate with the following remarks:

"Mr. President—If no other gentleman desires to "address the Convention, I will exercise the usual par-"liamentary privilege accorded to the Chairman of a "committee reporting a measure—that of closing the "debate, by assigning a few reasons why the measure "before you should be adopted. In common with all "others here, I feel that this is a solemn hour, and I "congratulate the Convention that the spirit that pre-"vails is both fraternal and patriotic—that whatever of "irritation or suspicion had prevailed in the earlier "hours of our session, has been, in a great degree, "dissipated, and has given way to a juster appreciation "of the motives and the conduct of each other. In "the committee the majority yielded to the minority "all the time that they desired for deliberation; and "since the report has been made, the majority in the "Convention has also yielded to the wishes of the mi-"nority in this respect, and every delegate who desired "to do so, has addressed the Convention in explanation "of his vote, and has taken as much time as, in his "judgment, was necessary to his purpose. If, in "the earlier stages of our proceedings, it has been "thought, as it has been said by some gentlemen, that "an undue celerity of movement was pressed by the "majority, I beg those gentlemen to believe that this "conduct on our part was dictated solely by our con-"victions of duty, and not from any—the least—desire "to precipitate others into a vote before they were pre-"pared to give it understandingly. Time was deemed "by the friends of independent State action to be either "success or defeat in the inauguration of this great "movement—success if there was a prompt and une-"quivocal withdrawal from the Union—or, defeat, if "time was used to delay and to dishearten. You who "were opposed to such action from a sense of duty, "would necessarily be for all such delays as would aid "in accomplishing its defeat; we who were for it, from "a like sense of duty, were necessarily in favor of a "prompt decision of the question. Each has acted, "doubtless, upon well-founded ideas of duty. All that "was necessary to a better understanding of each other, "was a belief in that fact, a belief in the good faith of "each other; and I rejoice that to-day has furnished "ample evidence that we now mutually entertain that "belief; and, on the part of the majority, I return "thanks to the venerable delegate from Lauderdale, "(Mr. Posey,) who, though compelled to vote against "this ordinance, yet has characterized the conduct of "the majority in this matter as giving evidence of "'wisdom, discretion, and a spirit of conciliation.'

"As to the measure itself (the ordinance and reso-"lutions), whatever merit it possesses, is the result of "consultation between the majority and minority of the "committee. I am sure that the members of that com-"mittee will indulge me in alluding to what passed in "its sessions. The majority decidedly preferred to "adopt a simple ordinance of secession, but determined, "for the sake of harmony, to do all in their power to "disarm prejudice and to bring about a fraternal feel-"ing; they did not hesitate to yield their own cher-"ished desire in this particular, when my friend from "Madison (Mr. Clemens) proposed to amend our pro-"posed ordinance by adding thereto the preamble and "resolutions, which form a part of his report. It is "well known that some of the people have been led to "believe that the friends of secession desired to erect "Alabama either into a monarchy or into an inde-"pendent State, repudiating an alliance with other "States. As for myself, I can truly declare that I "have never met with any friend of secession enter-"taining such views. The proposition submitted by "my friend from Madison (Mr. Clemens), being in "perfect accordance with the wishes and desires of the "majority, and amply refuted these misconceptions, "the one which we would have preferred to have voted "upon separately, was at once agreed to, and the result "is the measure now before us for consideration.

"On the first day of our session a resolution was "unanimously adopted declaring that the people of the "State would resist the Administration of Lincoln for "the causes and upon the principles there enunciated. "On the question of resistance, then, there is no differ-"ence in this body. All are for resistance; but there is "a difference between members as to the mode, the "manner of resistance. Some believe that when the "rights of our people are denied or assailed by the par-

"ties to the Federal compact, or by the Government, "that secession from this compact is the rightful reme- "dy. Others believe that secession is wrong, and that "the remedy is revolution. A careful reading of the "ordinance on your table will show that the resistance "therein provided may be called revolution, disunion, "or secession, as each member may desire. The cap- "tion styles it 'An Ordinance to dissolve the Union,' "etc. In the body of the ordinance the people of "the State are 'withdrawn from the compact,' etc. It "is true that the mode of resistance is organic; it is "an organic co-operation, not of States, but of the "people of this State in resistance to wrong. In this "respect it harmonizes differences. Another differ- "ence, both in the popular mind and in that of dele- "gates, is, that resistance should be by co-operation of "States, and not by independent State action. That "difference has been harmonized by the conjunction "of the ordinance and resolutions, as reported by the "committee. Co-operation and separate State action, "as far as they can be effected under our obligation to "the Federal compact and in harmony with the princi- "ples of State sovereignty, have been joined in this "measure. It is true there are a class of Co-opera- "tionists whose views are not met by this measure; "those who have advocated co-operation to secure sub- "mission—to defeat resistance. But there are none of "that character here. While the friends of indepen- "dent State action in this ordinance do obtain a declara- "tion as to the rights of the people of Alabama; and "as to our determination to sustain them, the friends "of co-operation, for the purpose of effectual resistance, "also obtain a declaration of our desire and purpose to "unite with all of the slaveholding States who enter- "tain a like purpose, in confederated or co-operative "resistance, and in a confederate government upon the "principles of the Federal Constitution.

"As far as it was possible, then, to do so without

"yielding principles, the friends of resistance have used "every reasonable effort to meet on a common ground. "And I rejoice in the belief that the effort has been "successful, and that there will be a far greater una-"nimity manifested when the vote shall be taken on "this measure, than was even hoped for when we first "met in this hall. From the remarks of gentlemen to-"day, many will be compelled to vote against this "measure by reason of restrictions of their people, who "otherwise would vote for it. I sincerely respect these "motives, and think those occupying such positions "act correctly in their premises.

"Mr. President, we are fortunate in having the "example of our Revolutionary fathers sustaining the "plan of action here proposed—separate State action "and then co-operation in confederating together. "South Carolina, after several months deliberation, "with a view of resisting British aggression, formed a "State government early in the year 1776. Virginia "did so in June, 1776, declaring her separate and inde-"pendent secession from the Government of Great "Britain. Afterwards, on the 4th of July, 1776, the "Congress of the United States agreed upon and "adopted a joint Declaration of Independence. It was "after the colonies had acted separately and indepen-"dently, that both the Declaration of Independence "and the Articles of Confederation and the Constitu-"tion of the United States were severally adopted. "The friends of independent State action have also "cause to congratulate themselves, that as far as the "people of the Southern States have spoken, they have "unanimously expressed themselves in favor of inde-"pendent State action.

"South Carolina, Mississippi and Florida have each "already acted independently. In this Convention a "majority are known to be in favor of that kind of "action. We have already received information that "a majority of delegates in favor of such action has "been elected, both in Georgia and Louisiana. I com-"mend this significant fact to all who feel disposed to "condemn an independent State movement.

"Some have been disposed to think that this is a "movement of politicians, and not of the people. This "is a great error. Who, on a calm review of the past, "and reflection upon what is daily occurring, can rea-"sonably suppose that the people of South Carolina, "Georgia, Florida, Alabama, Mississippi and Louisiana, "who have already elected Conventions favorable to "dissolution, and the people of Arkansas, Tennessee, "North Carolina and Virginia, who are contemplating "an assembling in their several Conventions, have been "mere puppets in the hands of politicians? Who can "for a moment thus deliberately determine that all "these people in these various States, who are so "attached to their government, have so little intelli-"gence that they can be thus blindly driven into revo-"lution, without cause, by designing and evil-minded "men against the remonstrances of conservative men? "No, sir; this is a great popular movement, based "upon a wide-spread, deep-seated conviction that the "forms of government have fallen into the hands of a "sectional majority, determined to use them for the "destruction of the rights of the people of the South. "This mighty flood-tide has been flowing from the "popular heart for years. You, gentlemen of the "minority, have not been able to repress it; we of the "majority have not been able to add a particle to its "momentum. We are each and all driven forward "upon this irresistible tide. The rod that has smitten "the rock from which this flood flows, has not been in "Southern hands. The rod has been Northern and "sectional aggression and wrong, and that flood-tide "has grown stronger and stronger as days and years "have passed away, in proportion as the people have "lost all hope of a constitutional and satisfactory "solution of these vexed questions. In this connec-

"tion I would say a few words upon the proposition to "submit the ordinance of dissolution to a popular vote. "This proposition is based upon the idea that there is a "difference between the people and the delegate. It "seems to me that this is an error. There is a differ- "ence between the representatives of the people in the "law-making body and the people themselves, because "there are powers reserved to the people by the Con- "vention of Alabama, and which the General Assembly "cannot exercise. But in this body is all power—no "powers are reserved from it. The people are here in "the persons of their deputies. Life, Liberty and "Property are in our hands. Look to the ordinances "adopting the Constitution of Alabama. It states 'we, "the people of Alabama,' etc., etc. All our acts are "supreme, without ratification, because they are the "acts of the people acting in their sovereign capacity. "As a policy, submission of this ordinance to a popular "vote is wrong. In the first place, we have gone too "far to recede with dignity and self-respect. It could "not well be effected before the 4th of March. The "policy is at war with our system of government. "Ours is not a pure Democracy—that is, a govern- "ment by the people; though it is a government of "the people. Ours is a representative government, "and whatever is done by the representative in accord- "ance with the Constitution is law; and whatever is "done by the deputy in organizing government, is the "people's will.

"The policy, too, is one of recent suggestion; if I "am not mistaken, it was never proposed and acted "upon previous to 1837. Certainly the Fathers did "not approve it. The Constitutions of the original "Thirteen States were adopted by Conventions, and "were never referred to the people.

"The Constitution of the United States was adopted "by the several State Conventions, and in no instance "was it submitted to the people for ratification. Coming "down to a later day, and coming home to the action "of our State sires, we find another example against "such submission. The Constitution of the State of "Alabama was never submitted for popular ratification. "One other and most important consideration is, that "looking to the condition of the popular mind of the "minority of the people on this question, such a course "will but tend to keep up strife and contention among "ourselves. Such a submission, it is clear to my mind, "will but result in a triumph of the friends of secession "—and an additional amount of irritation and preju- "dice be thus engendered in the minds of the defeated "party. Some gentlemen seem to think that in dis- "solving the Union we hazard the 'rich inheritance' "bequeathed to us. For one, I make a distinction "between our liberties and the powers which have been "delegated to secure them. Those liberties have never "been alienated—are inalienable. The State Govern- "ments were formed to secure and protect them. The "Federal Government was made the common agent of "the States for the purpose of securing them in our "intercourse with each other and the foreign powers. "The course we are about to adopt makes no war on "our liberties—nor, indeed, upon our institutions—nor "upon the Federal Constitution. It is but a dismissal "of the agent that first abuses our institutions with a "view to destroy our rights, and then turns the very "powers we delegated to him for our protection against "us for our injury. These powers were originally pos- "sessed by the people of the sovereign States, and "when the common agent abuses them, it seems to me "but the dictate of common sense, as well as an act of "self-preservation, that the States should withdraw "and resume them. The ordinance withdraws those "once delegated by Alabama, and the resolutions ac- "companying it propose to meet our sister States in "Convention and to confederate with them on the basis "of the very constitution which was the bond of com-

"pact and union between Alabama and the other States "of the Union. We propose to do as the Israelites did "of old, under Divine direction to withdraw our people "from under the power that oppresses them, and, in "doing so, like them, to take with us the Ark of the "Covenant of our liberties.

"There is but one more point upon which I desire to "say a few words. My venerable friend from Lauder-"dale asked us to forbear pressing the minority to "sign the ordinance. In my opinion it is not a neces-"sity that it be signed by members. Its signature "does not necessarily express approval of the act. "Signing it is but an act of attestation, in one sense, as "when the President of the Senate signs an act of the "General Assembly which he has voted against. I am "willing to vote for all reasonable delay to enable "members to consult their constituents. But I beseech "gentlemen to bear in mind that when the ordinance is "signed, the absence of the signature of any members "will be a notice to our enemies that we are divided as "a people, and that there are those in our midst who "will not support the State in its hour of peril. The "signature of the ordinance, while waiving no vote "given against it, while giving up no opinion, is an "evidence of the highest character that the signer will "support his country.

"It will give dignity, strength, unity to the State in "which we live, and by which each of its citizens should "be willing to die if its exigencies demand it. I now "ask that the vote may be taken."

The question being upon the adoption of the ordinance, the vote was taken by ayes and noes, and resulted—ayes 61, noes 39. Seven of the minority party had gone over to the majority under the lead of Mr. Clemens. Mr. President Brooks announced the result of the vote, and declared that Alabama was a free, sovereign, and independent State. The obligation of secrecy was removed at once from the proceedings of the Convention and the doors thrown open.

The vast multitude which had assembled in and about the Capitol, thronging the corridors and vestibule in anxious expectation of the news, as soon as the doors were opened, burst into the lobbies in a fever of excitement and enthusiasm. The Senate Chamber, within hearing of the Convention Hall, had been thronged with citizens from an early hour, who had listened to speeches from distinguished men, and whose rapturous applause had constantly reached the ears of the Convention. Now the rush to the lobbies, to the galleries, and to the floor of the Convention Chamber, resembled the rush of a mountain torrent. In an instant salvos of artillery heralded the event, and banners were displayed in all parts of the little city. As if by magic, an immense flag of Alabama was thrown across the hall, and was greeted with cheer upon cheer until the rafters fairly rang with the applause. Mr. YANCEY presented the flag in the name of the ladies of Alabama, and paid a splendid tribute to the ardor of female patriotism. It was accepted by Mr. ALPHEUS BAKER in one of those glowing speeches for which he was so famous, in which the word-painting was so brilliant and electric as to carry captive every heart.

Throughout the day the roar of peaceful guns continued; more flags leaped every moment to the wind, until the air was heavy with the vast expanse of gorgeous bunting. Speeches of congratulation were being made by eloquent orators to the wild populace; and everywhere was seen an enthusiasm such as perhaps never before in the annals of the world greeted the birth of a new government.

On the 16th of January the report of the special committee of thirteen upon the formation of a provisional and permanent government between the seceding States, was taken up by the Convention on motion of Mr. YANCEY. The report favored the formation of confederate relations with such of the Southern States as might desire it, upon the basis of the Constitution of the United States. It advised the election of delegates to the Provisional Congress called to meet at Montgomery, Feb. 4. The opponents of secession took the ground that a new Convention should be called to pass upon the formation of a permanent government. There still lingered a hope that while Alabama was untrammeled by a new alliance, she was in a better condition to renew at any moment her connection with the United States. Mr. YANCEY said that "the proposition "has a tendency to reopen the question of secession, "by bringing up the issue of a reconstruction of the "Federal Government; it allows such an issue to be "made; it invites it, in fact." Said he: "From the "signs of the times it would seem that coercive mea- "sures were to be adopted. If so, about the time of "such an election the people will be bearing the "burthens of such a contest. Commercial and agricul- "tural interests will be suffering. Debts will be hard "to pay. Provisions will be scarce. Perhaps death "at the hands of the enemy will have come to the "doors of many families. Men's minds thus sur- "rounded and affected by strong personal and selfish "considerations, will not be in that calm and well-bal- "anced condition which is favorable to a correct and "patriotic judgment of the question. The very state "of things will perhaps exist which our Black Repub- "lican enemies predict will exist, and which they sneer- "ingly rely upon to force our people to ask for re-ad- "mission into the Union."

These remarks of Mr. YANCEY show conclusively that he believed it to be the purpose of the advocates of a new Convention to gain time and thus to enable the State to seize the first opportunity to return to the Union. A motion that the plan for a Confederate States Constitution should be submitted for ratification or rejection to a new Convention to be elected by the people, was laid upon the table by a vote of 49 in favor of laying it upon the table, and 39 opposed to tabling.

The Convention adjourned until March 4th. Before dispersing, the President, Mr. BROOKS, said: "We are "free, and shall any of us cherish any idea of a recon-"struction of the old government, whereby Alabama "will again link her rights, her fortunes and her destiny "in a Union with the Northern States? If any of "you hold to such a fatal opinion, let me entreat you, "as you value the blessings of equality and freedom, "dismiss it at once. There is not, cannot be, any secu-"rity or peace for us in a reconstructed government of "the old material. I must believe that there is not a "friend or advocate of reconstruction in this large body. "The people of Alabama are now independent; sink "or swim, live or die, they will continue free, sovereign "and independent. Dismiss the idea of a reconstruc-"tion of the old Union now and forever."

On the 12th of March the permanent Constitution for the Confederate States was submitted to the Alabama Convention. Mr. JEMISON, of Tuskaloosa, advocated its submission to a direct vote of the people. He said that there was great dissatisfaction in some sections of the State because the ordinance of secession had not been so submitted. It would be impossible now to plead want of time or necessity for hasty action. Mr. MORGAN, of Dallas, opposed submission of the instrument to the people. He said:

"The people would never ratify by a direct vote. "This doctrine of a direct vote of the people on ratifi-"cation was absurd and odious. A reference would "give rise to many distracting questions. The African "slave trade would be brought in; the question of Re-"construction, with all its agitating features, would be "brought in, and many other questions of sufficient "abstract merit to excite the people and arouse opposi-"tion, but of no useful importance. Our fathers never "would have ratified the old Constitution by a direct "vote."

It was argued by the friends of submission that the existing Convention, having adopted the ordinance of secession, was *functus officio*; that the formation of a new government by Alabama with certain States, was new matter demanding a new voice from the people. It was said that the proposed Constitution had been framed by deputies elected by the Convention and not by the people, and that the people had nothing to say as to the ordinance of secession, the election of a Provisional Government, or the formation of a permanent Constitution. Now they were to be deprived of an opportunity of voting upon the kind of government under which they were to live. Mr. SMITH, of Tuskaloosa, said: "They find themselves under a new gov-"ernment, and in amazement exclaim, who did this? "They find themselves in the hands of a new Congress, "and exclaim—who elected this new Congress? Who "authorized it? The answer is, 'We are the People.' "Sir, that 'we are the people' in any but a "representative sense, is absurd. It is the flimsy "excuse for usurpations; it has been the characteris-"tic of legislative tyrannies in all ages of the world, "from the Areopagus to Cromwell's Parliament."

Mr. JEMISON'S proposed amendment to the committee's report, providing for the meeting of a new Convention to pass upon the Constitution, was finally voted down by—ayes 36, noes 53.

The Confederate States Constitution was then ratified by the Alabama Convention, only five votes being cast against it.

On Tuesday, March 12, a resolution was unanimously adopted by the Convention approving the election of JEFFERSON DAVIS President, and ALEXANDER H. STEPHENS Vice-President, of the Provisional Government of the Confederate States of America.